Discover

Contents

California

Throughout this book, we use these icons to highlight special recommendations:

 The Best...
Lists for everything from bars to wildlife – to make sure you don't miss out

 Don't Miss
A must-see – don't go home until you've been there

Local Knowledge | Local experts reveal their top picks and secret highlights

 Detour
Special places a little off the beaten track

If you like...
Lesser-known alternatives to world-famous attractions

These icons help you quickly identify reviews in the text and on the map:

 Sights

 Eating

 Drinking

 Sleeping

 Information

This edition written and researched by

Brid............................on,
Alison ....vers,

ACC. No: 03140094

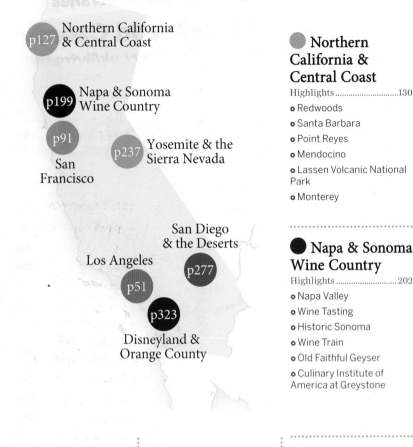

Northern California & Central Coast

Highlights 130
- Redwoods
- Santa Barbara
- Point Reyes
- Mendocino
- Lassen Volcanic National Park
- Monterey

Napa & Sonoma Wine Country

Highlights 202
- Napa Valley
- Wine Tasting
- Historic Sonoma
- Wine Train
- Old Faithful Geyser
- Culinary Institute of America at Greystone

Los Angeles

Highlights 54
- Hollywood
- South Bay Bicycle Trail
- Getty Center & Getty Villa
- Griffith Observatory
- Venice Beach Boardwalk
- La Brea Tar Pits & Page Museum

San Francisco

Highlights 94
- Golden Gate Park
- California Cuisine
- Alcatraz Island
- Vintage Trains & Cable Cars
- North Beach
- Mission District

Yosemite & the Sierra Nevada

Highlights 240
- Yosemite National Park
- Lake Tahoe
- Hunt for Gold
- Sequoia & Kings Canyon National Parks
- Mono Lake
- Bodie State Historic Park

Contents

San Diego & the Deserts

Highlights 280

- Balboa Park
- San Diego Zoo & Safari Park
- Old Town San Diego
- Joshua Tree National Park
- Palm Springs
- Death Valley National Park

Disneyland & Orange County

Highlights 326

- Disneyland
- Disney California Adventure
- Bowers Museum of Cultural Art
- Huntington Beach
- Laguna Beach
- Newport Beach

Plan Your Trip

This Is California	6
California Map	8
California's Top 25 Experiences	10
California's Top Itineraries	32
Month by Month	42
What's New	46
Get Inspired	47
Need to Know	48

On the Road

Los Angeles 51

Highlights	54
Best...	58
Walking Tour	60
Long Beach	*83*

San Francisco 91

Highlights	94
Best...	98
Walking Tour	100

Northern California & Central Coast .. 127

Highlights	130
Best...	134
Itineraries	136
Marin County	**138**
Marin Headlands	138
Sausalito	142
Tiburon	144
Muir Beach	145
Stinson Beach	146
Point Reyes Station	146
Point Reyes National Seashore	148
North Coast & the Redwoods	**151**
Berkeley	*151*

Contents

On the Road

Bodega Bay 152

Sonoma Coast State Beach 153

Salt Point State Park .. 153

Mendocino 154

Humboldt Redwoods State Park & Avenue of the Giants 158

Ferndale 159

Eureka 163

Arcata 165

Redwood National & State Parks 166

Prairie Creek Redwoods State Park .. 167

Klamath 168

Del Norte Coast Redwoods State Park 168

Jedediah Smith Redwoods State Park . 169

Lassen National Park & Northern Mountains 169

Lassen Volcanic National Park 170

Mt Shasta 171

Mt Shasta City & McCloud 171

Central Coast 173

Pescadero 173

Año Nuevo State Reserve 175

Santa Cruz 175

Monterey 178

Carmel-by-the-Sea 183

Big Sur 185

Point Piedras Blancas .. 189

San Luis Obispo 189

Santa Barbara 191

🔵🔵🔵⚫

Napa & Sonoma Wine Country .. 199

Highlights 202

Best... 206

Itineraries 208

Napa Valley 212

Napa Valley Wineries . 212

Napa 214

Yountville 217

St Helena 219

Calistoga 221

Around Calistoga 224

Sonoma Valley 225

Sonoma Valley Wineries 226

Sonoma & Around ... 227

Jack London State Historic Park 231

Healdsburg & the Russian River 232

Russian River Area Wineries 232

Healdsburg 233

Dry Creek Valley 234

🔵🔵🔵

Yosemite & the Sierra Nevada 237

Highlights 240

Best... 244

Itineraries 246

Lake Tahoe 248

Tahoe Ski & Snowboard Resorts 248

South Lake Tahoe & Stateline 249

Western Shore 251

Tahoe City 251

Truckee & Donner Lake 253

Yosemite National Park 254

Sequoia & Kings Canyon 263

Kings Canyon National Park 264

Sequoia National Park 265

Eastern Sierra 266

Mono Lake 266

Mammoth Lakes 268

Manzanar National Historic Site 270

Alabama Hills 271

Gold Country 271

Nevada City 272

Marshall Gold Discovery State Historic Park 273

Sacramento 273

🔵🔵🔵

San Diego & the Deserts 277

Highlights 280

Best... 284

Itineraries 286

San Diego 288

In Focus | **Survival Guide**

Palm Springs 306

**Joshua Tree
National Park** 313

Route 66 316

Los Angeles to
Barstow 316

*Mojave National
Preserve* 316

**Death Valley
National Park** 317

● ● ● ●

Disneyland &
Orange
County 323

Highlights 326

Best... 330

Itineraries 332

**Disneyland &
Anaheim** 334

**Orange County
Beaches** 344

Huntington Beach 344

Newport Beach &
Around 345

Laguna Beach 348

California Today 352

History 354

Family Travel 362

Way of Life 366

The Arts 369

California Cuisine 373

**Beaches & Outdoor
Activities** 378

Land & Wildlife 383

Directory 388

Accommodation........ 388

Business Hours 389

Climate 389

Customs 390

Discount Cards 390

Electricity 391

Food 391

Gay & Lesbian
Travelers............ 391

Health 392

Insurance 392

Internet Access 392

Legal Matters............ 393

Money............ 393

Public Holidays........ 394

Safe Travel 395

Telephone 396

Time............ 396

Tourist Information ... 396

Travelers with
Disabilties 397

Visas 397

Transport 398

Getting There
& Away............ 398

Getting Around.......... 399

Behind the Scenes ... 405

Index 406

**How to Use This
Book** 414

Our Writers 416

This Is California

Everyone heads to the Golden State to find fame and fortune – but you can do better. Come for the landscape, stay for sensational food, and glimpse the future in the making on America's creative coast.

California is older than it seems. Coastal bluffs and snow-capped peaks created over millennia of tectonic upheavals threatened to shake California right off the continent. And after unchecked 19th-century mining, logging and oil drilling threatened to undermine its ancient natural splendors, California's pioneering environmentalists rescued about 2.5 million acres of old-growth trees. Conservation initiatives by John Muir and his Sierra Club created Yosemite National Park and Redwood National & State Parks, and though Unesco named them World Heritage sites, visitors call them simply breathtaking.

Every time they sit down to eat, Californians have nationwide impact. Since California produces most US fresh produce and specialty meats, minor menu decisions go a long way. Californians are taking trendsetting stands on mealtime moral dilemmas: certified organic versus spray-free, grass-fed versus grain-finished, farm-to-table versus urban-garden grown, veganism versus humanely raised meats. But no matter what you order, it's likely to be local and creative, and it better be good – Californians compulsively share their dining experiences via social-media platforms like Facebook, Twitter and Yelp, all created here. For a chaser, try a stiff drink: California produces the nation's most prestigious wines, and has more breweries than any other state.

Californians are once again getting by on their wits. From the Gold Rush to the dot-com bubble, California has survived booms and busts – and the current US recession is no different. Trends are started here not by moguls in offices, but by a motley crowd of surfers, artists and dreamers concocting the out-there ideas behind skateboarding, interactive art and biotechnology. The Creative Class research institute predicts that California has the talent and technology to stage another economic comeback – and if you linger in California galleries and cafes, you may actually see the future coming.

> Trends are kick-started here by a motley crowd of surfers, artists and dreamers.

Cable car (p97), San Francisco

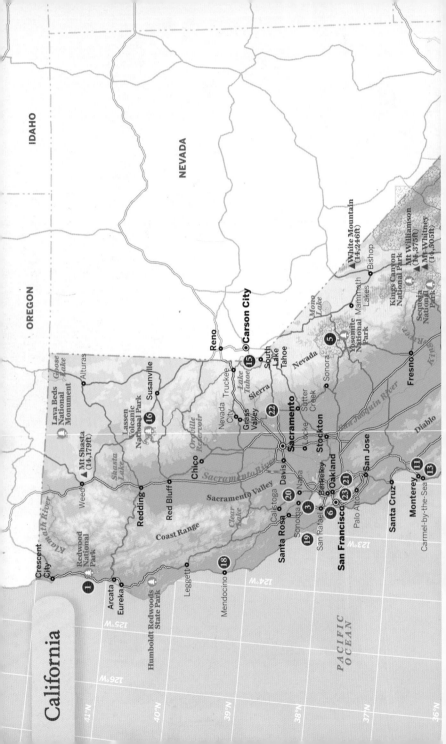

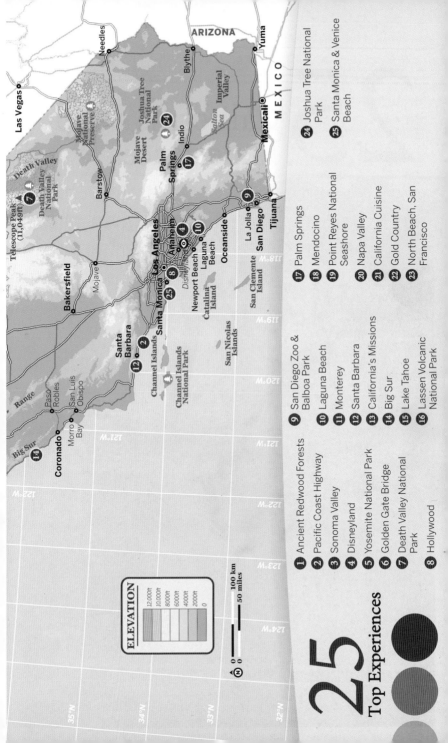

25 Top Experiences

1. Ancient Redwood Forests
2. Pacific Coast Highway
3. Sonoma Valley
4. Disneyland
5. Yosemite National Park
6. Golden Gate Bridge
7. Death Valley National Park
8. Hollywood
9. San Diego Zoo & Balboa Park
10. Laguna Beach
11. Monterey
12. Santa Barbara
13. California's Missions
14. Big Sur
15. Lake Tahoe
16. Lassen Volcanic National Park
17. Palm Springs
18. Mendocino
19. Point Reyes National Seashore
20. Napa Valley
21. California Cuisine
22. Gold Country
23. North Beach, San Francisco
24. Joshua Tree National Park
25. Santa Monica & Venice Beach

ELEVATION

12,000ft
10,000ft
8000ft
6000ft
4000ft
2000ft
0

100 km
50 miles

25 California's Top Experiences

Ancient Redwood Forests

Ditch the cell phone and hug a tree, man. And why not start with the world's tallest trees: redwoods? California's towering giants grow along much of the coast, from Big Sur north to the Oregon border. It's possible to cruise past these trees – or even drive right through them at old-fashioned tourist traps – but nothing compares to the awe you'll feel while walking underneath these ancient ones. Meditate at Muir Woods National Monument (p147), the Avenue of the Giants (p158) or Redwood National & State Parks (p166).

Redwood National Park (p166)

JOHN ELK III/LONELY PLANET IMAGES ©

Pacific Coast Highway

Make your escape from traffic-jammed freeways and cruise the coast in the slow lane (p36). California's coastal highways snake past sea cliffs and beach towns. PCH (the generic term for the route) connects the dots between major coastal cities, too: surfin' San Diego, rocking LA and beatnik San Francisco. In between, you'll uncover hidden beaches, rustic seafood shacks, and wooden seaside piers for catching sunsets over the Pacific. Pacific Coast Hwy, Big Sur

Sonoma Valley

As winemaking in the neighboring Napa Valley grows ever more dizzyingly upscale, here (p225) sun-dappled vineyards are surrounded by pastoral ranchlands. The uniqueness of *terroir* is valued most in this down-to-earth wine country, where you may taste new vintages straight from the barrel inside a tin-roofed shed while playing with the winemaker's pet dog. Who cares if it's not noon yet? Relax and enjoy your late-harvest zinfandel with a scoop of white-chocolate ice cream drizzled with organic olive oil. This is Sonoma; conventions need not apply.

The Best...
Dining Spots

CHEZ PANISSE
Taste the revolution Alice Waters started in Berkeley. (p151)

FERRY BUILDING
Mind-blowing restaurants and a farmers market. (p102)

PRADO
Mediterranean cuisine and luscious seafood. (p302)

CAFÉ BEAUJOLAIS
Romantic Cal-French in 19th-century surrounds. (p156)

MADRONA MANOR
A retro-formal Victorian mansion with artful California haute cuisine. (p235)

The Best...
Day Hikes

HALF DOME
Super-strenuous hike but worth every second. (p259)

GRIFFITH PARK
For spectacular views of LA and the Hollywood sign. (p67)

JULIA PFEIFFER BURNS STATE PARK
Bring the kids along to beachfront waterfalls. (p187)

POINT LOBOS STATE NATURAL RESERVE
Watch as the wildflowers come out in May and June. (p183)

MUIR WOODS NATIONAL MONUMENT
The closest redwoods to San Francisco. (p147)

Disneyland

④

Where orange groves and walnut trees once grew, there Walt Disney built his dream, throwing open the doors of his Magic Kingdom in 1955. Today, Disneyland (p334) is SoCal's most-visited tourist attraction. Inside Anaheim's mega-popular theme parks, beloved cartoon characters waltz arm-in-arm down Main Street USA and fireworks explode over Sleeping Beauty Castle on hot summer nights. If you're a kid, or just hopelessly young at heart, who are we to say that Disneyland can't really be 'The Happiest Place on Earth'?

It's a Small World, Disneyland

Yosemite National Park

⑤

At Yosemite National Park (p254), meander through wildflower-strewn meadows in valleys carved by glaciers, avalanches and earthquakes. Everything looks bigger here, whether you're getting splashed by thunderous waterfalls that tumble over sheer cliffs, staring up at granite domes or walking in ancient groves of giant sequoias. Perch at Glacier Point during a full moon or drive the high country's dizzying Tioga Rd in summer.

Golden Gate Bridge

Sashay out onto San Francisco's iconic bridge (p102) to spy on cargo ships threading through pylons painted 'International Orange,' then take in 360-degree views of the rugged Marin Headlands, far-off downtown skyscrapers, and Alcatraz Island. Watch the boats with billowing sails tack across the bay, and the chilly surfers wipe out near Fort Point.

Death Valley National Park

Just uttering the name brings up visions of broken-down pioneer wagon trains and parched lost souls crawling across desert sand dunes. But the most surprising thing about Death Valley (p317) is how full of life it really is. Spring wildflower blooms explode with a painter's palette of hues across camel-colored hillsides. Feeling adventurous? Twist your way up narrow canyons cluttered with geological oddities, stand atop volcanic craters formed by violent prehistoric explosions, or explore Wild West mining ghost towns where fortunes have been lost – and found.

Hollywood

The studios have moved, but Hollywood (p64) and its pink-starred Walk of Fame still attracts millions of wide-eyed visitors every year. Like an aging starlet making a comeback, this once-gritty urban neighborhood in LA is undergoing a rebirth of cool, blossoming with hip hotels, restored movie palaces and glitzy bars. Snap a photo outside Grauman's Chinese Theatre or inside Hollywood & Highland's Babylon Court with the Hollywood sign as a backdrop – go ahead, we know you can't resist. Hollywood Walk of Fame, Los Angeles

The Best...
Beaches

SOUTH LAKE TAHOE
Try your sand with a panoramic dose of mountain vistas. (p249)

SANTA BARBARA
Sandy swimming beaches line the city tip to toe. (p193)

LAGUNA BEACH
You can't go wrong with volleyball, basketball courts and excellent swimming. (p348)

HUNTINGTON BEACH
Ogle the surfers, and put in if you dare. (p344)

San Diego Zoo & Balboa Park

A rare urban SoCal green space, Balboa Park (p291) is where San Diegans come to play (when they're not at the beach, naturally). Bring the family and spend the day immersed in more than a dozen art, cultural and science museums, or just marveling at the Spanish revival architecture while sunning yourself along El Prado promenade. Glimpse exotic wildlife and ride the 'Skyfari' cable car at San Diego's world-famous zoo (p296), or see a show at the Old Globe Theatre (p305), a reconstruction of the Shakespearean original. Polar bear, San Diego Zoo

The Best...
Drives

FOXEN CANYON WINE TRAIL
Hidden canyons among oak-covered hills. (p196)

MT SHASTA
Take the Everitt Memorial Hwy almost to the top of the mountain. (p171)

TIOGA ROAD
Highway 120 E goes through the best of Yosemite's back country; passable only in summer. (p258)

17-MILE DRIVE
A scenic journey through Pebble Beach, between Pacific Grove and Carmel. (p184)

AVENUE OF THE GIANTS
A 32-mile detour through the heart of redwood country. (p158)

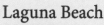

10 Laguna Beach

In Orange County, Huntington Beach draws the hang-loose trust-fund surfer crowd, while teens and yachties play in the soap-opera fantasyland of Newport Beach. But further south, Laguna Beach (p348) beckons, with its sophisticated blend of money and SoCal culture. Oh, and natural beauty: startlingly beautiful seascapes led an early-20th-century artists' colony to take root here. Laguna's bohemian past still peeks out in downtown's art galleries, historic arts-and-crafts bungalows tucked among multimillion-dollar mansions and the annual Festival of Arts and Pageant of the Masters (p43).

Monterey

Forget those hypnotizing Hollywood visions of sun-soaked SoCal beaches. Northern California's hurly-burly fishing villages are made for heartier outdoors lovers. Hop aboard a whale-watching cruise out into Monterey Bay National Marine Sanctuary (p178), some of whose denizens of the deep also swim in Cannery Row's ecologically sound aquarium (p180). Soak up the authentic maritime atmosphere on the coast, or head downtown among flowering gardens and adobe-walled buildings from California's Mexican past. Jellyfish, Monterey Bay Aquarium

11

DOUGLAS STEAKLEY/LONELY PLANET IMAGES ©

12

Santa Barbara

Egotistically calling itself the 'American Riviera,' – but that's not such a stretch – Santa Barbara (p191) is so idyllic, you just have to sigh. Waving palm trees, sugar-sand beaches, boats bobbing by the harbor – it'd be a travel cliche if it wasn't the truth. California's 'Queen of the Missions' is a beauty, as are downtown's red-roofed, whitewashed adobe buildings all rebuilt in harmonious historical style after a devastating 1925 earthquake. Come escape just for the day, or maybe a wine-drenched weekend in the country. Santa Barbara County Courthouse (p192)

13

California's Missions

If you road-trip along the coast between San Diego (p288) and Sonoma (p225), you can't help but follow in the footsteps of early Spanish conquistadors and Catholic priests. Foremost among those colonists was peripatetic Padre Junípero Serra, who founded many of California's 21 historical missions in the late 18th century. Some have been authentically restored; others are just the ruins of an era long past. Mission Santa Barbara (p192)

EDDIE BRADY/LONELY PLANET IMAGES ®

Big Sur

Nestled up against mossy, mysterious-looking redwood forests, the rocky Big Sur (p185) coast is a secretive place. Get to know it like the locals do, especially if you want to find hidden hot springs and beaches where the sand is tinged purple or where ginormous jade has been found. Time your visit for May, when waterfalls peak, or after summer-vacation crowds have left but sunny skies still rule. Don't forget to look skyward to catch sight of endangered California condors taking wing above the cliffs on thermal winds.

The Best...
Historic Architecture

HEARST CASTLE
Take a tour of the largest private residence ever built in the US. (p190)

LOS ANGELES UNION STATION
The last of the grand railroad stations in the USA. (p87)

AHWAHNEE HOTEL
Yosemite's swank lodge is a national historic landmark. (p261)

OLD TOWN
Twinned with the nearby Gaslamp Quarter, forming two eras a few miles apart. (p293)

The Best...
Maritime Museums

MONTEREY
Hundreds of artifacts spanning California's history. (p181)

SAN DIEGO
Features the 1863 *Star of India* and the USS *Midway* aircraft carrier. (p289)

SANTA BARBARA
Hands-on exhibits and virtual reality make this a fabulous destination for kids. (p193)

POINT ARENA LIGHTHOUSE
One of the lighthouses on the West Coast you can still enter. (p154)

USS PAMPANITO
Tall folks will want to watch their heads on this WWII submarine. (p103)

15

RICHARD CUMMINS/LONELY PLANET IMAGES ©

Lake Tahoe

Tucked high in the Sierra Nevada mountains, this all-seasons adventure base camp revolves around the USA's second-deepest lake (p248). In summer, startlingly clear blue waters lead to splashing, kayaking or even scuba diving. Meanwhile, mountain-bikers careen down epic single-track and hikers stride along trails threading through thick forests. After fun in the sun, you can retreat to a cozy lakefront cottage and toasts s'mores in the firepit. When the lake turns into a winter wonderland, gold-medal ski resorts keep downhill fanatics, punk snowboarders and Nordic traditionalists more than satisfied.

LEE FOSTER/LONELY PLANET IMAGES ©

Lassen Volcanic National Park

This alien landscape bubbles over with roiling mud pots, noxious sulfur vents and steamy fumaroles, not to mention its colorful cinder cones and crater lakes. You won't find the engulfing crowds of more famous national parks at this off-the-beaten-path destination, but Lassen (p170) still offers peaks to be conquered, azure waters, forested campsites, and boardwalks through Bumpass Hell that will leave you awestruck by the terrible beauty. Fumaroles, Bumpass Hell (p171)

Palm Springs

A star-studded oasis (p306) in the Mojave since the days of Frank Sinatra's Rat Pack, 'PS' is a chic desert resort getaway. Lounge by your Mid-Century Modern hotel's swimming pool; go art-golfing, gallery hopping or vintage shopping; and then drink cocktails from sunset till dawn. Feeling less loungey? Break a sweat on hiking trails through desert canyons across Native American tribal lands, or scramble to a summit in the San Jacinto Mountains, reached via an aerial tramway (p307).

TIM MCCAIG/ISTOCKPHOTO ©

Mendocino

Mendocino (p154) is the North Coast's sandcastle. Nothing restores the soul like a ramble out onto craggy headland cliffs and among berry brambles. In summer, fragrant bursts of lavender and jasmine drift along fog-laden winds. Year-round surf is never out of earshot, and driftwood-littered beaches are reminders of the sea's power. Originally a 19th-century port built by New Englanders, Mendocino today belongs to bohemians who would scoff at puritanical virtues, favoring art and nature's outdoor temple for their religions instead. Point Cabrillo Lighthouse (p154), Mendocino

18

The Best...
Unique Experiences

KINETIC SCULPTURE MUSEUM
If you miss the race in May, check out some of its former champion kinetic contraption entries. (p160)

MYSTERY SPOT
Travel back in time for optical illusions and campy good fun. (p175)

MADONNA INN
Is it possible to get tooth decay from a hotel? (p191)

ALCATRAZ ISLAND
Sure, everyone goes, but it's a prison. On an island. In the middle of the bay. (p107)

Point Reyes National Seashore ⑲

If just one park could encapsulate Northern California, Point Reyes (p148) would get our vote. Step across the San Andreas fault – like the bassist in the band playing the state's geological rhythm of shake, rattle 'n' roll. Stand out by the lighthouse at what truly feels like land's end and peer through binoculars at migratory whales. Witness the raucous birthing and mating antics of elephant seals at Chimney Rock, then hike among herds of tule elk and drive out to windswept beaches. Chimney Rock (p149)

LEE FOSTER/LONELY PLANET IMAGES ©

The Best...
Wildlife Watching

POINT REYES NATIONAL SEASHORE
Whales, elk and marine mammals galore. (p148)

ANÕ NUEVO STATE RESERVE
A beach crowded with noisy elephant seals. (p175)

YOSEMITE NATIONAL PARK
Keep your eyes peeled for bears and mule deer. (p254)

MOJAVE NATIONAL PRESERVE
Scan the Joshua tree landscape for desert tortoises, coyotes and jackrabbits. (p316)

20 Napa Valley

A trip to Napa Valley (p212) lives up to the lore: visitors cruise the Silverado Trail on bicycles in search of the perfect cabernet, soak in the region's luxuriant spas and order dinner off visionary menus of celebrity chefs. Among the endless fields of grapes and rolling, oak-dotted hills, this is a beautiful place to get pampered. Book a limo to transport you to your wine-tasting appointments, or dodge that pesky traffic in a hot-air balloon.

WES WALKER/LONELY PLANET IMAGES ©

California Cuisine

The Golden State has seen more than its fair share of boom times and busts, and Hollywood starlets come and go, but for epicures, the prize remains the same: California's food and wine. As you travel up and down the coast, tasting samples from surfer-worthy fish tacos at seafood shacks to farm-to-table feasts on chefs' seasonal menus in San Francisco, you'll have just cause to pat your belly blissfully more than once.

21

22

Gold Country

'Go west, young man!' could have been the rallying cry of tens of thousands of immigrants who invaded during California's Gold Rush. Today, the Sierra Nevada foothills (p271) are a stronghold of Golden State history, tainted by banditry, bordellos and bloodlust. Hwy 49, which winds past sleepy townships and abandoned mines, is a gateway to swimming holes and rafting, and the fruits of some of California's oldest vines. Exhibit, Marshall Gold Discovery State Historic Park (p273)

North Beach, San Francisco

Scale the heart-stopping stairway streets in a neighborhood that has attracted bebop jazz musicians, Civil Rights agitators, topless dancers and Beat poets. With its tough climbs and giddy vistas, North Beach (p97) is a place with more sky than ground, an area that was civilized but never entirely tamed. Seek out clouds of green parrots as they shriek and flutter over bohemian hillside cottages, before you descend back to earth for a perfect frothy espresso or a scoop of gelato. Columbus Ave, North Beach

The Best...
Desserts

DOWNTOWN BAKERY & CREAMERY
Baked goods to die for in Healdsburg. (p235)

BREAD & CIE
Trays full of tasty delights in the Hillcrest section of San Diego. (p302)

BI-RITE CREAMERY
Get in line for the fresh salted-caramel ice cream. (p117)

NICKEL DINER
Maple-glazed bacon donut. Need we say more? (p80)

Joshua Tree National Park

Chalk up your hands and try not to look down as you tackle the boulders of Joshua Tree National Park (p313). The longest climbs are not much more than 100ft or so, but there are many challenging technical routes, and most can be easily top-roped for training. Not a rock hound? Hike its landscape of desert-fan-palm oases or kick up some trail dust with a mountain-bike exploration of its 4WD roads. Or just drive to Keys View for vistas of the Coachella Valley and the Salton Sea.

The Best...
Geology

LA BREA TAR PITS
Ancient fossils excavated from the bubbling ooze. (p68)

LAVA BEDS
Go underground to crawl through lava tubes and claustrophobic passageways. (p173)

DEATH VALLEY NATIONAL PARK
Salt flats, mineral-painted hills and saw-toothed miniature mountains. (p317)

KINGS CANYON & SEQUOIA NATIONAL PARKS
Explore caves with trippy stalactites and stalagmites. (p263)

25

Santa Monica & Venice Beach

Who needs LA traffic? Hit the beach instead. Posh Santa Monica (p71) grants instant happiness. Learn to surf, ride a solar-powered Ferris wheel, dance under the stars on an old-fashioned pier, let the kids explore the aquarium's tidal touch pools or dip your toes in the water and let your troubles float away. Did we mention jaw-dropping sunsets? Then join the parade of new-agers, muscled bodybuilders, goth punks and hippie tribal drummers at nearby Venice Beach (p72), where everyone lets their freak flag fly. BMX freestyler, Venice Beach

California's
Top Itineraries

San Francisco to Wine Country Bay Area Roundup

5 DAYS

Explore San Francisco then head north to visit the natural attractions and famed grape-growing regions just beyond. Budget two nights in the city, and the rest in the wilds of Marin and chic Wine Country.

Idaho

Nevada

WINE COUNTRY
MARIN COUNTY
SAN FRANCISCO

PACIFIC OCEAN

MEXICO

❶ San Francisco (p102)

In the hilly 7-sq-mile peninsula that is dashing, innovative and ever-evolving San Francisco, uncover the alleyways of **Chinatown** and wander the mural-adorned **Mission District**. Then brave the fog on a cruise over to evocative **Alcatraz** and visit a colony of blubbery sea lions sunning themselves on the floating docks at **Fisherman's Wharf**. Lose yourself on a sunny day in **Golden Gate Park**, stopping to smell the flowers where hippies danced during 1967's Summer of Love, and gawking at the rare critters and marine beasts on display at the **Academy of Sciences**.

SAN FRANCISCO ➡ MARIN COUNTY
🚗 **20 minutes** From downtown over Hwy 101. ⚓ **30 minutes** From San Francisco Ferry Building to Sausalito.

❷ Marin County (p138)

Escape the city via the landmark **Golden Gate Bridge**, stopping for photographs of San Francisco from the viewpoints in Marin. Choose from hiking across the **Marin Headlands**, taking the ferry from **Tiburon** over

to Angel Island to go kayaking, hiking and mountain-biking, or kicking back and letting the little ones run wild at the play structures of the **Bay Area Discovery Museum**. Meander north along the Marin County coast, passing the tall redwood trees of **Muir Woods National Monument**. Pause to bury your toes in the sand at small-town **Stinson Beach** on your way to view elk and elephant seals on the bluffs of wildly beautiful **Point Reyes National Seashore**.

MARIN COUNTY ➡ WINE COUNTRY
🚗 **20 minutes** Point Reyes Station to Sonoma via Hwy 116.

❸ Wine Country (p210)

Beyond the quaint Hitchcock-movie location of Bodega Bay, country roads wind through **Russian River Valley** vineyards. Truck east across Hwy 101, then turn south to tipple in the heart of Northern California's renowned Wine Country, orbiting stylish **Napa** and its countrified, still-chic cousin **Sonoma**. Taste your way through the cabernets and chardonnays and reserve ahead for dinner at one of the chichi French eateries in **Yountville**. Soak your road-weary bones in a mud bath in **Calistoga** and swim some laps in a spring-fed pool before looping back to San Francisco.

Redwood trees, Muir Woods National Monument (p147)
PHOTOGRAPHER: STEPHEN SAKS/LONELY PLANET IMAGES ©

5 DAYS

Los Angeles to Orange County Beaches
SoCal Dreaming

Get a taste of Southern California life with an infusion of big-city sophistication, a romp through some fabulous beaches and some theme parks the kids will never forget. If you visit in summertime, plan to spend more time at the beach.

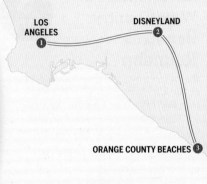

LOS ANGELES ①

DISNEYLAND ②

ORANGE COUNTY BEACHES ③

PACIFIC OCEAN

❶ Los Angeles (p62)

Kick things off in Los Angeles, where top-notch attractions, beaches and tasty food form an irresistible trifecta. After you've traipsed along the star-studded sidewalks of clubby **Hollywood**, dived into the arts and cultural scenes **Downtown** or **Mid-City**, and snapped photos of the Hollywood sign from Griffith Observatory, you'll be ready to party on **Sunset Blvd**. On your next day, **Santa Monica** beckons with a carnival pier, creative restaurants and boutiques. Move on to nearby Venice for primo people-watching on the **Venice Boardwalk**. If you have time, dig deeper into LA culture on a literary or city history tour with **Esotouric**, or visit the hilltop **Getty Center**. Good **shopping** can be found across the city; stars frequent **Robertson Blvd**.

LOS ANGELES ➲ DISNEYLAND
🚗 **45 minutes** Via I-5.

❷ Disneyland (p340)

In Anaheim, make a date with a mouse named Mickey at perfectly 'imagineered' Disneyland, and try to hold on as the **Space Mountain** roller coaster attempts to whirl you into an alternate universe. Stick around until the sun goes down for the nightly **fireworks** that burst over Sleeping Beauty Castle and the artificial snow that falls in winter. Next door, **Disney California Adventure** celebrates the Golden State, with thrill rides and night-time spectaculars. Both parks are not far from **Knott's Berry Farm**, which has an Old West theme and frighteningly fun rides.

DISNEYLAND ➲ ORANGE COUNTY BEACHES
🚗 **30 minutes** To Huntington Beach via SR22 and SR39.

❸ Orange County Beaches (p344)

Take a day off in **Huntington Beach**, aka 'Surf City USA.' Rent a board, play beach volleyball, build a bonfire at day's end – whatever – just kick back and chill. Make a stop in **Newport Beach** for soap-opera-worthy people-watching by the piers, and consider taking the ferry to car-free **Balboa Island** for a ramble around its promenade. Then roll south to **Laguna Beach**, a former artists' colony with over two dozen public beaches to spoil you, and a protected inlet frequented by divers and snorkelers.

Cyclists, Venice Beach (p72), Los Angeles
PHOTOGRAPHER: DAVID PEEVERS/LONELY PLANET IMAGES ©

10 DAYS

San Francisco to Los Angeles
A Tale of Two Cities

With 10 days, you can compare and contrast California's two rival cities and savor everything in between. Spend a few days roaming the famous hills and fog of San Francisco before puttering south along the coast to take the pulse of eclectic LA.

Idaho

Nevada

1 SAN FRANCISCO

MONTEREY PENINSULA 2

3 BIG SUR

SANTA BARBARA 4

5 LOS ANGELES

PACIFIC OCEAN

MEXICO

1 San Francisco (p102)

Start with a taste test through the **Ferry Building** and a stroll along the bay. Hop a cable car to **Fisherman's Wharf** to ogle the sea lions at Pier 39, and set sail for the former prison and thriving bird habitat at **Alcatraz**. Cap off the day with a ramble across the **Golden Gate Bridge**. The following day, check out the city's biggest green space and some of its best museums in **Golden Gate Park**, and do some shopping in the nearby **Haight** or in downtown's **Union Square**. Swim the tide of humanity in **Chinatown** and then settle in for a quiet coffee in **North Beach**. Book dinner at one of the city's destination restaurants, and shake it 'til dawn at a **SoMa** club.

SAN FRANCISCO ➔ MONTEREY PENINSULA
🚗 **Two hours** Via Hwy 101.

2 Monterey Peninsula (p178)

Stop by **Carmel-by-the-Sea** to tour its exquisite Spanish mission and for coastal views of dramatic Monterey pines. Visit John Steinbeck country at Monterey's restored **Cannery Row**, and allow a few hours to marvel at the marine life of the **Monterey Bay Aquarium**.

MONTEREY PENINSULA ➔ BIG SUR
🚗 **One hour** Hwy 1.

3 Big Sur (p185)

At the fabled stretch of shoreline called Big Sur, stroll **Pfeiffer Beach** and stay at a nearby inn or campground. Continuing south, take a gander at the opulent hilltop pleasure dome of **Hearst Castle**.

BIG SUR ➔ SANTA BARBARA
🚗 **Four hours** Via Hwy 1 and Hwy 101.

4 Santa Barbara (p191)

Vying for the coveted Southern California beauty prize is Santa Barbara, where you should meander along **Stearns Wharf** and take a dip in one of its many beaches. Visit the **Mission Santa Barbara** on your way into town, and spend the night in the Mediterranean-style downtown.

SANTA BARBARA ➔ LOS ANGELES
🚗 **Two hours** Hwy 101. 🚆 **Three hours**

5 Los Angeles (p62)

It's unlikely you'll see a celebrity (head to Malibu or Robertson Blvd for that), but the **Hollywood Walk of Fame** and **Grauman's Chinese Theatre** are a nod to Hollywood's yesteryear. For a backstage look at what's being filmed today, catch a **Universal Studios** tour. Check out **Griffith Park**, America's largest urban park, for views of the **Hollywood sign** and the Museum of the American West. Just south of the park, **Los Feliz** and **Silverlake** are non-touristy neighborhoods good for strolling. The next day, go **Downtown**, tour the Walt Disney Concert Hall and get a cocktail at the rooftop bar at the Standard hotel. Or spend the day cruising the beach towns from **Malibu** to **Manhattan Beach**.

Golden Gate Bridge (p102), San Francisco
PHOTOGRAPHER: LEE FOSTER/LONELY PLANET IMAGES ©

10 DAYS

San Diego to Avenue of the Giants
Pacific Coast & Tall Trees

Can't avert your eyes from the Pacific Ocean? Harbor a secret desire to hug some stratospheric trees? Take this classic road trip from San Diego, tracing the coast north until the road ducks through sky-high redwoods.

Idaho

6 HUMBOLDT REDWOODS STATE PARK

Nevada

5 SAN FRANCISCO

BIG SUR 4

LOS ANGELES 3 **2 LAGUNA BEACH**

PACIFIC OCEAN

SAN DIEGO 1

MEXICO

① San Diego (p288)

Give yourself two days to soak up the sun and sights in this pleasant SoCal city. Start with some animal spectaculars and rides at **SeaWorld**, and let the kids go nuts at the petting pools. Then go wiggle your toes around in the hot sand at **Mission Beach** and try to stay standing during a surfing lesson. Budget most of the following day for the museums, gardens and the overall atmosphere of **Balboa Park**, making certain to see some of the 3000 animals at its world-famous **zoo**. Pass the evening enjoying the nightlife in downtown's **Gaslamp Quarter**.

SAN DIEGO ○ LAGUNA BEACH

🚗 **Two hours** Via I-5.

② Laguna Beach (p348)

Continue north to artsy **Laguna Beach**, the quintessential California beach town. Stop by the **Laguna Art Museum** and peruse the galleries on S Coast Hwy. For swimming, **Main Beach** is your best bet.

LAGUNA BEACH ○ LOS ANGELES

🚗 **One hour** Via I-5.

③ Los Angeles (p62)

Ditch the car to ramble along the **South Bay Bicycle Trail**, then gawk at LA's prehistoric past at the gooey **La Brea Tar Pits**. In Downtown LA, Frank Gehry's **Walt Disney Concert Hall** and the collection at the **Museum of Contemporary Art** are highlights.

LOS ANGELES ○ BIG SUR

🚗 **Four hours** Via Hwy 101 and Hwy 1.

④ Big Sur (p185)

Navigate the soupy fog clinging to the coast and bask in the region's bohemian history with an overnight stay in an oceanside yurt at **Treebones Resort**, and a browse in the welcoming **Henry Miller Memorial Library**. Keep the camera handy to snap the postcard views from **Julia Pfeiffer Burns State Park**.

BIG SUR ○ SAN FRANCISCO

🚗 **Three hours** Via Hwy 1 and Hwy 101.

⑤ San Francisco (p102)

Bite into inspiring California cooking at the **Ferry Building**, then hop a boat over to infamous **Alcatraz** prison, aka 'The Rock.' For panoramic bay views, it's all aboard a **cable car** between **downtown** and **North Beach** or **Fisherman's Wharf**.

SAN FRANCISCO ○ HUMBOLDT REDWOODS STATE PARK

🚗 **3½ hours** Via Hwy 101.

⑥ Humboldt Redwoods State Park (p158)

Work your way north on Hwy 101 to **Leggett**, where your magical mystery tour of the Redwood Coast really begins. In **Humboldt Redwoods State Park**, encounter some of the tallest trees on Earth along the **Avenue of the Giants**.

Marina, San Diego (p288)
PHOTOGRAPHER: WITOLD SKRYPCZAK/LONELY PLANET IMAGES ©

2 DAYS

San Francisco to Los Angeles California's Greatest Hits

Jump off for a whirlwind tour of the state. You'll experience its two most exciting cities, wildlife-rich coastline, high granite mountains, a patchwork quilt of vineyards, and a desiccated desert wilderness.

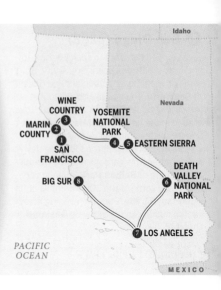

❶ San Francisco (p102)

Take a bell-clanging trip aboard the city's fabled **cable cars** and traipse the creaky wooden floors at **City Lights** bookstore. Wander through the **Ferry Building** and grab lunch, then check out the latest show at the spacious **San Francisco Museum of Modern Art**. Explore **Golden Gate Park**, survey amazing plant life inside the steamy **Conservatory of Flowers**, and take a stroll at sunset along **Ocean Beach**.

SAN FRANCISCO ○ MARIN COUNTY

🚗 **20 minutes** From downtown over Hwy 101.
⚓ **30 minutes** From San Francisco Ferry Building to Sausalito.

❷ Marin County (p138)

Head north over the Golden Gate Bridge into the heart-stopping hills of Marin, calling at the headlands viewpoint of **Point Bonita Lighthouse** and the hushed redwood grove at **Muir Woods**. Continue north to the animal-spotting bonanza of **Point Reyes National Seashore**.

MARIN COUNTY ○ WINE COUNTRY

🚗 **20 minutes** Point Reyes Station to Sonoma via Hwy 116.

❸ Wine Country (p210)

Put all your senses into play with a seaweed wrap and a hot-spring bath in the spa town of **Calistoga** and book a meal to remember at one of the destination restaurants in **Yountville** or **Healdsburg**. Naturally, don't think of missing the opportunity to go wine tasting in **Napa Valley** and the other regional wineries.

WINE COUNTRY ○ YOSEMITE NATIONAL PARK

🚗 **Four hours** Via Hwy 120.

❹ Yosemite National Park (p254)

Descend into **Yosemite Valley**, and you'll understand the lure of this landscape. Give yourself at least two days to explore Yosemite's trails, splash in the **Merced River** and romp through soaring groves of **giant sequoias**. Splurge for an overnight stay or a meal at the historic **Ahwahnee Hotel** to experience its classic grandeur.

Poppies, Big Sur (p185)
PHOTOGRAPHER: JAN STROMME/LONELY PLANET IMAGES ©

⑥ Death Valley National Park (p317)

Detour east to feel a wall of heat and witness the unusual geology of Death Valley National Park. Drive around its odd array of mineral deposits, learn about the area's mining history and then overnight at one of the accommodation options in **Furnace Creek** to cool off in a spring-fed pool.

DEATH VALLEY NATIONAL PARK ➲ LOS ANGELES

🚗 **Five to 5½ hours** Via Hwy 395.

⑦ Los Angeles (p62)

Spend one day inland, looking for your favorite star on the **Hollywood Walk of Fame** and admiring historic theaters and architecture **Downtown**. Head to the beaches the next day, including shopping Abbot Kinney Blvd in **Venice** and Third Street Promenade in **Santa Monica**.

LOS ANGELES ➲ BIG SUR

🚗 **5½ hours** Via Hwy 101 and Hwy 1.

⑧ Big Sur (p185)

Four hours from LA, stop in to gawk at the grandeur of **Hearst Castle**. Once you arrive at the stretch of coast called Big Sur, take a stroll on the purplish sand at **Pfeiffer Beach**. End the adventure with a cliffside dinner at **Nepenthe**.

YOSEMITE NATIONAL PARK ➲ EASTERN SIERRA

🚗 **Two hours** Yosemite Valley to Mono Lake via Hwy 120 (closed in winter). 🚌 **2½ hours**

⑤ Eastern Sierra (p266)

Continue to the Eastern Sierra along Hwy 120, losing elevation to reach the haunting vista of **Mono Lake**, then head south on the mountain-hemmed Eastern Sierra Scenic Byway, with a stop at the geological curiosity of **Devils Postpile National Monument**. Complete the day in the **Alabama Hills**, watching the sunset seep into steely silver mountains and ginger-orange hills.

EASTERN SIERRA ➲ DEATH VALLEY NATIONAL PARK

🚗 **Two hours** Alabama Hills to Furnace Creek via Hwy 190.

California Month by Month

Top Events

⭐ **Tournament of Roses**, January

✳️ **Festival of Arts & Pageant of the Masters**, July

⭐ **Pride Month**, June

⭐ **Coachella Music & Arts Festival**, April

✳️ **Cinco de Mayo**, May

January

⭐ **Tournament of Roses**

Before the Rose Bowl college football game, this famous New Year's parade of flower-festooned floats, marching bands and prancing equestrians draws over 100,000 spectators to Pasadena, a Los Angeles suburb.

🧧 **Chinese New Year**

Firecrackers, parades, lion dances and street food celebrate the lunar new year, falling in late January or early February. Some of California's biggest celebrations happen in San Francisco and LA.

February

◎ **Modernism Week**

Do you dig Palm Springs' retro vibe, baby? Join other Mid-Century Modern aficionados in mid-February for more than a week of architectural tours, art shows, film screenings, expert lectures and swingin' cocktail parties.

🐾 **Wildlife Watching**

Don't let winter storms drive you away from the coast! February is prime time for spotting migratory whales offshore, colonies of birthing and mating elephant seals, roosting monarch butterflies and hundreds of bird species along the Pacific Flyway.

March

⭐ **Dinah Shore Weekend & White Party**

Palm Springs' lesbian social event of the year sees pool parties, dancers and mixers coinciding with the LPGA golf tournament

May Kinetic Grand Championship

in late March or early April. For men, the four-day White Party gets crazy over Easter weekend.

April

⭐ Coachella Music & Arts Festival

Indie no-name rock bands, cult DJs and superstar rappers and pop divas all converge outside Palm Springs for a three-day musical extravaganza in mid-April. Bring lots of sunscreen and drink tons of water.

◉ Doo Dah Parade

Affectionately known as the twisted sister of Pasadena's world-famous Rose Parade, this offbeat, inventive and zany procession of artistically whimsical floats and unpredictable frolickers sashays down Colorado Blvd in late April.

⭐ San Francisco International Film Festival

Forget about seeing stars in Hollywood. The Americas' longest-running film festival has been lighting up San Francisco since 1957, with a slate of over 150 independent-minded films, including provocative premieres from around the globe in late April and early May.

May

❁ Cinco de Mayo

¡Viva Mexico! Margaritas, music and merriment commemorate the victory of Mexican forces over the French army at the Battle of Puebla on May 5, 1862. LA and San Diego really do it up in style.

◉ Calaveras County Fair & Jumping Frog Jubilee

Taking inspiration from Mark Twain's famous short story, this Gold Rush–era pioneer settlement offers old-fashioned family fun over a long weekend in mid-May, with country-and-western musicians, rodeo cowboys and a celebrated frog-jumping contest.

✈ Bay to Breakers

Jog costumed (although no longer naked or intoxicated) during San Francisco's annual pilgrimage from the Embarcadero to Ocean Beach on the third Sunday in May. Watch out for those participants dressed as salmon, who run 'upstream' from the finish line!

✈ Kinetic Grand Championship

Over Memorial Day weekend, this 'triathlon of the art world' merits a three-day, 38-mile race from Arcata to Ferndale on the North Coast. Competitors outdo each other in inventing human-powered, self-propelled and sculptural contraptions to make the journey.

June

⭐ Pride Month

Out and proud since 1970, California's LGBTQ pride celebrations take place throughout June, with costumed parades, coming-out parties, live music, DJs and more. The biggest, bawdiest celebrations are in San Francisco and LA; San Diego celebrates in mid-July.

July

⭐ Reggae on the River

Come party with the 'Humboldt Nation' of hippies, Rastafarians, tree huggers and other beloved NorCal freaks for two days of live reggae bands, arts and crafts, barbecue, juggling, unicycling, camping and swimming in mid-July.

August

⭐ Old Spanish Days Fiesta

Santa Barbara celebrates its early Spanish, Mexican and American *rancho* culture with parades, rodeo events, crafts exhibits and live music and dance shows, all happening in early August.

◉ Perseids

Peaking in mid-August, these annual meteor showers are the best time to catch shooting stars with your naked eye or a digital camera. Head away from urban light pollution to places like Joshua Tree and Death Valley National Parks in SoCal's deserts.

September

✳ Monterey Jazz Festival

Cool trad-jazz cats, fusion magicians and world-beat drummers all line up to play at one of the world's longest-running jazz festivals, featuring outdoor concerts and more intimate shows on the Central Coast over a long weekend in mid-September.

October

🍷 Vineyard Festivals

All month long under sunny skies, California's wine counties celebrate bringing in the harvest from the vineyards with star chef food-and-wine shindigs, grape-stomping 'crush' parties and barrel tastings, with some events starting earlier in September.

✳ Festival of Arts & Pageant of the Masters

Exhibits by hundreds of working artists and a pageant of masterpiece paintings 're-created' by actors keep Orange County's Laguna Beach plenty busy during July and August.

◉ California State Fair

A million people come to ride the giant Ferris wheel, cheer on pie-eating contestants and horseback jockeys, browse the blue-ribbon agricultural and arts-and-crafts exhibits, taste California wines and microbrews, and listen to live bands for two weeks in late July.

✳ Comic-Con International

Affectionately known as 'Nerd Prom,' the alt-nation's biggest annual convention of comic-book geeks, sci-fi and animation lovers, and pop-culture memorabilia collectors brings out-of-this-world costumed madness to San Diego in late July.

November

Día de los Muertos

Mexican communities honor dead ancestors on November 2 with costumed parades, sugar skulls, graveyard picnics, candlelight processions and fabulous altars. Join the colorful festivities in San Francisco, LA and San Diego.

Death Valley '49ers

Take a trip back to California's hardy 19th-century Gold Rush days during this annual encampment at Furnace Creek, with old-timey campfire singalongs, cowboy poetry readings, horseshoe tournaments and a Western art show in early November.

December

Mavericks

South of San Francisco, Half Moon Bay's monster big-wave surfing competition only takes place when winter swells top 50ft, usually between December and March. When the surf's up, invited pro surfers have 24 hours to fly in from around the globe.

Parade of Lights

Spicing up the Christmas holiday season with nautical cheer, brightly bedecked and illuminated boats float through many harbors, notably Orange County's Newport Beach and San Diego. San Francisco and LA host winter-wonderland parades on land.

New Year's Eve

Out with the old, in with the new: millions get drunk, resolve to do better, and the next day nurse hangovers while watching college football. Some cities and towns put on alternative, alcohol-free First Night street festivals.

Far left: July Pageant of the Masters exhibit, Festival of Arts **Left: November** Toys and decorations for Día de los Muertos

PHOTOGRAPHERS: (FAR LEFT) DAVID PEEVERS/LONELY PLANET IMAGES ©; (LEFT) WITOLD SKRYPCZAK/LONELY PLANET IMAGES ©

What's New

For this new edition of Discover California, our authors have hunted down the fresh, the revamped, the transformed, the hot and the happening. For up-to-the-minute reviews and recommendations, see lonelyplanet.com/usa/california.

1 FOOD TRUCKS
Sure, there have always been roadside taco trucks in California. But recently, a gourmands' street-food revolution has taken over, especially in Los Angeles and the San Francisco Bay Area. See also p115.

2 DISNEYLAND
It's a Small World got dolled up, Captain EO returned, the Pixar Play Parade and World of Color spectacular debuted and Ariel's Undersea Adventure and Cars Land opened. See p334 and p375.

3 DOWNTOWN LOS ANGELES
Swing by the high-fidelity Grammy Museum (p63) at the new LA Live entertainment complex, then explore the city's Mexican American heritage at La Plaza de Cultura y Artes (p63).

4 GLBT HISTORY MUSEUM
San Francisco flies the rainbow flag with pride at the country's first ever stand-alone museum dedicated solely to the gay, lesbian, bisexual and transgender cultural experience (☎ 415-621-1107; www.glbthistory.org /museum; 4127 18th St; admission $5, free on 1st Wed of month; ⊙11am-7pm Tue-Sat, noon-5pm Sun & Mon).

5 WINE COUNTRY GOES 'GREEN'
Earthy cooking renews chefs' locavarian, grass-fed and organic roots, vineyards become solar powered and biodynamic, and ever more boutique hotels jump on the eco-bandwagon too. See p210.

6 SAN DIEGO'S EAST VILLAGE
Popping up around Petco Park you'll find gastropubs, epicurean pizzerias, bistros and bars that are making stiff competition for the Gaslamp Quarter. See p288.

7 HALF DOME HIKING PERMITS
Wanna summit Yosemite National Park's most iconic granite dome? Even day hikers now need permits, which sell out online months in advance – plan ahead, folks. See p258.

8 SHOREBREAK HOTEL
Party animals still rule in Huntington Beach, but this hip downtown boutique property is upping the sophistication ante with a 'surf concierge,' yoga studio and dog-friendly lodgings. See p344.

9 CALIFORNIA STATE PARK CLOSURES
Due to an ongoing fiscal crisis, more than 60 state parks are slated to shut their gates to the public in 2012. Visit www.parks .ca.gov for updates. See also p384.

Get Inspired

📖 Books

○ **Cannery Row** (1945) Before you visit Monterey, read John Steinbeck's true-to-life account.

○ **LA Confidential** (1990) James Ellroy's novel about the seedy world of 1950s Los Angeles.

○ **My First Summer in the Sierra** (1911) Find out why John Muir felt passionate enough to found the Sierra Club.

○ **Slouching Towards Bethlehem** (1968) Musings by Joan Didion.

○ **Tripmaster Monkey** (1989) Maxine Hong Kingston on the Chinese American community in San Fran's turbulent '60s.

🎞 Films

○ **Dirty Harry** Do you feel lucky enough to see San Francisco on the big screen? Do you, punk?

○ **Fast Times at Ridgemont High** Every LA high school in the '80s had its own version of Jeff Spicoli.

○ **LA Story** Steve Martin drives 25ft to his neighbor's house.

○ **Vertigo** The quintessential 'San Francisco meets Hitchcock' classic.

○ **Chinatown** Roman Polanski's version of the LA water wars.

🎵 Music

○ **California Love** (2Pac and Dr Dre) The rappers' ode to California, from Long Beach to Sacktown.

○ **Californication** (Red Hot Chili Peppers) Anthony Kiedis' journey to the dark side of Hollywood.

○ **Los Angeles** (X) Exene Cervenka and John Doe's post punk homage to their city.

○ **Surfin' USA** (Beach Boys) Like a page out of a Southern California beach-town atlas.

🖱 Websites

○ **Discover LA** (www.disco verlosangeles.com) Where to surf, dine and sun.

○ **San Francisco Travel** (www.sanfrancisco.travel) Official info about the city's unique offerings.

○ **San Diego Convention & Visitors Bureau** (www.sandiego.org) Amusement parks, historic neighborhoods and microbreweries.

○ **California Parks & Recreation** (www.parks .ca.gov) California's state parks.

○ **National Park Service** (www.nps.gov/state /ca) National parks and monuments in California.

Short on time?

This list will give you an instant insight into the state.

Read *My California: Journeys by Great Writers* offers a memorable romp through California with contemporary authors from Pico Iyer to Michael Chabon.

Watch *Sideways* shows a bachelors' journey through the Santa Barbara wine country, maligning merlot and scoring points for pinot.

Listen *Sittin' on the Dock of the Bay* by Otis Redding might make you seek out a houseboat hideaway.

Log on www.visitcalifornia .com is the official state tourism site.

Poppies, San Diego (p288)
PHOTOGRAPHER: RICHARD CUMMINS/LONELY PLANET IMAGES ©

Need to Know

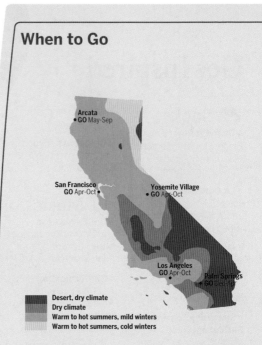

Currency
US dollars ($)

Language
English

ATMs
Available everywhere.

Credit Cards
Accepted almost universally.

Visas
Generally not required for citizens of Visa Waiver Program (VWP) countries, but only with ESTA approval (apply online at least 72 hours in advance).

Cell Phones
The only foreign phones that work in the USA are GSM multiband models.

Wi-Fi
In most lodgings and cafes.

Internet Access
Internet cafes are common. Most libraries and some accommodations have free computers.

Driving
Traffic in cities and coastal areas can be nightmarish. Avoid rush hours.

Tipping
15% to 20% in restaurants, 10% to 15% for taxis, bars $1 per drink, porters $2 per bag.

When to Go

Arcata
• GO May–Sep

San Francisco
GO Apr–Oct •

Yosemite Village
• GO Apr–Oct

Los Angeles
GO Apr–Oct

Palm Springs
GO Dec–Apr

- Desert, dry climate
- Dry climate
- Warm to hot summers, mild winters
- Warm to hot summers, cold winters

High Season (Jun–Aug)
- Accommodation prices up 50% to 100% on average
- Major holidays even busier and more expensive
- Summer is low season in the desert, where temperatures exceed 100°F (38°C)

Shoulder Season (Apr–May & Sep–Oct)
- Crowds and prices drop off, especially along the coast and in the mountains
- Mild temperatures; many sunny days
- Weather typically wetter in spring, drier in autumn

Low Season (Nov–Mar)
- Accommodation rates drop by the coast, not always in cities
- Chilly temperatures, frequent rainstorms and heavy snowfalls in the mountains
- Winter is peak season in SoCal's desert regions

Advance Planning

- **Two months before** Shop for airfares online; book accommodations in popular areas.

- **One month before** Set up special tours of film studios; make reservations at in-demand restaurants.

- **One week before** Buy Disneyland tickets if you don't want to stand in line; choose from a mountain of options and plan a rough itinerary.

Your Daily Budget

Budget up to $75

o Hostel dorm beds: $25–40

o Skip theme parks and plan around 'free admission' days at museums

o Find farmers markets for cheap eats

Midrange $75–200

o Two-star motel or hotel double room: $75–150

o Rental car: from $30 per day, excluding insurance and gas

Top End more than $200

o Three-star lodging: from $150 per night in high season

o Three-course meal in top restaurant: $75 plus wine

Exchange Rates		
Australia	A$1	$1.04
Canada	C$1	$0.98
Euro zone	€1	$1.30
China	Y10	$1.58
Japan	¥100	$1.29
Mexico	MXN10	$0.75
New Zealand	NZ$1	$0.80
UK	£1	$1.55

For current exchange rates see www .xe.com.

What to Bring

o **Clothing** Pack good walking shoes. Dress to impress in LA. Bring a jacket for summer in San Francisco.

o **ID** Required to rent cars or use internet services.

o **Insurance** Obtain international insurance for renting a car.

Arriving in California

o Los Angeles International Airport

Taxis $30 to $55, 30 minutes to one hour

Door-to-door shuttles $16 to $25

Free Shuttle C to LAX Transit Center or Metro FlyAway bus ($7) to Downtown LA

o San Francisco International Airport

Taxis $35 to $50, 25 to 50 minutes

Door-to-door shuttles $15 to $20

BART to downtown every 15 minutes from 6am to 11:45pm ($8.10, 30 minutes)

Getting Around

o **Air** Inexpensive flights between LA and San Francisco save time.

o **Boat** Ferries ply the San Francisco Bay.

o **Bus** Greyhound and Amtrak run inexpensive (but time-consuming) options between most major towns.

o **Car** Required in Napa Valley and throughout much of the coast and eastern backcountry.

o **Train** Runs only between Los Angeles, Santa Barbara, San Luis Obispo, Salinas (near Monterey) and Oakland/East Bay.

Accommodations

o **B&Bs** Every coastal town has at least a dozen; quaint and romantic but can be pricey.

o **Camping** Very popular, from luxury tents to bare-bones primitive national-park sites.

o **Hostels** Independent hostels and HI are popular, especially along the coast in larger cities.

o **Hotels** The higher the tariff, the more amenities.

o **Motels** Ubiquitous along highways or in heavily visited areas.

o **Resorts** From swish lodges to casual outdoorsy spots.

o **Spas** Many Wine Country hotels now double as spas.

Be Forewarned

o **Driving distances** LA to San Francisco is about seven hours, and it's another five or six hours to the redwoods.

o **Earthquakes** Small tremors happen daily, but are rarely felt.

o **Smog** Smog and heat can make an unhealthy combination. Watch for reports for advice on staying inside.

Los Angeles

Ah, Los Angeles: land of star-struck dreams and Tinseltown magic. You may think you know what to expect from LA: celebrity worship, plastic-surgery junkies, endless traffic, earthquakes, wildfires...

True, your waitress today might be tomorrow's starlet and you may well encounter artificially enhanced blondes and phone-clutching honchos weaving lanes at 80mph, but LA is intensely diverse and brimming with fascinating neighborhoods and characters that have nothing to do with the 'Industry' (entertainment, to the rest of us). Its UN of cooking has pushed the boundaries of American cuisine for generations. Arts and architecture? Frank Lloyd Wright to Frank Gehry. Music? The Doors to Dr Dre and Dudamel.

So do yourself a favor and leave your preconceptions in the suitcase. LA's truths are not doled out on the silver screen or gossip rags: rather, you will discover them in everyday interactions. Chances are, the more you explore, the more you'll enjoy.

Pacific Park (p72), Santa Monica
LOU JONES/LONELY PLANET IMAGES ©

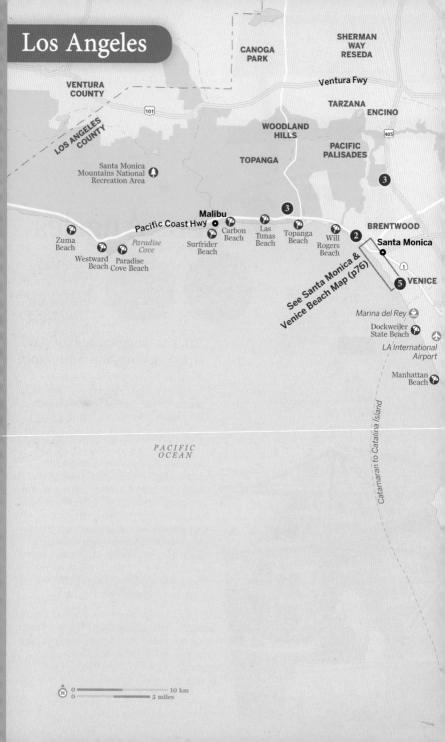

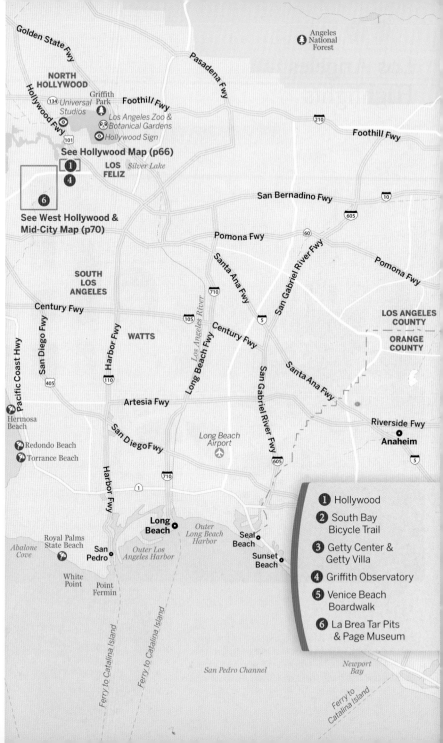

Golden State Fwy

NORTH HOLLYWOOD

Hollywood Fwy

134 *Universal Studios*

Griffith Park

Foothill Fwy

Los Angeles Zoo & Botanical Gardens

101

Hollywood Sign

Pasadena Fwy

Angeles National Forest

210

Foothill Fwy

See Hollywood Map (p66)

❶

❹

LOS FELIZ

Silver Lake

San Bernadino Fwy

10

❻

See West Hollywood & Mid-City Map (p70)

605

Pomona Fwy

60

SOUTH LOS ANGELES

Santa Ana Fwy

San Gabriel River Fwy

Pomona Fwy

Century Fwy

710

105

Los Angeles River

WATTS

Century Fwy

5

LOS ANGELES COUNTY

ORANGE COUNTY

Pacific Coast Hwy

San Diego Fwy

Harbor Fwy

Long Beach Fwy

405

110

Santa Ana Fwy

Artesia Fwy

San Gabriel River Fwy

Hermosa Beach

Redondo Beach

Torrance Beach

San Diego Fwy

Long Beach Airport

Riverside Fwy

Anaheim

5

Harbor Fwy

710

605

1

Outer Long Beach Harbor

Long Beach

Seal Beach

Sunset Beach

Abalone Cove

Royal Palms State Beach

San Pedro

Outer Los Angeles Harbor

White Point

Point Fermin

❶ Hollywood

❷ South Bay Bicycle Trail

❸ Getty Center & Getty Villa

❹ Griffith Observatory

❺ Venice Beach Boardwalk

❻ La Brea Tar Pits & Page Museum

Ferry to Catalina Island

Ferry to Catalina Island

San Pedro Channel

Newport Bay

Ferry to Catalina Island

Los Angeles Highlights

① Hollywood

Hollywood (p64) has been synonymous with motion pictures since Cecil B DeMille shot one of the world's first full-length feature films in a Hollywoodland barn in 1914. LA took center stage in the world of popular culture and has been there ever since. Hollywood Museum

Need to Know

STUDIO TOURS Try to book tours two weeks in advance
CELEBRITY-SPOTTING TIP Keep an eye out for packs of photographers **For more, see p64**.

Hollywood Don't Miss List

BY LERON GUBLER, MASTER OF
CEREMONIES, HOLLYWOOD WALK
OF FAME

1 HOLLYWOOD MUSEUM

This museum (p65) is a great place to spend a few hours looking at movies costumes, posters and memorabilia, celebrity cars like Cary Grant's Rolls Royce, and film sets including Hannibal Lecter's cell from *Silence of the Lambs*. It's in the historic Max Factor Building – a former speakeasy – and the ground-floor rooms each have a unique color scheme designed to complement the different hair colors of actresses.

2 MOVIE PALACES

There are so many fantastic, restored motion-picture palaces in Hollywood (see p73). Disney has its premieres at the El Capitan, which also has a Wurlitzer pipe organ. The Egyptian was the first themed movie palace and began the concept of dazzling premieres with klieg lights. The Pantages has a spectacular lobby, with grand, vaulted ceilings and art-deco chandeliers. And of course there's Grauman's Chinese Theatre (p64).

3 STUDIO TOURS

For the real flavor of what Hollywood's all about, do a studio tour (p74) at Paramount or Warner Brothers. You get to see working studios in action, and the groups are small. The guides take you around to the prop shop, and you are able to watch shows being filmed. You also tour the backlots and find out about the movies filmed there.

4 HOLLYWOOD WALK OF FAME

It's free! We currently have 2449 stars on the Walk (p64), and average about 24 new ones each year. Besides the stars, 46 buildings along Hollywood Blvd and Vine have historic markers detailing what happened there.

5 SUNSET RANCH

This stable (www.sunsetranchhollywood.com) has been in business for over 70 years, and is very 'old Hollywood.' It does sunset horseback rides through Griffith Park to Burbank that are a fun experience because the views are just great. You have all kinds of vistas, including the Hollywood sign, the Griffith Observatory and Downtown LA.

South Bay Bicycle Trail

This two-lane beach thoroughfare (p73), known in LA as 'The Strand,' mixes LA's two favorite things: freeways and looking good. Hundreds of bikini-clad bicyclists and oiled-up in-line skaters glide along a flat, pothole-free 'street,' which runs along the beach from Will Rogers State Beach to Torrance Beach. Go ahead, just try to make the 22-mile-long journey without singing Randy Newman's 'I Love LA.'

Getty Center & Getty Villa

One of the top museums for European art in the US, the Getty Center (p75) isn't just about the art. Plan on spending a day soaking up the sun on the lawn, wandering the garden maze or enjoying one of the special events (film noir, traveling Da Vinci exhibits etc). If you can't get to the ancient world, you can make it to the Getty Villa (p71), a Roman-, Greek- and Etruscan-filled treasure trove. Getty Center

EPI/IMAGEBROKER ©

Griffith Observatory

Cosmically informing Angelenos since 1935, this observatory (p67), located in gigantic Griffith Park, underwent a $100-million refurbishment last decade. Check out its out-of-this-world astronomical exhibits and check its calendar for viewings on clear evenings. To see the best foliage and views in all of Griffith Park (including views of the Hollywood sign), ramble the 2-mile trail from the Fern Dell area to the observatory.

Venice Beach Boardwalk

Dodgy glass-pipe vendors, thong bikinis, steroid-laden muscle men with their pit bulls...what isn't there to love about Venice Beach (p72)? Perhaps nowhere on Earth are folks more inclined to let their freak flag fly high. If you're looking for stereotypical California wingnuts, this is certainly the place. More kid-friendly are the Venice Canals, just two blocks east of the beach.

La Brea Tar Pits & Page Museum

If ever there was a cautionary tale about watching your step, it would use as its setting the *gotcha!* ooze of the La Brea Tar Pits (p68). Check out the remains of saber-toothed cats, mammoths and other unlucky animals who miscalculated and were doomed to fossilize here. You can also watch staff archaeologists excavate, clean and sort fossils in the museum's 'Fishbowl Lab.'

Los Angeles' Best...

Street Markets

Original Farmers Market (p81) LA's 'original' farmers market – started in 1934 – sports about a dozen inexpensive eateries.

Grand Central Market (p79) Packed and lively, with permanent restaurants and booths

Santa Monica (www .smgov.net/farmers_market) On Arizona Ave between 4th St and Ocean Ave on Wednesday mornings, and between 2nd and 4th Sts Saturday mornings; Wednesday is less crowded.

Olvera St (p62) Mexican market at LA's original European settlement site.

Places to Take Kids

Santa Monica Pier (p71) Rides, games, souvenirs, all along a fabulous beach.

La Brea Tar Pits (p68) Kids will love this giant fossil sandbox.

Griffith Park (p67) Hiking trails, picnic spots and a kid-friendly observatory and zoo.

Hollywood & Highland (p64) Redeveloped mall replaces grit with campiness in downtown Hollywood.

Beaches

Zuma Beach (p69) Stunningly gorgeous Malibu's even more stunningly gorgeous beach.

Santa Monica (p71) Extra-wide, hugely popular beach that's packed on weekends with families escaping the inland heat.

Manhattan Beach (p81) Glamorous condos, swank shops and surfers.

Venice (p72) An amusing sideshow of beachside bodybuilders, fire dancers, assorted fabulous freaks and people-watching galore.

Need to Know

Places to See Art

○ **Los Angeles County Museum of Art** (p72) Ancient art through to Kandinsky, with Friday evening jazz.

○ **Getty Center** (p75) A billion-dollar architecturally impressive art museum with equally impressive gardens and city views.

○ **Getty Villa** (p71) Head back in artistic time 2000 years for Roman, Greek and Etruscan examples.

○ **Museum of Contemporary Art** (p63) Art as modern as LA.

Left: Santa Monica Pier;
Above: Grand Central Market

ADVANCE PLANNING

○ **Two months before** See which TV shows are taping; call or email for free audience tickets.

○ **One month before** Sign up for VIP studio tours.

○ **Two weeks before** Book your hotels and make restaurant reservations.

RESOURCES

○ **Discover Los Angeles** (www.discoverlosangeles.com) Official information.

○ **LA.com** (www.la.com) Clued-in guide to shopping, dining, nightlife and events.

○ **LA Weekly** (www.laweekly.com) Free alternative news and listings magazine.

○ **Los Angeles Times** (www.latimes.com) The west's leading daily.

○ **Sig Alert** (www.sigalert.com) Real-time traffic information for LA-area freeways.

○ **US Geological Survey** (earthquake.usgs.gov) Up-to-the-minute earthquake updates.

○ **Los Angeles Magazine** (www.lamage.com) Glossy lifestyle monthly with useful restaurant guide.

○ **South Coast Air Quality Management District** (www.aqmd.gov) Hourly air-quality forecasts and advisories.

○ **KCRW 89.9FM** (www.kcrw.org) National Public Radio (NPR) station based in Santa Monica with cutting-edge music and well-chosen public affairs programming.

GETTING AROUND

○ **Bus** LA buses: not just for the pre-teen or desperate anymore.

○ **Car** An extension of your very existence in LA; Santa Monica to Hollywood can take 45 minutes to an hour.

○ **Metro** Not nearly comprehensive enough but an impressive effort.

○ **Walking** Best within neighborhoods: Santa Monica, Silver Lake, Venice.

BE FOREWARNED

○ **Drugs** Venice Beach, Hollywood and Downtown LA see their fair share of shady behavior.

○ **Freeways** Traffic is ubiquitous during rush 'hour,' which runs from 5am to 9am and 3pm to 7pm.

Los Angeles Walking Tour

Downtown is the most historical, fascinating part of LA. There's great architecture, world-class music, top-notch art, superb dining and a Fashion District.

WALK FACTS

- **Start** LA Live
- **Finish** Union Station
- **Distance** 3.8 miles
- **Duration** Four hours

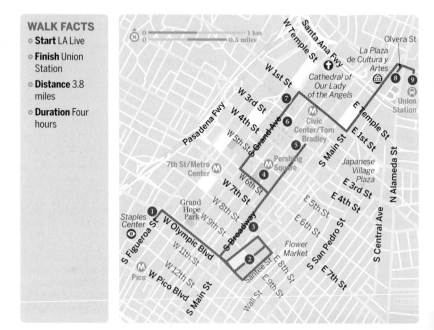

1 Grammy Museum & LA Live

The Grammy Museum is easily the highlight of LA Live. Learn about different musical genres through the interactive exhibits, watch live footage and see Michael's glove.

2 Fashion District

The axis of the Fashion District, this 90-block nirvana for shopaholics is at the intersection of 9th and Los Angeles Streets, where the fashionistas and designers congregate.

3 Broadway Theatre District

Highlighted by the still-running Orpheum Theatre, built in 1926, Broadway was LA's entertainment hub with no fewer than a dozen theaters built in a riot of styles, from beaux arts to East Indian to Spanish Gothic.

4 Pershing Square

The hub of Downtown's historic core, Pershing Square was LA's first public park in 1866 and is now enlivened by public art, summer concerts, and a holiday-season ice rink.

5 Grand Central Market

On the ground floor of a 1905 beaux-arts building where architect Frank Lloyd Wright once kept an office, stroll along the sawdust-sprinkled aisles beneath old-timey ceiling fans, past stalls piled high with mangoes, peppers and jicamas.

6 Museum of Contemporary Art

A collection that arcs from the 1940s to the present, and includes works by Mark Rothko, Dan Flavin, Joseph Cornell and other big-shot contemporary artists, is housed in a postmodern building by Arata Isozaki.

7 Walt Disney Concert Hall

Frank Gehry pulled out all the stops for his iconic concert venue, a molten blend of steel, music and psychedelic architecture.

8 Pueblo de Los Angeles

Here's where LA's first colonists settled in 1781. El Pueblo preserves the city's oldest buildings, some dating back to its days as a dusty, lawless outpost.

9 Union Station

A glamorous Mission revival achievement with art-deco accents, Union Station opened in 1939 as America's last grand rail station. The marble-floored main hall, with cathedral ceilings, original leather chairs and grand chandeliers, is breathtaking. Charles Bukowski worked at the historic Terminal Annex post office just north of the station, inspiring his 1971 novel *Post Office*.

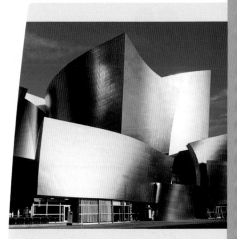

Los Angeles in...

Allow for traffic and don't try to pack too much in.

ONE DAY

Fuel up at the **Waffle** and then go star-searching on the **Hollywood Walk of Fame** along revitalized Hollywood Blvd. Up your chances of spotting actual celebs by hitting the boutiques on paparazzi-infested **Robertson Blvd** and having lunch at the **Ivy**. Then drive to lofty **Getty Center**, before heading west to the **Venice Boardwalk** to see the seaside sideshow. Watch the sunset over the ocean in **Santa Monica**.

TWO DAYS

Take our walking tour around **Downtown LA**. Stop for lunch at **Bottega Louie**, the **Grand Central Market** or **Philippe the Original**. Head to **Griffith Park** to snap a photo of the Hollywood sign, then meander around the **Museum of the American West** or the **zoo**. If there's time, check out the shops and restaurants in **Los Feliz** and **Silver Lake**. Top off the day with cocktails at the rooftop bar at the **Standard Downtown LA**.

Walt Disney Concert Hall (p63)
RICHARD CUMMINS/LONELY PLANET IMAGES ©

Discover Los Angeles

Sights

Los Angeles may be vast and amorphous, but the areas of visitor interest are fairly well defined. About 12 miles inland, Downtown LA is the region's hub, combining great architecture and culture with global-village pizzazz. Northwest of Downtown, there's sprawling Hollywood and nearby hip 'hoods Los Feliz and Silver Lake. West Hollywood is LA's center of urban chic and the gay and lesbian community, while Long Beach, at six o'clock from Downtown, is a bustling port with big-city sophistication.

South of Hollywood, Mid-City's main draw is Museum Row, while further west are ritzy Beverly Hills and the Westside communities of Westwood and Brentwood. Santa Monica is the most tourist- and pedestrian-friendly beach town; others include swish-but-low-key Malibu and bohemian Venice.

At a Glance

- **Downtown** (p77) Cultural institutions, entertainment venues and fabulous architecture.

- **Hollywood** (p64) Movie-industry flash and a marvelous urban park.

- **West Hollywood** (p67) LA's gay ground zero, plus chic shopping and nightclubs galore.

- **Mid-City** (p68) Museum Row and a classic farmers market.

- **Santa Monica** (p71) Beachside, laid-back and pedestrian friendly.

Downtown & Around

Crowds fill Downtown's performance and entertainment venues, and young professionals and artists have moved by the thousands into new lofts, attracting bars, restaurants and galleries. See also the walking tour, p60.

EL PUEBLO DE LOS ANGELES & AROUND

Compact, colorful and car-free, this historic district is an immersion in LA's Spanish–Mexican roots. Its spine is **Olvera Street**, a festive tack-o-rama where you can chomp on tacos and stock up on handmade candy and folkloric trinkets.

Wall of Fame, Hollywood Museum (p65)
DAVID PEEVERS/LONELY PLANET IMAGES ©

FREE **AVILA ADOBE**   Historic Home
(📞213-628-1274, Olvera St; ⏱9am-4pm) This
1818 ranch home claims to be the city's
oldest existing building. It's decorated
with period furniture, and a video documents history and highlights about the
neighborhood.

**LA PLAZA DE
CULTURA Y ARTES**   Cultural Museum
(Map p60; www.lapca.org; 501 Main St; adult/
student/senior $9/5/7; ⏱noon-7pm Wed-Sun;
P) This new museum (opened 2010)
chronicles the Mexican American experience in Los Angeles, in exhibits about city
history from the Zoot Suit Riots to the
Chicana (Latina women's) movement.
Calle Principal re-creates Main Street in
the 1920s.

It adjoins **La Placita** (Our Lady Queen of
Angels Church; 535 N Main St; ⏱8am-8pm),
built in 1822 and a sentimental favorite
with LA's Latino community. Peek inside
for a look at the gold-festooned altar and
painted ceiling.

UNION STATION   Landmark
(Map p60; 800 N Alameda St; **P**) This majestic 1939 edifice is the last of America's
grand rail stations; its glamorous art-deco
interior can be seen in *Blade Runner,
Bugsy, Rain Man* and many other movies.

FREE **WALT DISNEY CONCERT
HALL**   Concert Hall, Architecture
(Map p60; www.laphil.com; 111 S Grand Ave) This
gleaming concert venue, designed by
Frank Gehry, is a gravity-defying sculpture
of curving and billowing stainless-steel
walls that conjure visions of a ship adrift
in a cosmic sea. The auditorium feels like
the inside of a finely crafted instrument
clad in walls of smooth Douglas fir. Check
the website for details of free guided and
audio tours. Disney Hall is the home of
the Los Angeles Philharmonic.

**CATHEDRAL OF OUR LADY OF THE
ANGELS**   Church
(Map p60; www.olacathedral.org; 555 W Temple
St; ⏱6:30am-6pm Mon-Fri, 9am-6pm Sat,
7am-6pm Sun) Architect José Rafael Moneo
mixed Gothic proportions with bold

Angels Flight

Part novelty act, part commuter
train for the lazy, **Angels Flight**
(1901; www.angelsflight.com; per ride
25¢; ⏱6:45am-10pm) is a funicular
billed as the 'shortest railway in the
world' (298ft). The adorable cars
chug up and down the steep incline
connecting Hill and Olive Sts.

contemporary design for the main church
(built 2002) of LA's Catholic archdiocese.
It teems with art (note the contemporary
tapestries of saints by John Nava), lit with
serene light through alabaster panes.

**MUSEUM OF
CONTEMPORARY ART**   Art Museum
(MoCA; Map p60; www.moca.org; 250 S Grand
Ave; adult/child/student & senior $10/free/5,
5-8pm Thu free; ⏱11am-5pm Mon & Fri, to 8pm
Thu, to 6pm Sat & Sun) MoCA offers headline-
grabbing special exhibits; its permanent
collection presents heavy hitters from
the 1940s to the present. It's in a building
by Arata Isozaki; many consider it his
masterpiece.

South Park

The southwestern corner of Downtown,
South Park isn't a park but an emerging
neighborhood, including Staples Center
arena (p84), LA's Convention Center and
LA Live, which includes a dozen restaurants, live-music venues, a 54-story hotel
tower and the 7100-seat Nokia Theatre,
home to the MTV Music Awards and
American Idol finals.

GRAMMY MUSEUM   Museum
(Map p60; www.grammymuseum.org; 800 W
Olympic Blvd; adult/child/senior & student
$12.95/10.95/11.95; ⏱11:30am-7:30pm Mon-Fri,
10am-7:30pm Sat & Sun) The highlight of LA
Live. Music lovers will get lost in interactive exhibits, which define, differentiate
and link musical genres, while live footage
strobes from all corners. You can glimpse
GnR's bass drum, Lester Young's tenor, Yo

Yo Ma's cello and Michael's glove. Interactive sound chambers allow you and your friends to try your hand at mixing and remixing, singing and rapping.

Hollywood, Los Feliz & Silver Lake

Aging movie stars know that a facelift can quickly pump up a drooping career, and the same has been done with the legendary **Hollywood Blvd** (Map p66), preened and spruced up in recent years. Though it still hasn't recaptured its Golden Age (1920s–1940s) glamour, much of its late-20th-century seediness is gone.

Historic movie palaces bask in restored glory, Metro Rail's Red Line makes access easy, some of LA's hottest bars and nightclubs have sprung up here, and even 'Oscar' has found a permanent home in the Kodak Theatre, part of the vast shopping and entertainment complex called Hollywood & Highland.

The most interesting mile runs between La Brea Ave and Vine St, along the **Hollywood Walk of Fame**, which honors more than 2000 celebrities with brass stars embedded in the sidewalk. For interesting historical tidbits about local landmarks, keep an eye out for the sign markers along here, or join a guided walking tour operated by Red Line Tours.

Following Hollywood Blvd east beyond Hwy 101 (Hollywood Fwy) takes you to the neighborhoods of **Los Feliz** (los *fee*-liss) and **Silver Lake**, both boho-chic enclaves with offbeat shopping, funky bars and a hopping cuisine scene.

The Metro Red Line serves central Hollywood (Hollywood/Highland and Hollywood/Vine stations) and Los Feliz (Vermont/Sunset station) from Downtown LA and the San Fernando Valley.

HOLLYWOOD BOULEVARD

GRAUMAN'S CHINESE THEATRE
Cinema

(Map p66; 6925 Hollywood Blvd) Even the most jaded visitor may thrill in the Chinese Theater's famous forecourt at the heart of the Hollywood Walk of Fame, where generations of screen legends have left their imprints in cement: feet, hands, dreadlocks (Whoopi Goldberg), and even magic wands (the young *Harry Potter* stars). Actors dressed as Superman, Marilyn Monroe and the like pose for

Grauman's Chinese Theatre

Detour:
Universal Studios Hollywood

One of the world's oldest and largest continuously operating movie studios, **Universal** (Map p52; www.universalstudioshollywood.com; 100 Universal City Plaza; admission over/under 48in $77/69; ☽daily, hr vary) first opened to the public in 1915, when studio head Carl Laemmle invited visitors at a quaint 25¢ each (including a boxed lunch) to watch silent films being made.

Your chances of seeing an actual movie shoot are approximately nil at Universal's current theme-park incarnation, yet generations of visitors have had a ball here. Start with the 45-minute narrated **Studio Tour** aboard a giant, multicar tram that takes you past working soundstages and outdoor sets. Also prepare to survive a shark attack à la *Jaws* and an 8.3-magnitude earthquake. It's hokey but fun.

Among the dozens of other attractions, **King Kong in 3-D** scares the living daylights, the **Simpsons Ride** is a motion-simulated romp 'designed' by Krusty the Klown, and you can splash down among the dinos of **Jurassic Park**, while **Special Effects Stages** illuminate the craft of movie-making. **Water World** may have bombed as a movie, but the live-action show is a runaway hit, with stunts including giant fireballs and a crash-landing seaplane. Note: kids may be too short or too easily spooked for many attractions.

Parking is $12, or arrive via Metro Red Line.

photos (for tips), and you may be offered free tickets to TV shows.

KODAK THEATRE — Theater
(Map p66; www.kodaktheatre.com; adult/child & senior $15/10; ☽10:30am-4pm, closed irregularly) Real-life celebs sashay along the Kodak's red carpet for the Academy Awards – columns with names of Oscar-winning films line the entryway. Pricey 30-minute tours take you inside the auditorium, VIP room and past an actual Oscar statuette. Cirque du Soleil presents **Iris** (www.cirque dusoleil.com; tickets $43-253) here, a new film-themed performance.

HOLLYWOOD SIGN — Landmark
(Map p52) LA's most recognizable land-mark first appeared atop its hillside perch in 1923 as an advertising gimmick for a real-estate development called Hollywood Land. Each letter is 50 feet tall and made of sheet metal. It's illegal to hike up to the sign, but there are many places where you can catch good views, including the Hollywood & Highland shopping and

entertainment complex, Griffith Park and the top of Beachwood Dr.

HOLLYWOOD MUSEUM — Museum
(Map p66; www.thehollywoodmuseum.com; 1660 N Highland Ave; adult/student & senior/child $15/12/5; ☽10am-5pm Wed-Sun) The slightly musty museum is a 35,000-sq-ft shrine to the stars, crammed with kitsch, costumes, knickknacks and props from Charlie Chaplin to *Glee*.

HOLLYWOOD BOWL & AROUND — Amphitheater
(off Map p66; ☏323-850-2000; www.hollywood bowl.com; 2301 N Highland Ave; ☽concerts late Jun-Sep) Summer concerts at the Holly-wood Bowl have been a great LA tradition since 1922. This 18,000-seat hillside amphitheater is the summer home of the LA Philharmonic, and is also host to big-name rock, jazz and blues acts. For in-sight into the Bowl's storied history, visit the **Hollywood Bowl Museum** (www .hollywoodbowl.com/visit/museum.cfm; 2301 N Highland Ave; admission free; ☽10am-8pm Tue-Sat, 4-7pm Sun mid-Jun–mid-Sep, 10am-5pm

65

DISCOVER LOS ANGELES SIGHTS

Hollywood

66

500 m

0.25 miles

Hollywood

⊙ Sights
Egyptian Theatre .... (see 9)
1 El Capitan Theatre B2
2 Grauman's Chinese Theatre B2
3 Hollywood Museum C3
4 Kodak Theatre B2

⊙ Sleeping
5 Hollywood Roosevelt Hotel B2
6 Magic Castle Hotel A1

⊗ Eating
7 Musso & Frank Grill D2
8 Waffle F3

⊙ Entertainment
9 American Cinematheque C2
10 ArcLight & Cinerama Dome F4
11 Catalina Bar & Grill C3
12 Drai's F3

⊙ Shopping
13 Amoeba Music E4
14 Space 1520 .... E3

Tue-Fri mid-Sep–mid-Jun). The Bowl grounds are open to the public daytimes.

GRIFFITH PARK   Park
(Map p52; www.laparks.org/dos/parks /griffithpk; admission free; ⊙6am-10pm, trails close at dusk; P ♦) America's largest urban park is five times the size of New York's Central Park. It embraces an outdoor theater, zoo, observatory, museum, antique trains, golf, tennis, playgrounds, bridle paths, 53 miles of hiking trails, Batman's caves and the Hollywood Sign. The **Ranger Station** (4730 Crystal Springs Dr) has maps.

GRIFFITH OBSERVATORY   Observatory
(www.griffithobservatory.org; 2800 Observatory Rd; admission free, planetarium shows adult/ child/senior $7/3/5; ⊙noon-10pm Tue-Fri, 10am-10pm Sat & Sun, closed occasional Tue; P ♦) Above Los Feliz loom the iconic triple domes of this 1935 observatory, which boasts a super-techie planetarium and films in the Leonard Nimoy Event Horizon Theater. During clear night-time skies, you can often peer through the telescopes at heavenly bodies.

LOS ANGELES ZOO & BOTANICAL GARDENS   Zoo
(Map p52; www.lazoo.org; 5333 Zoo Dr; adult/ child/senior $14/9/11; ⊙10am-5pm; P ♦) Make friends with 1100 finned, feathered and furry creatures, including in the Campo Gorilla Reserve and the Sea Cliffs, which replicate the California coast complete with harbor seals.

MUSEUM OF THE AMERICAN WEST   Museum
(www.autrynationalcenter.org; 4700 Western Heritage Way; adult/child/students & seniors $10/4/6, free 2nd Tue each month; ⊙10am-4pm Tue-Fri, to 5pm Sat & Sun; P ♦) Exhibits on the good, the bad and the ugly of America's westward expansion rope in even the most reluctant of cowpokes. Star exhibits include an original stagecoach, a Colt firearms collection and a nymph-festooned saloon. Its affiliated **Southwest Museum of the American Indian** (234 Museum Dr) is scheduled to reopen in 2013.

West Hollywood
Rainbow flags fly proudly over Santa Monica Blvd. Celebs keep gossip rags happy by misbehaving at clubs on the fabled Sunset Strip. Welcome to the city of West Hollywood (WeHo), 1.9 sq miles of pure personality.

Boutiques on Robertson Blvd and Melrose Ave purvey the sassy and chic for Hollywood royalty, Santa Monica Blvd is gay central, WeHo's eastern precincts are filled with Russian speaking émigrés, and Sunset Blvd bursts with clubs, chichi hotels and views across LA. WeHo's also a hotbed of cutting-edge interior design, particularly along the **Avenues of Art and Design** around Beverly Blvd and Melrose Ave.

PACIFIC DESIGN CENTER   Design Center
(Map p70; www.pacificdesigncenter.com; 8687 Melrose Ave; ⊙9am-5pm Mon-Fri) Some 130 galleries fill the monolithic blue and green 'whales' of the Cesar Pelli–designed Pacific Design Center (a red whale should open by 2012). Visitors are welcome to window-shop, though most sales are to the trade. Parking is $6 per hour.

SUNSET STRIP · Neighborhood

The famed Sunset Strip – Sunset Blvd between Laurel Canyon Blvd and Doheny Dr – has been a favorite nighttime playground since the 1920s. The **Chateau Marmont** and clubs such as Ciro's (now the **Comedy Store**), Mocambo and the Trocadero (both now defunct) were favorite hangouts for Hollywood high society, from Bogart to Bacall, Monroe to Sinatra.

Today the strip is still nightlife central, although it's lost much of its cutting edge. It's a visual cacophony dominated by billboards and giant advertising banners draped across building facades.

Mid-City

Mid-City encompasses an amorphous area east of West Hollywood, south of Hollywood, west of Koreatown and north of I-10 (Santa Monica Fwy). There's plenty of street parking and validated parking at the farmers market and the adjacent Grove shopping mall.

LA BREA TAR PITS · Historic Site

Between 10,000 and 40,000 years ago, tarlike bubbling crude oil trapped saber-toothed cats, mammoths and other extinct Ice Age critters, which are still being excavated at La Brea Tar Pits. Check out their fossilized remains at the **Page Museum** (Map p70; www.tarpits.org; 5801 Wilshire Blvd; adult/child/senior & student $11/5/8, free first Tue each month; ☻9:30am-5pm; 👪). New fossils are being discovered all the time, and an active staff of archaeologists works behind glass. Parking is $7.

PETERSEN AUTOMOTIVE MUSEUM · Museum

(Map p70; www.petersen.org; 6060 Wilshire Blvd; adult/child/student/senior $10/3/5/8; ☻10am-6pm Tue-Sun; 👪) A four-story ode to the auto, the museum exhibits shiny vintage cars galore, plus a fun LA streetscape showing how the city's growth has been shaped by the automobile. Parking is $8.

Left: La Brea Tar Pits; **Below:** Memorial wall, Museum of Tolerance
(LEFT) DAVID PEEVERS/LONELY PLANET IMAGES ©; (BELOW) DAVID PEEVERS/LONELY PLANET IMAGES ©

Beverly Hills & Westside

The mere mention of Beverly Hills conjures up images of fame and wealth, reinforced by film and TV. Opulent mansions flank manicured grounds on palm-lined avenues, especially north of **Sunset Boulevard**, while legendary **Rodeo Drive** is three solid blocks of style for the Prada and Gucci brigade.

Several city-owned parking lots and garages offer up to two hours free parking.

MUSEUM OF TOLERANCE   Museum (www.museumoftolerance.com; 9786 W Pico Blvd; adult/child/student & senior $15/12/11; ⏱10am-5pm Mon-Thu, to 3:30pm Fri, 11am-5pm Sun; P 👫) This museum uses interactive technology to make visitors confront racism and bigotry. There's a particular focus on the Holocaust, including Nazi-era artifacts and letters by Anne Frank. A history wall celebrates diversity, exposes intolerance and champions rights in America. Reservations recommended.

Malibu

Malibu has been synonymous with celebrities since the early 1930s. Clara Bow and Barbara Stanwyck were the first to stake out their turf in what became known as the **Malibu Colony** and the earliest Hollywood elite to Barbra and Leo have lived here ever since.

Along Malibu's spectacular 27-mile stretch of the Pacific Coast Hwy, where the Santa Monica Mountains plunge into the ocean, are some fine beaches, including **Las Tunas**, **Point Dume**, **Zuma** and the world-famous surfing spot **Surfrider**. Rising behind Malibu is **Malibu Creek State Park**, part of the Santa Monica Mountains National Recreation Area and laced with hiking trails. Malibu has no real center, but you'll find the greatest concentration of restaurants and

69

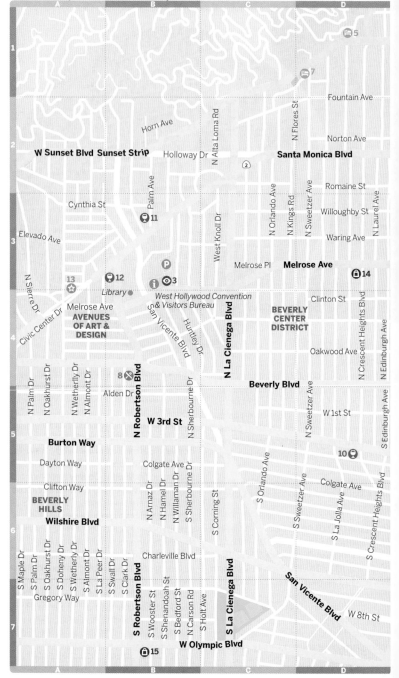

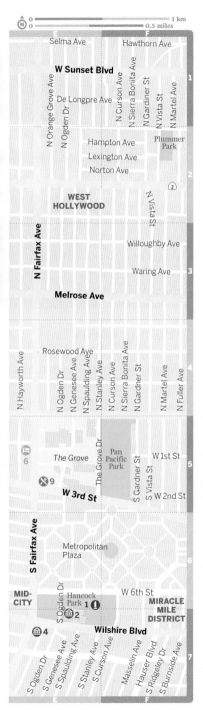

West Hollywood & Mid-City

◎ Sights
1 La Brea Tar Pits E6
2 Los Angeles County Museum of
   Art E7
3 Pacific Design Center B3
   Page Museum .... (see 1)
4 Petersen Automotive Museum E7

🛏 Sleeping
5 Chateau Marmont D1
6 Farmer's Daughter Hotel E5
7 Standard Hollywood D1

⊗ Eating
   Gumbo Pot .... (see 9)
8 Ivy B4
9 Original Farmers Market E5

❂ Drinking
10 El Carmen D5
11 Eleven B3
12 The Abbey B3

⊕ Entertainment
13 Troubadour A3

ⓐ Shopping
14 Fred Segal D3
15 It's a Wrap B7

shops near the century-old **Malibu Pier**. The most likely star-spotting venue is the **Malibu Country Mart shopping center** (3835 Cross Creek Rd).

GETTY VILLA   Art Museum
(www.getty.edu; 17985 Pacific Coast Hwy; admission free; ⊙10am-5pm Wed-Mon; P) Malibu's cultural star – a replica Roman villa that's a fantastic showcase of Greek, Roman and Etruscan antiquities. Admission is by timed ticket (no walk-ins). See also the Getty Center (p75). Parking is $15.

Santa Monica

Santa Monica (Map p76) is the belle by the beach, mixing urban cool with a laid-back vibe.

Tourists, teens and street performers make car-free, chain-store-lined **Third Street Promenade** the most action-packed zone. For more local flavor, shop celeb-favored **Montana Avenue** or down-homey **Main Street**, backbone of the neighborhood once nicknamed 'Dogtown'

RICHARD CUMMINS/LONELY PLANET IMAGES ©

Don't Miss Los Angeles County Museum of Art

LACMA is one of the country's top art museums and the largest in the western USA. The collection in the new Renzo Piano–designed **Broad Contemporary Art Museum** (B-CAM) includes seminal pieces by Jeff Koons, Roy Lichtenstein and Andy Warhol, and two gigantic works in rusted steel by Richard Serra.

Other LACMA pavilions brim with paintings, sculpture and decorative arts: Rembrandt, Cézanne and Magritte; ancient pottery from China, Turkey and Iran; photographs by Ansel Adams and Henri Cartier-Bresson; and a jewel box of a Japanese pavilion. There are often headline-grabbing touring exhibits. Parking is $10.

NEED TO KNOW

Map p70; www.lacma.org; 5905 Wilshire Blvd; adult/child under 17yr/student & senior $15/free/10; ☾noon-8pm Mon, Tue & Thu, noon-9pm Fri, 11am-8pm Sat & Sun

as birthplace of skateboard culture. Rent bikes or in-line skates from many outlets along the beach.

SANTA MONICA PIER Amusement Park (Map p76; www.santamonicapier.org; admission free, unlimited rides under/over 7 $16/22; ☾24hr; 👫) Kids love the venerable 1908 pier, where attractions include a quaint 1922 carousel, a tiny aquarium with touch tanks and the **Pacific Park** (www.pacpark .com) amusement park crowned by a solar-powered Ferris wheel.

BERGAMOT STATION ARTS CENTER Art Galleries & Museum (2525 Michigan Ave; ☾10am-6pm Tue-Sat; P) Art fans gravitate inland toward this avant-garde center, a former trolley stop that now houses 35 galleries and the progressive **Santa Monica Museum of Art** (www.smmoa.org; 2525 Michigan Ave; suggested donation $5; ☾11am-6pm Tue-Sat).

Venice

Venice (Map p76) was created in 1905 by eccentric tobacco heir Abbot Kinney as an amusement park, called 'Venice of America,' complete with Italian *gondolieri* who poled visitors around canals. Most of the waterways have since been paved over, but those that remain are flanked by flower-festooned villas, easily accessed from either Venice or Washington Blvds.

 Activities

Cycling & In-line Skating

Anyone who's ever watched tourism footage of LA (or the opening of *Three's Company*) knows about skating or riding on the **South Bay Bicycle Trail** (Map p76). This paved path parallels the beach for 22 miles, from just north of Santa Monica to the South Bay, with a detour around the yacht harbor at Marina del Rey. Mountain-bikers will find the **Santa Monica Mountains** (Map 52) a suitably challenging playground. You'll find lots of good information at www .labikepaths.com.

There are numerous bike-rental shops, especially along the beaches.

PERRY'S CAFÉ & RENTALS
Bike Rentals
(Map p76; 📞310-939-0000; www.perryscafe .com; Ocean Front Walk; bikes per hr/day $10/25; 🕙9:30am-5:30pm) Several locations on the bike path. They also rent body boards ($8/17 per hour/day). Cash only.

Hiking

For a quick ramble, head to **Griffith Park** (Map p52) or **Runyon Canyon** (off Map p66; www.runyon-canyon.com), both just a hop, skip and jump from frenzied Hollywood Blvd. The latter is a favorite playground of hip and fitness-obsessed locals and their dogs, which roam mostly off-leash. You'll have fine views of the Hollywood Sign, the city and, on clear days, all the way to the beach. Runyon's southern trailhead is at the end of Fuller St, off Franklin Ave.

Runyon Canyon is on the eastern edge of the 150,000-acre **Santa Monica**

♥ If You Like...
Historic Movie Palaces

If you like Grauman's Chinese Theatre (p64), take a gander at these spectacular 1920s and 1930s shrines to film.

1 EL CAPITAN THEATRE
(Map p66; 📞323-467-7674; www.elcapitan .go.com; 6838 Hollywood Blvd, Hollywood) Disney shows first-run movies at this flamboyant East India–styled 1926 theater.

2 EGYPTIAN THEATRE
(Map p66; 📞323-466-3456; www.egyptian theatre.com; 6712 Hollywood Blvd, Hollywood) Home of the nonprofit American Cinematheque, the palm-tree-framed 1922 theater – also built by Sid Grauman – screens classic films and offers monthly behind-the-scenes tours.

3 ORPHEUM THEATRE
(www.laorpheum.com; 842 S Broadway) Now a concert venue, this 1926 beaux-arts building in the Broadway Theatre District) has hosted *American Idol* auditions and sports a Wurlitzer organ.

4 LOS ANGELES THEATRE
(www.losangelestheatre.com; 615 S Broadway) Though now only available for private functions, this 1931 French-baroque-inspired beauty was host to the premier of Charlie Chaplin's *City Lights*. In the Broadway Theatre District).

Mountains National Recreation Area (Map p52; 📞805-370-2301; www.nps.gov /samo). This hilly, tree- and chaparral-covered park follows the outline of Santa Monica Bay from just north of Santa Monica all the way north across the Ventura County line to Point Mugu.

Swimming & Surfing

LA pretty much defines beach culture, yet be prepared: the Pacific is generally chilly; in colder months you'll want a wet suit. Water temperatures peak at about 70°F (21°C) in August and September. Water quality varies; for updated conditions check the 'Beach Report Card' at www .healthebay.org.

Surfing novices can expect to pay up to $120 for an up to two-hour private lesson or $65 to $75 for a group lesson, including board and wet suit. Contact these surfing schools for details:

Learn to Surf LA   Surf School
(www.learntosurfla.com)

Malibu Long Boards   Surf School
(www.malibulongboards.com)

Surf Academy   Surf School
(www.surfacademy.org)

 Tours

ESOTOURIC   History, Literature
(☎ 323-223-2767; www.esotouric.com; bus tours $58) Hip, offbeat, insightful and entertaining walking and bus tours themed around literary lions (Chandler to Bukowski), famous crime sites (Black Dahlia) and historic neighborhoods.

SIX TASTE   Culinary, Walking
(☎ 888-313-0936; www.sixtaste.com; tours $55-65) Walking tours of restaurants in LA neighborhoods, including Downtown, Little Tokyo, Chinatown, Thai Town and Santa Monica.

RED LINE TOURS   Walking, Bus
(☎ 323-402-1074; www.redlinetours.com; tours from $25) 'Edutaining' walking tours of Hollywood and Downtown using headsets that cut out traffic noise.

STARLINE TOURS   Bus
(☎ 323-463-333, 800-959-3131; www.starline tours.com; tours from $39) Narrated bus tours of the city, stars' homes and theme parks.

Studio Tours

Did you know it takes a week to shoot a half-hour sitcom? Or that you rarely see ceilings on TV because the space is filled with lights and lamps? You'll learn these and other fascinating nuggets while touring a working studio. Action is slowest during 'hiatus' (May to August). Reservations recommended; bring photo ID.

Surfing

EDDIE BRADY/LONELY PLANET IMAGES ©

Don't Miss **Getty Center**

Triple delights: stellar art collection (Renaissance to David Hockney), Richard Meier's soaring architecture and Robert Irwin's ever-evolving gardens. On clear days, add breathtaking views of the city and ocean to the list. Visit in the late afternoon after the crowds have thinned. See also Getty Villa (p71). Parking is $15, or Metro bus 761 stops here.

NEED TO KNOW

Map p52; www.getty.edu; 1200 Getty Center Dr; admission free; ⏱10am-5:30pm Sun & Tue-Thu, to 9pm Fri & Sat

---

PARAMOUNT STUDIOS Studio Tour (off Map p66; ☎323-956-1777; www.paramount studios.com; 5555 Melrose Ave, Hollywood; tours $45; ⏱Mon-Fri by reservation) The only studio in Hollywood proper runs two-hour tram tours of its historic lot. Group size is limited to eight per tram. No two tours are alike, and access to stages varies daily, but they might include the sets of *Dr Phil* or *Nip/Tuck*. Minimum age 12.

SONY PICTURES STUDIOS Studio Tour (☎323-520-8687; www.sonypicturesstudios tours.com; 10202 W Washington Blvd, Culver City; tour $33; ⏱tours 9:30am, 10:30am, 1:30pm & 2:30pm Mon-Fri; Ⓟ) Two-hour walk-

ing tours include possible visits to sound stages where *Men in Black*, *Spider-Man*, *Charlie's Angels* and other blockbusters were filmed. Munchkins hopped along the Yellow Brick Road in the *Wizard of Oz*, filmed when this was the venerable MGM studio.

WARNER BROS STUDIOS Studio Tour (☎818-972-8687; www.wbstudiotour.com; 3400 Riverside Dr, Burbank; tours $45; ⏱8:30am-4pm Mon-Fri, extended hr Mar-Sep) This 2¼-hour, fun yet authentic look behind the scenes kicks off with a video of WB's greatest hits (*Rebel Without a Cause, Harry Potter* etc) before you travel by mini-tram to sound

Santa Monica & Venice Beach

0 —————— 500 m
0 —————— 0.25 miles

Santa Monica & Venice Beach

◉ Sights
1 Carousel A3
2 Pacific Park Amusement Park............A3
3 Santa Monica Pier Aquarium..............A3
4 Third St Promenade B2

❸ Activities, Courses & Tours
5 Perry's Café & Rentals A1
6 Perry's Café & Rentals A4

🛏 Sleeping
7 Embassy Hotel Apartments B1
8 Hotel Erwin..A6

✖ Eating
9 Gjelina..B7
10 Santa Monica Farmers Market..........B2
11 Santa Monica Place B2

❸ Drinking
12 Copa d'Oro B2

ⓐ Shopping
13 Fred Segal B2

stages, backlot sets and technical departments. Tours leave roughly every half-hour. Minimum age eight. Parking $7.

 **Festivals & Events**

TOURNAMENT OF ROSES   Parade
(☎626-449-4100; www.tournamentofroses.com) New Year's Day cavalcade of flower-festooned floats along Pasadena's Colorado Blvd, followed by the Rose Bowl football game.

FIESTA BROADWAY   Street Fair
(☎310-914-0015; www.fiestabroadway.la) Mexican-themed fair along historic Broadway in Downtown, with perform-ances by Latino stars. Last Sunday in April.

WEST HOLLYWOOD HALLOWEEN CARNIVAL   Street Fair
(☎323-848-6400; www.visitwesthollywood .com) Eccentric, and often NC-17-rated, costumes fill Santa Monica Blvd, on October 31.

🛏 Sleeping

For seaside life, base yourself in Santa Monica, Venice or Long Beach. Cool-hunters and party people will be happiest in Hollywood or WeHo; culture-vultures, in Downtown.

Downtown

STANDARD DOWNTOWN LA   Hotel $$
(📞 213-892-8080; www.standardhotel.com; 550 S Flower St; r from $165; ❊@☎☎) This 207-room design-savvy hotel in a former office building goes for a young, hip and shag-happy crowd – the rooftop bar fairly pulses – so don't come here with kids or to get a solid night's sleep. Mod, minimalist rooms have platform beds and peek-through showers. Parking is $33.

FIGUEROA HOTEL   Historic Hotel $$
(📞 213-627-8971, 800-421-9092; www.figueroa hotel.com; 939 S Figueroa St; r $148-184, ste $225-265; ❊@☎☎) A rambling 1920s oasis across from LA Live, the Fig welcomes guests with a richly tiled Spanish-style lobby that segues to a sparkling pool and buzzy outdoor bar. Rooms are furnished in a world-beat mash-up of styles (Morocco, Mexico, Zen...), comfy but varying in size and configuration. Parking is $12.

Hollywood

HOLLYWOOD ROOSEVELT HOTEL   Hotel $$$
(Map p66; 📞 323-466-7000, 800-950-7667; www.holly woodroosevelt.com; 7000 Hollywood Blvd; r from $269; ❊@☎☎) This venerable hotel has hosted elite players since the first Academy Awards were held here in 1929. It pairs a palatial Spanish lobby with sleek Asian contemporary rooms, a busy pool scene

and rockin' restos: Public and 25 Degrees burger bar. Parking is $33.

MAGIC CASTLE HOTEL   Hotel $$
(Map p66; 📞 323-851-0800, 800-741-4915; www.magiccastlehotel.com; 7025 Franklin Ave; r $154-304; ❊☎☎👤) Walls are thin, but this renovated former apartment building around a courtyard boasts contemporary furniture, attractive art, comfy bathrobes and fancy bath amenities. Most rooms have a separate living room. For breakfast: freshly baked goods and gourmet coffee on your balcony or poolside. Ask about access to the namesake private club for magicians. Parking is $10.

West Hollywood & Mid-City

STANDARD HOLLYWOOD   Hotel $$
(Map p70; 📞 323-650-9090; www.standardhotel .com; 8300 W Sunset Blvd; r $165-250, ste from $350; ❊@☎☎) This white-on-white property on the Sunset Strip is a scene with Astroturf-fringed pool offering a view across LA and sizable shagadelic rooms

235

Tournament of Roses
RICHARD CUMMINS/LONELY PLANET IMAGES ©

GREG BALFOUR EVANS/ALAMY ©

Don't Miss **Venice Boardwalk**

Freak show, human zoo and wacky carnival, the Venice Boardwalk is an essential LA experience. This cauldron of counter-culture is the place to get your hair braided or a *qi gong* back massage, or pick up cheap sunglasses or a woven bracelet. Encounters with bodybuilders, hoop dreamers, a Speedo-clad snake charmer or an in-line-skating Sikh minstrel are pretty much guaranteed, especially on hot summer afternoons. Alas, the vibe gets a bit creepy after dark.

NEED TO KNOW
Ocean Front Walk; Map p76

with silver beanbag chairs, orange-tiled bathrooms and Warhol poppy-print curtains. Parking is $29.

FARMER'S DAUGHTER HOTEL Motel $$
(Map p70; ☎ 323-937-3930; www.farmersdaugh terhotel.com; 115 S Fairfax Ave; r $219-269; ❋ @ 🛜 ☲ 🛉) Opposite the Original Farmers Market, Grove and CBS Studios, this perennial pleaser gets high marks for its sleek 'urban cowboy' look. Parking is $18.

CHATEAU MARMONT Historic Hotel $$$
(Map p70; ☎ 323-656-1010; www.chateau marmont.com; 8221 W Sunset Blvd; r $415, ste $500-875; ❋ 🛜 ☲) Its French-flavored indulgence may look dated, but this faux-chateau has long attracted A-listers – Greta Garbo to Bono – with its legendary discretion. The garden cottages are the most romantic. Parking is $28.

Beverly Hills

BEVERLY HILLS HOTEL Hotel $$$
(☎ 310-276-2251, 800-283-8885; www.beverly hillshotel.com; 9641 Sunset Blvd; r from $530; ❋ @ 🛜 ☲) The legendary Pink Palace from 1912 oozes opulence. The pool deck is classic, the grounds are lush, and the Polo Lounge remains a clubby lunch spot

for the well heeled and well dressed. Rooms are comparably old-world, with gold accents and marble tiles. Parking is $33.

Santa Monica & Venice

HOTEL ERWIN   Hotel $$

(Map p76; 310-452-1111; www.jdvhotels.com; 1679 Pacific Ave, Venice; r from $169; ✴ @ 🛜) A worthy emblem of Venice. Rooms aren't the biggest and in most there's a low traffic hum, but you're steps from the beach and your room features graffiti- or anime-inspired art and honor bar containing sunglasses and '70s-era soft drinks. The rooftop bar offers spellbinding coastal vistas. Parking is $28.

**EMBASSY HOTEL
APARTMENTS**   Boutique Hotel $$

(Map p76; 310-394-1279; www.embassyhotel apts.com; 1001 3rd St, Santa Monica; r $169-390; P @) This hushed 1927 Spanish-colonial hideaway delivers charm by the bucket. A rickety elevator takes you to units oozing old-world flair and equipped with internet. Kitchens make many rooms well suited to do-it-yourselfers. No air-con.

Long Beach

QUEEN MARY HOTEL   Cruise Ship $$

(562-435-3511; www.queenmary.com; 1126 Queens Hwy, Long Beach; r $110-395; ✴ @ 🛜) Take a trip without leaving the dock aboard this grand ocean liner (p79). Staterooms brim with original art-deco details – avoid the cheapest ones that are on the inside. Rates include admission to guided tours. Parking is $12 to $15.

 Eating

Downtown

For browsing, try the food stalls of the **Grand Central Market** (Map p60; 317 S Broadway; 🕘9am-6pm).

BOTTEGA LOUIE   Italian $$

(213-802-1470; www.bottegalouie.com; 700 S Grand Ave; mains $11-18; 🕘breakfast, lunch & dinner) The wide marble bar at Bottega Louie has become a magnet for the artsy loft set and office workers alike. The open-kitchen crew, in chef's whites, grills

Malibu (p69)

house-made sausage and wood-fires thin-crust pizzas in the white-on-white, big-as-a-gym dining room. Always busy, always buzzy.

NICKEL DINER   Diner $
(www.5cdiner.com; 524 S Main St; mains $8-14; ⊙8am-3:30pm Tue-Sun, 6pm-11pm Tue-Sat) In Downtown's boho historic district, this red vinyl joint feels like a throwback to the 1920s. Ingredients are 21st century, though: artichokes stuffed with quinoa salad, burgers piled with poblano chiles. Must-try dessert: maple-glazed bacon donut.

PHILIPPE THE ORIGINAL   Diner $
(www.philippes.com; 1001 N Alameda St; sandwiches $6-7.50; ⊙6am-10pm; P) LAPD hunks, stressed-out attorneys and Midwestern vacationers all flock to this legendary 'home of the French dip sandwich,' dating back to 1908 at the edge of Chinatown. Order your choice of meat on a crusty roll dipped in au jus, and hunker down at the tables on the sawdust-covered floor. Coffee is just 10¢ (no misprint). Cash only.

Hollywood, Los Feliz & Silver Lake

MUSSO & FRANK GRILL   Bar, Grill $$
(Map p66; ☏323-467-7788; 6667 Hollywood Blvd; mains $12-35; ⊙11am-11pm Tue-Sat) Hollywood history hangs thickly in the air at the boulevard's oldest eatery. Waiters balance platters of steaks, chops, grilled liver and other dishes harking back to the days when cholesterol wasn't part of our vocabulary. Service is smooth, so are the martinis.

⌖WAFFLE   New American $
(Map p66; ☏323-465-6901; www.thewaffle.us; 6255 W Sunset Blvd; most mains $9-12; ⊙6:30am-2:30am Sun-Thu, to 4:30am Fri & Sat) After a night out clubbing, do you really feel like filling yourself with garbage? Us, too. But the Waffle's 21st-century diner food – cornmeal-jalapeño waffles with grilled chicken, carrot-cake waffles, mac and cheese, samiches, heaping salads – is organic and locally sourced, so it's (almost) good for you.

UMAMI BURGER   Burgers $$
(www.umamiburger.com; 4655 Hollywood Blvd; burgers $9-17; ⊙lunch & dinner; P🛉) With a

Pier, Manhattan Beach

spacious brick interior framed by rusted iron, this is by far the grooviest Umami in the fledgling empire. It does the staples everyone loves (the Umami, the SoCal and the Truffle), as well as a *carnitas* (Mexican braised pork) and a Jurky (jerk turkey) burger. The wine bar offers $4 artisan drafts or glasses of wine, and $5 'smash burgers' at happy hour (3pm to 7pm).

West Hollywood & Mid-City

IVY   American **$$$**

(Map p70; ☏ 310-274-8303; www.theivyla .com; 113 N Robertson Blvd; mains $20-38; ☺11:30am-11pm Mon-Fri, 11am-11pm Sat, 10am-11pm Sun) In the heart of Robertson's fashion frenzy, the Ivy's picket-fenced porch and rustic cottage are *the* power lunch spot. Chances of catching B-lister (possibly A-lister) babes nibbling on a carrot stick or studio execs discussing sequels over the lobster omelet are excellent.

ORIGINAL FARMERS MARKET   Market **$**

(Map p70; cnr 3rd St & S Fairfax Ave; 🍴) The market hosts a dozen worthy, budget-priced eateries, most *alfresco*. Try the classic diner Du-par's, Cajun-style cooking at the Gumbo Pot, ¡Loteria! Mexican grill or Singapore's Banana Leaf.

Malibu

REEL INN   Seafood **$$**

(www.reelinnmalibu.com; 18661 Pacific Coast Hwy; fresh grilled fish $12-25; ☺lunch & dinner; 🅿) Across PCH from the ocean, this shambling shack with counter service and picnic tables serves up fish and seafood for any budget and many styles, including grilled, fried or Cajun. The cole-slaw, potatoes and Cajun rice (included in most meals) have fans from Harley riders to beach bums and families. It's an easy detour from Topanga State Park or the Getty Villa (p71).

Santa Monica & Venice

To shop with gourmands for fresh veg-etables, cheeses, meats and herbs, check

If You Like... Beaches

If you like digging your toes in the sand or riding the Pacific's waves, the LA area has plenty of places to indulge your California dreaming.

1 EL MATADOR
Small beach hideaway, about 2.5 miles northwest of Zuma Beach, hemmed in by battered rock cliffs and strewn with giant boulders. Wild surf; not suitable for children. Clothing optional (unofficially).

2 VENICE BEACH
(Map p76) LA's most outlandish beach, with a nonstop parade of friends and freaks. Drum circle in the sand on Sundays.

3 MANHATTAN BEACH
(Map p52) The most upmarket of the South Bay beach cities (Redondo, Hermosa and Manhattan), where surfers still rule the waves.

4 MALIBU LAGOON/SURFRIDER BEACH
(Map p52) Legendary surf beach with superb swells and extended rides. Water quality is only so-so. The lagoon is great for bird-watching.

5 SANTA MONICA
(Map p76) Along the South Bay Bicycle Trail, this spacious stretch of sand lures volleyball players and families.

out **Santa Monica farmers market** (Map p76; www.smgov.net/portals/farmersmarket).

GJELINA   Californian **$$**

(Map p76; ☏ 310-450-1429; www.gjelina.com; 1429 Abbot Kinney Blvd, Venice; dishes $8-25; ☺lunch & dinner) Whether you carve out a slip on the communal table between the hipsters and yuppies or get your own slab of wood on the rustic stone terrace, you will dine on delicious and imaginative small plates (think chanterelles and gravy on toast or raw yellowtail spiced with chili and mint and drenched in olive oil and blood orange), and sensational thin-crust, wood-fired pizza.

SANTA MONICA
PLACE
Shopping Center **$$**

(Map p76; www.santamonicaplace.com; 3rd fl, cnr Third St & Broadway, Santa Monica;  **)** We wouldn't normally eat at a mall, but the indoor-outdoor dining deck sets standards: Latin-Asian fusion at Zengo (think Peking duck tacos), sushi at Ozumo, wood-oven-baked pizzas at Antica. Most restaurants have seating with views across adjacent rooftops – some to the ocean. Stalls in the market do *salumi* to soufflés.

Drinking

EDISON
Fashionable Bar

(www.edisondowntown.com; 108 W 2nd St, enter off Harlem Alley; ⏰**5pm-2am Wed-Fri, 6pm-2am Sat)** *Metropolis* meets *Blade Runner* at this industrial-chic basement boîte, where you'll sip mojitos surrounded by turbines from Edison's days as a boiler room. It's all tarted up nicely with cocoa leather couches and three cavernous bars.

ROOFTOP BAR@STANDARD
DOWNTOWN LA
Bar

(550 S Flower St; ⏰**noon-1:30am)** The scene at this outdoor lounge, swimming in a sea of skyscrapers, is libidinous, intense and more than a bit surreal. There are vibrating waterbed pods for lounging, hot-bod servers and a pool for cooling off if it all gets too steamy. Velvet rope on weekends.

FORMOSA CAFE
Bar

(☎**323-850-9050; 7156 Santa Monica Blvd, Hollywood)** Bogie and Bacall used to knock 'em back at this watering hole, and today you can use all that nostalgia to soak up mai tais and martinis.

EL CARMEN
Tequila Bar

(Map p70; ☎**323-852-1552; 8138 W 3rd St, Mid-City;** ⏰**5pm-2am Mon-Fri, 7pm-2am Sat & Sun)** Beneath mounted bull heads and *lucha libre* (Mexican wrestling) masks, this tequila temple dispenses cocktails based on over 100 tequilas. Industry-heavy crowd.

COPA D'ORO
Lounge

(Map p76; www.copadoro.com; 217 Broadway; ⏰**6pm-2am Mon-Fri, 8pm-2am Sat & Sun)** Old-school, handcrafted cocktails from a well of top-end liquors and a produce bin of fresh herbs, fruits, juices and a few veggies too. The rock tunes and the smooth, dark ambience don't hurt.

Queen Mary

Detour:
Long Beach

Long Beach is the other half of the port of Los Angeles, with an industrial edge that has been worn smooth in its humming downtown and restyled waterfront.

Long Beach's 'flagship' is the **Queen Mary** (www.queenmary.com; 1126 Queens Hwy; adult/child/senior from $25/13/22; ⏰10am-6pm), a grand (and supposedly haunted!) British ocean liner, permanently moored here. Larger and fancier than the *Titanic*, it transported royals, dignitaries, immigrants and troops during its 1001 Atlantic crossings between 1936 and 1964. Parking is $12.

Kids will probably have a better time at the **Aquarium of the Pacific** (www .aquariumofpacific.org; 100 Aquarium Way; adult/child/senior $25/13/22; ⏰9am-6pm; ⏣) – a high-tech romp through an underwater world in which sharks dart, jellyfish dance and sea lions frolic. Imagine the thrill of petting a shark! Parking is $8 to $15. *Queen Mary* and aquarium combination tickets cost $36/20 for adult/child three to 11 years.

Entertainment

The freebie *LA Weekly* and the *Los Angeles Times* Calendar section are your best sources for plugging into the local scene. Buy tickets at box offices or through **Ticketmaster** (📞213-480-3232; www.ticketmaster .com). Half-price tickets to many shows are sold online by **LAStageTIX** (www .theatrela.org).

Cinemas

Movie-going is serious business in LA; it's not uncommon for viewers to sit through the end credits, out of respect for friends and neighbors. In addition to the classic Hollywood theaters like Grauman's Chinese and El Capitan, venues listed here are noteworthy for their upscale atmosphere. Tickets for most theaters can be booked online or through **Moviefone** (📞from any LA area code 777-3456).

ARCLIGHT   Cinema
(Map p66; 📞323-464-4226; www.arclight cinemas.com; 6360 W Sunset Blvd, Hollywood) This cineastes' favorite multiplex offers plush seating and no commercials before films (only trailers). Look for the landmark geodesic Cinerama Dome.

AMERICAN CINEMATHEQUE   Classic Cinema
(📞323-466-3456; www.americancinematheque .com) Hollywood (Map p66; Egyptian Theatre, 6712 Hollywood Blvd); Santa Monica (off Map p76; Aero Theatre, 1328 Montana Ave) Eclectic film fare from around the world for serious cinephiles, often followed by chats with the actors or director.

Live Music

TROUBADOUR   Live Music
(Map p70; www.troubadour.com; 9081 Santa Monica Blvd, West Hollywood; ⏰Mon-Sat) The Troub did its part in catapulting the Eagles and Tom Waits to stardom, and it's still a great place to catch tomorrow's headliners. The all-ages policy ensures a mixed crowd that's refreshingly low on attitude. Mondays are free.

SPACELAND   Live Music
(www.clubspaceland.com; 1717 Silver Lake Blvd, Silver Lake) Mostly local alt-rock, indie, skate-punk and electrotrash bands take the stage here in the hopes of making it big. Beck and the Eels played some of their early gigs here.

CATALINA BAR & GRILL   Jazz
(Map p66; www.catalinajazzclub.com; 6725 W Sunset Blvd, Hollywood; cover $12-35, plus dinner

or 2 drinks; ⊙ Tue-Sun) LA's premier jazz club has a ho-hum location but top-notch acts, including Ann Hampton Calloway and Karen Akers.

Nightclubs

DRAI'S
Club

(Map p66; www.draishollywood.com; 6250 Hollywood Blvd; ⊙10pm-3am Tue-Sat) The W Hotel rooftop is the domain of this classic Vegas after-hours club. If you dig bling and surgical enhancements, hip-hop and the sweaty pulse of a packed dance floor, you will be in Shangri La. Wednesday and Friday are the big nights.

LITTLE TEMPLE
Club

(www.littletemple.com; 4519 Santa Monica Blvd; ⊙9pm-2am Wed-Sun) This Buddha-themed lounge still brings global grooves to the people via live acts and local DJs. Fans of good reggae, funk and Latin rhythms shake their collective ass here. Admission prices vary.

Sports

DODGER STADIUM
Baseball

(www.dodgers.com; 1000 Elysian Park Dr, Downtown) LA's Major League Baseball team plays from April to October in this legendary stadium.

STAPLES CENTER
Basketball, Ice Hockey

(Map p60; www.staplescenter.com; 1111 S Figueroa St, Downtown) All the high-tech trappings fill this flying-saucer-shaped home to the Lakers, Clippers and Sparks basketball teams, and the Kings ice hockey team. Headliners – Britney Spears to Katy Perry – also perform here.

🛍 Shopping

Fashion-forward fashionistas (and paparazzi) flock to Robertson Blvd (between Beverly Blvd and W 3rd St) or Melrose Ave (between San Vicente and La Brea) in West Hollywood, while bargain hunters

Left: Little Temple; **Below:** Grauman's Chinese Theatre (p64)

(LEFT) BRENT WINEBRENNER/LONELY PLANET IMAGES ©; (BELOW) DAVID PEEVERS/LONELY PLANET IMAGES ©

haunt Downtown's **Fashion District** (Map p60; 213-488-1153; www.fashiondistrict.org), a frantic, 90-block trove of stores, stalls and showrooms where discount shopping is an Olympian sport. If money is no object, Beverly Hills beckons with international couture, jewelry and antiques, especially along Rodeo Dr, which is ground central for groovy tunes, while east of here Silver Lake has cool kitsch and collectibles, especially around Sunset Junction (Hollywood and Sunset Blvds). Santa Monica has good boutique shopping on high-toned Montana Ave and eclectic Main St, while the chain store brigade (H&M to Banana Republic) has taken over Third Street Promenade. In nearby Venice, you'll find cheap and crazy knickknacks along the Venice Boardwalk, although locals prefer Abbot Kinney Blvd with its fun mix of art, fashion and new-age emporiums.

FRED SEGAL   Clothing

West Hollywood (Map p70; 323-651-4129; 8100 Melrose Ave; P); Santa Monica (Map p76;

310-458-9940; 500 Broadway; P) Cameron and Gwyneth are among the stars kitted out at this kingpin of LA fashion boutiques, where you can also stock up on beauty products, sunglasses, gifts and other essentials.

IT'S A WRAP   Clothing

Mid-City (Map p70; www.itsawrap.com; 1164 S Robertson Blvd); Burbank (3315 W Magnolia Blvd) Dress like a movie star – in their actual clothes! It's a Wrap sells wardrobe castoffs – tank tops to tuxedos – worn by actors and extras working on TV or movie shoots. Tags are coded, so you'll know whose clothing you can brag about wearing.

AMOEBA MUSIC   Music

(Map p66; www.amoeba.com; 6400 W Sunset Blvd, Hollywood; 10:30am-11pm Mon-Sat, 11am-9pm Sun; P) Our friends call it 'Hot-moeba' for good reason: all-star staff and listening stations help you sort through

85

over half a million new and used CDs, DVDs, videos and vinyl, and there are free in-store live shows.

SPACE 1520   Mall
(Map p66; www.space1520.com; 1520 N Cahuenga Blvd; ⊙11am-9pm Mon-Fri, 10am-10pm Sat, to 9pm Sun; P) The hippest mini-mall in Hollywood, this designer construct of brick, wood, concrete and glass is home to classic and trend-setting mini-chains such as Umami Burger and the Hennesy & Ingalls art and design bookstore.

ℹ Information

Dangers & Annoyances

Despite what you see in the movies, walking around LA is generally safe. Downtown's Skid Row, an area roughly bounded by 3rd, Alameda, 7th and Main Sts, has plenty of homeless folks, as does Santa Monica.

Money

Travelex (☎310-659-6093; US Bank, 8901 Santa Monica Blvd, West Hollywood; ⊙9am-5pm Mon-Thu, to 6pm Fri, to 1pm Sat)

Tourist Information

Downtown LA (☎213-689-8822; http://discoverlosangeles.com; 685 S Figueroa St; ⊙8:30am-5pm Mon-Fri)

Hollywood (☎323-467-6412; http://disco verlosangeles.com; Hollywood & Highland complex, 6801 Hollywood Blvd; ⊙10am-10pm Mon-Sat, to 7pm Sun)

Santa Monica (☎310-393-7593, 800-544-5319; www.santamonica.com) Visitor center (1920 Main St; ⊙9am-6pm); Information kiosk (☎1400 Ocean Ave; ⊙9am-5pm Jun-Aug, 10am-4pm Sep-May)

ℹ Getting There & Away

Air

Los Angeles International Airport (LAX; www .lawa.org; 1 World Way, Los Angeles) is one of the world's busiest, located on the coast between Venice and the South Bay city of Manhattan Beach.

Locals love Bob Hope Airport (BUR; www .bobhopeairport.com; 2627 N Hollywood Way, Burbank), commonly called Burbank Airport, in the San Fernando Valley. It has delightful art-deco

Blue-whale exhibit, Aquarium of the Pacific (p83)

Los Angeles for Children

Keeping the rug rats happy is child's play in LA.

The sprawling Los Angeles Zoo (p67) in family-friendly Griffith Park is a sure bet. Dino fans dig the Page Museum at the La Brea Tar Pits (p68). For live sea creatures, head to the Aquarium of the Pacific (p79); teens might get a kick out of the ghost tours of the *Queen Mary* (p79).

Among LA's amusement parks, Santa Monica Pier (p72) is meant for kids of all ages. Activities for younger children are more limited at Universal Studios Hollywood (p65).

style, easy-to-use terminals and proximity to Hollywood, Downtown and Pasadena.

To the south, on the border with Orange County, Long Beach Airport (LGB; www.long beach.gov/airport; 4100 Donald Douglas Dr, Long Beach) is convenient for Disneyland.

Bus

LA's hub for Greyhound (✆213-629-8401, 800-231-2222; www.greyhound.com; 1716 E 7th St) is in an unsavory part of Downtown, so avoid arriving after dark. Some northbound buses stop at the terminal in Hollywood (✆323-466-6381; 1715 N Cahuenga Blvd), and a few southbound buses also pass through Long Beach (✆562-218-3011; 1498 Long Beach Blvd).

Car & Motorcycle

All the major international car-rental agencies have branches at airports and throughout Los Angeles. If you haven't booked, use the courtesy phones in airport arrival areas at LAX.

Train

Amtrak trains roll into Downtown's historic Union Station (✆800-872-7245; www.amtrak.com; 800 N Alameda St) from across California and the country. The *Pacific Surfliner* travels daily to San Diego ($36, 2¾ hours), Santa Barbara ($29, 2¾ to 3¼ hours) and San Luis Obispo ($40, 5½ hours).

ⓘ Getting Around

To/From the Airport

At LAX, door-to-door shared-ride vans operated by Prime Time (✆800-473-3743; www.prime timeshuttle.com) and Super Shuttle (✆310-782-

6600; www.supershuttle.com) leave from the lower level of all terminals. Typical fares to Santa Monica, Hollywood or Downtown are $20, $25 and $16, respectively. Disneyland Express (✆714-978-8855; www.grayline.com) travels at least hourly between LAX and Disneyland-area hotels for one way/round trip $22/$32.

Curbside dispatchers will summon a taxi for you. There's a flat fare of $46.50 to Downtown LA. Otherwise, metered fares ($2.85 at flag fall plus $2.70 per mile) average $30 to Santa Monica, $42 to Hollywood and up to $90 to Disneyland. There is a $4 surcharge for taxis departing LAX.

LAX Flyaway Buses (✆866-435-9529; www.lawa.org/flyaway) depart LAX terminals every 30 minutes, from about 5am to midnight, nonstop to both Westwood ($5, 30 minutes) and Union Station ($7, 45 minutes) in Downtown LA.

Other public transportation is slower and less convenient but cheaper. From the lower level outside any terminal, catch a free shuttle bus to parking lot C, next to the LAX Transit Center, hub for buses serving all of LA. You can also take shuttle bus G to Aviation Station and the Metro Green Line light rail, from where you can connect to the Metro Blue Line and Downtown LA or Long Beach (40 minutes).

Bicycle

Most buses have bike racks and bikes ride for free, although you must securely load and unload it yourself. Bikes are also allowed on Metro Rail trains except during rush hour (6:30am to 8:30am and 4:30pm to 6:30pm weekdays).

Car & Motorcycle

Driving in LA doesn't need to be a hassle (a GPS device helps), but be prepared for some of the worst traffic in the country during rush hour (roughly 7:30am to 9am and 4pm to 6:30pm).

Parking at motels and cheaper hotels is usually free, while fancier ones charge from $8 to $36. Valet parking at nicer restaurants, hotels and nightspots is commonplace, with rates ranging from $2.50 to $10.

Public Transportation

Trip-planning help is available via LA's Metro (☎800-266-6883; www.metro.net), which operates about 200 bus lines and six subway and light-rail lines:

Blue Line Downtown (7th St/Metro Center) to Long Beach.

Expo Line Downtown (7th St/Metro Center) to Culver City, via Exposition Park (scheduled opening: winter 2011–12).

Gold Line Union Station to Pasadena and East LA.

Green Line Norwalk to Redondo Beach, with shuttle to LAX.

Purple Line Downtown to Koreatown.

Red Line Union Station to North Hollywood, via Downtown, Hollywood and Universal Studios.

Tickets cost $1.50 per boarding (get a transfer when boarding if needed). There are no free transfers between trains and buses, but 'TAP card' unlimited ride passes cost $5/20/75 (plus $1 for the reusable card) per day/week/month. Purchase train tickets and TAP cards at vending machines in stations, or visit www.metro.net for other vendors.

Local DASH minibuses (☎your area code + 808-2273; www.ladottransit.com; 50¢) serve Downtown and Hollywood. Santa Monica–based Big Blue Bus (☎310-451-5444; www.bigbluebus .com, $1) serves much of the Westside and LAX. Its Line 10 Freeway Express connects Santa Monica with Downtown LA ($2; one hour).

Gay & Lesbian LA

The rainbow flag flies especially proudly in 'Boystown,' along Santa Monica Blvd in West Hollywood, which is lined with dozens of bars, cafes, restaurants, gyms and clubs. Most places cater to gay men. Silver Lake, LA's original gay enclave, has evolved from largely leather and Levi's to encompass both cute hipsters of all ethnicities to an older contingent. Long Beach also has a significant gay neighborhood.

If nightlife isn't your scene, the gay community has plenty of other ways to meet. **Will Rogers State Beach** ('Ginger Rogers' to her friends) in Santa Monica is LA's unofficial gay beach. **Long Beach Pride Celebration** (www.longbeachpride .com; ☾late May) is a warm-up for **LA Pride** (www.lapride.org; ☾mid-Jun), a weekend of nonstop partying and a parade down Santa Monica Blvd.

LA's essential gay bar and restaurant is **The Abbey** (Map p70; www.abbeyfood andbar.com; 692 N Robertson Blvd; mains $9-24; ☾9am-2am). Take your pick of preening and partying spaces spanning a leafy patio to a slick lounge, and enjoy flavored martinis and upscale pub grub. Other venues include **Eleven** (Map p70; www .eleven.la; 8811 Santa Monica Blvd; mains $13-29; ☾6-10pm Tue-Sun, 11am-3pm Sat & Sun), a glam spot that occupies a historic building, serves New American cuisine and offers different theme nights; **Akbar** (www.akbarsilverlake.com; 4356 W Sunset Blvd), which has the best jukebox in town, a casbah atmosphere, and a crowd that's been known to change from hour to hour; and **MJ's** (www.mjsbar.com; 2810 Hyperion Ave), a popular contempo hangout for dance nights, 'porn star of the week' and cruising; it has a young but diverse crowd.

Your 15 Minutes of Fame

Come on, haven't you always dreamed of seeing your silly mug on TV? Well, LA has a way of making dreams come true, but you have to do your homework before coming to town. Here are some leads to get you started.

Sitcoms and game shows usually tape between August and March before live audiences. To nab free tickets, check with **Audiences Unlimited** (✆818-260-0041; www.tvtickets.com). For tickets to the *Tonight Show* at **NBC Studios** (3000 W Alameda Ave, Burbank), check www.nbc.com/nbc/footer/tickets.shtml.

Although many game shows tape in LA, the chances of becoming a contestant are greatest on *The Price is Right*, at **CBS Television City** (www.cbs.com/daytime /price; 7800 Beverly Blvd, Mid-City).

Taxi

Except for taxis lined up outside airports, train stations, bus stations and major hotels, it's best to phone for a cab. Fares are metered: $2.85 at flag fall plus $2.70 per mile. Taxis serving the airport accept credit cards, though sometimes grudgingly. Some recommended companies:

Checker (✆800-300-5007)

Independent (✆800-521-8294)

Yellow Cab (✆800-200-1085)

San Francisco

Get to know the world capital of weird from the inside out, from mural-lined alleyways named after poets to clothing-optional beaches on a former military base. But don't be too quick to dismiss San Francisco's wild ideas. Bio-tech, gay rights, personal computers, cable cars and organic fine dining were once considered outlandish too, before San Francisco introduced these underground ideas into the mainstream decades ago. San Francisco's morning fog erases the boundaries between land and ocean, reality and infinite possibility.

Rules are never strictly followed here, but bliss is. Golden Gate Bridge and Alcatraz are entirely optional – San Franciscans mostly admire them from afar – leaving you free to pursue inspiration in the beauty of Golden Gate Park, the city's flamboyantly painted Victorians and its funky Mission galleries. Just don't be late for your sensational, sus-tainable dinner: in San Francisco, you can find happiness and eat it too.

Conservatory of Flowers (p106), Golden State Park

San Francisco
RUDY SULGAN/CORBIS ©

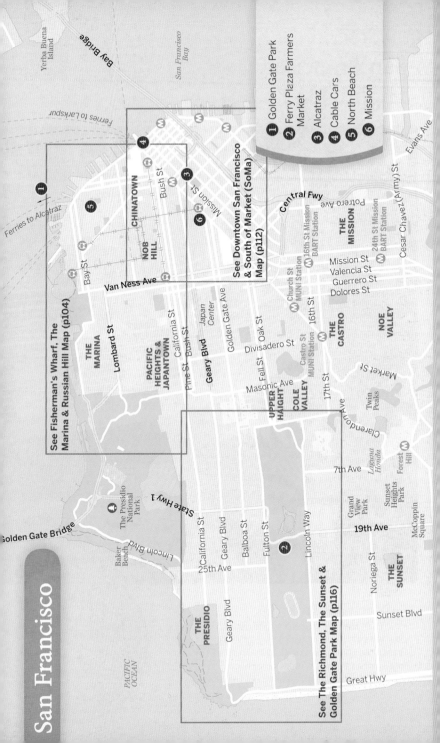

San Francisco

1. Golden Gate Park
2. Ferry Plaza Farmers Market
3. Alcatraz
4. Cable Cars
5. North Beach
6. Mission

See Fisherman's Wharf, The Marina & Russian Hill Map (p104)

See Downtown San Francisco & South of Market (SoMa) Map (p112)

See The Richmond, The Sunset & Golden Gate Park Map (p116)

Yerba Buena Island

Bay Bridge

San Francisco Bay

Ferries to Larkspur

Ferries to Alcatraz

CHINATOWN

NOB HILL

Bay St

Bush St

Mission St

Van Ness Ave

Central Fwy

Potrero Ave

THE MISSION

16th St Mission BART Station

24th St Mission BART Station

Cesar Chavez (Army) St

Evans Ave

Mission St
Valencia St
Guerrero St
Dolores St

Church St MUNI Station

16th St

THE CASTRO

NOE VALLEY

Castro St MUNI Station

17th St

Market St

THE MARINA

Lombard St

PACIFIC HEIGHTS & JAPANTOWN

Japan Center

California St

Golden Gate Ave

Divisadero St

Fell St

Oak St

Geary Blvd

Pine St

Bush St

Masonic Ave

UPPER HAIGHT

COLE VALLEY

Clarendon Ave

Twin Peaks

7th Ave

Laguna Honda

Forest Hill

Grand View Park

Sunset Heights Park

19th Ave

McCoppin Square

Golden Gate Bridge

The Presidio National Park

THE PRESIDIO

Baker Beach

Lincoln Blvd

State Hwy 1

PACIFIC OCEAN

California St

Geary Blvd

Balboa St

Fulton St

25th Ave

Lincoln Way

Noriega St

THE SUNSET

Sunset Blvd

Great Hwy

Geary Blvd

San Francisco Highlights

Golden Gate Park

When San Franciscans refer to 'the park,' there's only one that gets the definite article. Everything that San Franciscans hold dear is in Golden Gate Park (p102): free spirits, free music, redwoods, Frisbee, protests, fine art, bonsai and buffalo. California Academy of Sciences (p110)

Need to Know

CAR-FREE WEEKENDS Eastern JFK Drive closes to cars on weekends and holidays **DISCOUNTS** Both park museums give discounts to MUNI riders **For more, see p106**.

Golden Gate Park Don't Miss List

BY BRENT DENNIS, ASSISTANT DIRECTOR OF OPERATIONS, GOLDEN GATE PARK

1 MH DE YOUNG MEMORIAL MUSEUM

When I bring people to the park for the first time, the first place I take them is the De Young's top-floor observation tower (p106; pictured left). In addition to the museum's superb collection, the 360-degree views from here are awe-inspiring. Past the greenness of the park, you can see from the Panhandle all the way to the ocean.

2 CALIFORNIA ACADEMY OF SCIENCES

You see the wavy green roof of the Academy (p110) from the top of the De Young, and when you go there you realize what a fantastic vantage point it is as well. The roof was specifically designed to attract butterflies and insects. It's also the world's largest LEED platinum museum, and the building contains so many architectural and engineering feats.

3 CONSERVATORY OF FLOWERS

I tell everyone that the Conservatory (p106) has the best oxygen in San Francisco. It's a Victorian-era-style greenhouse – the first building erected in the park – and it's a literal jungle inside, with exhibits of tropical, carnivorous and aquatic plants. On a cool day, your glasses fog over when you walk into the humid environment.

4 JAPANESE TEA GARDEN

The garden (p108) was recently renovated and feels very authentic now. The trees are maintained bonsai-style, and the rocks and plants in the green garden are symbolically placed. It has very traditional and beautiful statues and a pagoda, plus wooden bridges and koi ponds, and cherry trees that flower in spring. It's a very spiritual place to many people.

5 BOTANICAL GARDENS

The botanical collection is unique because of San Francisco's climate. A visit to the gardens (p108) is like walking through a global garden because we can grow plants from temperate zones around the world. The redwood grove seems like nature's cathedral – the towering trees disappear into the clouds on foggy days and make you feel dwarfed by their size.

California Cuisine

Today the number one San Francisco tourist attraction is no longer the Golden Gate Bridge, but food, including the local, sustainable, seasonal bounty at Bay Area farmers markets (suc as at the Ferry Building, p102). San Francisco has more award-winning chefs per capita than any other US city, and enough exciting eateries to keep you in a perpetual swoon throughout your visit.

2

roasted
pork loin

braised
carrots 16 lb
in herb butter

3 Alcatraz Island

Housing infamous criminals like Al Capone the lighthouse-topped bay island of Alcatraz (p107) later became the site of an American Indian occupation. Pace the stark prison via a self-guided audio tour, as inmates recount their stories of life on 'The Rock.' Named by Spanish explorers for its bird colonies ('alcatraz' means pelican in Spanish), the island is still a sanctuary and breeding ground for seabirds.

LEE FOSTER/LONELY PLANET IMAGES ©

Vintage Trains & Cable Cars 4

To see the city sights in old-fashioned style, board a historic F-line streetcar to cruise down Market St and skim along the Embarcadero piers. Feeling more adventurous? Nab a spot on a cable car (p125) running board and cling to the pole as it crests Nob Hill then plummets and clangs its bell as it heads toward the bay.

North Beach 5

Shrill, green parrots streak through the skies of North Beach (p118), a longtime Italian and literary neighborhood with sidewalk cafes, scrumptious restaurants, scores of nightclubs and boozy watering holes, and one of the San Francisco's best bookstores, **City Lights** (www.citylights.com; **261 Columbus Ave;** ⏰**10am-midnight**). Score a scoop of gelato or a bracing espresso and loaf around the greens of Washington Sq.

Mission District 6

If the sun's to be found anywhere on a foggy San Francisco day, there's a good chance it's beaming in Mission (p118). Join a mural tour (p108) for an overview of expressive neighborhood art and then feast on the best burritos in town. At night, cross paths with mariachis for hire as you bar hop along Mission and Valencia Sts.

San Francisco's Best…

Cheap Thrills

○ **Golden Gate Bridge** (p102) Ramble the city's iconic gateway.

○ **Ferry Plaza Farmers Market** (p102) Sample fresh fruit and snacks.

○ **TIX Bay Area** (p119) Half-price, same-day theater tickets.

○ **Bay Ferries** (p124) Set sail across the bay at sunset.

○ **MH de Young Memorial Museum tower** (p106) A free bird's-eye view of Golden Gate Park and the city beyond.

Places for People-Watching

○ **Caffe Trieste** (p118) North Beach's most evocative cafe.

○ **Café Flore** (p119) Sidewalk cafe where pretty boys gather.

○ **Crissy Field** (p104) A nonstop parade of joggers, kite flyers and dog walkers.

○ **Dolores Park** (p121) The site for soccer games, street basketball, nonstop political protests, competitive tanning and other favorite local sports.

Kid Magnets

○ **California Academy of Sciences** (p110) Attractions include a butterfly-filled Rainforest Dome, a walk-through aquarium and lots of exotic creepy crawlies.

○ **Pier 39** (p103) Blubbery sea lions push, shove and bark.

○ **Musée Mecanique** (p103) An antique arcade housing old-fashioned musical and mechanical curiosities.

○ **Exploratorium** (p103) A hands-on science museum.

Foggy-Day Treats

○ **USS Pampanito** (p103) You won't notice gray weather aboard this restored WWII submarine.

○ **Castro Theatre** (p121) A chandelier-lit movie palace featuring Wurlitzer preludes.

○ **Warming Hut** (p104) Curl up with a cappuccino and gaze out at the Golden Gate Bridge.

○ **Precita Eyes Mural Tours** (p108) Vibrant murals are the perfect antidote to a monochrome day.

ADVANCE PLANNING

○ **Two weeks before** Buy tickets for Alcatraz Island, especially if you plan to visit on a weekend or in summer.

○ **One month before** Make dinner reservations for top restaurants.

RESOURCES

○ **Craig's List** (http://sfbay.craigslist.org) The Bay Area's definitive community bulletin board.

○ **San Francisco Chronicle** (www.sfgate.com) Northern California's largest daily newspaper.

○ **San Francisco Visitors Information Center** (www.onlyinsanfrancisco.com) Lots of city maps and information.

○ **511** (www.511.org) Website and phone number for public transportation and traffic information.

○ **Eater SF** (http://sf.eater.com) The latest on SF food, nightlife and bars.

○ **Open Table** (www.opentable.com) Make reservations at restaurants and browse discount deals.

○ **Flavorpill** (www.flavorpill.com/sanfrancisco) Live music, lectures, art openings and movie premieres.

○ **Bay Area Reporter** (www.ebar.com) Free GLBT community paper.

○ **Bay Times** (www.sfbaytimes.com) Another free GLBT community paper.

GETTING AROUND

○ **Bus** MUNI buses provide extensive coverage of the city, but can be slow.

○ **Cable car** A perennial favorite, but limited to a few lines in the northeast part of the city.

○ **Taxi** Easy to hail downtown.

○ **Train** BART trains run from the airport to downtown with a few stops in between, and MUNI streetcars radiate south and west from there.

BE FOREWARNED

○ **Weather** Pack warm clothes: it can get chilly any time of the year.

Left: Pier 39, Fisherman's Wharf;
Above: Golden Gate Bridge

San Francisco Walking Tour

Conquer some of San Francisco's famous hills with this itinerary. Along the way, you'll pass through cinematic alleyways in Chinatown, savor the flavors of Italian North Beach, meet wild parrots and take in beautiful views.

WALK FACTS

- **Start** Dragon Gate
- **Finish** Coit Tower
- **Distance** 1.3 miles
- **Duration** Two to 2½ hours

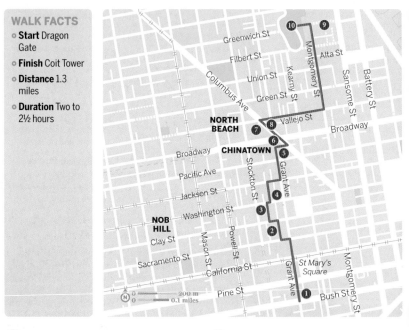

① Dragon Gate

Enter this ornate archway – donated by Taiwan in 1970 – and walk up Grant Ave past dragon lamps and pagoda-topped souvenir shops. The attractions here were created as a signature 'Chinatown Deco' look by forward-thinking Chinatown business leaders in the 1920s.

② Waverly Place

This is the namesake for one of the main characters in Amy Tan's bestselling *The Joy Luck Club*. Look up from this alley street to admire prayer flags and red lanterns gracing ornamentally painted temple balconies,

③ Spofford Alley

Sun Yat-sen plotted the overthrow of China's last emperor at No 36, and the 1920s saw bootleggers' gun battles in this alley, but Spofford has mellowed with age. In the evenings you'll hear the shuffling of mah-jong tiles and *erhu* (a two-stringed Chinese fiddle) warming up at local senior centers.

④ Ross Alley

Alternately known as Manila, Spanish and Mexico St after the working girls who once worked this block, mural-lined Ross Alley is occasionally pimped out for Hollywood productions, including *Karate Kid II* and *Indiana Jones & the Temple of Doom*.

⑤ Jack Kerouac Alley

Follow the aroma of tea shops and roast duck to another evocative alley, where the pavement is embedded with a Kerouac ode to San Francisco: 'The air was soft, the stars so fine, and the promise of every cobbled alley so great...'.

⑥ City Lights

Enter past the Dante-inspired sign warning 'Abandon All Despair, Ye Who Enter Here' to get into this literary landmark. Head upstairs to the Poetry section, open a book at random and read one poem. (If it's Allen Ginsberg's epic *Howl,* you could be here awhile.)

⑦ Molinari

After your food for thought, address that growling belly. Get your dream panini sandwich to go (house-cured salami highly recommended) and some *vino* for a picnic atop Telegraph Hill.

⑧ Caffe Trieste

But first, fuel up for the altitude gain with a shot of espresso at the back table where Francis Ford Coppola drafted his script for *The Godfather*. Play some opera on the jukebox and keep your eyes peeled for Poet Laureate Lawrence Ferlinghetti.

⑨ Greenwich Street Steps

Reach the top of Telegraph Hill on a passageway lined with cottages and terraced gardens. Choose your spot for a picnic in the company of wild parrots.

⑩ Coit Tower

This iconic tower was financed by the firefighter-obsessed heiress Lillie Hitchcock Coit, who rarely missed a fire or a firefighter's funeral. She even had the firehouse emblem embroidered on her bedsheets. Check out the once-controversial murals and ascend the elevator for panoramic views of the bay.

San Francisco In...

ONE DAY

Grab a leather strap on the **Powell-Hyde cable car** and hold on: you're in for hills and thrills. Hop off at **Lombard St** and Sterling Park for photo ops and views of the **Golden Gate Bridge**. Next explore the waterfront: check out the vintage arcade at **Musée Mechanique** and watch sea lions salute the setting sun at **Pier 39**. End the evening with shivers on a night tour of **Alcatraz**. Afterwards head to the Ferry Building and celebrate your great San Francisco escape with bubbly and oysters at **Hog Island Oyster Company** or Dungeness crab noodles at **Slanted Door**.

TWO DAYS

Spend the morning on our San Francisco walking tour, then take BART to the Mission and view the mural-covered garage doors lining **Balmy Alley**. Break for burritos, then hoof it to the **Haight** for flashbacks at vintage boutiques and the Summer of Love site: **Golden Gate Park**. Glimpse Golden Gate Bridge views atop the **MH de Young Museum**, then take a walk on the wild side in the **California Academy of Sciences** rainforest dome.

Discover San Francisco

At a Glance

○ **The Bay & Embarcadero** (p102)
A landmark bridge, foodie heaven and a famous island prison.

○ **Fisherman's Wharf** (p103) Gawk at sea lions and play in an old-time arcade.

○ **South of Market** (SoMa; p105) Top museums and nightclubs, just a quick stroll from downtown.

○ **Golden Gate Park** (p106) Excellent museums and gardens in the city's main green space.

Ferry Building
LEE FOSTER/LONELY PLANET IMAGES ©

◎ Sights

The Bay & The Embarcadero

GOLDEN GATE BRIDGE Bridge
(Map p93; ☏ 415-921-5858; www.goldengate .org; Fort Point Lookout, Marine Dr; southbound car $6, carpools free) San Franciscans have passionate views on every subject, but especially their signature landmark. Cinema buffs believe Hitchcock had it right: seen from below at **Fort Point**, the 1937 brige induces a thrilling case of *Vertigo*. Fog aficionados prefer the north-end lookout at Marin's **Vista Point**, to watch gusts billow through bridge cables like dry ice.

FERRY BUILDING Historic Building
(Map p112; www.ferrybuildingmarket place.com; Embarcadero) Slackers have the right idea at the Ferry Building, the transport hub turned gourmet emporium where no one's in a hurry to leave. Boat traffic tapered off after the grand hall and clock tower were built in 1898, and by the 1950s the building was literally overshadowed by a freeway overpass. But after the freeway collapsed in the 1989 Loma Prieta Earthquake, the city revived the Ferry Building as a tribute to San Francisco's monumental good taste. On weekends the **Ferry Plaza Farmers Market** fans out around the south end of the building like a fabulous garnish.

Civic Center & The Tenderloin

ASIAN ART MUSEUM Museum
(Map p112; ☏ 415-581-3500; www.asianart.org; 200 Larkin St; adult/student $12/7; ◷10am-

5pm Tue, Wed, Fri-Sun, to 9pm Thu; ⛛) Civic Center may be landlocked, but it has an unrivalled view of the Pacific thanks to this museum. Cover 6000 years and thousands of miles here in under an hour, from racy ancient Rajasthan miniatures to futuristic Japanese manga (graphic novels) via priceless Ming vases and even a Bhutan collection. The Asian has worked diplomatic wonders with a rotating collection of 17,000 treasures that bring Taiwan, China and Tibet together, unite Pakistan and India, and strike a harmonious balance among Japan, Korea and China.

CITY HALL   Historic Building
(Map p112; ☎415-554-4000, tour info 415-554-6023, art exhibit line 415-554-6080; www.ci.sf .ca.us/cityhall; 400 Van Ness Ave; ⊙8am-8pm Mon-Fri, tours 10am, noon & 2pm; ⛛) From its Gilded Age dome to the avant-garde art in the basement, City Hall is quintessentially San Franciscan. Rising from the ashes of the 1906 earthquake, this beaux arts building has seen historic firsts under its splendid Tennessee pink marble and Colorado limestone rotunda: America's first sit-in on the grand staircase in 1960, protesting red-baiting McCarthy hearings; the 1977 election and 1978 assassination of openly gay Supervisor Harvey Milk; and 4037 same-sex marriages performed in 2004, until the state intervened.

Fisherman's Wharf
MUSÉE MECANIQUE   Museum
(Map p104; ☎415-346-2000; www.musee mecanique.org; Pier 45, Shed A; admission free; ⊙10am-7pm Mon-Fri, to 8pm Sat & Sun; ⛛) A few quarters let you start bar brawls in coin-operated Wild West saloons, peep at belly-dancers through a vintage Mutoscope, save the world from Space Invaders and get your fortune told by an eerily lifelike wooden swami at this vintage arcade.

USS PAMPANITO   Historic Site
(Map p104; ☎415-775-1943; www.maritime.org; Pier 45; adult/child $10/4; ⊙9am-5pm) Explore a restored WWII submarine that survived six tours of duty, while listening to submariners' tales of stealth mode and sudden attacks in a riveting audio tour ($2) that makes surfacing afterwards a relief (caution claustrophobes).

PIER 39   Landmark
(Map p104; ☎415-981-1280; www.pier39.com; at Beach St & Embarcadero; ⛛) Ever since they first hauled out here in 1990, 300 to 1300 sea lions have spent winter through summer bellyflopped on these yacht docks. While bulls jostle for prime sunning location on the piers, boardwalk B-boyers compete for street-dance supremacy and kids wage battles of the will with parents over souvenir teddy bears.

The Marina & Russian Hill
EXPLORATORIUM   Museum
(Map p104; ☎415-561-0360; www.exploratorium .edu; 3601 Lyon St; adult/child $15/10, incl Tactile Dome $20; ⊙10am-5pm Tue-Sun; ⛛) Budding Nobel Prize winners swarm this hands-on discovery museum that's been blowing minds since 1969, answering the questions you always wanted to ask in science class: does gravity apply to skateboarding, do robots have feelings and do toilets flush counterclockwise in Australia? One especially far-out exhibit is the **Tactile Dome**, a pitch-black space that you can crawl, climb and slide through (advance reservations required). It's moving to Piers 15 and 17 in 2013.

PALACE OF FINE ARTS   Monument
(Map p104; www.lovethepalace.org; Palace Dr) When San Francisco's 1915 Panama-Pacific expo was over, SF couldn't bear to part with this Greco-Roman plaster palace. California Arts and Crafts architect Bernard Maybeck's artificial ruin was recast in concrete, so that future generations could gaze up at the rotunda relief to glimpse Art under attack by Materialists, with Idealists leaping to her rescue.

LOMBARD ST   Hill
(Map p104; 900 block; admission free; ⊙all day) Known as the 'world's crookedest street,' Lombard St has a natural 27% grade – far too steep for automobiles in

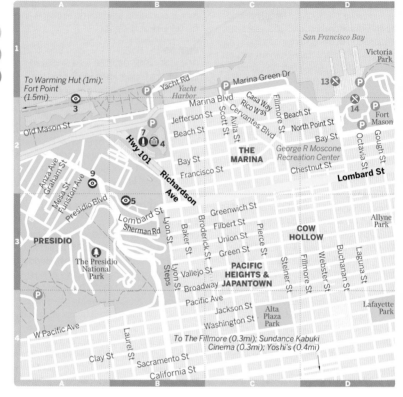

the 1920s. Property owners came up with the idea to install a series of curves. The result is what you see today: a red-brick street with eight sweeping turns, divided by lovingly tended flower beds and 250 steps rising on either side. (Vermont St, on Potrero Hill, between 20th and 22nd Sts, may actually be 'crookeder,' but don't bother trekking across town: Lombard St is prettier.)

The Presidio

PRESIDIO VISITORS CENTER
Historic Building

(Map p104; ☏ 415-561-4323; www.nps.gov/prsf; cnr Montgomery St & Lincoln Blvd; ⏱ 9am-5pm) The Presidio's military role ended in 1994, when the 1480-acre plot became part of the Golden Gate National Recreation Area. Today the only wars waged around here are interstellar ones in George Lucas' screening room in the **Letterman Digital Arts Center**, right by the Yoda statue.

CRISSY FIELD
Park

(Map p104; www.crissyfield.org; 603 Mason St; ⏱ sunrise-sunset, Center 9am-5pm) War is now officially for the birds at this former military airstrip, restored as a tidal marsh and reclaimed by knock-kneed coastal birds. On blustery days, bird-watch from the shelter of Crissy Field Center, which has a cafe counter facing the field with binoculars. Join joggers and puppies romping beachside trails that were once oil-stained asphalt, and on foggy days stop by the certified green **Warming Hut** (off Map p104; 983 Marine Dr; ⏱ 9am-5pm) to thaw out with Fair Trade coffee, browse field guides and sample honey made by Presidio honeybees.

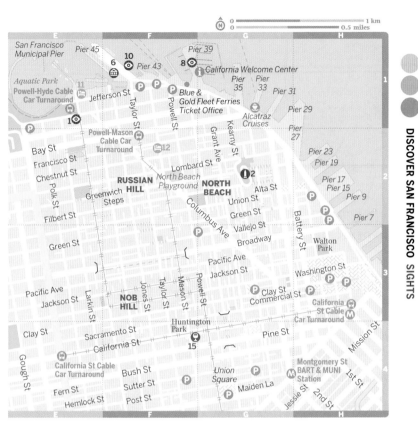

FORT POINT   Historic Building
(off Map p104; ☎415-561-4395; www.nps.gov
/fopo; Marine Dr; ☿10am-5pm Thu-Mon)
Despite its impressive guns, this Civil War
fort saw no action – at least until Alfred
Hitchcock shot scenes from *Vertigo* here,
with stunning views of the Golden Gate
Bridge from below.

BAKER BEACH   Outdoors
(Map p93) The city's best beach, with
windswept pines uphill, craggy cliffs and a
whole lot of exposed goosebumps on the
breezy, clothing-optional north end.

South Of Market (SoMa)
SAN FRANCISCO MUSEUM OF
MODERN ART   Museum
(SFMOMA; Map p112; ☎415-357-4000; www
.sfmoma.org; 151 3rd St; adult/student/child
$18/11/free, 1st Tue of month free; ☿11am-
6pm Fri-Tue, to 9pm Thu) Swiss architect
Mario Botta's light-filled brick box leans
full-tilt toward the horizon, with curators
similarly inclined to take forward-thinking
risks on Matthew Barney's poetic videos
involving industrial quantities of Vaseline
and Olafur Eliasson's outer-space light
installations. SFMOMA has arguably the
world's leading photography collection,
with works by Ansel Adams, Daido Mori-
yama, Diane Arbus, Edward Weston, William Eggleston and Dorothea Lange, and
since its 1995 grand reopening coincided
with the tech boom, SFMOMA became
an early champion of new media art.
Sculpture sprouts from the new rooftop
garden, and a $480-million expansion is
underway to accommodate 1100 major
modern works donated by the Fisher family (local founders of Gap). Go Thursday

Fisherman's Wharf, The Marina & Russian Hill

⦿ Sights
1 Blazing Saddles E1
2 Coit Tower... G2
3 Crissy Field.. A2
4 Exploratorium B2
5 Letterman Digital Arts Center B3
6 Musée Mecanique F1
7 Palace of Fine Arts................................ B2
8 Pier 39 .... F1
9 Presidio Visitors Center A2
10 USS Pampanito F1

☺ Sleeping
11 Argonaut Hotel E1
12 San Remo Hotel F2

✖ Eating
13 Greens.. D1
14 Off the Grid D2

☕ Drinking
15 Top of the Mark F4

nights after 6pm for half-price admission and the most artful flirting in town.

CONTEMPORARY JEWISH MUSEUM
Museum

(Map p112; ☎415-655-7800; www.jmsf.org; 736 Mission St; adult/student/child $10/8/free; ☺11am-5:30pm Fri-Tue, 1-8:30pm Thu) In 2008, architect Daniel Liebskind re-shaped San Francisco's 1881 power plant with a blue steel extension to form the Hebrew word *l'chaim* ('to life'). Inside this architectural statement are lively shows, ranging from a retrospective of modern art instigator and Bay Area native Gertrude Stein to Linda Ellia's *Our Struggle: Artists Respond to Mein Kampf,* for which 600 artists from 17 countries were invited to alter one page of Hitler's book.

The Richmond

CALIFORNIA PALACE OF THE LEGION OF HONOR
Museum

(Map p116; ☎415-750-3600; http://legionof honor.famsf.org; 100 34th Ave; adult/child $10/6, $2 discount with Muni ticket, 1st Tue of month free; ☺9:30am-5:15pm Tue-Sun) A nude sculptor's model who married well and collected art with a passion, 'Big Alma' de Bretteville Spreckels gifted this museum to San Francisco. Featured artworks range from Monet waterlilies to John Cage soundscapes, Iraqi ivories to R Crumb comics – part of the Legion's Achenbach Collection of 90,000 graphic artworks.

CLIFF HOUSE
Historic Building

(Map p116; www.cliffhouse.com; 1090 Point Lobos Ave) Built by populist millionaire Adolph Sutro in 1863 as a workingman's resort, Cliff House is now in its fourth incarnation as an upscale (overpriced) restaurant. Three of the resort's attractions remain: hiking trails around the splendid ruins of **Sutro Baths**, wintertime views of sea lions frolicking on **Seal Rock**, and the **Camera Obscura** (admission $2; ☺11am-sunset), a Victorian invention projecting sea views inside a small building.

Inside Golden Gate Park

MH DE YOUNG MEMORIAL MUSEUM
Museum

(Map p116; ☎415-750-3600; www.famsf.org /deyoung; 50 Hagiwara Tea Garden Dr; adult/child $10/free, $2 discount with Muni ticket, 1st Tue of month free; ☺9:30am-5:15pm Tue, Thu, Sat & Sun, to 8:45pm Fri) Follow sculptor Andy Goldsworthy's artificial fault-line in the sidewalk into Herzog & de Meuron's sleek, copper-clad building that's oxidizing to green, blending into the park. Don't be fooled by the de Young's camouflaged exterior: shows here boldly broaden artistic horizons from Oceanic ceremonial masks and Balenciaga gowns to sculptor Al Farrow's cathedrals built from bullets. Access to the tower viewing room is free, and worth the wait for the elevator.

CONSERVATORY OF FLOWERS
Garden

(Map p116; ☎15-666-7001; www.conservatory offlowers.org; Conservatory Dr West; adult/child $7/2; ☺10am-4pm Tue-Sun) Flower power is alive inside the newly restored 1878 Victorian conservatory, where orchids sprawl out like Bohemian divas, lilies float contemplatively and carnivorous plants reek of insect belches.

JOHNNY HAGLUND/LONELY PLANET IMAGES ©

Don't Miss **Alcatraz**

Almost 150 years before Guantanamo came into existence, a rocky island in the middle of San Francisco Bay became the nation's first military prison: Alcatraz. Civil War deserters were kept in wooden pens along with Native American 'unfriendlies,' including 19 Hopis who refused to send their children to government boarding schools where Hopi religion and language were banned.

In 1934 the Federal Bureau of Prisons took over Alcatraz to make a public example of bootleggers and other gangsters. 'The Rock' only averaged 264 inmates at one time, but its A-list criminals included Chicago crime boss Al Capone, Harlem poet-mafioso 'Bumpy' Johnson, and Morton Sobell, found guilty of Soviet espionage along with Julius and Ethel Rosenberg. Though Alcatraz was considered escape-proof, in 1962 the Anglin brothers and Frank Morris floated away on a makeshift raft and were never seen again.

Since sending guards and supplies to the island cost more than putting up prisoners at the Ritz, the prison was closed in 1963. Native American leaders occupied the island from 1969 to 1971 to protest US occupation of Native lands; their standoff with the FBI is commemorated in a dockside museum and 'This is Indian Land' water-tower graffiti.

Ferries depart for Alcatraz from behind the Pier 33 ticket booth, but book tickets online at least two weeks ahead in summer. Day visits include captivating audio tours, with prisoners and guards recalling cell house life, while popular, creepy twilight tours are led by park rangers.

NEED TO KNOW

Map p93; ☎ 415-981-7625; www.alcatrazcruises.com, www.nps.gov/alcatraz; adult/child day $26/16, night $33/19.50; ⏰ call center 8am-7pm, ferries every 30min 9am-3:55pm, plus 6:10pm & 6:45pm

STRYBING ARBORETUM & BOTANICAL GARDENS
Garden

(Map p116; ☎415-661-1316; www.strybing.org; 1199 9th Ave; admission $7; ⏰9am-6pm Apr-Oct, 10am-5pm Nov-Mar) There's always something blooming in these 70-acre gardens. The Garden of Fragrance is designed for the visually impaired, and the California native plant section explodes with color when the native wildflowers bloom in early spring, right off the redwood trail.

JAPANESE TEA GARDEN
Garden

(Map p116; http://japaneseteagardensf.com; Hagiwara Tea Garden Dr; adult/child $7/5, Mon, Wed, Fri before 10am free; ⏰9am-6pm;) Mellow out in the Zen Garden, admire doll-sized trees that are pushing 100, and sip toasted-rice green tea under a pagoda in this picturesque 5-acre garden founded in 1894.

Activities

BLAZING SADDLES
Bicycle Rental

(Map p104; ☎415-202-8888; www.blazingsaddles.com; 2715 Hyde St; bikes per hr/day from

$8/$32; ⏰8am-7:30pm, weather permitting;) From this bike rental shop's Fisherman's Wharf outposts, cyclists can cross the Golden Gate Bridge and take the Sausalito ferry back to SF.

Tours

PRECITA EYES MURAL TOURS
Walking

(☎415-285-2287; www.precitaeyes.org; 2981 24th St; adult $12-15, child $5; ⏰11am, noon & 1:30pm Sat & Sun) Muralists lead two-hour tours on foot or bike covering 60 to 70 murals in a six- to 10-block radius of mural-bedecked **Balmy Alley**; proceeds fund mural upkeep.

CHINATOWN ALLEYWAYS TOURS
Walking

(☎415-984-1478; www.chinatownalleywaytours.org; adult/child $18/5; ⏰11am Sat & Sun) Neighborhood teens lead two-hour tours for up-close-and-personal peeks into Chinatown's past (weather permitting). Book

five days ahead or pay double for Saturday walk-ins; cash only. Tour meeting points vary.

⭐ Festivals & Events

LUNAR NEW YEAR   Cultural
(www.chineseparade.com) Firecrackers, legions of tiny-tot martial artists and a 200ft dancing dragon make this parade at the end of February the highlight of San Francisco winters.

BAY TO BREAKERS   Quirky
(www.baytobreakers.com; race registration $44-48) Run costumed or naked from Embarcadero to Ocean Beach the third Sunday in May, while joggers dressed as salmon run upstream.

CARNAVAL   Cultural
(www.carnavalsf.com) Shake your tail feathers through the Mission on Memorial Day weekend in late May.

FOLSOM STREET FAIR   Quirky
(www.folsomstreetfair.com) Enjoy public spankings for local charities on the last Sunday in September.

JAZZ FESTIVAL   Music
(www.sfjazz.org) Old schoolers and hot new talents jam around the city in late October.

🛏 Sleeping

Union Square
ORCHARD GARDEN
HOTEL   Boutique Hotel $$
(Map p112; ☎415-399-9807; www.theorchard gardenhotel.com; 466 Bush St; r $179-249; ❄@🛜) SF's first all-green-practices hotel has soothingly quiet rooms with luxe touches, like Egyptian-cotton sheets, plus an organic rooftop garden.

SABRINA DALBESIO/LONELY PLANET IMAGES ©

Don't Miss **California Academy of Sciences**

Architect Renzo Piano's landmark LEED-certified green building houses 38,000 weird and wonderful animals in a four-story rainforest and split-level aquarium, all under a 'living roof' of California wildflowers. After dark, the wild rumpus starts at kids'-only Academy Sleepovers, and over-21 NightLife Thursdays (6pm to 10pm, $10) – when rainforest-themed cocktails encourage strange mating rituals among shy internet daters.

NEED TO KNOW

Map p116; 📞415-321-8000; www.calacademy.org; 55 Concourse Dr; adult/child $29.95/24.95, $3 discount with Muni ticket; 🕙9:30am-5pm Mon-Sat, 11am-5pm Sun; 🚼

HOTEL TRITON   Boutique Hotel **$$**
(Map p112; 📞415-394-0500, 800-800-1299; www.hotel-tritonsf.com; 342 Grant Ave; r $169-239; ✳@🛜) The lobby looks straight out of a comic book, and rooms are whimsically designed and ecofriendly; least-expensive rooms are tiny and celeb suites are named after Carlos Santana and Jerry Garcia. Don't miss tarot-card readings and chair massages during nightly happy hour.

HOTEL DES ARTS   Quirky **$$**
(Map p112; 📞415-956-3232; www.sfhoteldesarts .com; 447 Bush St; r $139-199, without bath $99-149; 🛜) A budget hotel for art freaks, with rooms painted by underground artists –

it's like sleeping inside an art installation. Standard rooms are less exciting, but clean and good value; bring earplugs.

Civic Center & The Tenderloin

PHOENIX MOTEL   Motel **$$**
(Map p112; 📞415-776-1380, 800-248-9466; www.jdvhospitality.com; 601 Eddy St; r incl breakfast $119-169; P🛜🏊) The city's rocker crash pad draws artists and hipsters to a vintage-1950s motor lodge with tropical decor in the gritty Tenderloin. Check out the shrine to actor Vincent Gallo, opposite Room 43, and happening lounge Chambers. Bring earplugs. Parking is free.

North Beach

HOTEL BOHÈME Boutique Hotel **$$**
(📞 415-433-9111; www.hotelboheme.com; 444 Columbus Ave; r $174-194; @ 📶) Like a love letter to the jazz era, the Bohème has moody 1950s orange, black and sage-green color schemes. Inverted Chinese umbrellas hang from ceilings and photos from the Beat years decorate the walls. Rooms are smallish, and some front on noisy Columbus Ave, but the hotel is smack in the middle of North Beach's vibrant street scene.

SAN REMO HOTEL Hotel **$**
(Map p104; 📞 415-776-8688, 800-352-7366; www.sanremohotel.com; 2237 Mason St; d $65-99; @ 📶) One of the city's best values, the 1906 San Remo has old-fashioned charm. Rooms are simply done with mismatched turn-of-the-century furnishings, and all share bathrooms. Note: least-expensive rooms have windows onto the corridor, not the outdoors; no elevator.

Fisherman's Wharf

ARGONAUT HOTEL Hotel **$$$**
(Map p104; 📞 415-563-0800, 866-415-0704; www.argonauthotel.com; 495 Jefferson St; r $205-325; P ✳ 📶 ♿) Built as a cannery in 1908, the nautical-themed Argonaut has century-old wooden beams, exposed brick walls, and porthole-shaped mirrors. All rooms have ultra-comfy beds and CD players, but some are tiny and get limited sunlight; pay extra for mesmerizing bay views.

South Of Market (SoMa)

HOTEL VITALE Hotel **$$$**
(Map p112; 📞 415-278-3700, 888-890-8688; www.hotelvitale.com; 8 Mission St; d $239-379; ✳ @ 📶) Behind that skyscraper exterior is a soothing spa-hotel, with silky-soft 450-thread-count sheets and rooftop hot tubs; upgrade to bay-view rooms.

🌿 **GOOD HOTEL** Motel **$$**
(Map p112; 📞 415-621-7001; www.thegoodhotel.com; 112 7th St; r $109-169; P @ 📶 ♨) A revamped motor lodge that places a premium on green, with reclaimed wood headboards, light fixtures of repurposed bottles, and fleece bedspreads made of recycled soda bottles. The vibe is upbeat and there's a pool across the street and bikes for rent, but the neighborhood is sketchy.

The Haight

🌿 **RED VICTORIAN** Quirky **$$**
(📞 415-864-1978; www.redvic.net; 1665 Haight St; r $149-229, without bath $89-129, incl breakfast; 📶) The '60s live on at the tripped-out Red Vic. The 18 rooms have themes such as Sunshine, Flower Children and the Summer of Love; only four have baths, but all come with breakfast in the organic cafe. Wi-fi in the lobby; no elevator.

 Eating

The Embarcadero

🌿 **SLANTED DOOR** Vietnamese, Californian **$$**
(Map p112; 📞 415-861-8032; www.slanteddoor.com; 1 Ferry Bldg; lunch $13-24, dinner $18-36; ⏱lunch & dinner) California ingredients, Continental influences and Vietnamese flair with a sparkling bay outlook, from

Downtown San Francisco & South of Market (SoMa)

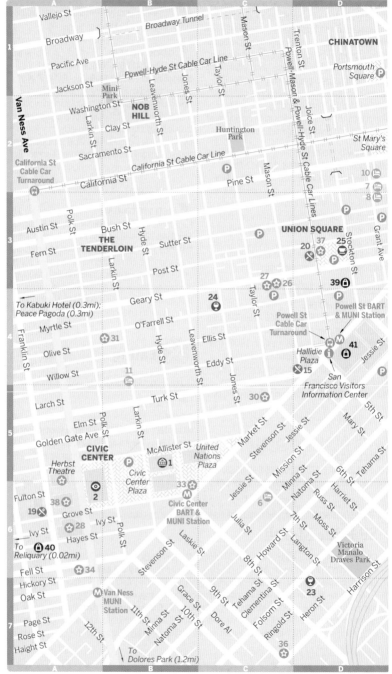

Vallejo St

Broadway Tunnel

Broadway

Pacific Ave

Jackson St

CHINATOWN

Powell-Hyde St Cable Car Line

Mason St

Trenton St

Portsmouth Square

Van Ness Ave

Mini Park

Washington St

NOB HILL

Larkin St

Leavenworth St

Jones St

Taylor St

Powell-Mason & Powell-Hyde St Cable Car Lines

Joice St

St Mary's Square

Clay St

Huntington Park

Sacramento St

California St Cable Car Turnaround

California St Cable Car Line

California St

Pine St

Mason St

10

7

8

Austin St

Polk St

Bush St

Hyde St

Sutter St

UNION SQUARE

Stockton St

Grant Ave

Fern St

THE TENDERLOIN

Larkin St

Post St

20

37

25

Geary St

27

26

24

Powell St BART & MUNI Station

39

To Kabuki Hotel (0.3mi); Peace Pagoda (0.3mi)

Myrtle St

O'Farrell St

Taylor St

Powell St Cable Car Turnaround

Franklin St

31

Olive St

Hyde St

Leavenworth St

Ellis St

Hallidie Plaza

41

Willow St

Eddy St

Jones St

15

San Francisco Visitors Information Center

Jessie St

Larch St

Turk St

30

5th St

Elm St

Polk St

Larkin St

Market St

Stevenson St

Jessie St

Mary St

Golden Gate Ave

CIVIC CENTER

McAllister St

United Nations Plaza

Mission St

6th St

Tehama St

Herbst Theatre

Civic Center Plaza

33

Minna St

Natoma St

Russ St

Harriet St

Fulton St

38

2

Jessie St

6

7th St

Moss St

19

Grove St

Ivy St

Civic Center BART & MUNI Station

Julia St

Langton St

Victoria Manalo Draves Park

28

Ivy St

Polk St

Harrison St

To Reliquary (0.02mi)

40

Hayes St

Laskie St

Howard St

8th St

Fell St

Stevenson St

34

Hickory St

Oak St

Van Ness MUNI Station

11th St

Grace St

9th St

Tehama St

Clementina St

Folsom St

Ringold St

Heron St

23

Page St

12th St

Minna St

10th St

Dore Al

Natoma St

36

Rose St

Haight St

To Dolores Park (1.2mi)

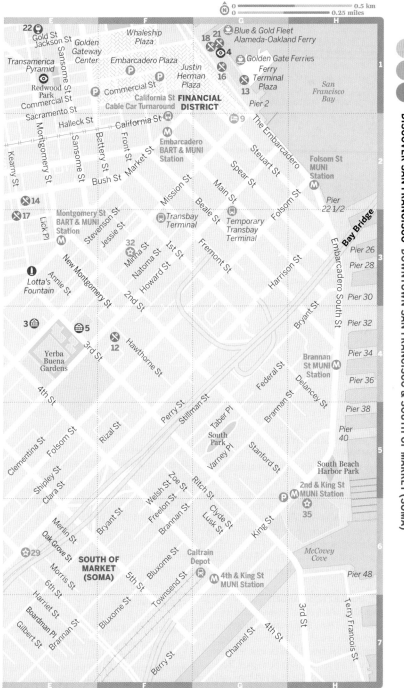

0.5 km
0.25 miles

22 Gold St
Jackson St
Golden Gateway Center
Whaleship Plaza
18 21 Blue & Gold Fleet
Alameda-Oakland Ferry
4

Transamerica Pyramid
Embarcadero Plaza
Justin Herman Plaza
16
Golden Gate Ferries
Ferry Terminal Plaza

Redwood Park
Commercial St
Commercial St
California St
13 Pier 2

Sacramento St
Halleck St
California St
California St Cable Car Turnaround
FINANCIAL DISTRICT
9
The Embarcadero
San Francisco Bay

Kearny St
Montgomery St
Sansome St
Battery St
Front St
Market St
Bush St
Embarcadero BART & MUNI Station
Steuart St
Folsom St MUNI Station

Sansome St
Mission St
Spear St
Main St
Folsom St
Pier 22 1/2

14
17
Lick Pl
Montgomery St BART & MUNI Station
Stevenson St
Jessie St
Beale St
Transbay Terminal
Temporary Transbay Terminal
Harrison St
Embarcadero South St
Bay Bridge
Pier 26
Pier 28

New Montgomery St
Annie St
32 Minna St
Natoma St
1st St
Fremont St
Pier 30

Lotta's Fountain
2nd St
Howard St
Bryant St
Pier 32

3 **5**
Yerba Buena Gardens
3rd St
12 Hawthorne St
Federal St
Brannan St MUNI Station
Pier 34
Pier 36

4th St
Perry St
Stillman St
Delancey St
Brannan St
Pier 38

Clementina St
Folsom St
Rizal St
Taber Pl
South Park
Varney Pl
Stanford St
Pier 40

Shipley St
Clara St
Welsh St
Zoe St
Ritch St
Clyde St
Lusk St
King St
South Beach Harbor Park
2nd & King St MUNI Station
35

Merlin St
Oak Grove St
Bryant St
Freelon St
Brannan St
McCovey Cove

29
Morris St
SOUTH OF MARKET (SOMA)
5th St
Bluxome St
Caltrain Depot
4th & King St MUNI Station
Pier 48

6th St
Harriet St
Boardman Pl
Brannan St
Gilbert St
Bluxome St
Townsend St
3rd St
4th St
Terry Francois St

Channel St
Berry St

Downtown San Francisco & South of Market (SoMa)

⊙ **Sights**
1	Asian Art Museum	B5
2	City Hall	A6
3	Contemporary Jewish Museum	E4
4	Ferry Building Marketplace	G1
5	San Francisco Museum of Modern Art (SFMOMA)	E4

⊛ **Sleeping**
6	Good Hotel	C6
7	Hotel des Arts	D2
8	Hotel Triton	D3
9	Hotel Vitale	G2
10	Orchard Garden Hotel	D2
11	Phoenix Motel	B4

⊗ **Eating**
12	Benu	F4
13	Boulette's Larder	G1
14	Boxed Foods	E2
15	farmerbrown	D4
16	Ferry Plaza Farmers Market	G1
17	Gitane	E3
18	Hog Island Oyster Company	G1
19	Jardinière	A6
20	Michael Mina	D3
21	Slanted Door	G1

⊙ **Drinking**
22	Barrique	E1
23	Bloodhound	D7
24	Bourbon & Branch	C4
25	Emporio Rulli Caffè	D3

⊛ **Entertainment**
26	American Conservatory Theater	C3
27	Curran Theatre	C3
28	Davies Symphony Hall	A6
29	EndUp	E6
30	Golden Gate Theatre	C5
31	Great American Music Hall	B4
32	Harlot	F3
33	Orpheum Theatre	B6
34	Rickshaw Stop	A6
35	San Francisco Giants	H6
36	Stud	C7
37	TIX Bay Area	D3
38	War Memorial Opera House	A6

⊙ **Shopping**
39	Macy's	D3
40	Nancy Boy	A6
41	Westfield Shopping Center	D4

award-winning chef-owner Charles Phan. Reserve ahead or picnic on takeout from the Open Door stall.

🌿 HOG ISLAND OYSTER COMPANY
Seafood $$

(Map p112; ☎ 415-391-7117; www.hogisland oysters.com; 1 Ferry Bldg; oyster samplers $15-30; ⏱ 11:30am-8pm Mon-Fri, 11am-6pm Sat & Sun) Sustainably farmed, local Tomales Bay oysters served raw or cooked to perfection, with superb condiments and a glass of Sonoma bubbly. From 5pm to 7pm on Mondays and Thursdays, oysters are half-price and pints are $4.

🌿 BOULETTE'S LARDER
Californian $$

(Map p112; ☎ 415-399-1155; www.boulettes larder.com; 1 Ferry Bldg; breakfast $7.50-16.50, lunch $9-20, brunch $7-22; ⏱ breakfast Mon-Fri, lunch Mon-Sat, brunch Sun) Dinner theatre doesn't get better than brunch at Boulette's communal table, amid the swirl of chefs preparing for dinner service. Inspired by the truffled eggs and beignets? Get spices and mixes at the counter.

Union Square

MICHAEL MINA
Californian $$$

(Map p112; ☎ 415-397-9222; www.michaelmina .net; 252 California St; lunch menus $49-59, dinner mains $35-42; ⏱ Mon-Fri lunch, dinner nightly) The James Beard Award winner has reinvented his posh namesake restaurant as a lighthearted take on French-Japanese cooking – there's still caviar and lobster, but also foie gras PB&J and lobster pot pie. Reservations essential, or grab bar bites and cocktails at the bar.

FARMERBROWN
Modern American, Organic $$

(Map p112; ☎ 415-409-3276; www.farmerbrown sf.com; 25 Mason St; mains $12-23; ⏱ 6-10:30pm Tue-Sun, weekend brunch 11am-2pm) A rebel from the wrong side of the block, dishing up seasonal watermelon margaritas with a cayenne-salt rim, ribs that stick to yours and coleslaw with kick. Chef-owner Jay Foster works with local organic and African American farmers to provide food with actual soul, in a shotgun-shack setting with live funk bands.

Financial District

GITANE Mediterranean $$
(Map p112; ☎415-788-6686; www.gitane restaurant.com; 6 Claude Lane; mains $15-25; ☻5:30pm-midnight Tue-Sat, bar to 1am; ☞)
Slip out of the Financial District and into something more comfortable at this boudoir-styled bistro, featuring Basque- and Moroccan-inspired stuffed squash blossoms, silky pan-seared scallops, herb-spiked lamb tartare and craft cocktails.

BOXED FOODS Sandwiches $
(Map p112; www.boxedfoodscompany.com; 245 Kearny St; dishes $8-10; ☻8am-3pm Mon-Fri; ☞) The SF salad standard is set here daily, with organic greens topped by tart goat cheese, smoked bacon, wild strawberries and other local treats. Grab hidden seating in back, or get yours to go to the Transamerica Pyramid redwood grove.

Civic Center & The Tenderloin

JARDINIÈRE Californian $$$
(Map p112; ☎415-861-5555; www.jardiniere.com; 300 Grove St; mains $18-38; ☻dinner) Opera arias can't compare to the high notes hit by James Beard Award winner, Iron Chef and Top Chef Master Traci des Jardins, who lavishes braised oxtail ravioli with summer truffles and stuffs crispy pork belly with salami and Mission figs. Go Mondays, when $45 scores three market-inspired, decadent courses with wine pairings, or enjoy post–SF Opera meals in the bar downstairs.

Chinatown

CITY VIEW Chinese $
(☎415-398-2838; 662 Commercial St; small plates $3-5; ☻11am-2:30pm Mon-Fri, 10am-2:30pm Sat & Sun) Take your seat in a sunny dining room and your pick from carts

Detour:
Off the Grid

Some 30 **food trucks** (Map p104; http://offthegridsf.com; Fort Mason parking lot; dishes under $10; ☻5-10pm Fri; ☙) circle their wagons at SF's largest mobile-gourmet hootenanny (other nights/locations attract less than a dozen trucks; see website). Arrive before 6:30pm or expect a 20-minute wait for Chairman Bao's clamshell buns stuffed with duck and mango, Roli Roti's free-range herbed roast chicken, or dessert from The Crème Brûlée Man. Cash only; take dinner to nearby docks for Golden Gate Bridge sunsets.

loaded with delicate shrimp and leek dumplings, tender black-bean asparagus and crisp Peking duck and other tantalizing, ultrafresh dim sum.

HOUSE OF NANKING Chinese $$
(☎415-421-1429; 919 Kearny St; starters $5-8, mains $9-15; ☻11am-10pm Mon-Fri, noon-10pm Sat, noon-9pm Sun) Bossy service with bravura cooking. Supply the vaguest outlines for your dinner – maybe seafood, nothing deep-fried, perhaps some greens – and within minutes you'll be devouring pan-seared scallops, sautéed pea shoots and garlicky noodles.

North Beach

COTOGNA Italian $$
(☎415-775-8508; www.cotognasf.com; 470 Pacific Av; mains $14-24; ☻noon-3pm & 7-10pm Mon-Sat; ☞) No wonder chef-owner Michael Tusk won the 2011 James Beard Award: his rustic Italian pastas and toothsome pizzas magically balance a few pristine, local flavors. Book ahead; the $24 prix-fixe is among SF's best dining deals.

The Richmond, The Sunset & Golden Gate Park

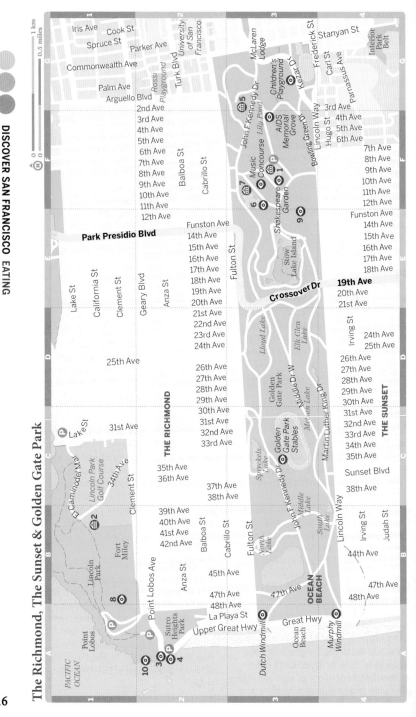

The Richmond, The Sunset & Golden Gate Park

⊚ Sights
1 California Academy of Sciences F3
2 California Palace of the Legion
    of Honor..B1
3 Camera Obscura A2
4 Cliff House...A2
5 Conservatory of Flowers.....................G3
6 Japanese Tea Garden F3
7 MH de Young Memorial Museum F3
8 Seal Rocks B1
9 Strybing Arboretum & Botanical
    Gardens...E3
10 Sutro Baths..A2

IDEALE   Italian **$$**

(☎415-391-4129; 1315 Grant Ave; ☺5:30-10:30pm Mon-Sat, 5-10pm Sun) SF's most authentic Italian restaurant, with a Roman chef that grills a mean fish and whips up gorgeous truffled zucchini – but order anything with bacon or meat and Tuscan-staff-recommend wine, and everyone goes home happy.

MOLINARI   Italian, Sandwiches **$**

(☎415-421-2337; 373 Columbus Ave; sandwiches $5-8; ☺9am-5:30pm Mon-Fri, 7:30am-5:30pm Sat) Grab a number and wait your turn ogling Italian wines and cheeses, and by the time you're called, the scent of house-cured salami dangling from the rafters and Parma prosciutto will have made your choice for you.

The Marina & Cow Hollow

GREENS   Vegetarian **$$**

(Map p104; ☎415-771-6222; www.greensres taurant.com; Fort Mason Center, bldg A; mains $7-20; ☺noon-2:30pm Tue-Sat, 5:30-9pm Mon-Sat, 9am-4pm Sun; 🖉) In a converted army barracks, enjoy Golden Gate views, smoky-rich black bean chili with pickled jalapeños and roasted eggplant panini. All Greens' dishes are meat-free and organic, mostly raised on a Zen farm in Marin – sure beats army rations.

South Of Market (SoMa)

BENU   Californian, Fusion **$$$**

(Map p112; ☎415-685-4860; www.benusf.com; 22 Hawthorne St; mains $25-40; ☺5:30-10pm Tue-Sat) SF has refined fusion cuisine over 150 years, but no one rocks it quite like chef Corey Lee, who remixes local fine-dining staples and Pacific Rim flavors with a SoMa DJ's finesse. Velvety Sonoma foie gras with tangy, woodsy yuzu-sake glaze makes tastebuds bust wild moves, while Dungeness crab and black truffle custard bring such outsize flavor to faux-shark's fin soup, you'll swear there's Jaws in there. The tasting menu is steep ($160) and beverage pairings add $110, but you won't want to miss star-sommelier Yoon Ha's flights of fancy – including a rare 1968 Madeira with your soup.

The Mission

LA TAQUERÍA   Mexican **$**

(☎415-285-7117; 2889 Mission St; burritos $6-8; ☺11am-9pm Mon-Sat, 11am-8pm Sun) No debatable tofu, saffron rice, spinach tortilla or mango salsa here: just classic tomatillo or mesquite salsa, marinated, grilled meats and flavorful beans inside a flour tortilla – optional housemade spicy pickles and sour cream highly recommended.

RANGE   Californian **$$**

(☎415-282-8283; www.rangesf.com; 842 Valencia St; mains $20-28; ☺5:30-10pm Sun-Thu, to 11pm Fri & Sat; 🖉) Inspired American dining is alive and well within Range. The menu is seasonal Californian, prices are reasonable and the style is repurposed industrial chic – think coffee-rubbed pork shoulder served with microbrewed beer from the blood-bank refrigerator.

BI-RITE CREAMERY   Ice Cream **$$**

(☎415-626-5600; http://biritecreamery.com; 3692 18th St; ice cream $3.25-7; ☺11am-10pm Sun-Thu, to 11pm Fri & Sat) Velvet ropes at clubs seem pretentious in laid-back San Francisco, but at organic Bi-Rite Creamery they make perfect sense: lines wrap around the corner for legendary salted-caramel ice cream with housemade hot fudge.

If You Like…
San Francisco's Neighborhoods

If you like touring the city's eclectic enclaves, we think you'll like exploring these historic and happening areas.

1 NORTH BEACH
(Map p104) Boutiques outnumber bohemians in the neighborhood where the Beat poets once howled, and tough stairway climbs lead to giddy vistas with wild parrots squawking overhead.

2 CHINATOWN
(Map p112) Stroll beneath the pagoda-style roofs and dragon lanterns of the shopping streets, and listen for the clack of mah jong tiles in quiet alleyways.

3 THE CASTRO
(Map p93) The heart of San Francisco's queer community, where you'll find scores of restaurants and bars and one of the city's most ornate arthouse cinemas.

4 THE MISSION
(Map p93) Visit the oldest building in the city, tour colorful alley murals, devour a chunky burrito, and then kick back with the hipsters at a buzzing outdoor bar.

5 THE HAIGHT
(Map p93) The legendary intersection of Haight and Ashbury Sts was the place to be in the psychedelic '60s; now vintage boutiques co-mingle with head shops at this gateway to Golden Gate Park.

Drinking

Downtown & South Of Market (SoMa)

EMPORIO RULLI CAFFÈ Cafe
(Map p112; www.rulli.com; 333 Post St; ⏲7:30am-7pm) Ideal people-watching atop Union Sq, with excellent espresso and pastries to fuel up for shopping, plus wine by the glass afterward.

BLOODHOUND Bar
(Map p112; www.bloodhoundsf.com; 1145 Folsom St; ⏲4pm-2am) The murder of crows painted on the ceiling is definitely an omen: nights at Bloodhound assume mythic proportions with top-shelf booze served in Mason jars and pool marathons. SF's best food trucks often park out front; ask the barkeep to suggest a pairing.

Union Square

BARRIQUE Bar
(Map p112; www.barriquesf.com; 461 Pacific Ave; ⏲3pm-10pm Tue-Sat) Roll out the barrel: get your glass of high-end small-batch vino straight from the cask, directly from the vineyard. Settle into white-leather sofas in back, near the casks, with artisan cheese and charcuterie plates.

Civic Center & The Tenderloin

BOURBON & BRANCH Bar
(Map p112; ☎415-346-1735; www.bourbon andbranch.com; 501 Jones St; ⏲Wed-Sat by reservation) 'Don't even think of asking for a cosmo' reads one of many House Rules at this revived speakeasy, complete with secret exits from its Prohibition-era heyday. For top-shelf gin and bourbon cocktails in the Library, use the buzzer and the password 'books.'

North Beach

CAFFE TRIESTE Cafe
(www.caffetrieste.com; 601 Vallejo St; ⏲6:30am-11pm Sun-Thu, 6:30am-midnight Fri & Sat; 🛜) Look no further for inspiration: Francis Ford Coppola drafted *The Godfather* here under the mural of Sicily, and Poet Laureate Lawrence Ferlinghetti still swings by en route to City Lights. With opera on the jukebox and weekend accordion jam sessions, this is North Beach at its best, since 1956.

TOSCA CAFE Cocktail Bar
(http://toscacafesf.com; 242 Columbus Ave; ⏲5pm-2am Tue-Sun) Come early for your pick of opera on the jukebox and red

circular booths, and stay late for Irish-coffee nightcap crowds and chance sightings of Sean Penn, Bono or Robert De Niro.

The Mission
ZEITGEIST
Bar
(www.zeitgeistsf.com; 199 Valencia St; ⏰9am-2am) When temperatures tip over 70°F (21°C), bikers and hipsters converge on Zeitgeist's huge outdoor beer garden (minus the garden) for 40 brews on tap pulled by SF's toughest lady barkeeps and late-night munchies courtesy of the Tamale Lady.

The Castro
CAFÉ FLORE
Cafe
(2298 Market St; ⏰7am-1am; 📶) The see-and-be-seen, glassed-in corner cafe at the center of the gay universe. Eavesdrop on blind dates with bracing cappuccino or knee-weakening absinthe.

SAMOVAR TEA LOUNGE
Teahouse
(498 Sanchez St; ⏰10am-11pm; 📶) Iron pots of tea with scintillating side dishes, from savory pumpkin dumplings to chocolate brownies with green-tea mousse.

The Haight & Hayes Valley
TORONADO
Bar
(www.toronado.com; 547 Haight St; ⏰6pm-1am)Bow before the chalkboard altar that lists 50 microbrews and hundreds more bottled, including spectacular seasonal microbrews. Bring cash, come early and stay late, with a sausage from Rosamunde next door to accompany seasonal ales.

 # Entertainment

Big events sell out fast in SF. Scan the free weeklies, the *San Francisco Bay Guardian* and the *SF Weekly,* and see what half-price and last-minute tickets you can find at **TIX Bay Area** (Map p112; 📞415-433-7827; Union Sq at 251 Stockton St; ⏰11am-6pm Tue-Thu, to 7pm Fri & Sat). Tickets are sold on the day of the

Detour:
Ocean Beach

Golden Gate Park ends in the blustery **Ocean Beach** (Map116; 📞415-561-4323; www.parksconservancy .org; ⏰sunrise-sunset), too chilly for bikini-clad clambakes but ideal for wet-suited pro surfers braving rip tides (casual swimmers beware). Bonfires are permitted in designated fire-pits only; no alcohol allowed.

performance for cash only. For tickets to theater shows and big-name concerts in advance, call **Ticketmaster** (📞415-421-8497) or **BASS** (📞415-478-2277).

Nightclubs

EL RIO
Club
(📞415-282-3325; www.elriosf.com; 3158 Mission St; admission $3-8) Free-form funky grooves worked by regulars of every conceivable ethnicity and orientation. 'Salsa Sundays' are legendary – arrive at 3pm for lessons – and other nights feature oyster happy hours, eclectic music, and shameless flirting on the garden patio.

DNA LOUNGE
Club
(www.dnalounge.com; 375 11th St; admission $3-25) SF's mega-club hosts live bands and big-name DJs. Second and fourth Saturdays bring Bootie, the kick-ass original mashup party; Monday's Goth Death Guild means shuffle-dancing and free tea service.

HARLOT
Club
(Map p112;www.harlotsf.com; 46 Minna St; admission $10-20, free 5-9pm Wed-Fri; ⏰Wed-Sat) Aptly named after 10pm, when the bordello-themed lounge cuts loose to house Thursdays, indie-rock Wednesdays, and women-only Fem Bar parties.

Live Music

THE FILLMORE — Live Music

(off Map p104; www.thefillmore.com; 1805 Geary Blvd; tickets from $20) Hendrix, Zeppelin, Janis – they all played the Fillmore. The legendary venue that launched the psychedelic era has the posters to prove it upstairs, and hosts arena acts in a 1250-seat venue where you can squeeze in next to the stage.

YOSHI'S — Jazz

(off Map p104; www.yoshis.com; 1300 Fillmore St; tickets $12-50) San Francisco's definitive jazz club draws the world's top talent to the historic African and Japanese American Fillmore jazz district, and serves pretty good sushi besides.

GREAT AMERICAN MUSIC HALL — Live Music

(Map p112; www.musichallsf.com; 859 O'Farrell St; admission $12-35) Previously a bordello and a dance hall, this ornate venue now hosts rock, country, jazz and world music artists. Arrive early to stake your claim to front-row balcony seats with a pint and a passable burger.

BOTTOM OF THE HILL — Live Music

(www.bottomofthehill.com; 1233 17th St; admission $5-12; ☺Tue-Sat) Top of the list for breakthrough bands, from notable local alt-rockers like Deerhoof to newcomers worth checking out by name alone (Yesway, Stripmall Architecture, Excuses for Skipping) in *Rolling Stone*'s favorite SF venue; cash only.

RICKSHAW STOP — Live Music

(Map p112; www.rickshawstop.com; 155 Fell St; admission $5-35) Noise-poppers, eccentric rockers and crafty DJs cross-pollinate hemispheres with something for everyone: bad-ass banghra nights, Latin explosion bands, lesbian disco, and mainstay Thursday 18+ Popscene.

Theater

Musicals and Broadway spectaculars play at a number of downtown theaters. **SHN** (☏415-512-7770; www.shnsf.com) hosts touring Broadway shows at opulent **Orpheum**

Gay/Lesbian/Bi/Trans San Francisco

Singling out the best places to be queer in San Francisco is almost redundant. Though the Castro is a gay hub and the Mission is a magnet for lesbians, the entire city is gay-friendly. Top GLBT venues include the followng:

Stud (Map p112; ☏415-252-7883; www.studsf.com; 399 9th St; admission $5-8; ☺5pm-3am) Rocking the gay scene since 1966, and branching out beyond leather daddies with rocker-grrrl Mondays, Tuesday drag variety shows, raunchy comedy/karaoke Wednesdays, Friday art-drag dance parties, and performance-art cabaret whenever hostess-DJ Anna Conda gets it together.

Lexington Club (☏415-863-2052; 3464 19th St; ☺3pm-2am) Odds are eerily high you'll develop a crush on your ex-girlfriend's hot new girlfriend here over strong drink, pinball and tattoo comparisons – go on, live dangerously at SF's most famous/notorious full-time lesbian bar.

EndUp (Map p112; ☏415-646-0999; www.theendup.com; 401 6th St; admission $5-20; ☺10pm-4am Mon-Thu, 11pm-11am Fri, 10pm Sat to 4am Mon) Home of Sunday 'tea dances' (gay dance parties) since 1973, though technically the party starts Saturday. Bring a change of clothes and EndUp watching the sunrise on Monday over the freeway on-ramp.

Theatre (Map p112; 1192 Market St), **Curran Theatre** (Map p112; 445 Geary St), and 1920s **Golden Gate Theatre** (Map p112; 1 Taylor St). But the pride of SF is its many indie theaters that host original, solo and experimental shows, including the following.

AMERICAN CONSERVATORY THEATER Theater
(Map p112; ACT; ☎415-749-2228; www.act-sf .org; 415 Geary St) San Francisco's most famous mainstream venue has put on original landmark productions of Tony Kushner's *Angels in America* and Robert Wilson's *Black Rider,* with a libretto by William S Burroughs and music by the Bay Area's own Tom Waits.

BEACH BLANKET BABYLON Comedy, Cabaret
(☎415-421-4222; www.beachblanketbaby lon.com; 678 Green St; seats $25-78) San Francisco's longest-running comedy cabaret keeps the belly laughs coming with giant hats, killer drag and social satire with bite. Spectators must be 21-plus, except at matinees.

Classical Music, Opera & Dance

DAVIES SYMPHONY HALL Classical Music
(Map p112; ☎415-864-6000; www.sfsym phony.org; 201 Van Ness Ave) Home of nine-time Grammy-winning SF Symphony, conducted with verve by Michael Tilson Thomas from September to May here – don't miss Beethoven.

WAR MEMORIAL OPERA HOUSE Opera
(Map p112; ☎415-864-3330; www.sfopera .com; 301 Van Ness Ave) Rivaling City Hall's grandeur is the 1932 home to **San Francisco Opera** (www.sfopera.com) from June through December and the **San Francisco Ballet** (www.sfballet.org) from January through May. Student tickets and standing-room tickets go on sale two hours before performances.

ODC THEATER Dance
(☎415-863-9834; www.odctheater.org; 3153 17th St) For 40 years, redefining dance with risky, raw performances and the sheer joy

If you're wowed by the bay views from Fort Point (p105) and Crissy Field (p104), spend a fog-free day scaling some of the city's best vantage points.

1 **COIT TOWER**
(Map p104; ☎415-362-0808; admission free, elevator rides $5; ☑10am-6pm) Climb the giddy, steep Filbert St or Greenwich St steps to the top of Telegraph Hill where you'll find this peculiar 210ft projectile – a monument to San Francisco firefighters, financed by eccentric heiress Lillie Hitchcock Coit. Completed in 1934, the historic landmark boasts Diego Rivera–style WPA murals and 360-degree views of downtown from the tower-top viewing platform.

2 **TOP OF THE MARK**
(Map p104; ☎415-616-6916; www.topofthemark .com; 999 California St; cover $5-15; ☑5pm-midnight Sun-Thu, 4pm-1am Fri & Sat) Sashay across the dance floor of this view bar and feel on top of the world. Cocktails will set you back $15 plus cover, but watch the sunset and then try to complain.

3 **DOLORES PARK**
(off Map p112) Take the J-Church MUNI train to 20th St for a sweeping cityscape framed by palm trees and hunky sunbathers.

4 **TWIN PEAKS**
(Map p93) Almost dead-center of the city, the bay-to-breakers vistas from this unmistakable landmark beckon visitors day and night. Bring a jacket and watch birds surf the thermal currents.

of movement with performances September through December, and 200 dance classes a week.

Cinemas

CASTRO THEATRE Cinema
(www.thecastrotheatre.com; 429 Castro St; adult/ child $10/7.50) Showtunes on a Wurlitzer are the overture to independent cinema, silver-screen classics and unstoppable audience participation.

SUNDANCE KABUKI CINEMA — Cinema

(off Map p104; www.sundancecinemas.com/kabuki.html; 1881 Post St; tickets $10-14) Trendsetting green multiplex with GMO-free popcorn, reserved seating in cushy recycled-fiber seats and the frankly brilliant Balcony Bar, where you can slurp seasonal cocktails during your movie.

ROXIE CINEMA — Cinema

(www.roxie.com; 3117 16th St; adult/child $10/6.50) Independent gems, insightful documentaries and rare film noir you won't find elsewhere, in a landmark 1909 cinema recently upgraded with Dolby sound.

Sports

SAN FRANCISCO GIANTS — Baseball

(Map p112; http://SanFrancisco.giants.mlb.com; AT&T Park; tickets $5-135; ☉ season Apr-Oct) Watch and learn how the World Series is won – bushy beards, women's underwear and all. The city's National League baseball team draws crowds to AT&T Park and its solar-powered scoreboard; the Waterfront Promenade offers a free view of right field.

SAN FRANCISCO 49ERS — Football

(www.49ers.com; Candlestick Park; tickets from $59; ☉ season Aug-Dec) For NFL football, beer and garlic fries, head to Candlestick Park.

🔒 Shopping

San Francisco has big department stores and name-brand boutiques around Union Sq, including **Macy's** (Map p112; www.macys.com; 170 O'Farrell Street) and the sprawling new **Westfield Shopping Centre** (Map p112; www.westfield.com/San Francisco; 865 Market St; ☉ 9:30am-9pm Mon-Sat, 10am-7pm Sun), but special, only-in-SF stores are found in the Haight, the Castro, the Mission and Hayes Valley (west of Civic Center).

NANCY BOY — Beauty

(Map p112; www.nancyboy.com; 347 Hayes St; ☉ 11am-7pm Mon-Fri, to 6pm Sat & Sun) Wear these highly effective moisturizers, pomades and sun balms with pride, all locally made with plant oils and tested on boyfriends, never animals.

GOLDEN GATE FORTUNE COOKIE COMPANY — Food & Drink

(56 Ross Alley; admission free; ☉ 8am-7pm) Make a fortune in San Francisco at this bakery, where cookies are stamped out on old-fashioned presses and folded over your customized message ($0.50 each). Cash only; $0.50 tip for photo requested.

ℹ️ Information

Dangers & Annoyances

Keep your city smarts and wits about you, especially at night in SoMa, the Mission and the Haight. Unless you know where you're going, avoid the sketchy, depressing Tenderloin (bor-

Castro Theatre (p121)

Cable Cars

Andrew Hallidie's 1873 contraptions have held up miraculously well on San Francisco's slopes, and groaning brakes and clanging brass bells only add to the carnival-ride thrills. Cable cars stop almost every block on California and Powell-Mason lines, and stop every block on north–south stretches of the Powell-Hyde line. To board on hills, act fast: leap onto the baseboard and grab the closest leather hand-strap. Here are route highlights:

Powell-Hyde Cable Car Golden Gate Bridge pops in and out of view, and you can hop off at the zig-zagging Lombard St or go straight to Ghirardelli Square.

Powell-Mason Cable Car Route crosses North Beach and ends in Fisherman's Wharf.

California St Cable Car History buffs and crowd-shy visitors prefer this line, in operation since 1878. Heads west through Chinatown and climbs Nob Hill. The Van Ness terminus is a few blocks northwest of Japantown.

MUNI (see p125) operates the lines, which run from about 6am to 1am daily, with scheduled departures every three to 12 minutes. Standard fare is $6 for a single ride; all-day unlimited rides $14. Tickets are available onboard, but you'll need exact change.

dered east–west by Powell and Polk Sts and north–south by O'Farrell and Market Sts), Skid Row (6th St between Market and Folsom Sts) and Bayview-Hunters Point. To cut through the Tenderloin, take Geary or Market Sts – still seedy, but tolerable. Panhandlers and homeless people are a fact of life in the city. People will probably ask you for spare change, but donations to local non-profits stretch further. For safety, don't engage with panhandlers at night or around ATMs. Otherwise, a simple 'I'm sorry,' is a polite response.

Tourist Information

California Welcome Center (Map p104; ☎ 415-981-1280; www.visitcwc.com; Pier 39, Bldg P, ste 241b; ☺10am-5pm) Handy for travel information, brochures, maps and help booking accommodations.

San Francisco Visitors Information Center (Map p112; ☎ 415-391-2000; www.onlyinSan Francisco.com; lower level, Hallidie Plaza; ☺9am-5pm Mon-Fri, 9am-3pm Sat & Sun) Maps, guidebooks, brochures, accommodations help.

✪ Getting There & Away

Air

The Bay Area has three major airports: San Francisco International Airport (SFO; www .flysfo.com), 14 miles south of downtown SF, off Hwy 101; Oakland International Airport, a few miles across the bay; and San José International Airport, at the southern end of the bay. The majority of international flights use SFO.

Bus

Until the new terminal is complete in 2017, SF's intercity hub remains the Temporary Transbay Terminal (Map p112; Howard & Main Sts), where you can catch buses on AC Transit (www.actransit .org) to the East Bay, Golden Gate Transit (http:// goldengatetransit.org) north to Marin and Sonoma Counties, and SamTrans (www.samtrans.com) south to Palo Alto and the Pacific coast. Greyhound (☎ 800-231-2222; www.greyhound.com) buses leave daily for Los Angeles ($56.50, eight to 12 hours), Truckee near Lake Tahoe ($33, 5½ hours), and other destinations.

Car & Motorcycle

All major car-rental operators (Alamo, Avis, Budget, Dollar, Hertz, Thrifty) are represented at the airports, and many have downtown offices.

Ferry

For Alcatraz Cruises, see p107.

Blue & Gold Fleet Ferries (Map p104; www .blueandgoldfleet.com) The Alameda–Oakland Ferry runs from the Ferry Building to Jack London Sq in Oakland ($6.25, 30 minutes). Ferries to Tiburon, Sausalito and Angel Island run from Pier 41 at Fisherman's Wharf.

Golden Gate Ferries (Map p112; ☑415-923-2000; www.goldengateferry.org; ⊙6am-10pm Mon-Fri, 10am-6pm Sat & Sun) Regular services run from the Ferry Building to Larkspur and Sausalito in Marin County. Transfers are available to MUNI bus services, and bicycles permitted.

Train

CalTrain (Map p112; www.caltrain.com; cnr 4th & King Sts) Links San Francisco to the South Bay, including Palo Alto (Stanford University) and San Jose.

Amtrak (☑800-872-7245; www.amtrak california.com) Offers low-emissions, leisurely travel to and from San Francisco. *Coast Starlight*'s spectacular 35-hour run from Los Angeles to Seattle stops in Oakland, and the *California Zephyr* takes its sweet time (51 hours) traveling from Chicago through the Rockies to Oakland. Both have sleeping cars and dining/lounge cars with panoramic windows.

ⓘ Getting Around

For Bay Area transit options, departures and arrivals, check ☑511 or www.511.org.

To/From the Airport

BART (Bay Area Rapid Transit; www.bart.gov; one way $8.10) Offers a fast, direct ride to downtown San Francisco.

SamTrans (www.samtrans.com; one way $5) Express bus KX gets you to Temporary Transbay Terminal in about 30 minutes.

SuperShuttle (☎800-258-3826; www.supershuttle.com; one way $17) Door-to-door vans depart from baggage-claim areas, taking 45 minutes to most SF locations.

Taxis To downtown San Francisco costs $35 to $50.

Car & Motorcycle

If you can, avoid driving in San Francisco: street parking is harder to find than true love, and meter readers are ruthless. Convenient downtown parking lots are at Embarcadero Center, 5th and Mission Sts, Union Sq, and Sutter and Stockton Sts.

BART

Bay Area Rapid Transit (BART; ☎415-989-2278; www.bart.gov; ⊙4am-midnight Mon-Fri, 6am-midnight Sat, 8am-midnight Sun) is a subway system linking SFO, the Mission District, downtown, San Francisco and the East Bay. The fastest link between Downtown and the Mission District also offers transit to SF airport.

MUNI

MUNI (Municipal Transit Agency; www.sfmuni.com) operates bus, streetcar and cable-car lines. Two cable-car lines leave from Powell and Market Sts; a third leaves from California and Market Sts. Standard fare for buses or streetcars is $2, and tickets are good on buses or streetcars (not BART or cable cars) for 90 minutes; cable-car fare is $6 for a single ride. Tickets are available on board, but you'll need exact change.

A **MUNI Passport** (one-/three-/seven-days $14/21/27) allows unlimited travel on all MUNI transport, including cable cars; it's sold at San Francisco's Visitor Information Center (p123) and at the TIX Bay Area kiosk at Union Sq and from a number of hotels. A seven-day **City Pass** (adult/child $69/39) covers Muni and admission to five attractions.

Taxi

Fares run about $2.25 per mile, plus 10% tip (starting at $1); meters start at $3.50.

Northern California & Central Coast

Northern California and the state's central coastline encompass a bonanza of natural vistas and bountiful wildlife. In Marin, you'll see wizened ancient redwoods blocking the sun, herds of elegant tule elk, plus leaping gray whales off the cape of wind-scoured Point Reyes.

Continuing north, craggy cliffs, towering redwoods and windswept bluffs define the wild, scenic and even slightly foreboding coast, where spectral fog has fostered the world's tallest trees and a maverick spirit pervades. The northern mountains, including the snowcapped peaks of Mt Shasta and Lassen Volcanic National Park, contain California's remote frontier, where vast expanses of wilderness are divided by rivers and streams, and dotted with cobalt lakes, horse ranches, and alpine pinnacles. South of San Francisco, flower-power Santa Cruz and the historic port town of Monterey are gateways to the rugged lands of the bohemian Big Sur coast and the central coast towns of laid-back San Luis Obispo and idyllic Santa Barbara.

Monterey (p178)

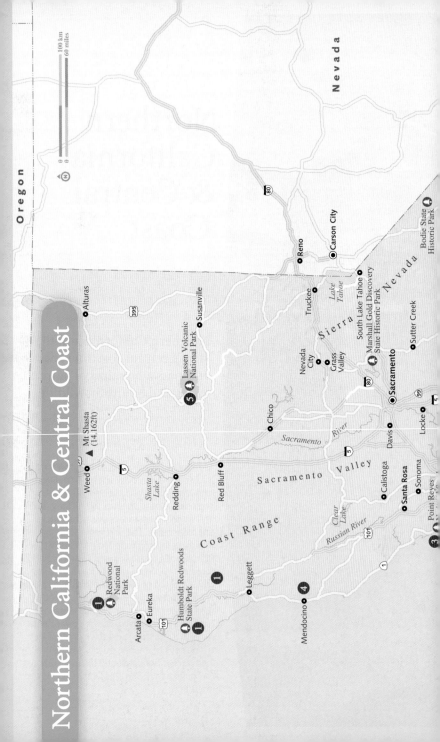

Northern California & Central Coast

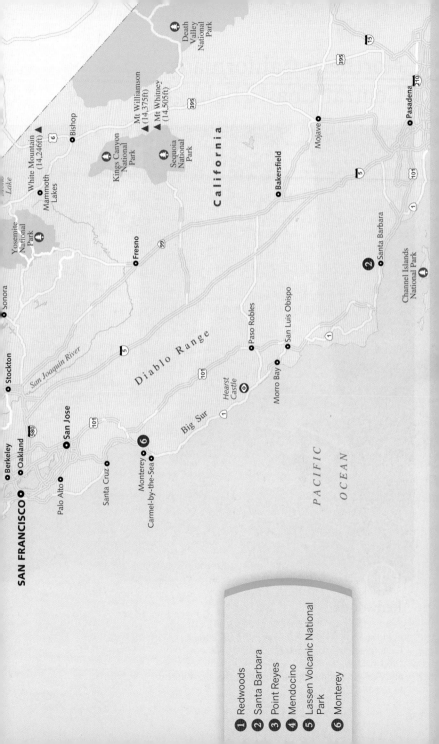

Northern California & Central Coast Highlights

Redwoods

Coast redwoods, the tallest living things on earth, are found in a narrow, 450-mile-long strip (p151) along California's coast between Big Sur and southern Oregon. They can live for 2200 years, grow to 378ft tall and achieve a diameter of 22ft at the base, with bark up to 12in thick.

Need to Know

TOP TIP Redwoods thrive on fog; bring warm clothes, non-slip shoes and rain gear for hikes **BEST TIME TO VISIT** Driest season from May though September **For more, see p151**

Redwoods Don't Miss List

BY JENNIFER BENITO, DIRECTOR OF OUTREACH, SAVE THE REDWOODS LEAGUE

1 HUMBOLDT REDWOODS STATE PARK

This park (p158) has lots of guides and is great for families because kids can learn a lot during a visit. It also has a number of good trails for hiking and cycling, plus a number of other outdoor activities you can do such as swimming and horseback riding. The Founders Grove and Rockefeller Forest were set aside for preservation a long time ago and are particularly amazing.

2 AVENUE OF THE GIANTS

Avenue of the Giants (p158) is a scenic drive that runs through Humboldt Redwoods State Park, and it parallels Hwy 101. People usually drive the 30-something miles through the trees, but it also hosts the annual Avenue of the Giants Marathon. Being outside and directly under the canopy of these massive trees is breathtaking – and it sure takes your mind off running!

3 BIG BASIN REDWOODS STATE PARK

Big Basin (p177) is California's oldest state park. It's located in the Santa Cruz Mountains and contains the largest ancient redwood stand south of San Francisco. What's so unexpected about visiting here is the sheer number of ancient trees that can be found so close to the cities.

4 JEDEDIAH SMITH REDWOODS STATE PARK

It feels like the trees get larger the further north you go in California, and this place (p169) is almost at the top of the state. I like it because it's so quiet, lush and serene, with hardly any people – just nature and the surrounding forest.

5 MONTGOMERY WOODS STATE RESERVE

This ancient forest (p159) has inspired photographers, artists – and even accountants – for generations. There's an overwhelming sense of peace and quiet, like you need to speak in a hushed voice. We're working with scientists from UC Berkeley and Humboldt State University to monitor growth in a designated plot here so the information can be used to protect redwoods in the future.

Santa Barbara

Just a 90-minute drive north of LA, Santa Barbara (p191) basks smugly in its near-perfection. Tucked between the Santa Ynez Mountains and the ocean, the city's red-tiled roofs, white-stucco buildings, Spanish mission, and Mediterranean vibe have long given credence to its claim to the title of the American Riviera. Its mild weather and bevy of surfing and swimming beaches don't hurt either.

Point Reyes

Wander through town for a stroll, pick up some cheese and picnic supplies at Tomales Bay Foods & Cowgirl Creamery and head out to the Point Reyes National Seashore (p148) to watch whales blow by in the late winter. Spend an afternoon kayaking in nearby Tomales Bay. Are you really only 1½ hours from San Francisco? Point Reyes Lighthouse (p149)

Mendocino

The coastal headland town of Mendo-cino (p154) is beloved by weekenders. Browse the charming upscale shops and art galleries, then explore the lighthouse and wildlife preserve north of its picket-fence-lined core. Dramatic cypress trees stand watch over the booming ocean surf and solitary coves, and you can canoe through the largest tidal estuary in the northern half of the state.

Lassen Volcanic National Park

California's stand-in for Yellowstone, Lassen (p170) is the state's ultimate geology lesson, with crunchy cinder cones, bubbling mud pots and steaming vents that stink like eggs months past their sell-by date. Though it last erupted in 1915, towering 10,000ft Lassen Peak is still considered to be an active volcano, though you might not want to ponder that as you survey its hard-won summit views.

Monterey

Trippy jellyfish, tangly kelp-forest creatures, graceful rays and boisterous sea otters en-liven the awesome Monterey Bay Aquarium (p180). Make a point of stopping by the tanks during feeding times, when divers hand-feed the sharks, and nattily plumed penguins waddle and jostle. In Old Monterey, travel back through time to wander the myriad 19th-century adobe buildings of Monterey State Historic Park (p179). Monterey Bay Aquarium

Northern California & Central Coast's Best...

Beaches

○ **Pfeiffer Beach** (p187) Big Sur's most dramatic beach.

○ **East Beach** (p193) Santa Barbara's downtown, kid-friendly beach.

○ **Point Piedras Blancas** (p189) Come for the historic lighthouse, stay for the elephant seals, peregrine falcons and otters.

○ **Stinson Beach** (p146) Good for long strolls and views of Point Reyes and San Francisco.

Charming Downtowns

○ **Carmel-by-the-Sea** (p183) Galleries, upscale boutiques and fairy-tale cottages attract shoppers, art collectors and dogs.

○ **Sausalito** (p142) Take the ferry to the Bay Area's fave vacation village.

○ **Mendocino** (p154) One-of-a-kind shops line the downtown drag.

○ **Ferndale** (p159) Handmade ironworks and a general store in a darling town.

Places to Take Kids

○ **Bay Area Discovery Museum** (p142) Parents will enjoy the cove's view of the bay; preschoolers will love the hands-on exhibits.

○ **Santa Cruz Beach Boardwalk** (p176) A beachfront amusement park with carnival rides.

○ **Monterey Bay Aquarium** (p180) Ogle the psychedelic jellyfish and touch tidepool animals.

○ **Lassen Volcanic National Park** (p170) For an illustrative example of what you learned in science class.

Need to Know

Outdoor Adventures

- **Salt Point State Park** (p153) Wild berries, rough-and-tumble coastline and animal species galore.

- **Lava Beds National Monument** (p173) Stark, moonlike landscapes, cave tours, and 10,000-year-old rock paintings and petroglyphs.

- **Mt Shasta** (p171) Worth the haul, if you're into that whole stunningly gorgeous mountain wilderness thing.

- **Point Reyes National Seashore** (p148) Just watch out for the elk in rutting season.

ADVANCE PLANNING

- **Two months before** Research outdoor activities and buy whatever gear you need.

- **One month before** Make your reservations at Chez Panisse (p151).

- **Two months before** Look up festivals and events around the state.

- **Two weeks before** Break in your boots for all of the hiking you'll do around Big Sur.

RESOURCES

- **Redwood National & State Parks** (www.nps.gov /redw) Official information.

- **Muir Woods National Monument** (www.nps.gov /muwo) Plan your visit in advance.

- **Marin Headlands** (www .nps.gov/goga) Info on Marin Headlands and Golden Gate National Parks.

- **Big Sur California** (www.bigsurcalifornia .org) Information on lodging, restaurants and parklands.

- **West Marin Chamber of Commerce** (www.point reyes.org) Information on lodging near Point Reyes.

GETTING AROUND

- **Walking** The best way to explore compact downtown areas including San Luis Obispo, Monterey and Santa Barbara.

- **Ferry** From San Francisco, the best way to visit Sausalito or Tiburon.

- **Bus** Not convenient for the further reaches, but a great way to reach Muir Woods.

- **Car** Will allow you the most freedom to explore the redwoods and coast.

- **Amtrak** Its *Coast Starlight* route runs between Los Angeles, Santa Barbara, San Luis Obispo and Salinas.

BE FOREWARNED

- **Coast** Many people have been killed, both on- and offshore. Watch your step while hiking, and keep an eye out for riptides, sharks and storms.

- **Tidepools** Read posted information or online guides to ensure you don't hurt the fragile ecosystem.

- **Costs** The Central California Coast can be quite an expensive destination for accommodations.

- **Climate** Redwoods thrive in fog, so dress accordingly.

Northern California & Central Coast Itineraries

Take your time as you tour miles of evocative coastline and forests of giant redwoods, contemplating the rhythm of the crashing Pacific surf and the fortitude of the sky-high trees.

5 DAYS

UKIAH TO NORTHERN REDWOOD COAST

Redwood Country

Don't let the distance scare you off; visiting the redwoods is an easy trip from the Bay Area in five days (or even less). To save time, take Hwy 101 instead of the coast. Stop first in **(1) Ukiah** for a stress-relieving soak in one of the local hot-spring resorts and a visit to the tranquil old-growth redwood stand at Montgomery Woods State Reserve. The next day you'll enter the **(2) Southern Redwood Coast** with a drive through Avenue of the Giants. You can spend an entire day hiking the area and craning your neck to see the tops of the ancient trees, but be sure to reach **(3) Ferndale** by nightfall to stay in one of the adorable town's 'butterfat mansion' B&Bs. Spend the next day in **(4) Arcata**, a university town where the smell of biodiesel fuel and patchoulis hangs in the air. Take a walk along the wildlife sanctuary on Humboldt Bay to spot scores of water birds. Spend the rest of your time on the **(5) Northern Redwood Coast**, hiking the moss-covered Fern Canyon or admiring the giant redwoods in Lady Bird Johnson Grove.

5 NORTHERN REDWOOD COAST
4 ARCATA
3 FERNDALE
2 SOUTHERN REDWOOD COAST

1 MENDOCINO
1 UKIAH

2 BODEGA BAY
3
POINT REYES
NATIONAL
SEASHORE

MONTEREY **4**
BIG SUR **5**

HEARST CASTLE **6**

SANTA BARBARA **7**

Top Left: Victoria Inn, Ferndale (p159); **Top Right:** Sea lions, Monterey (p178)

(TOP LEFT) WITOLD SKRYPCZAK/LONELY PLANET IMAGES ©;
(TOP RIGHT) RICHARD MILLS/LONELY PLANET IMAGES ©

1 WEEK

REDWOOD NATIONAL PARK TO SANTA BARBARA

Cruising the Coast

Start a lazy road trip that follows the water's edge, leaving Redwood National Park and retracing forested Hwy 101 south until you join coastal Hwy 1. Pass the afternoon and evening in the North Coast jewel of **(1) Mendocino**, exploring its rocky headlands and cozying up for the night at one of its picturesque lodgings. The next day, call in at **(2) Bodega Bay** to relive *The Birds* and scan the water for breaching whales at Bodega Head. For a wildlife bonanza of tule elk, elephant seals and even more whales, wind your way to the stark shoreline bluffs of the **(3) Point Reyes National Seashore**. After seeing what lives above the water, venture on to the world-famous aquarium in **(4) Monterey** to see the slippery creatures that thrive underneath the waves. You could spend a lifetime pondering the wild and solitary **(5) Big Sur** area – the most dazzling section of California coastline – but reserve a place to stay so you can linger for the sunset. Book advance tickets for a tour of the opulent **(6) Hearst Castle**, and then plant yourself in the warm sand in **(7) Santa Barbara**.

Discover Northern California & Central Coast

At a Glance

○ **Marin County** Rugged headlands, wild beaches and organic local agriculture, all just across the bridge from San Francisco.

○ **Central Coast** (p173) A personality-packed stretch of coastline with dazzling beaches.

○ **North Coast** (p151) Soaring redwood forests cluster close to quaint towns.

○ **Northern Mountains** (p169) Remote and impressive mountain peaks.

MARIN COUNTY

If there's a part of the Bay Area that consciously attempts to live up to the California dream, it's Marin County. Just across the Golden Gate Bridge from San Francisco, the region has a wealthy population that cultivates a seemingly laid-back lifestyle. Towns may look like idyllic rural hamlets, but the shops cater to cosmopolitan and expensive tastes. The 'common' folk here eat organic, vote Democrat and drive hybrids.

Nature is what makes Marin County such an excellent day trip or weekend escape from San Francisco.

Marin Headlands

The headlands rise majestically out of the water at the north end of the Golden Gate Bridge, their rugged beauty all the more striking given the fact that they're only a few miles from San Francisco's urban core. As trails wind through the headlands, they afford stunning views of the sea, the Golden Gate Bridge and San Francisco, leading to isolated beaches and secluded spots for picnics.

◉ Sights

After crossing the Golden Gate Bridge, exit immediately at Alexander Ave, then dip left under the highway and head out west for the expansive views and hiking trailheads. Conzelman Rd snakes up into the hills, where it eventually forks. Conzelman Rd continues west, becoming a steep, one-lane road as it descends to Point Bonita. From here it continues to Rodeo Beach and Fort Barry.

Point Bonita Lighthouse
ROBERTO GEROMETTA/LONELY PLANET IMAGES ©

McCullough Rd heads inland, joining Bunker Rd toward Rodeo Beach.

HAWK HILL
Hill

About 2 miles along Conzelman Rd is Hawk Hill, where thousands of migrating birds of prey soar along the cliffs from late summer to early fall.

POINT BONITA LIGHTHOUSE
Lighthouse

(www.nps.gov/goga/pobo.htm; ⏰12:30-3:30pm Sat-Mon) At the end of Conzelman Rd, this lighthouse is a breathtaking half-mile walk from a small parking area. From the tip of Point Bonita, you can see the distant Golden Gate Bridge and beyond it the San Francisco skyline. It's an uncommon vantage point of the bay-centric city, and harbor seals haul out nearby in season. To reserve a spot on one of the free monthly full-moon tours of the promontory, call ☎415-331-1540.

FREE MARINE MAMMAL CENTER
Animal Rescue center

(☎415-289-7325; www.marinemammalcenter .org; ⏰10am-5pm; 👪) Set on the hill above Rodeo Lagoon, the newly expanded Marine Mammal Center rehabilitates injured, sick and orphaned sea mammals before returning them to the wild, and has educational exhibits about these animals and the dangers they face. During the spring pupping season the center can have up to several dozen orphaned seal pups on site and you can often see them before they're set free.

Activities

Hiking

At the end of Bunker Rd sits Rodeo Beach, protected from wind by high cliffs. From here the **Coastal Trail** meanders 3.5 miles inland, past abandoned military bunkers, to the **Tennessee Valley Trail**. It then continues 6 miles along the blustery headlands all the way to Muir Beach.

Sleeping

MARIN HEADLANDS HOSTEL
Hostel $

(☎415-331-2777; www.norcalhostels.org/marin; Bldg 941, Fort Barry, Marin Headlands; dm $22-26, r $72-92; @) Wake up to grazing deer and dew on the ground at this spartan 1907 military compound snuggled in the woods. It has comfortable beds and two well-stocked kitchens, and guests can gather round a fireplace in the common room, shoot pool or play ping-pong. Most importantly, the Hostelling International (HI) hostel is surrounded by hiking trails.

Information

Information is available from the Golden Gate National Recreation Area (GGNRA; ☎415-561-4700; www.nps.gov/goga) and the Marin Headlands Visitors Center (☎415-331-1540; www.nps.gov/goga/marin-headlands.htm;

Marin Public Transportation

The **West Marin Stagecoach** (☎415-526-3239; www.marintransit.org/stage.html; fare $2) runs three minibus routes to reach Marin coast destination towns:

Route 61 Daily from Marin City to Stinson Beach and Bolinas, and weekend and holiday service from the Sausalito ferry

Route 62 Tuesday, Thursday and Saturday service from San Rafael to Point Reyes Station, Bolinas and Stinson Beach

Route 68 Daily from San Rafael to Point Reyes Station and Inverness

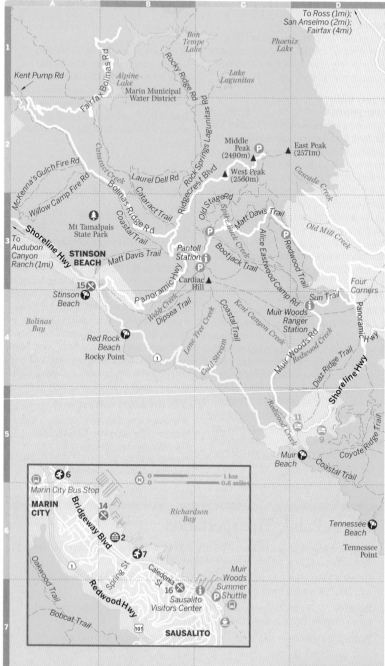

To Ross (1mi);
San Anselmo (2mi);
Fairfax (4mi)

Kent Pump Rd

Bon Tempe Lake

Alpine Lake

Phoenix Lake

Lake Lagunitas

Fairfax Bolinas Rd

Rocky Ridge Rd

Marin Municipal Water District

Cataract Creek

McKenna's Gulch Fire Rd

Willow Camp Fire Rd

Laurel Dell Rd

Cataract Trail

Bolinas Ridge Rd

Coastal Trail

Ridgecrest Blvd

Rock Springs Lagunitas Rd

Middle Peak (2490m)

West Peak (2560m)

East Peak (2571m)

Cascade Creek

Old Stage Rd

Matt Davis Trail

Old Mill Creek

Mt Tamalpais State Park

Shoreline Hwy

To Audubon Canyon Ranch (1mi)

STINSON BEACH

Matt Davis Trail

Pantoll Station

Spike Buck Creek

Bootjack Trail

Alice Eastwood Camp Rd

Redwood Trail

Four Corners

Sun Trail

15

Stinson Beach

Panoramic Hwy

Cardiac Hill

Dipsea Trail

Webb Creek

Lone Tree Creek

Coastal Trail

Kent Canyon Creek

Muir Woods Ranger Station

Bolinas Bay

Red Rock Beach
Rocky Point

Cold Stream

Muir Woods Rd

Redwood Creek

Diaz Ridge Trail

Shoreline Hwy

Panoramic Hwy

Redwood Creek

11

9

Coyote Ridge Trail

Muir Beach

Coastal Trail

Tennessee Beach

Tennessee Point

6
Marin City Bus Stop

MARIN CITY

Bridgeway Blvd

14

2

7

Richardson Bay

0 ___ 1 km
0 ___ 0.6 miles

Oakwood Trail

Spring St

Redwood Hwy

Caledonia St

16

Sausalito Visitors Center

Muir Woods Summer Shuttle

Bobcat Trail

101

SAUSALITO

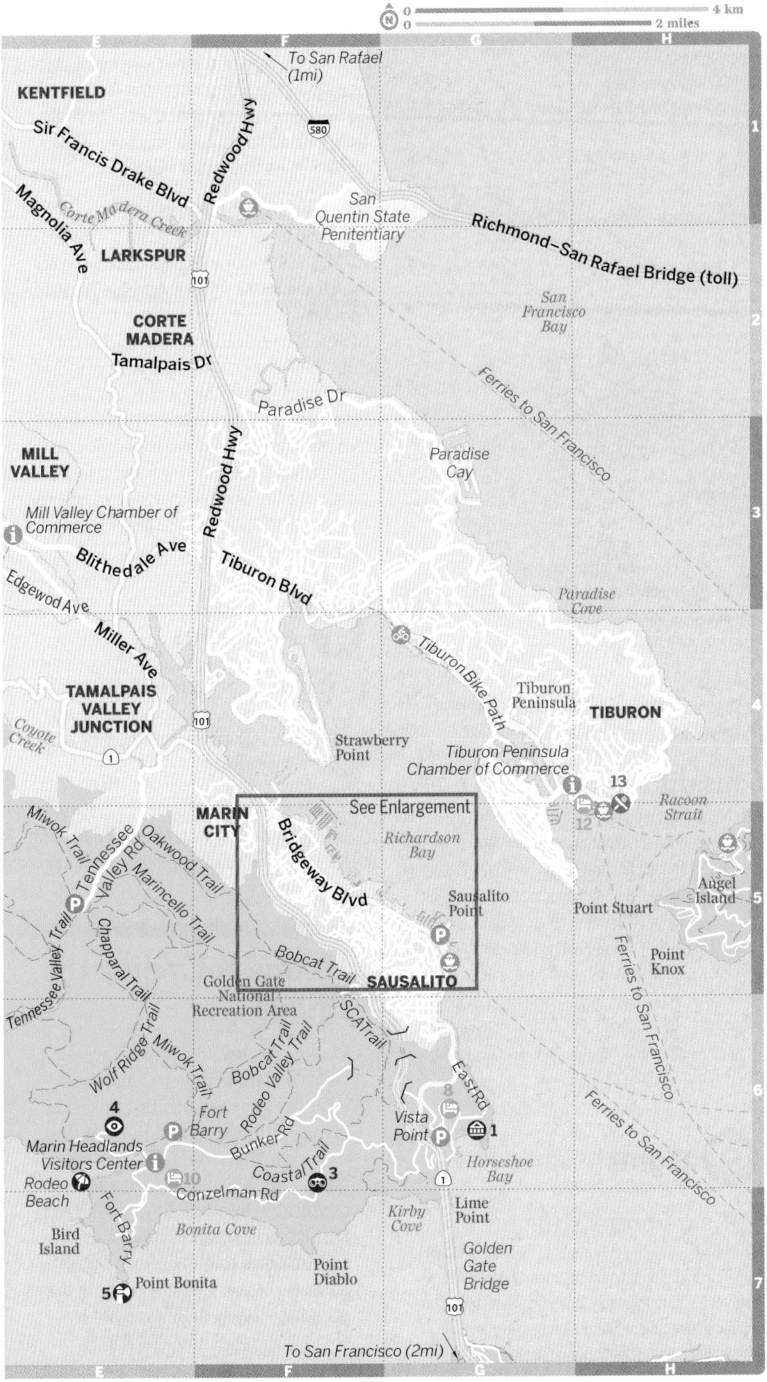
0 4 km
0 2 miles
To San Rafael (1mi)
KENTFIELD
Sir Francis Drake Blvd
Redwood Hwy
580
San Quentin State Penitentiary
Magnolia Ave
Corte Madera Creek
LARKSPUR
Richmond–San Rafael Bridge (toll)
101
San Francisco Bay
CORTE MADERA
Tamalpais Dr
Ferries to San Francisco
Paradise Dr
MILL VALLEY
Redwood Hwy
Paradise Cay
Mill Valley Chamber of Commerce
Blithedale Ave
Tiburon Blvd
Edgewood Ave
Paradise Cove
Miller Ave
Tiburon Bike Path
TAMALPAIS VALLEY JUNCTION
Tiburon Peninsula
TIBURON
Coyote Creek
Strawberry Point
Tiburon Peninsula Chamber of Commerce
13
See Enlargement
MARIN CITY
Racoon Strait
12
Miwok Trail
Tennessee Valley Rd
Oakwood Trail
Bridgeway Blvd
Richardson Bay
Marincello Trail
Angel Island
Sausalito Point
Point Stuart
Tennessee Valley Trail
Chapparal Trail
Bobcat Trail
Point Knox
SAUSALITO
Golden Gate National Recreation Area
SCA Trail
Wolf Ridge Trail
Miwok Trail
Bobcat Trail
Rodeo Valley Trail
East Rd
8
4
Fort Barry
Vista Point
1
Bunker Rd
Marin Headlands Visitors Center
Horseshoe Bay
Rodeo Beach
10
Coastal Trail
3
Conzelman Rd
Kirby Cove
Lime Point
Fort Barry
Bonita Cove
Bird Island
Golden Gate Bridge
Point Diablo
5
Point Bonita
To San Francisco (2mi)
E
F
G
H
1
2
3
4
5
6
7

Marin County

◎ Sights
1 Bay Area Discovery Museum.............G6
2 Bay Model Visitor Center...................B6
3 Hawk Hill F6
4 Marine Mammal Center......................E6
5 Point Bonita Lighthouse E7

⊕ Activities, Courses & Tours
6 Mike's Bikes...A5
7 Sea Trek B6

⊜ Sleeping
8 Cavallo Point...G6
9 Green Gulch Farm & Zen
   Center..D5
10 Marin Headlands Hostel E6
11 Pelican Inn...D5
12 Water's Edge Hotel.............................H5

⊗ Eating
13 Caprice H5
14 Fish B6
   Murray Circle.............................. (see 8)
15 Parkside Cafe A3
   Sam's Anchor Cafe....................(see 12)
16 Sushi Ran..B7

◎9:30am-4:30pm), in an old chapel off Bunker Rd near Fort Barry.

Sausalito

Perfectly arranged on a secure little harbor on the bay, Sausalito is undeniably lovely. Named for the tiny willows that once populated the banks of its creeks, it's a small settlement of pretty houses that tumble neatly down a green hillside into a well-heeled downtown. Much of the town affords the visitor uninterrupted views of San Francisco and Angel Island, and due to the ridgeline at its back, fog generally skips past it.

Sights

FREE **BAY MODEL VISITOR CENTER**　　　Museum
(📞415-332-3871; www.spn.usace.army.mil/bmvc; 2100 Bridgeway Blvd; ◎9am-4pm Tue-Fri, plus 10am-5pm Sat & Sun in summer; 👪)
One of the coolest things in town, fas-

cinating to both kids and adults, is the Army Corps of Engineers' visitor center. Housed in one of the old Marinship warehouses, it's a 1.5-acre hydraulic model of San Francisco Bay and the delta region. Self-guided tours take you over and around it as the water flows.

BAY AREA DISCOVERY MUSEUM　　　Museum
(📞415-339-3900; www.baykidsmuseum.org; adult/child $10/8; ◎9am-4pm Tue-Fri, 10am-5pm Sat & Sun; 👪) Just under the north tower of the Golden Gate Bridge, at East Fort Baker, this excellent hands-on activity museum is specifically designed for children. Permanent (multilingual) exhibits include a wave workshop, a small underwater tunnel and a large outdoor play area with a shipwreck to romp around. A small cafe has healthy nibbles.

Activities

Sausalito is great for **bicycling**, whether for a leisurely ride around town, a trip across the Golden Gate Bridge or a longer-haul journey.

SEA TREK　　　Kayaking
(📞415-488-1000; www.seatrek.com; Schoonmaker Point Marina; single/double kayaks per hr

Hiking & Cycling the Bridge

Walking or cycling across the Golden Gate Bridge to Sausalito is a fun way to avoid traffic, get some great ocean views and bask in that refreshing Marin County air. It's a fairly easy journey, mostly flat or downhill when heading north from San Francisco (cycling back to the city involves one big climb out of Sausalito). You can also simply hop on a ferry back to SF (see p144).

JOHN ELK III/LONELY PLANET IMAGES ©

$20/35) On a nice day, Richardson Bay is irresistible. Kayaks and stand-up paddleboards can be rented here, near the Bay Model Visitor Center. No experience is necessary, and lessons and group outings are also available.

MIKE'S BIKES　　　Bicycle Rental
(☎415-332-3200; 1 Gate 6 Rd; 24hr $40) At the north end of Bridgeway Blvd near Hwy 101, this shop rents out road and mountain bikes. Supplies are limited and reservations aren't accepted.

Sleeping & Eating

CAVALLO POINT　　　Hotel $$$
(☎415-339-4700; www.cavallopoint.com; 601 Murray Circle, Fort Baker; r from $280; ❄@☎☀☺) Spread out over 45 acres of the Bay Area's most scenic parkland, Cavallo Point is a buzz-worthy lodge that flaunts a green focus, a full-service spa and easy access to outdoor activities. Choose from richly renovated rooms in the landmark Fort Baker officers' quarters or more contemporary solar-powered accommodations with exquisite bay views

(including a turret of the Golden Gate Bridge).

FISH　　　Seafood $$
(www.331fish.com; 350 Harbor Dr; mains $13-25; ⏲11:30am-8:30pm; ♿) Chow down on seafood sandwiches, oysters and Dungeness crab roll with organic local butter at redwood picnic tables facing Richardson Bay. A local leader in promoting fresh and sustainably caught fish, this place has wonderful wild salmon in season, and refuses to serve the farmed stuff. Cash only.

MURRAY CIRCLE　　　American $$
(☎415-339-4750; www.cavallopoint.com/dine.html; 601 Murray Circle, Fort Baker; mains $17-29; ⏲7-11am & 11:30am-2pm Mon-Fri, to 2:30pm Sat & Sun, 5:30-10pm Sun-Thu, to 11pm Fri & Sat) At the Cavallo Point lodge, dine on locally sourced meats, seafood and produce, like grass-fed organic burgers or Dungeness crab BLT, in a clubby dining room topped by a pressed-tin ceiling. Reservations recommended for lunch and dinner, especially for seating on the panoramic-view balcony. Save room for the butterscotch soufflé.

SUSHI RAN Sushi $$

(☏415-332-3620; www.sushiran.com; 107 Caledonia St; sushi $4-19) Many Bay Area residents claim this place is the best sushi spot around. A wine and sake bar next door eases the pain of the long wait for a table.

ⓘ Getting There & Away

Driving to Sausalito from San Francisco, take the Alexander Ave exit (the first exit after the Golden Gate Bridge) and follow the signs into Sausalito. There are five municipal parking lots in town, and street parking is difficult to find.

The ferry is a fun and easy way to travel to Sausalito. Golden Gate Ferry (☏415-455-2000; www.goldengateferry.org; one way $9.25) operates to and from the San Francisco Ferry Building six to nine times daily and takes 30 minutes. The Blue & Gold Fleet (☏415-705-8200; www.blueandgoldfleet.com; Pier 41, Fisherman's Wharf; one way $10.50) sails to Sausalito four to five times daily from the Fisherman's Wharf area in San Francisco. Both ferries operate year-round and transport bicycles for free.

Tiburon

At the end of a small peninsula pointing out into the center of the bay, Tiburon is blessed with gorgeous views. The name comes from the Spanish *Punta de Tiburon* (Shark Point). Take the ferry from San Francisco, browse the shops on Main St, grab a bite to eat and you've seen Tiburon. The town is also a jumping-off point for nearby **Angel Island**, a pleasant spot for hiking and cycling and the site of the West Coast's historic immigration station.

🛏 Sleeping & Eating

WATER'S EDGE HOTEL Hotel $$

(☏415-789-5999; www.watersedgehotel.com; 25 Main St; r incl breakfast $169-499; ❄@🛜) This hotel, with its deck extending over the bay, is exemplary for its tasteful modernity. Rooms have an elegant minimalism that combines comfort and style, and all afford an immediate view of the

Left: Sculpture, Tiburon; **Below:** Angel Island
(LEFT) LEE FOSTER/LONELY PLANET IMAGES ©; (BELOW) LEE FOSTER/LONELY PLANET IMAGES ©

bay. The rooms with rustic, high wood ceilings are quite romantic.

SAM'S ANCHOR CAFE Seafood $$
(www.samscafe.com; 27 Main St; mains $17-28; ⏱11am-10pm Mon-Fri, from 9:30am Sat & Sun) Sam's has been slinging seafood and burgers since 1920, and though the entrance looks like a shambling little shack, the area out back has unbeatable views. On a warm afternoon, you can't beat a cocktail or a tasty plate of sautéed prawns on the deck.

CAPRICE American $$$
(☎415-435-3400; www.thecaprice.com; 2000 Paradise Dr; mains $18-49; ⏱5-10pm Tue-Sun, plus 11am-3pm Sun) Splurge-worthy and romantic, book a table here at sunset for riveting views of Angel Island, the Golden Gate Bridge and San Francisco. Caprice mostly features seafood, though other standouts include the artichoke bisque and the filet mignon. Take a peek at the fireplace downstairs – it's constructed into the coast bedrock. A three-course midweek dinner ($25) is easier on the wallet.

🛈 **Getting There & Away**

Blue & Gold Fleet (☎415-705-8200; one way $10.50) sails daily from either Pier 41 or the Ferry Building in San Francisco to Tiburon; ferries dock right in front of the Guaymas restaurant on Main St. You can transport bicycles for free. From Tiburon, ferries also connect regularly to Angel Island.

Muir Beach

The turnoff to Muir Beach from Hwy 1 is marked by the longest row of mailboxes on the North Coast. Muir Beach is a quiet little town with a nice beach, but it has no direct bus service. Just north of Muir Beach there are superb views up and down the coast from the **Muir Beach Overlook**; during WWII, watch was kept

145

from the surrounding concrete lookouts for invading Japanese ships.

Pelican Inn (415-383-6000; www .pelicaninn.com; 10 Pacific Way; r incl breakfast $190-265;) is the only commercial establishment in Muir Beach. The downstairs restaurant and pub (mains $9 to $34) is an Anglophile's dream and perfect for pre- or post-hike nourishment.

Green Gulch Farm & Zen Center (415-383-3134; www.sfzc.org; 1601 Shoreline Hwy; s $90-135, d $160-205, d cottage $300-350, all with 3 meals; @) is a Buddhist retreat in the hills above Muir Beach. The center's accommodations are elegant, restful and modern, and delicious buffet-style vegetarian meals are included.

Stinson Beach

Positively buzzing on warm weekends, Stinson Beach is 5 miles north of Muir Beach. The town flanks Hwy 1 for about three blocks and is densely packed with galleries, shops, eateries and B&Bs. The beach itself is often blanketed with fog, and when the sun's shining it's blanketed with surfers, families and gawkers. There are views of Point Reyes and San Francisco on clear days, and the beach is long enough for a vigorous stroll. From San Francisco it's nearly an hour's drive, though on weekends plan for toe-tapping traffic delays.

Three-mile-long **Stinson Beach** is a popular surf spot, but swimming is advised from late May to mid-September only; for updated weather and surf conditions call 415-868-1922. The beach is one block west of Hwy 1.

Audubon Canyon Ranch (415-868-9244; www.egret.org; donations requested; 10am-4pm Sat, Sun & holidays mid-Mar–mid-Jul) is about 3.5 miles north of town on Hwy 1, in the hills above the Bolinas Lagoon. A major nesting ground for great blue herons and great egrets, viewing scopes are set up on hillside blinds where you can watch these magnificent birds congregate to nest and hatch their chicks in tall redwoods.

Parkside Cafe (415-868-1272; www.parksidecafe.com; 43 Arenal Ave; mains $9-25; 7:30am-9pm Mon-Fri, from 8am Sat & Sun) is famous for its hearty breakfasts and lunches, and noted far and wide for its excellent coastal cuisine. Reservations are recommended for dinner.

Point Reyes Station

Though the railroad stopped coming through in 1933 and the town is small, Point Reyes Station is nevertheless the hub of West Marin. Dominated by dairies and ranches, the region was invaded by artists in the 1960s. Today it's an interesting blend of art galleries and tourist shops.

Golden Gate National Recreation Area
WALTER BIBIKOW/GETTY IMAGES ©

LEE FOSTER/LONELY PLANET IMAGES ©

Don't Miss **Muir Woods National Monument**

Walking through an awesome stand of the world's tallest trees is an experience to be had only in Northern California and a small part of southern Oregon. The old-growth redwoods at **Muir Woods**, just 12 miles north of the Golden Gate Bridge, is the closest redwood stand to San Francisco. The trees were initially eyed by loggers, and Redwood Creek, as the area was known, seemed ideal for a dam. Those plans were halted when congressman and naturalist William Kent bought a section of Redwood Creek and, in 1907, donated 295 acres to the federal government. President Theodore Roosevelt made the site a national monument in 1908, the name honoring John Muir, naturalist and founder of environmental organization the Sierra Club.

Muir Woods can become quite crowded, especially on weekends. Try to come midweek, early in the morning or late in the afternoon, when tour buses are less of a problem. Even at busy times, a short hike will get you out of the densest crowds and onto trails with huge trees and stunning vistas. A lovely cafe serves local and organic goodies and hot drinks that hit the spot on foggy days.

The 1-mile **Main Trail Loop** is a gentle walk alongside Redwood Creek to the 1000-year-old trees at **Cathedral Grove**; it returns via **Bohemian Grove**, where the tallest tree in the park stands 254ft high. The **Dipsea Trail** is a good 2-mile hike up to the top of aptly named **Cardiac Hill**.

The parking lot fills up during busy periods, so consider taking the summer shuttle operated by **Marin Transit**. The 40-minute shuttle connects with four Sausalito ferries arriving from San Francisco.

NEED TO KNOW

Muir Woods (415-388-2595; www.nps.gov/muwo; adult/child under 16 $5/free; 8am-sunset); Marin Transit (www.marintransit.org; round trip adult/child $3/1; weekends & holidays late-May–Sep)

Sleeping & Eating

Cute little cottages, cabins and B&Bs are plentiful in and around Point Reyes. The **West Marin Chamber of Commerce** (☎415-663-9232; www.pointreyes.org) has numerous listings, as does the **Point Reyes Lodging Association** (www.ptreyes.com).

HOLLY TREE INN　　Inn, Cottages $$
(☎415-663-1554, 800-286-4655; www.holly treeinn.com; Silver Hills Rd; r incl breakfast $130-180, cottages $190-265) This inn, off Bear Valley Rd, has four rooms and three private cottages in a beautiful setting. The **Sea Star Cottage** is a romantic refuge at the end of a small pier on Tomales Bay.

BOVINE BAKERY　　Bakery $
(11315 Hwy 1; ⊙6:30am-5pm Mon-Thu, 7am-5pm Sat & Sun) Don't leave town without sampling something buttery from possibly the best bakery in Marin. A bear claw (a large sweet pastry) and an organic coffee are a good way to kick off your morning.

🖉OSTERIA STELLINA　　Italian $$
(☎415-663-9988; www.osteriastellina.com; 11285 Hwy 1; mains $15-25; ⊙11:30am-2:30pm

& 5-9pm; 🖉) This place specializes in rustic Italian cuisine, with pizza and pasta dishes and Niman Ranch meats. Head over Tuesday nights for lasagna and live music, and definitely make reservations for the weekend.

🖉TOMALES BAY FOODS & COWGIRL CREAMERY　　Market $$
(☎415-663-9335; www.cowgirlcreamery.com; 80 4th St; ⊙10am-6pm Wed-Sun; 🖉) A local market in an old barn selling picnic items, including gourmet cheeses and organic produce. Reserve a spot in advance for the small-scale artisanal cheesemaker's demonstration and tasting ($5), where you can watch the curd-making and cutting, then sample a half-dozen of the fresh and aged cheeses. All of the milk is local and organic, with vegetarian rennet in all its soft cheeses.

Point Reyes National Seashore

The windswept peninsula Point Reyes is a rough-hewn beauty that has always lured marine mammals and migratory birds as well as scores of shipwrecks.

Bark hut, Kule Loklo

EMILY RIDDELL/LONELY PLANET IMAGES ©

Don't Miss **Point Reyes Lighthouse**

At the very end of Sir Francis Drake Blvd, with wild terrain and ferocious winds, this spot feels like the ends of the earth and offers the best **whale-watching** along the coast. The lighthouse sits below the headlands; to reach it requires descending over 300 stairs. Nearby **Chimney Rock** is a fine short hike, especially in spring when the wildflowers are blossoming. A nearby viewing area allows you to spy on the park's **elephant seal colony**.

On good-weather weekends and holidays from late December through mid-April, the road to Chimney Rock and the lighthouse is closed to private vehicles. Instead you must take a shuttle ($5, children under 17 free) from Drakes Beach.

NEED TO KNOW
☏ 415-669-1534; ⊙ 10am-4:30pm Thu-Mon

Point Reyes National Seashore has 110 sq miles of pristine ocean beaches, and the peninsula offers excellent hiking and camping opportunities. Be sure to bring warm clothing, as even the sunniest days can quickly turn cold and foggy.

 ## Sights & Activities

For an awe-inspiring view, follow the **Earthquake Trail** from the park headquarters at Bear Valley. The trail reaches a 16ft gap between the two halves of a once-connected fence line, a lasting testimonial to the power of the 1906 earthquake that was centered in this area. Another trail leads from the visitors center a short way to **Kule Loklo**, a reproduction of a Miwok village.

Limantour Rd, off Bear Valley Rd about 1 mile north of Bear Valley Visitor Center, leads to the Point Reyes Hostel (p150) and **Limantour Beach**, where a trail runs along Limantour Spit with Estero de Limantour on one side and Drakes Bay on the other. The **Inverness Ridge Trail** heads from Limantour Rd up to Mt Vision (1282ft), from where there are spectacular views of the entire national seashore. You can drive almost to the top of Mt Vision from the other side.

In Inverness and across the bay in Marshall (on Hwy 1, 8 miles north of Point Reyes Station), **Blue Waters Kayaking** (☎415-669-2600; www.bwkayak.com; kayak rental 2/4hr $50/60) has Tomales Bay tours, or rent a kayak and paddle around secluded beaches and rocky crevices solo; no experience necessary.

Pierce Point Rd continues to the huge windswept sand dunes at **Abbotts Lagoon**, full of peeping killdeer and other shorebirds. At the end of the road is Pierce Point Ranch, the trailhead for the 3.5-mile **Tomales Point Trail** through the **Tule Elk Reserve**. The plentiful elk are an amazing sight, standing with their big horns against the backdrop of Tomales Point, with Bodega Bay to the north, Tomales Bay to the east and the Pacific Ocean to the west.

🛏 Sleeping & Eating

🌿**POINT REYES HOSTEL**   Hostel **$**
(☎415-663-8811; www.norcalhostels.org/reyes; dm/r $24/68; @) Just off Limantour Rd,

this rustic HI property has bunkhouses with warm and cozy front rooms, big-view windows and outdoor areas with hill vistas, and a brand new LEED-certified building with four more private rooms in the works. It's in a beautiful secluded valley 2 miles from the ocean and surrounded by lovely hiking trails.

**DRAKES BAY OYSTER
COMPANY**   Seafood **$$**
(☎415-669-1149; www.drakesbayoyster.com; 17171 Sir Francis Drake Blvd, Inverness; 1 dozen oysters to go/on the half shell $15/24; ⏱8:30am-4:30pm) Drakes Bay and nearby Tomales Bay are famous for excellent oysters. Stop by to do some on-the-spot shucking and slurping, or pick some up to grill later.

ℹ Information

The park headquarters, Bear Valley Visitor Center (☎415-464-5100; Bear Valley Rd; ⏱9am-5pm Mon-Fri, from 8am Sat & Sun), is near Olema and has information and maps. You can also get information at the Point Reyes Lighthouse and the Ken Patrick Center (☎415-669-1250; ⏱10am-5pm Sat, Sun & holidays) at Drakes Beach. All visitor centers have slightly longer hours in summer.

Decorated car, Berkeley

Detour:
Berkeley

As the birthplace of the Free Speech and disability-rights movements, and the home of the hallowed halls of the University of California, Berkeley is no bashful wallflower. A national hot spot of (mostly left-of-center) intellectual discourse and one of the most vocal activist populations in the country, this infamous East Bay college town has an interesting mix of graying progressives and idealistic undergrads.

UNIVERSITY OF CALIFORNIA, BERKELEY

The Berkeley campus of the University of California (UCB, called 'Cal' by both students and locals) is the oldest university in the state. The **UC Berkeley Art Museum** (510-642-0808; www.bampfa.berkeley.edu; 2626 Bancroft Way; adult/student $10/7, 1st Thu each month free; 11am-5pm Wed-Sun) has 11 galleries showcasing a huge range of works, from ancient Chinese to cutting-edge contemporary. The complex also houses a bookstore, cafe and sculpture garden.

Officially called Sather Tower, the **Campanile** (elevator rides $2; 10am-4pm Mon-Fri, to 5pm Sat, to 1:30pm & 3-5pm Sun) was modeled on St Mark's Basilica in Venice. The 328ft spire offers fine views of the Bay Area, and at the top you can stare up into the carillon of 61 bells, ranging from the size of a cereal bowl to that of a Volkswagen.

GOURMET GHETTO

The section of Shattuck Ave north of University Ave is the 'Gourmet Ghetto,' home to lots of excellent eating establishments, including California cuisine landmark **Chez Panisse** (restaurant 510-548-5525, cafe 510-548-5049; www.chez panisse.com; 1517 Shattuck Ave; restaurant $60-95, cafe mains $18-29; restaurant dinner Mon-Sat, cafe lunch & dinner Mon-Sat).

Getting There & Away

By car you can get to Point Reyes a few different ways. The curviest is along Hwy 1, through Stinson Beach and Olema. More direct is to exit Hwy 101 in San Rafael and follow Sir Francis Drake Blvd all the way to the tip of Point Reyes. For the latter route, take the Central San Rafael exit and head west on 4th St, which turns into Sir Francis Drake Blvd. By either route, it's about 1½ hours to Olema from San Francisco.

Just north of Olema, where Hwy 1 and Sir Francis Drake Blvd come together, is Bear Valley Rd; turn left to reach the Bear Valley Visitor Center. If you're heading to the further reaches of Point Reyes, follow Sir Francis Drake Blvd through Point Reyes Station and out onto the peninsula (about an hour's drive).

NORTH COAST & THE REDWOODS

Get ready for a fabulous coastal drive, which cuts a winding course on isolated cliffs high above the crashing surf. Compared to the famous Big Sur coast, the serpentine stretch of Hwy 1 up the North Coast is more challenging, more remote and more real: passing farms, fishing towns and hidden beaches. North of Fort Bragg, Bay Area weekenders and antique-stuffed B&Bs give way to lumber wars, pot farmers and an army of carved bears. Last but not least, the route goes through a number of pristine, ancient redwood forests.

Bodega Bay

Bodega Bay is the first pearl in a string of sleepy fishing towns that line the North Coast and was the setting of Hitchcock's terrifying 1963 avian psycho-horror flick *The Birds*. The skies are free from bloodthirsty gulls today (though you best keep an eye on the picnic); it's Bay Area weekenders who descend en masse for extraordinary beaches, tide pools, whale-watching, fishing, surfing and seafood.

Sights & Activities

Surfing, beachcombing and sportfishing are the main activities here, the last of which requires advance booking. From December to April, the fishing boats host whale-watching trips, which are also good to book ahead.

BODEGA HEAD   Lookout
At the peninsula's tip, Bodega Head rises 265ft above sea level. To get there (and see the open ocean), head west from Hwy 1 onto Eastshore Rd, then turn right at the stop sign onto Bay Flat Rd. It's great for whale-watching. Landlubbers enjoy **hiking** above the surf, where several good trails include a 3.75-mile trek to Bodega Dunes Campground and a 2.2-mile walk to Salmon Creek Ranch. **Candy & Kites** (✆10am-5pm) is right along Hwy 1 in the middle of town – you can't miss it – selling kites to take advantage of all that wind.

**CHANSLOR RIDING
STABLES**   Horseback Riding
(✆707-875-3333; www.chanslor.com; 2660 Hwy 1, group rides $40-125) Just north of town, this friendly outfit leads horseback expeditions along the coastline and the rolling inland hills. Ron, the trip leader, is an amiable, sun-weathered cowboy straight from central casting; he recommends the Salmon Creek ride or calling ahead for weather-permitting moonlight rides. The 90-minute beach rides are donation based, and support a horse rescue program. Overnight trips in simple platform tents, which are excellent for families, can

also be arranged. If you book a ride, you can park your RV at the ranch for free.

**BODEGA BAY SPORTFISHING
CENTER**   Fishing, Whale-Watching
(✆707-875-3344; www.bodegacharters.com; 1410 Bay Flat Rd) Beside the Sandpiper Cafe, this outfit organizes full-day fishing trips ($135) and whale-watching excursions (three hours adult/child $35/25). It also sells bait, tackle and fishing licenses. Call ahead to ask about recent sightings.

Sleeping

BODEGA BAY LODGE & SPA   Lodge $$$
(✆707-875-3525, 888-875-2250; www.bodega baylodge.com; 103 Hwy 1; r $300-470; @ 🛜 🏊) Bodega's plushest, this small oceanfront resort has indulgent accommodations and a price tag to match. There is an ocean-view swimming pool, a whirlpool and a state-of-the-art fitness club. In the evenings it hosts wine tastings. The more expensive rooms have commanding views, but all have balconies, high-thread-count sheets, feather pillows and the usual amenities of a full-service hotel. The other pluses on-site include a golf course, Bodega Bay's best spa and a fine-dining restaurant, the **Duck Club** (✆707-875-3525; mains $16-37; ⏱7:30-11am & 6-9pm), which is the fanciest dining in town.

BODEGA HARBOR INN   Motel $$
(✆707-875-3594; www.bodegaharborinn.com; 1345 Bodega Ave; r $90-155; 🛜 🐾) Half a block inland from Hwy 1, surrounded by grassy lawns and furnished with both real and faux antiques, this modest blue-and-white shingled motel is the town's most economical option. Pets are allowed in some rooms for a fee of $15 plus a security deposit of $50. Freestanding cottages have BBQs.

Eating & Drinking

**SPUD POINT CRAB
COMPANY**   Seafood $
(www.spudpointcrab.com; 1860 Bay Flat Rd; mains $4-10; ⏱9am-5pm Thu-Tue; 👪) In the

classic tradition of dockside crab shacks, Spud Point serves salty-sweet crab cocktails and *real* clam chowder, served at picnic tables overlooking the marina. Take Bay Flat Rd to get here.

TERRAPIN CREEK CAFE & RESTAURANT
Californian $$
(☏707-875-2700; www.terrapincreekcafe.com; 1580 Eastshore Dr; mains $18-20; ⊙11am-2pm & 4:30-9pm Thu-Sun; ✈) Bodega Bay's most exciting upscale restaurant is run by a husband-wife team who espouse the Slow Food movement and serve local dishes sourced from the surrounding area. Modest comfort-food offerings like the pulled pork sandwich are artfully executed, while the Dungeness crab salad is fresh, briny and perfect. Jazz and warm light complete the atmosphere.

Sonoma Coast State Beach
Stretching 17 miles north from Bodega Head to Vista Trail, the glorious **Sonoma Coast State Beach** (☏707-875-3483) is actually a series of beaches separated by several beautiful rocky headlands. Some beaches are tiny, hidden in little coves, while others stretch far and wide. Most of the beaches are connected by vista-studded coastal hiking trails that wind along the bluffs. Exploring this area makes an excellent day-long adventure, so bring a picnic. Be advised however: the surf is often too treacherous to wade, so keep an eye on children.

◎ Sights & Activities

The following beaches are listed from south to north.

SALMON CREEK BEACH Beach
Situated around a lagoon, this has 2 miles of hiking and good waves for surfing.

PORTUGUESE BEACH & SCHOOLHOUSE BEACH Beach
Both are very easy to access and have sheltered coves between the rocky outcroppings.

DUNCAN'S LANDING Beach
Small boats unload near this rocky headland in the morning. A good place to spot wild flowers in the spring.

SHELL BEACH Beach
A boardwalk/trail leads to a stretch perfect for tide-pooling and beachcombing.

GOAT ROCK Beach
Famous for its harbor-seal colony who laze in the sun at the mouth of the Russian River.

Salt Point State Park
If you stop at only one park along the Sonoma Coast, make it 6000-acre **Salt Point State Park** (☏707-847-3221; per car

Bodega Head
LEE FOSTER/LONELY PLANET IMAGES ©

If You Like...
Beach Towns

If you like coastal towns such as Bodega Bay (p152), explore these Pacific settlements with a dash of salt spray:

1 GUALALA & ANCHOR BAY

Gualala sits square in the middle of the 'Banana Belt,' a stretch of coast known for unusually sunny weather. Founded as a lumber town in the 1860s, the downtown stretches along Hwy 1 and has a bustling commercial district with a great grocery store and some cute, slightly upscale shops. Just north, quiet Anchor Bay has several inns, a tiny shopping center and, heading north, a string of secluded, hard-to-find beaches.

2 POINT ARENA

This laid-back little town combines creature comforts with relaxed, eclectic California living. Sit by the docks a mile west of town at Arena Cove and watch surfers mingle with fishermen and hippies. Two miles north of town, the 10-story, 1908 **Point Arena Lighthouse** (www.pointarenalighthouse.com; adult/child $7.50/1; ⏱10am-3:30pm winter, to 4:30pm summer) is the only lighthouse in California you can ascend.

3 ELK

Thirty minutes north of Point Arena, itty-bitty Elk is famous for its stunning cliff-top views of 'sea stacks,' towering rock formations jutting out of the water.

4 MORRO BAY

Morro Bay is about 10 miles northwest of San Luis Obispo. Its biggest claim to fame is Morro Rock, a volcanic peak jutting dramatically from the ocean floor.

5 CAPITOLA

Six miles east of Santa Cruz is the little seaside town of Capitola, nestled quaintly between ocean bluffs and attracting affluent crowds. Downtown is laid out for strolling, with arty shops and touristy restaurants inside seaside houses.

$8), where sandstone cliffs drop dramatically into the kelp-strewn sea and hiking trails crisscross windswept prairies and wooded hills, connecting pygmy forests and coastal coves rich with tidepools. The 6-mile-wide park is bisected by the San Andreas Fault – the rock on the east side is vastly different from that on the west. Check out the eerily beautiful *tafonis*, honeycombed-sandstone formations, near Gerstle Cove.

Mendocino

Leading out to a gorgeous headland, Mendocino is the North Coast's salt-washed gem, with B&Bs surrounded by rose gardens, white-picket fences and New England–style redwood water towers. Bay Area weekenders walk along the headland among berry bramble and wildflowers, where cypress trees stand over dizzying cliffs. Nature's power is evident everywhere; from driftwood-littered fields and cave tunnels to the raging surf. The town itself is full of cute shops (no chains) and has earned the nickname 'Spendocino,' for its upscale goods.

◉ Sights

MENDOCINO ART CENTER   Gallery
(www.mendocinoartcenter.org; 45200 Little Lake St; ⏱10am-5pm Apr-Oct, to 4pm Tue-Sat Nov-Mar) Behind a yard of twisting iron sculpture, the city's art center takes up a whole tree-filled block, hosting exhibitions, the 81-seat Helen Schonei Theatre and nationally renowned art classes. This is also where to pick up the *Mendocino Arts Showcase* brochure, a quarterly publication listing all the happenings and festivals in town.

POINT CABRILLO LIGHTHOUSE   Lighthouse
(www.pointcabrillo.org; Point Cabrillo Dr; admission free; ⏱11am-4pm Sat & Sun Jan & Feb, daily Mar-Oct, Fri-Mon Nov & Dec) Restored in 1909, this lighthouse stands on a 300-acre wildlife preserve north of town, between

Russian Gulch and Caspar Beach. The head lighthouse-keeper's home is now a simple lodging (p156). Guided walks of the preserve leave at 11am on Sundays from May to September.

 Activities

CATCH A CANOE & BICYCLES, TOO!
Bicycle & Canoe Rental

(www.stanfordinn.com; Comptche-Ukiah Rd & Hwy 1; ☏9am-5pm) This friendly riverside outfit south of town rents bikes, kayaks and stable 'outrigger canoes' for trips up the 8-mile Big River tidal estuary, the longest undeveloped estuary in Northern California. No highways or buildings, only beaches, forests, marshes, streams, abundant wildlife and historic logging sites. Bring a picnic and a camera to enjoy the ramshackle remnants of century-old train trestles and majestic blue herons.

MENDOCINO HEADLANDS STATE PARK
Coastal Park

A spectacular park surrounds the village, with trails crisscrossing the bluffs and rocky coves. Ask at the visitor center about guided weekend walks, including spring wildflower walks and whale-watching.

Sleeping

ANDIRON
Cottages $$

(☏800-955-6478; www.theandiorn.com; 6051 N Hwy 1, Mendocino; r $99-149; ☏♨️👪🐾) Styled with hip vintage decor, this cluster of 1950s roadside cottages is a refreshingly playful option amid the stuffy cabbage-rose and lace aesthetic of Mendocino. Each cabin houses two rooms with complementing themes: 'Read' has old books, comfy vintage chairs, and hip retro eyeglasses while the adjoining 'Write' features a huge chalkboard and ribbon typewriter. A favorite for travelers? 'Here' and 'There,' themed with old maps, 1960s airline paraphernalia and collectables from North Coast's yesteryear.

STANFORD INN BY THE SEA
Inn $$

(☏707-937-5615, 800-331-8884; www.stanfordinn.com; cnr Hwy 1 & Comptche-Ukiah Rd; r $195-305; @♨️⚓🐾) This masterpiece of a lodge standing on 10 lush acres has

Waterfront restaurants, Capitola

Mendocino

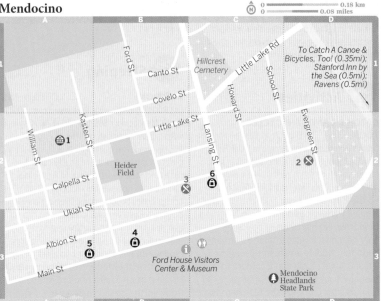

Mendocino

◎ Sights
1 Mendocino Art Center............................A2

✕ Eating
2 Café Beaujolais D2
3 Garden Bakery B2

🛍 Shopping
4 Compass Rose Leather........................B3
5 Twist A3
6 Village Toy Store..................................C2

wood-burning fireplaces, original art, stereos and top-quality mattresses in every room. Figure in a stroll in the organic gardens, where they harvest food for the excellent on-site restaurant, the solarium-enclosed pool and the hot tub, and it's a sublime getaway.

LIGHTHOUSE INN AT POINT CABRILLO
Historic B&B **$$**
(☎707-937-6124; 866-937-6124; www.point cabrillo.org; Point Cabrillo Dr; r $152-279) On 300 acres, in the shadow of Point Cabrillo Lighthouse, the light-keeper's house and several cottages have been turned into B&B rooms. Rates include a private night tour of the lighthouse and a five-course breakfast.

✕ Eating

CAFÉ BEAUJOLAIS
Californian, Fusion **$$**
(☎707-937-5614; www.cafebeaujolais.com; 961 Ukiah St; mains lunch $9-16, dinner $24-36; ⏰11:30am-2:30pm Wed-Sun, dinner from 5:30pm nightly) Mendocino's iconic, beloved country-Cal–French restaurant occupies an 1896 house restyled into a monochromatic urban-chic dining room, perfect for holding hands by candlelight. The refined, inspired cooking draws diners from San Francisco, who make this the centerpiece of their trip. The locally sourced menu changes with the seasons, but the Petaluma duck breast served with crispy skin is a gourmand's delight.

RAVENS
Californian **$$$**
(☎707-937-5615; www.ravensrestaurant.com; Stanford Inn by the Sea, Comptche-Ukiah Rd;

breakfast $11-15, mains $22-35; ⏱8-10:30am Mon-Sat, to noon Sun, plus 5:30-10pm daily; 🍴) Ravens brings haute-contemporary concepts to a completely vegetarian and vegan menu. Produce comes from the inn's own idyllic organic gardens, and the bold menu takes on everything from sea-palm strudel and portabella sliders to decadent (guilt-free) deserts.

GARDEN BAKERY
Bakery $

(☎707-937-0282; 10450 Lansing; baked goods $3-6; ⏱9am-4pm) Nearly every corner of Mendocino gets explored by hordes, but this little garden-side bakery still feels like a hidden gem. To describe the quality of the baked goods would invite hyperbole: they are *a-ma-zing*. The menu changes with the seasons and the baker's whim; one day, you're trying not to inhale the savory, cabbage-stuffed German pastry (a family recipe), on another you'll find apple cheddar croissants. If you show up early enough you'll get a taste of their renowned bear claw. If you don't find this place at first, keep looking: the bakery is located off the street, accessible by sidewalks that cut through the block.

🔒 Shopping

Mendocino's walkable streets are great for shopping, and the ban on chain stores ensures unique, often upscale gifts. There are many small galleries in town where one-of-a-kind artwork is for sale.

COMPASS ROSE LEATHER
Leather Goods

(45150 Main St) From hand-tooled belts and leather bound journals to purses and peg-secured storage boxes, the craftsmanship is unquestionable.

VILLAGE TOY STORE
Toys

(10450 Lansing St) Get a kite to fly on Bod-ega Head or browse the old-world selec-tion of wooden toys and games that you won't find in the chains – hardly anything requires batteries!

TWIST
Clothing

(45140 Main St) Twist stocks ecofriendly, natural-fiber clothing and lots of locally made clothing and toys.

Flower garden, Mendocino

Humboldt Redwoods State Park & Avenue of the Giants

Don't miss this magical drive through California's largest redwood park, **Humboldt Redwoods State Park** (Map p162; www.humboldtredwoods.org), which covers 53,000 acres – 17,000 of which are old-growth – and contains some of the world's most magnificent trees. It also boasts three-quarters of the world's tallest 100 trees. Tree huggers take note: these groves rival (and many say surpass) those in Redwood National Park, which is a long drive further north.

Exit Hwy 101 when you see the 'Avenue of the Giants' sign, take this smaller alternative to the interstate; it's an incredible, 32-mile, two-lane stretch. You'll find free driving guides at roadside signboards at both the avenue's southern entrance, 6 miles north of Garberville, near Phillipsville, and at the northern entrance, south of Scotia, at Pepperwood; there are access points off Hwy 101.

South of Weott, a volunteer-staffed **visitor center** (☎707-946-2263; ☉9am-5pm May-Sep, 10am-4pm Oct-Apr) shows videos and sells maps.

Three miles north, the **California Federation of Women's Clubs Grove** is home to an interesting four-sided hearth designed by renowned San Franciscan architect Julia Morgan in 1931 to commemorate 'the untouched nature of the forest.'

Primeval **Rockefeller Forest**, 4.5 miles west of the avenue via Mattole Rd, appears as it did a century ago. You quickly walk out of sight of cars and feel like you have fallen into the time of dinosaurs. It's the world's largest contiguous old-growth redwood forest, and contains about 20% of all such remaining trees. Check out the subtly variegated rings (count one for each year) on the cross sections of some of the downed giants that are left to mulch back into the earth over the next few hundred years.

In **Founders Grove**, north of the visitor center, the **Dyerville Giant** was knocked over in 1991 by another falling tree. A walk along its gargantuan 370ft length, with its wide trunk towering above, helps you appreciate how huge these ancient trees really are.

The park has over 100 miles of trails for hiking, mountain-biking and horseback riding. Easy walks include short nature trails in Founders Grove and Rockefeller Forest and **Drury-Chaney Loop Trail** (with berry picking in summer). Challenging treks include popular **Grasshopper Peak Trail**, south of the visitor center, which climbs to the 3379ft fire lookout.

Sleeping & Eating

BENBOW INN   Historic Resort $$
(☎707-923-2124, 800-355-3301; www.benbow inn.com; 445 Lake Benbow Dr; r $90-305, cottage

---

Drive-Thru Trees

Three carved-out (but alive!) redwoods await along Hwy 101, a bizarre holdover from a yesteryear road trip.

○ **Chandelier Drive-Thru Tree** Fold in your mirrors and inch forward, then cool off in the uberkitschy gift shop; in Leggett.

○ **Shrine Drive-Thru Tree** Look up to the sky as you roll through, on the Avenue of the Giants in Myers Flat. The least impressive of the three.

○ **Tour Thru Tree** Take exit 769 in Klamath, squeeze through a tree and check out an emu.

Detour:
Ukiah: Hot Springs & Ancient Trees

Opened in 1854, **Vichy** (☎707-462-9515; www.vichysprings.com; 2605 Vichy Springs Rd, Ukiah; lodge s/d $135/195, creekside r $195/245, cottages from $280; ✳🅢🅢) is the oldest continuously operating mineral-springs spa in California and the only warm-water, naturally carbonated mineral baths in North America. A century ago, Mark Twain, Jack London and Robert Louis Stevenson traveled here for the water's restorative properties. Day use costs $30 for two hours and $50 for a full day.

A clothing-optional resort that's beloved by locals, back-to-the-land hipsters, backpackers and liberal-minded tourists, **Orr Hot Springs** (☎707-462-6277; tent sites $45-50, d $140-160, cottages $195-230; ⏰10am-10pm; 🅢) has private tubs, a sauna, spring-fed rock-bottomed swimming pool, steam, massage and magical gardens. Day use costs $25 and d $20 on Mondays. Accommodation includes use of the spa and communal kitchen; some cottages have kitchens. Reservations are essential. To get there from Hwy 101, take N State St exit, go north a quarter of a mile to Orr Springs Rd, then 9 miles west. The steep, winding mountain road takes 30 minutes to drive.

Two miles west of Orr, 1140-acre **Montgomery Woods State Reserve** (Orr Springs Rd) protects five old-growth redwood groves, and some of the best groves within a day's drive from San Francisco. A 2-mile loop trail crosses the creek, winding through the serene forest.

$395-595; ✳🅢🅢) A monument to 1920s rustic elegance, the Redwood Empire's first luxury resort is a national historic landmark. Hollywood's elite once frolicked in the Tudor-style resort's lobby, where you can play chess by the crackling fire, and enjoy complimentary afternoon tea and evening hors d'oeuvres. Rooms have top-quality beds and antique furniture. The window-lined dining room (breakfast and lunch $10 to $15, dinner mains $22 to $32) serves excellent meals and the rib eye earns raves.

MIRANDA GARDENS RESORT Resort $$
(☎707-943-3011; www.mirandagardens.com; 6766 Ave of the Giants, Miranda; cottages with kitchen $165-275, without $115-175; 🅢🅢🅢) The best indoor stay along the avenue. The cozy, slightly rustic cottages have redwood paneling, some with fireplaces, and are spotlessly clean. The grounds – replete with outdoor ping pong and a play area for kids and swaying redwoods – have wholesome appeal for families.

RIVERBEND CELLARS Tasting Room $$
(www.riverbendcellars.com; 12990 Ave of the Giants, Myers Flat; ⏰11am-5pm) For something a bit more posh, pull over here. The El Centauro red – named for Pancho Villa – is an excellent estate-grown blend.

GROVES New American $$
(13065 Ave of the Giants, Myers Flat; ⏰5-9pm) This is the most refined eating option within miles, despite an aloof staff. The menu turns out simple, brick-oven pizzas, but spicy prawns and fresh salads are all artfully plated.

Ferndale

The North Coast's most charming town (Map p162) is stuffed with impeccable Victorians – known locally as 'butterfat mansions' because of the dairy wealth that built them. There are so many, in fact, that the entire place is a state and federal historical landmark. Dairy farmers built the town in the 19th century and it's still run by the 'milk mafia': you're not a local till you've lived here 40 years. A stroll

down Main St offers galleries, old-world emporiums and soda fountains.

Sights & Activities

Half a mile from downtown via Bluff St, enjoy short tramps through fields of wildflowers, beside ponds, past redwood groves and eucalyptus trees at 110-acre **Russ Park**. The **cemetery**, also on Bluff St, is amazingly cool with graves dating to the 1800s and expansive views to the ocean. Five miles down Centerville Rd, **Centerville Beach** is one of the few off-leash dog beaches in Humboldt County.

FREE KINETIC SCULPTURE
MUSEUM   Museum, Gallery
(580 Main St; ⏲10am-5pm Mon-Sat, noon-4pm Sun; 👪) This warehouse holds the fanciful, astounding human-powered contraptions used in the town's annual Kinetic Grand Championship. Shaped like giant fish and UFOs, these colorful piles of junk propel

racers over roads, water and marsh in the May event.

FERN COTTAGE   Historic Building
(📞707-786-4835; www.ferncottage.org; Centerville Rd; group tours per person $10; ⏲by appointment) This 1866 Carpenter Gothic grew to a 32-room mansion. Only one family ever lived here, so the interior is completely preserved.

**GINGERBREAD
MANSION**   Historic Building
(400 Berding St) An 1898 Queen Anne–Eastlake, this is the town's most photographed building. It held guests as a B&B for years, but has recently closed.

Sleeping

SHAW HOUSE   B&B $$
(📞707-786-9958, 800-557-7429; www.shaw house.com; 703 Main St; r $145-175, ste $225-275; 📶) Shaw House, an emblematic 'butter-fat palace,' was the first permanent struc-

Left: Gingerbread Mansion; **Below:** Redwood tree, Avenue of the Giants (p158)

(LEFT) CLASSICSTOCK/ALAMY ©; (BELOW) BILL GOZANSKY/ALAMY ©

ture in Ferndale, completed by founding father Seth Shaw in 1866. Today, it's California's oldest B&B, set back on extensive grounds. Original details remain, including painted wooden ceilings. Most of the rooms have private entrances, and three have private balconies over a large garden.

HOTEL IVANHOE Historic Hotel **$$**
(☎707-786-9000; www.ivanhoe-hotel.com; 315 Main St; r $95-145) Ferndale's oldest hostelry opened in 1875. It has four antique-laden rooms and an Old West–style 2nd-floor gallery, perfect for morning coffee. The adjoining saloon, with dark wood and lots of brass, is an atmospheric place for a nightcap.

 Eating

LOTUS ASIAN BISTRO & TEA ROOM Pan-Asian **$**
(www.lotusasianbistro.com; 619 Main St; mains $7-14; ☺11:30am-9pm Sat, Sun & Tue, 4-9pm Mon & Fri) Cherry-glazed beef, crispy scallion pancakes with pulled duck and udon bowls spiced with a ginger broth – the menu at this excellent Asian fusion bistro offers welcome diversity to Ferndale's lunch and dinner options.

POPPA JOE'S American **$**
(409 Main St; mains $5-7; ☺11am-8:30pm Mon-Fri, 6am-noon Sat & Sun) You can't beat the atmosphere at this diner, where trophy heads hang from the wall, the floors slant at a precarious angle and old men play poker all day. The American-style breakfasts are good, too – especially the pancakes.

 **Shopping**

BLACKSMITH SHOP & GALLERY Metal Goods
(☎707-786-4216; www.ferndaleblacksmith.com; 455 & 491 Main St) From wrought-iron art to

161

hand-forged furniture, this is the largest collection of contemporary blacksmithing in America.

ABRAXAS JEWELRY & LEATHER GOODS
Jewelry

(505 Main St) The pieces of locally forged jewelry here are extremely cool and moderately priced. The back room is filled with tons of hats.

Eureka

One hour north of Garberville, on the edge of the giant Humboldt Bay, lies Eureka (Map p162), the largest bay north of San Francisco. With strip-mall sprawl surrounding a lovely historic downtown, it wears its role as the county seat a bit clumsily. Despite a diverse and interesting community of artists, writers, pagans and other free-thinkers, Eureka's wild side slips out only occasionally – but mostly, it goes to bed early. Make for Old Town, a small district with colorful Victorians, good shopping and a revitalized waterfront. For nightlife, head to Eureka's trippy sister up the road, Arcata.

Sights

The free *Eureka Visitors Map,* available at tourist offices, details walking tours and scenic drives, focusing on architecture and history. **Old Town**, along 2nd and 3rd Sts from C St to M St, was once down-and-out, but has been refurbished into a buzzing pedestrian district. The F Street Plaza and Boardwalk run along the waterfront at the foot of F St.

ROMANO GABRIEL WOODEN SCULPTURE GARDEN
Art Installation

(315 2nd St) The coolest thing to gawk at downtown is this collection of whimsical outsider art that's enclosed by glass.

CARSON MANSION
Historic Building

(134 M St) Of Eureka's fine Victorian buildings the most famous is the ornate 1880s home of lumber baron William Carson. It took 100 men a full year to build. Today it's a private men's club. The **pink house** opposite, at 202 M St, is an 1884 Queen Anne Victorian designed by the same architects and built as a wedding gift for Carson's son.

Carson Mansion

WITOLD SKRYPCZAK/LONELY PLANET IMAGES ©

SEQUOIA PARK

Park

(www.sequoiaparkzoo.net; 3414 W St; park free, zoo adult/child $5.50/3.50; ☺zoo 10am-5pm May-Sep, Tue-Sun Oct-Apr; ⚑) A 77-acre old-growth redwood grove is a surprising green gem in the middle of a residential neighborhood. It has biking and hiking trails, children's playground and picnic areas, and a small zoo.

🛏 Sleeping

HOTEL CARTER & CARTER HOUSE VICTORIANS

Hotel, B&B $$$

(☎707-444-8067, 800-404-1390; www.carter house.com; 301 L St; r incl breakfast $159-225, ste incl breakfast $304-385; 🛜🍽) For those with a few extra bucks, the Hotel Carter and its associated Victorian rentals bear the standard for North Coast luxury. Recently constructed in period style, the hotel is a Victorian look-alike, holding rooms with top-quality linens and modern amenities; suites have in-room whirlpools and marble fireplaces. Unlike elsewhere, you won't see the innkeeper unless you want to. Guests have an in-room breakfast or can eat at the understated, elegant restaurant.

EAGLE HOUSE INN

Historic Inn $$

(☎707-444-3344; www.eaglehouseinn.com; 139 2nd St; r $105-205; 🛜⚑) This hulking Victorian hotel in Old Town has 24 rooms above a turn-of-the-century ballroom perfect for hide-and-seek. Rooms aren't overly stuffed with precious period furniture – carved headboards, floral-print carpeting and antique armoires – but some have bizarre touches (like the bright red spa tub that would fit in on an '80s adult film set). The coolest rooms are in the corner and have sitting areas in turrets looking over the street.

ABIGAIL'S ELEGANT VICTORIAN MANSION

B&B $$

(☎707-444-3144; www.eureka-california.com; 1406 C St; r $145-215) Inside this National Historic Landmark that's practically a living-history museum, the sweet-as-could-be innkeepers lavish guests with warm hospitality.

🍴 Eating & Drinking

HURRICANE KATE'S

Tapas $$

(www.hurricanekates.com; 511 2nd St; lunch mains $9-15, dinner mains $16-26; ☺11am-2:30pm &

Kinetic Grand Championship

5-9pm;) The favorite spot of local *bon vivants*, Kate's open kitchen pumps out pretty good, eclectic, tapas-style dishes and roast meats, but the wood-fired pizzas are the standout option. Full bar.

WATERFRONT CAFÉ OYSTER BAR
Seafood **$$**
(102 F St; mains lunch $8-13, dinner $13-20; ⏱9am-9pm) With a nice bay view and baskets of steamed clams, fish and chips, oysters and chowder, this is a solid bayside lunch. Top spot for Sunday brunch, with jazz and Ramos fizzes.

LOST COAST BREWERY
Brewery
(☎707-445-4480; 617 4th St; 📶) The roster of the regular brews at Eureka's colorful brewery might not knock the socks off a serious beer snob (and can't hold a candle to some of the others on the coast), but highlights include the Downtown Brown Ale, Great White and Lost Coast Pale Ale. After downing a few pints, the fried pub grub starts to look pretty tasty.

Arcata

The North Coast's most progressive town, Arcata (Map p162) surrounds a tidy central square that fills with college students, campers, transients and tourists. Sure, it occasionally reeks of patchouli and its politics lean far left, but its earnest embrace of sustainability has fostered some of the most progressive civic action in America. Here, garbage trucks run on biodiesel, recycling gets picked up by tandem bicycle, wastewater gets filtered clean in marshlands and almost every street has a bike lane.

 Sights

HUMBOLDT STATE UNIVERSITY
University
(HSU; www.humboldt.edu) The University on the northeastern side of town holds the Campus Center for Appropriate Technology (CCAT), a world leader in developing sustainable technologies; on Fridays at 2pm you can take a self-guided tour of the **CCAT House,** a converted residence

that uses only 4% of the energy of a comparably sized dwelling.

ARCATA MARSH & WILDLIFE SANCTUARY
Wildlife Sanctuary
(Map p162) On the shores of Humboldt Bay, this has 5 miles of walking trails and outstanding birding. The **Redwood Region Audubon Society** (www.rras.org; donation welcome) offers guided walks Saturdays at 8:30am, rain or shine, from the parking lot at I St's south end. Friends of Arcata Marsh offer guided tours Saturdays at 2pm from the **Arcata Marsh Interpretive Center** (☎707-826-2359; 569 South G St; tours free; ⏱9am-5pm).

 **Festivals & Events**

KINETIC GRAND CHAMPIONSHIP
Race
(www.kineticgrandchampionship.com) Arcata's most famous event is held Memorial Day weekend: people on amazing self-propelled contraptions travel 38 miles from Arcata to Ferndale.

Sleeping

HOTEL ARCATA
Historic Hotel **$$**
(☎707-826-0217, 800-344-1221; www.hotelarcata.com; 708 9th St; r $96-156; 📶) Anchoring the plaza, the renovated 1915 brick landmark has friendly staff, high ceilings and comfortable, old-world rooms of mixed quality. The rooms in front are an excellent perch for people-watching on the square, but the quietest face the back.

LADY ANNE INN
B&B **$$**
(☎707-822-2797; www.ladyanneinn.com; 902 14th St; r $125-140) Roses line the walkway to this 1888 mansion full of Victorian bric-a-brac. The frilly rooms are pretty, but there's no breakfast.

Eating & Drinking

 **FOLIE DOUCE**
New American **$$$**
(☎707-822-1042; www.holyfolie.com; 1551 G St; dinner mains $27-36; ⏱5:30-9pm Tue-Thu, to

165

10pm Fri-Sat; ) Just a slip of a place, but with an enormous reputation. The short but inventive menu features seasonally inspired bistro cooking, from Asian to Mediterranean, with an emphasis on local organics. Wood-fired pizzas ($14 to $19) are renowned. Sunday brunch, too. Reservations essential.

WILDFLOWER CAFE & BAKERY Cafe $$
(707-822-0360; 1604 G St; breakfast & lunch $5-8, dinner mains $15-16; 8am-8pm Sun-Wed;) Tops for vegetarians, this tiny storefront serves fab frittatas, pancakes and curries, and big crunchy salads.

SIX RIVERS BREWERY Brewpub
(www.sixriversbrewery.com; 1300 Central Ave, McKinleyville; mains $11-18; 11:30am-midnight Tue-Sun, from 4pm Mon) One of the first female-owned breweries in California, the 'brew with a view' kills it in every category: great beer, amazing community vibe, occasional live music and delicious hot wings. The spicy chili pepper ale is amazing.

❶ Getting There & Around

Only in Arcata: borrow a bike from **Library Bike** (www.arcata.com/greenbikes; 865 8th St) for a $20 deposit, which gets refunded when you return the bike – up to six months later!

Redwood National & State Parks

A patchwork of public lands jointly administered by the state and federal governments, the **Redwood National & State Parks** (Map p162) are a string of state and federally managed land that starts in the south at Redwood National Park and continues north through Prairie Creek Redwoods State Park (p167), Del Norte Coast Redwoods State Park (p168) and ends with Jedediah Smith Redwoods State Park (p169). A smattering of small towns break up the forested area, making it a bit confusing to get a sense of the parks as a whole. Prairie Creek and Jedediah Smith parks were originally land slated for clear-cutting, but in the '60s activists successfully protected them and today all these parks are an International Biosphere Reserve and World Heritage

Pinnacles National Monument

STEPHEN SAKS/LONELY PLANET IMAGES ©

DISCOVER NORTHERN CALIFORNIA & CENTRAL COAST REDWOOD NATIONAL & STATE PARKS

site. At one time the national park was to absorb at least two of the state parks, but that did not happen, and so the cooperative structure remains.

Little-visited compared to their southern brethren, the world's tallest living trees have been standing here for time immemorial, predating the Roman Empire by over 500 years. Prepare to be impressed.

◉ Sights & Activities

Just north of the southern visitor center, turn east onto Bald Hills Rd and travel 2 miles to **Lady Bird Johnson Grove**, one of the park's most spectacular groves, accessible via a gentle 1-mile loop trail. Continue for another 5 miles up Bald Hills to **Redwood Creek Overlook**. On the top of the ridgeline at 2100ft get views over the forest and the entire watershed – provided it's not foggy. Just past the overlook lies the gated turnoff for **Tall Trees Grove**, the location of several of the world's tallest trees. Rangers issue only 50 vehicle permits per day, but they rarely run out. Pick one up, along with the gate-lock combination, from the visitor centers. Allow four hours for the round-trip, which includes a 6-mile drive down a rough dirt road (speed limit 15mph) and a steep 1.3-mile one-way hike, which descends 800ft to the grove.

ⓘ Information

Unlike most national parks, there are no fees and no highway entrance stations at Redwood National Park, so it's imperative to pick up the free map at the park headquarters in Crescent City or at the Redwood Information Center (Kuchel Visitor Center; ☎707-464-6101; www.nps.gov /redw; Hwy 101; ☉9am-6pm Jun-Aug, to 5pm Sep-Oct & Mar-May, to 4pm Nov-Feb) in Orick.

Prairie Creek Redwoods State Park

Famous for virgin redwood and unspoiled coastline, this 14,000-acre section of Redwood National & State Parks has spectac-

♥ If You Like...
Wildlife-Watching

If you like the grazing elk at Prairie Creek Redwoods State Park (p167) and Point Reyes National Seashore (p148), detour to these spots to view animals that squawk, fly or swim:

1 PIEDRAS BLANCAS
At a signposted vista point 4.5 miles north of Hearst Castle, you'll find a bigger colony of elephant seals than the corpulent layabouts in Año Nuevo.

2 PINNACLES NATIONAL MONUMENT
(☎831-389-4486; www.nps.gov/pinn; per vehicle $5) Explore talus caves of napping bats and witness the elegant spectacle of enormous (and endangered) California condors at this craggy and out-of-the-way Central Valley park.

3 KLAMATH BASIN NATIONAL WILDLIFE REFUGES
(☎530-667-2231; www.fws.gov/klamathbasinrefuges; 4009 Hill Rd, Tulelake; ☉8am-4:30pm Mon-Fri, 10am-4pm Sat & Sun) These northeastern refuges provide habitat for a stunning array of birds migrating along the Pacific Flyway. During the spring and fall migration peaks, more than a million birds can fill the skies.

ular scenic drives and 70 miles of hiking trails, many of which are excellent for children. Pick up maps and information and sit by the river-rock fireplace at **Prairie Creek Visitor Center** (Map p162; ☎707-464-6101; ☉9am-5pm Mar-Oct, 10am-4pm Nov-Feb; ⊞). Kids will love the taxidermy dioramas with push-button, light-up displays. Outside, elk roam grassy flats.

◉ Sights & Activities

NEWTON B DRURY SCENIC PARKWAY
Scenic Drive
Just north of Orick is the turnoff for the 8-mile parkway, which runs parallel to Hwy 101 through untouched ancient redwood forests. It's worth the short detour

off the freeway to view the magnificence of these trees. Numerous trails branch off from roadside pullouts, including family- and ADA (American Disabilities Act)-friendly trails including Big Tree and Revelation Trail.

Hiking & Mountain Biking

There are 28 mountain-biking and hiking trails through the park, from simple to strenuous. Those tight on time or with mobility impairments should stop at **Big Tree**, an easy 100yd walk from the car park. Several other easy nature trails start near the visitor center, including **Revelation Trail** and **Elk Prairie Trail**. Stroll the recently reforested logging road on the **Ah-Pah Interpretive Trail** at the park's north end. The most challenging hike in this corner of the park is the truly spectacular 11.5-mile **Coastal Trail** which goes through primordial redwoods.

Just past the **Gold Bluffs Beach Campground** the road dead ends at **Fern Canyon**, where 60ft fern-covered sheer-rock walls can be seen from Steven Spielberg's *Jurassic Park 2: The Lost World*. This is one of the most photographed spots on the North Coast – damp and lush, all emerald green – and *totally* worth getting your toes wet to see.

Klamath

Giant metal-cast golden bears stand sentry at the bridge across the Klamath River announcing Klamath (Map p162), one of the tiny settlements that break up Redwood National & State Parks. With a gas station/market, a great diner and a casino, Klamath is basically a wide spot in the road. The Yurok Tribal Headquarters is here and the entire town and much of the surrounding area is the tribe's ancestral land. Klamath is roughly an hour north of Eureka.

Sights & Activities

The mouth of the **Klamath River** is a dramatic sight. Marine, riparian, forest and meadow ecological zones all converge: the birding is exceptional! For the best views, head north of town to Requa Rd and the **Klamath River Overlook** and picnic on high bluffs above driftwood-strewn beaches. On a clear day, this is one of the most spectacular viewpoints on the North Coast, and one of the best whale-watching spots in California. For a good hike, head north along the Coastal Trail. You'll have the sand to yourself at **Hidden Beach**; access the trail at the northern end of Motel Trees.

Just south of the river, on Hwy 101, follow signs for the scenic **Coastal Drive**, a narrow, winding country road (unsuitable for RVs and trailers) atop extremely high cliffs over the ocean. Come when it's not foggy, and mind your driving.

Del Norte Coast Redwoods State Park

Marked by steep canyons and dense woods, half the 6400 acres of this **park (vehicle per day $8)** are virgin redwood forest, crisscrossed by 15 miles of hiking

Trees of Mystery

It's hard to miss the giant statues of Paul Bunyan and Babe the Blue Ox towering over the parking lot at **Trees of Mystery** (707-482-2251; www.treesofmystery.net; 15500 Hwy 101; adult/child & senior $14/7; 8am-7pm Jun-Aug, 9am-4pm Sep-May;), a shameless tourist trap with a gondola running through the redwood canopy. The **End of the Trail Museum** located behind the Trees of Mystery gift shop has an outstanding collection of Native American arts and artifacts, and it's *free*.

trails. Even the most cynical of redwood-watchers can't help but be moved.

Pick up maps and inquire about guided walks at the Redwood National & State Parks Headquarters in Crescent City or the Redwood Information Center in Orick (p167).

Hwy 1 winds in from the coast at rugged, dramatic **Wilson Beach**, and traverses the dense forest, with groves stretching off as far as you can see.

Picnic on the sand at **False Klamath Cove**. Heading north, tall trees cling precipitously to canyon walls that drop to the rocky, timber-strewn coastline, and it's almost impossible to get to the water, except via gorgeous but steep **Damnation Creek Trail** or **Footsteps Rock Trail**.

Between these two, serious hikers will be most greatly rewarded by the Damnation Creek Trail. It's only 4 miles long, but the 1100ft elevation change and cliff-side redwood makes it the park's best hike. The unmarked trailhead starts from a parking area off Hwy 101 at mile mark 16.

Crescent Beach Overlook and picnic area has superb wintertime whale-watching. At the park's north end, watch the surf pound at **Crescent Beach**, south of Crescent City via Enderts Beach Rd.

Jedediah Smith Redwoods State Park

The northernmost park in the system of Redwood National & State Parks, the dense stands at **Jedediah Smith (day use $8)** are 10 miles northeast of Crescent City (via Hwy 101 east to Hwy 197). The redwood stands are so thick that few trails penetrate the park, but the outstanding 11-mile **Howland Hill scenic drive** cuts through otherwise inaccessible areas (take Hwy 199 to South Fork

Rd; turn right after crossing two bridges). It's a rough road, impassable for RVs, but if you can't hike, it's the best way to see the forest.

Stop for a stroll under enormous trees in **Simpson-Reed Grove**. If it's foggy at the coast it may be sunny here. There's a **swimming hole** and picnic area near the park entrance. An easy half-mile trail, departing from the far side of the campground, crosses the **Smith River** via a summer-only footbridge, leading to **Stout Grove**, the park's most famous grove. The **visitor center** (☎707-464-6101; ◔10am-4pm daily Jun-Aug, 10am-4pm Sat & Sun Sep, Oct, Apr & May) sells hiking maps and nature guides. If you wade in the river, be careful in the spring when currents are swift and the water cold.

LASSEN NATIONAL PARK & NORTHERN MOUNTAINS

The northeast corner is the remote, rugged, refreshingly pristine backyard of a

Redwood trees, Jedediah Smith Redwoods State Park
JIM ZUCKERMAN/CORBIS ©

state better known for sunny cities, sandy beaches and foggy groves of redwoods. Don't come here for the company (the towns are hospitable but tiny, with virtually no urban comforts); come to get lost in vast remoteness. Even the two principal attractions, Mt Shasta and Lassen Volcanic National Park, remain uncrowded (and sometimes snow-covered) at the peak of the summer.

Lassen Volcanic National Park

The dry, smoldering, treeless terrain within this 106,000-acre national park stands in stunning contrast to the cool, green conifer forest that surrounds it. That's the summer; in winter tons of snow ensures you won't get too far inside its borders. Still, entering the park from the southwest entrance is to suddenly step into another world. The lavascape offers a fascinating glimpse into the earth's fiery core. In a fuming display, the terrain is marked by roiling hot springs, steamy mud pots, noxious sulfur vents, fumaroles, lava flows, cinder cones, craters and crater lakes.

◉ Sights & Activities

Lassen Peak, the world's largest plug-dome volcano, rises 2000ft over the surrounding landscape to 10,457ft above sea level. Classified as an active volcano, its most recent eruption was in 1917, when it spewed a giant cloud of smoke, steam and ash 7 miles into the atmosphere. The national park was created the following year to protect the newly formed landscape. Some areas destroyed by the blast, including the aptly named **Devastated Area**, northeast of the peak, are recovering impressively. You can hike the **Lassen Peak Trail**, which has been under renovations for some time; check in with rangers before attempting to get to the top. An easy 1.3 mile hike partway up, to the Grandview viewpoint, is suitable for families. The 360-degree view from the top is stunning, even if the weather is a bit hazy.

Hwy 89, the road through the park, wraps around Lassen Peak on three sides and provides access to dramatic geothermal formations, pure lakes, gorgeous picnic areas and remote hiking trails.

Bumpass Hell area, Lassen Volcanic National Park

WITOLD SKRYPCZAK/LONELY PLANET IMAGES ©

In total, the park has 150 miles of **hiking trails**, including a 17-mile section of the Pacific Crest Trail. Experienced hikers can attack the Lassen Peak Trail; it takes at least 4½ hours to make the 5-mile round trip. Early in the season you'll need snow- and ice-climbing equipment to reach the summit. Near the Kom Yah-mah-nee visitor facility, a gentler 2.3-mile trail leads through meadows and forest to **Mill Creek Falls**. Further north on Hwy 89 you'll recognize the roadside **sulfur works** by its bubbling mud pots, hissing steam vent, fountains and fumaroles. At **Bumpass Hell** a moderate 1.5-mile trail and boardwalk lead to an active geothermal area, with bizarrely colored pools and billowing clouds of steam.

ⓘ Information

Park Headquarters (☎530-595-4444; www .nps.gov/lavo; 38050 Hwy 36; ⏰8am-4:30pm daily Jun-Sep, Mon-Fri Oct-May) About a mile west of the tiny town of Mineral, it's the nearest stop for refueling and supplies.

Mt Shasta

'When I first caught sight of it I was 50 miles away and afoot, alone and weary. Yet all my blood turned to wine, and I have not been weary since,' wrote naturalist John Muir of Mt Shasta in 1874. Mt Shasta's beauty is certainly intoxicating, and the closer you get the headier you begin to feel. Dominating the landscape, the mountain is visible for more than 100 miles from many parts of Northern California and southern Oregon. Though not California's highest peak (at 14,162ft it ranks fifth), Mt Shasta is especially magnificent because it rises alone on the horizon, unrivaled by other moutains.

The mountain and surrounding **Shasta-Trinity National Forest** (www.fs.fed.us/r5 /shastatrinity) are crisscrossed by trails and dotted with alpine lakes. It's easy to spend days or weeks camping, hiking, river rafting, skiing, mountain-biking and boating.

◎ Sights & Activities

You can drive almost the whole way up the mountain via the Everitt Memorial Hwy (Hwy A10) and see exquisite views at any time of year. Simply head east on Lake St from downtown Mt Shasta City, then turn left onto Washington Dr and keep going. **Bunny Flat** (6860ft), which has a trailhead for Horse Camp and the Avalanche Gulch summit route, is a busy place with parking spaces, information signboards and a toilet. The section of highway beyond Bunny Flat is only open from about mid-June to October, depending on snow, but if it's clear, it's worth the trouble. This road leads to **Lower Panther Meadow**, where trails connect the campground to a Wintu sacred spring, in the upper meadows near the **Old Ski Bowl** (7800ft) parking area. Shortly thereafter is the highlight of the drive, **Everitt Vista Point** (7900ft), where a short interpretive walk from the parking lot leads to a stone-walled outcrop affording exceptional views of Lassen Peak to the south, Mt Eddy and Marble Mountains to the west and the whole Strawberry Valley below.

MT SHASTA BOARD & SKI PARK   Snow Sports

(☎snow reports 530-926-8686; www.skipark .com; full-day lift tickets adult/child $39/20; ⏰9am-9pm Thu-Sat, to 4pm Sun-Tue) On the south slope of Mt Shasta, off Hwy 89 heading toward McCloud, this winter skiing and snowboarding park opens depending on snowfall. The park has a 1390ft vertical drop, over two-dozen alpine runs and 18 miles of cross-country trails. These are all exceptionally good for beginner and intermediate skiers, and the area makes a less-crowded alternative to the slopes around Lake Tahoe.

Mt Shasta City & McCloud

No town, no matter how lovely – and Mt Shasta City (population 3394) is lovely – could compete with the surrounding natural beauty here. Still, downtown itself is charming; you can spend hours poking around bookstores, galleries and boutiques. Orienting yourself is easy with Mt Shasta looming over the east side of town. The tiny, historic mill town of Mc-Cloud sits at the foot of the south slope of Mt Shasta, and is a quieter alternative to staying in Mt Shasta City. It's the closest settlement to Mt Shasta Board & Ski Park and is surrounded by natural beauty.

Sleeping

SHASTA MOUNTINN B&B $$
(☎530-926-1810; www.shastamountinn.com; 203 Birch St, Mt Shasta City; r without/with fireplace $130/175; @ 🛜) Only antique on the outside – inside, this bright Victorian farmhouse is all relaxed minimalism, bold colors and graceful decor. Each airy room has a designer mattress and exquisite views of the luminous mountain. Enjoy the expansive garden, wraparound deck and outdoor sauna. Not relaxed enough yet? There are also a couple of perfectly placed porch swings and on-site massage.

MCCLOUD RIVER MERCANTILE HOTEL Boutique Hotel $$
(☎530-964-2330; www.mccloudmercantile.com; 241 Main St; r $129-250; 🛜) Stoll up the stairs

to the 2nd floor of McCloud's central Mercantile and try not to fall in love; it's all high ceilings, exposed brick and a perfect marriage of preservationist class and modern panache. The rooms with antique furnishings are situated within open floor plans. Guests are greeted with fresh flowers and can drift to sleep on feather beds after soaking in claw-foot tubs. Certainly the best hotel in the Northern Mountains.

MCCLOUD HOTEL Historic Hotel $$
(☎530-964-2822; www.mccloudhotel.com; 408 Main St; r $100-235; ❄) Regal, butter-yellow and a whole block long, the grand hotel opposite the depot first opened in 1916 and has been a destination for Shasta's visitors ever since. The elegant historic landmark has been restored to a luxurious standard, and the included breakfast has gourmet flair. Many rooms have Jacuzzi tubs; one room is accessible for travelers with disabilities.

Eating

TRINITY CAFÉ Californian $$
(☎530-926-6200; 622 N Mt Shasta Blvd, Mt Shasta City; mains $17-28; ⏲5-9pm Tue-Sat)

Pigeon Point Light Station (p174)

Lava Beds National Monument

A wild landscape of charred volcanic rock and rolling hills, this remote **national monument** (📞530-667-8100; www.nps.gov/labe; 7-day entry per vehicle/hiker & cyclist $10/5, cash only) is reason enough to visit the region. Off Hwy 139, immediately south of Tule Lake National Wildlife Refuge, it's a truly remarkable 72-sq-mile landscape of volcanic features – lava flows, craters, cinder cones, spatter cones, shield volcanoes and amazing lava tubes.

Lava tubes are formed when hot, spreading lava cools and hardens when the surfaces get exposed to the cold air. The lava inside is thus insulated and stays molten, flowing away to leave an empty tube of solidified lava. Nearly 400 such tubular caves have been found in the monument, and many more are expected to be discovered. About two dozen or so are currently open for exploration by visitors.

On the south side of the park, the **visitors center** (📞530-667-2282, ext 230; ⏰8am-6pm, shorter hrs in winter) has free maps, activity books for kids and information about the monument and its volcanic features and history. Rangers loan flashlights, rent helmets and kneepads for cave exploration and lead summer interpretive programs, including campfire talks and guided cave walks. To explore the caves it's essential you use a high-powered flashlight, wear good shoes and long sleeves (lava is sharp), and not go alone.

The weathered Modoc **petroglyphs** at the base of a high cliff at the far northeastern end of the monument, called Petroglyph Point, are thousands of years old.

Trinity has long rivaled the Bay Area's best. The owners, who hail from Napa, infuse the bistro with a Wine Country feel and an extensive, excellent wine selection. The organic menu ranges from delectable, perfectly cooked steaks, savory roast game hen to creamy-on-the-inside, crispy-on-the-outside polenta. The warm, mellow mood makes for an overall delicious experience.

MOUNT SHASTA PASTRY Bakery $$
(610 S Mt Shasta Blvd, Mt Shasta City; mains $17-28; ⏰6am-2:30pm Mon-Sat, 7am-1pm Sun) Walk in hungry and you'll be plagued with an existential breakfast crisis: the potato and egg frittata topped with red peppers, ham and melted cheese, or the smoky breakfast burrito? The flaky croissants or peach cobbler? It also serves terrific sandwiches and gourmet pizza.

🌱**MOUNTAIN STAR CAFÉ** Vegetarian $
(241 Main St, McCloud; mains $7-9; ⏰8am-3pm) Deep within the creaking Mercantile,

this sweet lunch counter is a surprise, serving vegetarian specials made from locally sourced, organic produce. Some options on the menu during a recent visit included the morale biscuits and gravy, a garlicky tempeh Ruben, roast vegetable salad and a homemade oat and veggie burger.

CENTRAL COAST

Too often forgotten or dismissed as 'flyover' country between San Francisco and LA, this fairy-tale stretch of California coast is packed with wild Pacific beaches, misty redwood forests where hot springs hide, and rolling golden hills of fertile vineyards and farm fields.

Pescadero

A foggy speck of coastside crossroads between the cities of San Francisco and Santa Cruz, 150-year-old Pescadero is a close-knit rural town of sugar-lending neighbors and community pancake breakfasts. But on weekends the tiny downtown strains its seams with long-distance cyclists panting for carbohydrates and day trippers dive-bombing in from the oceanfront highway. With its cornucopia of tide-pool coves and parks of sky-blotting redwood canopy, city dwellers come here to slow down and smell the sea breeze wafting over fields of bushy artichokes.

◎ Sights & Activities

A number of pretty sand beaches speckle the coast, though one of the most interesting places to stop is **Pebble Beach**, a tide pool jewel a mile and a half south of Pescadero Creek Rd. As the name implies, the shore is awash in bite-sized eye candy of agate, jade and carnelians, and sandstone troughs are pockmarked by groovy honeycombed formations called tafoni.

PIGEON POINT LIGHT STATION   Lighthouse
(☎ 650-879-2120; www.parks.ca.gov/?page_id=533) Five miles south along the coast, the 115ft Light Station is one of the tallest lighthouses on the West Coast. The 1872 landmark had to close access to the Fresnel lens when chunks of its cornice began to rain from the sky, but the beam still flashes brightly and the bluff is a prime though blustery spot to scan for breaching gray whales. The Pigeon Point Lighthouse Hostel here is one of the best in the state.

🛏 Sleeping & Eating

🍃 PESCADERO CREEK INN
B&B   B&B $$
(☎ 888-307-1898; www.pescaderocreekinn.com; 393 Stage Rd; r $170-255; 🛜) Unwind in the private two-room cottage or one of the spotless Victorian rooms in a restored 100-year-old farmhouse. Afternoon wine and cheese features wine bottled by the owners, and organic ingredients from the creekside garden spice up a hot breakfast.

🍃 PIGEON POINT LIGHTHOUSE
HOSTEL   Hostel $
(☎ 650-879-0633; www.norcalhostels.org/pigeon; dm $24-26, r $72-98; @🛜) Not your workaday HI outpost, this highly coveted coastside hostel is all about location. Check in early to snag a spot in the outdoor hot tub, and contemplate roaring waves as the lighthouse beacon races through a starburst sky.

DUARTE'S TAVERN
American $$
(☎ 650-879-0464; www.duartestavern.com; 202 Stage Rd; mains $11-40) You'll rub shoulders with

Santa Cruz beach
JERRY ALEXANDER/LONELY PLANET IMAGES ©

fancy-pants foodies, spandex-swathed cyclists and dusty cowboys in spurs at this casual and surprisingly unpretentious fourth-generation family restaurant. Duarte's (pronounced DOO-arts) is the culinary magnet of Pescadero, and for many the town and eatery are synonymous. Feast on crab cioppino and a half-and-half split of the cream of artichoke and green chili soups, and bring it home with a wedge of olallieberry pie. Except for the unfortunate lull of Prohibition, the wood-paneled bar has been hosting the locals and their honored guests since 1894. Reservations recommended.

Año Nuevo State Reserve

More raucous than a full-moon beach rave, thousands of boisterous elephant seals party down year-round on the dunes of Año Nuevo point, their squeals and barks reaching fever pitch during the winter pupping season. The beach is 5 miles south of Pigeon Point and 27 miles north of Santa Cruz.

In the midwinter peak season, during the mating and birthing time from December 15 to the end of March, you must plan well ahead if you want to visit the reserve, because visitors are only permitted access through heavily booked guided tours. For the busiest period, mid-January to mid-February, it's recommended you book eight weeks ahead. If you haven't booked, bad weather can sometimes lead to last-minute cancellations.

The rest of the year, advance reservations aren't necessary, but visitor permits from the entrance station are required; arrive before 3pm from September through November and by 3:30pm from April through August.

Although the **park office** (☏650-879-2025, recorded information 650-879-0227; www.parks.ca.gov/?page_id=523) can answer general questions, high-season tour bookings must be made at ☏800-444-4445 or http://anonuevo.reserveamerica.com. When required, these tours cost $7, and parking is $10 per car year-round. From the ranger station it's a 3- to 5-mile round-trip hike on sand, and a visit takes two to three hours. No dogs are allowed on-site, and visitors aren't permitted for the first two weeks of December.

Santa Cruz

Santa Cruz has marched to its own beat since long before the Beat Generation. It's counterculture central, a touchy-feely, new-agey city famous for its leftie-liberal politics and live-and-let-live ideology.

On the waterfront is the famous beach boardwalk, and in the hills redwood groves embrace the University of California, Santa Cruz (UCSC) campus.

 Sights

One of the best things to do in Santa Cruz is simply stroll, shop and people-watch along **Pacific Ave** downtown. A 15-minute

Mystery Spot

A kitschy, old-fashioned tourist trap, Santa Cruz's **Mystery Spot** (☏831-423-8897; www.mysteryspot.com; 465 Mystery Spot Rd; admission $5, parking $5; ⏰10am-6pm Sun-Thu, 9am-7pm Fri & Sat late May-early Sep, 10am-4pm Sun-Thu, 10am-5pm Fri & Sat early Sep–late May; 👶) has scarcely changed since it opened in 1940. On a steeply sloping hillside, compasses seem to point crazily, mysterious forces push you around and buildings lean at odd angles. Make reservations, or risk being stuck waiting for a tour. It's 3 miles north of downtown: take Water St to Market St, turn left and continue on Branciforte Dr into the hills.

walk away is the beach and the **Municipal Wharf**, where seafood restaurants, gift shops and barking sea lions compete for attention. Ocean-view **West Cliff Dr** follows the waterfront southwest of the wharf, paralleled by a paved recreational path.

Sun-kissed Santa Cruz has warmer beaches than often-foggy Monterey. *Baywatch* it isn't, but 29 miles of coastline reveal a few Hawaii-worthy beaches, craggy coves, some primo surf spots and big sandy stretches where your kids will have a blast. Too bad fog ruins many a summer morning; it often burns off by the afternoon.

SANTA CRUZ BEACH BOARDWALK Amusement Park

(☎ 831-423-5590; www.beachboardwalk.com; 400 Beach St; per ride $3-5, all-day pass $30; ⏰ from 10am or 11am daily May-Sep; 👪) The West Coast's oldest beachfront amusement park, this 1907 boardwalk has a glorious old-school Americana vibe, with the smell of cotton candy mixing with the salt air, punctuated by the squeals of kids hanging upside down on carnival rides. Famous thrills include the Giant Dipper, a 1924 wooden roller coaster, and the 1911 Looff carousel, both National Historic Landmarks.

🌿 SEYMOUR MARINE DISCOVERY CENTER Museum

(www2.ucsc.edu/seymourcenter; end of Delaware Ave; adult/child 4-16yr $6/4; ⏰10am-5pm Tue-Sat, noon-5pm Sun year-round, plus 10am-5pm Mon Jul & Aug; 👪) Near Natural Bridges State Beach, this kids' educational center is part of UCSC's Long Marine Laboratory. Interactive natural-science exhibits include tidal touch pools and aquariums, while outside you can gawk at the world's largest blue-whale skeleton. Guided tours are usually given at 1pm, 2pm and 3pm daily; sign up in person an hour in advance (no reservations).

SANTA CRUZ SURFING MUSEUM Museum

(www.santacruzsurfingmuseum.org; 701 W Cliff Dr; admission by donation; ⏰noon-4pm Thu-Mon

Sep-Jun, 10am-5pm Wed-Mon Jul & Aug) A mile south of the wharf along the coast, the old lighthouse is packed with memorabilia, including vintage redwood surfboards. Fittingly, Lighthouse Point overlooks two popular surf breaks.

BIG BASIN REDWOODS STATE PARK
Park

(831-338-8860; www.bigbasin.org, www.parks .ca.gov; 21600 Big Basin Way; per car $10) Follow Hwy 236 northwest for nine twisting miles to this park, where nature trails loop past old-growth redwoods. A 12.5-mile one-way section of the Skyline to the Sea Trail ends at Waddell Beach on the coast, almost 20 miles northwest of Santa Cruz.

🛏 Sleeping

DREAM INN
Boutique Hotel $$$

(831-426-4330, 866-774-7735; www.dream innsantacruz.com; 175 W Cliff Dr; r $200-380; ❄@🛜🏊) Overlooking the wharf from a spectacular hillside perch, this retro-chic boutique-on-the-cheap hotel is as stylish as Santa Cruz gets. Rooms have all mod cons, while the beach is just steps away. Don't miss happy hour at Aquarius restaurant's ocean-view bar.

🌿 ADOBE ON GREEN B&B
B&B $$

(831-469-9866; www.adobeongreen.com; 103 Green St; r incl breakfast $149-199; 🛜) Peace and quiet are the mantras here, a short walk from Pacific Ave. The hosts are practically invisible, but their thoughtful touches are everywhere, from boutique-hotel amenities in spacious, stylish and solar-powered rooms to breakfast spreads from their organic gardens.

PELICAN POINT INN
Inn $$

(831-475-3381; www.pelicanpointinn-santa cruz.com; 21345 E Cliff Dr; ste $99-199; 🚹) Perfect for families, these roomy apartments near a kid-friendly beach are equipped with everything you'll need for a lazy

177

vacation, from kitchenettes to high-speed internet. Weekly rates available.

Eating

SOIF Bistro **$$$**
(☎ 831-423-2020; www.soifwine.com; 105 Walnut Ave; small plates $5-17, mains $19-28; ⏱ 5-10pm Sun-Thu, to 11pm Fri & Sat) Downtown is where *bon vivants* flock for a heady selection of 50 international wines by the glass, paired with a sophisticated, seasonally driven Euro-Cal menu. Expect taste-bud-ticklers like wild arugula salad with roasted apricot and curry-honey vinaigrette or baby back ribs with coffee-barbecue sauce. Live music some nights.

ZACHARY'S American **$**
(819 Pacific Ave; mains $6-11; ⏱ 7am-2:30pm Tue-Sun) At the scruffy brunch spot that locals don't want you to know about, huge portions of sourdough pancakes and blueberry cream-cheese coffee cake will keep you going all day. 'Mike's Mess' is the kitchen-sink standout.

Monterey

Working-class Monterey (Map p179) is all about the sea. What draws many tourists is the world-class aquarium, overlooking Monterey Bay National Marine Sanctuary, which protects dense kelp forests and a sublime variety of marine life, including seals and sea lions, dolphins and whales. The city possesses the best-preserved historical evidence of California's Spanish and Mexican periods, with many restored adobe buildings. An afternoon's wander through downtown's historic quarter promises to be more edifying than time spent in the tourist ghettos of Fisherman's Wharf and Cannery Row.

◉ Sights

CANNERY ROW Historic Site
John Steinbeck's novel *Cannery Row* immortalized the sardine-canning business that was Monterey's lifeblood for the first half of the 20th century. Back in Steinbeck's day, it was a stinky, hardscrabble, working-class melting pot, which the novelist described as 'a poem, a stink, a grating noise, a quality of light, a tone, a habit, a nostalgia, a dream.' Sadly, there's precious little evidence of that era now. A bronze **bust** of the Pulitzer Prize–winning writer sits at the bottom of Prescott Ave, just steps from the unabashedly commercial experience his row has devolved into, chock-a-block with chain restaurants and souvenir shops hawking saltwater taffy. Check out the **Cannery Workers Shacks** at the base of flowery Bruce Ariss Way, which have sobering explanations of the hard lives led by the Filipino, Japanese, Spanish and other immigrant laborers.

Cannery Row
LEE FOSTER/LONELY PLANET IMAGES ©

Monterey Peninsula

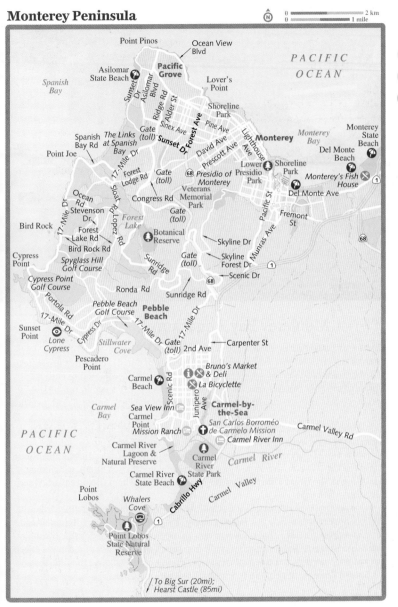

**MONTEREY STATE
HISTORIC PARK**   Historic Site

(📞cell phone audio tour 831-998-9458; www
.parks.ca.gov) Old Monterey is home to an
extraordinary assemblage of 19th-century
brick and adobe buildings, administered

as Monterey State Historic Park, all found
along a 2-mile self-guided walking tour
portentously called the Path of History.
You can inspect dozens of buildings,
many with charming gardens; expect
some to be open while others aren't,

GERALD FRENCH/CORBIS ©

Don't Miss **Monterey Bay Aquarium**

Monterey's most mesmerizing experience is its enormous aquarium, built on the former site of the city's largest sardine cannery. All kinds of aquatic creatures are on proud display, from kid-tolerant sea stars and slimy sea slugs to animated sea otters and surprisingly nimble 800lb tuna. The aquarium is much more than an impressive collection of glass tanks – thoughtful placards underscore the bay's cultural and historical contexts.

Every minute, upwards of 2000 gallons of seawater are pumped into the three-story **kelp forest**, re-creating as closely as possible the natural conditions you see out the windows to the east. The large fish of prey are at their charismatic best during mealtimes; divers hand-feed at 11:30am and 4pm. More entertaining are the sea otters, which may be seen basking in the **Great Tide Pool** outside the aquarium, where they are readied for reintroduction to the wild.

Even new-agey music and the occasional infinity-mirror illusion don't detract from the astounding beauty of jellyfish in the **Jellies Gallery**. To see fish – including hammerhead sharks and green sea turtles – that outweigh kids many times over, ponder the awesome **Open Sea** tank. Upstairs and downstairs you'll find **touch pools**, where you can get close to sea cucumbers, bat rays and tidepool creatures. Younger kids will love the interactive, bilingual **Splash Zone**, with penguin feedings at 10:30am and 3pm.

NEED TO KNOW

☏831-648-4888, tickets 866-963-9645; www.montereybayaquarium.org; 886 Cannery Row; adult/child 3-12yr $30/20; ⊙9:30am-6pm Mon-Fri, 9:30am-8pm Sat & Sun Jun-Aug, 10am-5pm or 6pm daily Sep-May; 🛜👪

according to a capricious schedule dictated by severe state-park budget cutbacks.

MONTEREY HISTORY & MARITIME MUSEUM
Museum

(☎831-372-2608; http://montereyhistory.org; 5 Custom House Plaza; admission $5, free after 3pm on 1st Tue of the month; ☉10am-5pm Tue-Sun) Near the waterfront, this voluminous modern exhibition hall illuminates Monterey's salty past, from early Spanish explorers to the roller-coaster–like rise and fall of the local sardine industry that brought Cannery Row to life in the mid-20th century. Highlights include a ship-in-a-bottle collection and the historic Fresnel lens from Point Sur Lightstation.

 **Activities**

FREE **DENNIS THE MENACE PARK**
Playground

(777 Pearl St; ☉10am-dusk, closed Tue Sep-May; ⛹) A must for fans of kick-ass playgrounds, this park was the brainchild of Hank Ketcham, the creator of the classic comic strip. This ain't your standard

dumbed-down playground, suffocated by Big Brother's safety regulations. With lightning-fast slides, a hedge maze and towering climbing walls, even some adults can't resist playing here.

Whale-Watching

You can spot whales off the coast of Monterey Bay year-round. The season for blue and humpback whales runs from late April to early December, while gray whales pass by from mid-December to mid-April. Tour boats depart from downtown's Fisherman's Wharf and also Moss Landing. Reserve trips at least a day in advance; be prepared for a bumpy, cold ride.

MONTEREY WHALE WATCHING
Boat Tours

(☎831-372-2203, tickets 800-979-3370; www.montereywhalewatching.com; 96 Fisherman's Wharf; 2½hr tour adult/child 3-12yr $40/30) Several daily departures.

MONTEREY BAY WHALE WATCH
Boat Tours

(☎831-375-4658; www.montereybaywhalewatch.com; 84 Fisherman's Wharf; 2½hr tour adult/

Monterey History & Maritime Museum

child 4-12yr from $38/27) Morning and afternoon departures.

Diving & Snorkeling

Monterey Bay offers world-renowned diving and snorkeling, including off **Lovers Point** in Pacific Grove and at **Point Lobos State Natural Reserve** near Carmel-by-the-Sea. You'll want a wet suit year-round.

MONTEREY BAY DIVE CHARTERS   Scuba Diving
(✆831-383-9276; www.mbdcscuba.com; scuba rental per day $79-89, shore/boat dive from $49/199) Rent a full scuba kit with wet suit, arrange small-group shore or boat dives or take a virgin undersea plunge by booking a three-hour beginners' dive experience ($159, no PADI certification required).

Kayaking & Surfing

MONTEREY BAY KAYAKS   Kayaking
(✆800-649-5357; www.montereybaykayaks.com; 693 Del Monte Ave; rental per day $30-50, tours adult/child from $50/40; ♨) Rents kay-

aks and stand-up paddle boarding (SUP) equipment and leads kayaking lessons and guided tours of Monterey Bay, including full-moon, sunrise and sunset trips, and family adventures.

SUNSHINE FREESTYLE SURF   Surfing
(✆831-375-5015; http://sunshinefreestyle.com; 443 Lighthouse Ave; rental per half-/full day surfboard $20/30, wet suit $10/15, boogie board $7/10) Monterey's oldest surf shop rents and sells all the gear you'll need. Staff grudgingly dole out tips.

🛏 Sleeping

CASA MUNRAS   Boutique Hotel $$
(✆831-375-2411, 800-222-2446; www.hotelcasamunras.com; 700 Munras Ave; r $185-279; @ 🛜 ➿ 🐾) Built around an adobe hacienda once owned by a 19th-century Spanish colonial don, chic modern rooms come with lofty beds and some gas fireplaces, all inside two-story motel-esque buildings. Splash in a heated outdoor pool, unwind at the tapas bar or take a sea-salt scrub in the tiny spa. Pet fee $50.

Point Lobos State Natural Reserve

COLTON INN   Motel **$$**
(📞831-649-6500, 800-848-7007; www.colton
inn.com; 707 Pacific St; r $109-199; ❄️ 🛜)
Downtown, this champ of a motel prides
itself on cleanliness and friendliness.
There's no pool and zero view, but staff
loan out DVDs, some rooms have real
log-burning fireplaces, hot tubs or kitch-
enettes, and there's even a dry sauna for
guests.

 Eating

FIRST AWAKENINGS   Brunch **$**
(www.firstawakenings.net; American Tin Cannery
Mall, 125 Oceanview Blvd; mains $5-12; ⏰7am-
2pm Mon-Fri, to 2:30pm Sat & Sun; 🚻) Sweet
and savory, all-American breakfasts and
lunches and bottomless pitchers of coffee
merrily weigh down outdoor tables at this
hideaway cafe. Order creative dishes like
'bluegerm' pancakes or the spicy 'Viva
Carnita' egg scramble.

**MONTEREY'S FISH
HOUSE**   Seafood **$$$**
(Map p179; 📞831-373-4647; 2114 Del Monte
Ave; mains $12-35; ⏰11:30am-2:30pm Mon-Fri,
5-9:30pm daily) Watched over by photos of
Sicilian fishermen, dig into dock-fresh seafood with an occasional Asian twist. Reservations are essential (it's so crowded), but
the vibe is island-casual: Hawaiian shirts
seem to be de rigueur for men. Try the
barbecued oysters or, for those stout of
heart, the Mexican squid steak.

• •
ℹ️ **Information**

**Monterey County Convention & Visitors
Bureau** (📞831-657-6400, 877-666-8373;
www.seemonterey.com; 401 Camino El Estero;
⏰9am-6pm Mon-Sat, to 5pm Sun) Ask for a free
Monterey County Film & Literary Map. Closes
one hour earlier November to March.

Carmel-by-the-Sea

Quaint Carmel-by-the-Sea (Map p179)
has the well-manicured feel of a country
club. Fairy-tale Comstock cottages, with
their characteristic stone chimneys and
pitched gable roofs, dot the town.

Founded as a seaside resort in the
1880s – fairly odd, given that its beach is
often blanketed in fog – Carmel quickly
attracted famous artists and writers,
such as Sinclair Lewis and Jack London,
and their hangers-on. An artistic flavor
survives in the more than 100 galleries
that line the town's immaculate streets.

 Activities

Not always sunny, **Carmel Beach** is a
gorgeous white-sand crescent, where
pampered pups excitedly run off-leash.

**POINT LOBOS STATE NATURAL
RESERVE**   Park
(Map p179; www.parks.ca.gov, www.pointlobos
.org; per car $10; ⏰8am-30min after sunset;
🚻) They bark, they bathe and they're fun
to watch – sea lions are the stars here at
Punta de los Lobos Marinos (Point of the
Sea Wolves), 4 miles south of Carmel,
where a dramatically rocky coastline of-
fers excellent tide-pooling.

The full perimeter hike is 6 miles,
but shorter walks take in wild scenery
too, including **Bird Island**, shady **Piney
Woods**, the historic **Whaler's Cabin** and
Devil's Cauldron, a whirlpool that gets
splashy at high tide.

🛏️ **Sleeping**

MISSION RANCH   Inn **$$$**
(Map p179; 📞831-624-6436, 800-538-8221;
www.missionranchcarmel.com; 26270 Dolores St;
r incl breakfast $135-285; 🛜) If woolly sheep
grazing on green fields within view of the
Pacific don't convince you to stay here,
perhaps knowing that actor and director
Clint Eastwood restored this historic
ranch will. Accommodations range from
shabby-chic rooms inside a converted
barn to a family-sized 1850s farmhouse.

SEA VIEW INN   B&B **$$**
(Map p179; 📞831-624-8778; www.seaviewinn
carmel.com; Camino Real btwn 11th & 12th Aves;
r incl breakfast $135-265; 🛜) At this intimate
retreat away from downtown's hustle,

Scenic Drive: 17-Mile Drive

WHAT TO SEE

Pacific Grove and Carmel are linked by the spectacularly scenic, if overhyped **17-Mile Drive** (Map p179), which meanders through Pebble Beach, a wealthy private resort. It's no chore staying within the 25mph limit – every curve in the road reveals another postcard vista, especially when wildflowers bloom. Cycling the route is enormously popular, but try to do it during the week, when traffic isn't as heavy, and ride with the flow of traffic, from north to south.

Using the self-guided touring map provided upon entry, you can easily pick out landmarks such as **Spanish Bay**, where explorer Gaspar de Portolá dropped anchor in 1769; treacherously rocky **Point Joe**, which in the past was often mistaken for the entrance to Monterey Bay and thus became the site of several shipwrecks; and **Bird Rock**, also a haven for harbor seals and sea lions. The ostensible pièce de résistance is the trademark **Lone Cypress**, which has perched on a seaward rock for more than 250 years.

Besides the coastal scenery, star attractions at Pebble Beach include world-famous **golf courses**, where a celebrity and pro tournament happens every February.

THE ROUTE

Operated as a toll road by the **Pebble Beach Company** (www.pebblebeach.com; per vehicle/bicycle $9.50/free), 17-Mile Drive is open from sunrise to sunset.

TIME & MILEAGE

There are five separate gates for the 17-Mile Drive; how far you drive and how long you take is up to you. For the most scenery, enter at Pacific Grove (off Sunset Dr) and exit at Carmel.

fireside nooks are made for reading or taking afternoon tea. The cheapest rooms with slanted ceilings are short on cat-swinging space, but the beach is nearby.

CARMEL RIVER INN   Inn $$$
(Map p179; ☏831-624-1575, 800-966-6490; www.carmelriverinn.com; 26600 Oliver Rd; d $159-319; ☎☀☂) Tucked off Hwy 1, this peaceful garden retreat south of Carmel's mission rents white-picket-fenced honeymooner and family cottages, many with fireplaces and kitchenettes, and simple country-style rooms. Pet fee $20.

Eating

Carmel's restaurant scene is more about old-world sidewalk atmosphere than sustenance. Most places open for breakfast, and stop serving dinner before 9pm.

LA BICYCLETTE   French, Italian $$$
(Map p179; www.labicycletterestaurant.com; Dolores St at 7th Ave; lunch mains $7-16, 3-course prix-fixe dinner $28; ⏱11:30am-4pm & 5-10pm) Rustic European comfort food using seasonal local ingredients packs canoodling couples into this bistro, with an open kitchen baking wood-fired oven pizzas. Excellent local wines by the glass are available.

MUNDAKA   Tapas $$
(www.mundakacarmel.com; San Carlos St btwn Ocean & 7th Aves; small plates $4-19; ⏱5:30-10pm Sun-Wed, 5:30-11pm Thu-Sat) This stone courtyard hideaway is a svelte escape from Carmel's stuffy 'newly wed and

nearly dead' crowd. Take Spanish tapas plates for a spin and sip the house-made sangria while DJs or flamenco guitars play.

BRUNO'S MARKET & DELI Deli, Groceries **$**
(Map p179; www.brunosmarket.com; cnr 6th & Junípero Aves; sandwiches $5-8; ⏱7am-8pm)
This small supermarket deli counter makes a saucy tri-trip beef sandwich and stocks all the accoutrements for a beach picnic, including Sparky's root beer from Pacific Grove.

ℹ Information

Downtown buildings have no street numbers, so addresses specify the street and nearest intersection too.

Carmel Chamber of Commerce (☎831-624-2522, 800-550-4333; www .carmelcalifornia.org; San Carlos St, btwn 5th & 6th Aves; ⏱10am-5pm) Free maps and information, including about local art galleries.

ℹ Getting There & Around

Carmel is 5 miles south of Monterey via Hwy 1. Find free unlimited parking in a municipal lot (cnr 3rd & Junípero Aves) behind the Vista Lobos building.

Big Sur

Big Sur is more a state of mind than a place you can pinpoint on a map. There are no traffic lights, banks or strip malls, and when the sun goes down, the moon and the stars are the only streetlights – if summer's dense fog hasn't extinguished them, that is. Much ink has been spilled extolling the raw beauty and energy of this precious piece of land shoehorned between the Santa Lucia Range and the Pacific Ocean,

but nothing quite prepares you for your first glimpse of the craggy, unspoiled coastline.

In the 1950s and '60s, Big Sur – so named by Spanish settlers living on the Monterey Peninsula, who referred to the wilderness as *el país grande del sur* ('the big country to the south') – became a retreat for artists and writers, including Henry Miller and Beat Generation visionaries such as Lawrence Ferlinghetti. Today Big Sur attracts self-proclaimed artists, new-age mystics, latter-day hippies and city slickers seeking to unplug and reflect more deeply on this emerald-green edge of the continent.

◉ Sights & Activities

All of the following places are listed north to south. Most parks are open from a half-hour before sunrise until a half-hour after sunset, with 24-hour campground access. At state parks, your parking fee ($10) receipt is valid for same-day entry

Coastal highway, Big Sur
JIM WARK/LONELY PLANET IMAGES ©

to all except Limekiln; don't skip paying the entry fee by parking illegally outside along Hwy 1.

BIXBY BRIDGE — Landmark

Under 15 miles south of Carmel, this landmark spanning Rainbow Canyon is one of the world's highest single-span bridges. Completed in 1932, it was built by prisoners eager to lop time off their sentences. There's a perfect photo-op pull-off on the bridge's north side. Before Bixby Bridge was constructed, travelers had to trek inland on what's now called the **Old Coast Rd**, which heads off opposite the pull-off, reconnecting after 11 miles with Hwy 1 near Andrew Molera State Park.

POINT SUR STATE HISTORIC PARK — Lighthouse

(☎831-625-4419; www.pointsur.org; adult/child 6-17yr $10/5, moonlight tour $15/10; ☉tour schedules vary) Just over 6 miles south of Bixby Bridge, Point Sur rises like a green velvet fortress. This imposing volcanic rock looks like an island, but is actually connected to land by a sandbar. Atop the rock is the 1889 stone lightstation, which operated until 1974. Ocean views and tales of the lighthouse keepers' family

lives are engrossing. Meet your tour guide at the locked gate a quarter-mile north of Point Sur Naval Facility, usually at 10am Saturday and Sunday year-round, and 1pm Wednesday from November through March. Tours also depart at 2pm Wednesday and Saturday from April to October, when monthly full-moon tours are also available. Call ahead to confirm tour schedules. Arrive early because space is limited (no reservations).

ANDREW MOLERA STATE PARK — Park

(☎831-667-2315; www.parks.ca.gov; per vehicle $10) Named after the farmer who first planted artichokes in California, this oft-overlooked park is a trail-laced pastiche of grassy meadows, waterfalls, ocean bluffs and rugged beaches offering excellent wildlife-watching. Look for the turnoff just over 8 miles south of Bixby Bridge.

From the parking lot, a half-mile walk along the beach-bound trail leads to a first-come, first-served campground, from where a gentle quarter-mile spur trail leads past the 1861 redwood **Cooper Cabin**, Big Sur's oldest building. Otherwise, keep hiking on the main trail out toward a beautiful beach where the Big Sur River runs into the ocean and

Bixby Bridge

condors can occasionally be spotted circling overhead.

PFEIFFER BIG SUR STATE PARK   Park

(☎831-667-2315; www.parks.ca.gov; per vehicle $10) Named after Big Sur's first European settlers, who arrived in 1869, Pfeiffer Big Sur is the largest state park in Big Sur. Hiking trails loop through redwood groves and head into the adjacent Ventana Wilderness. The most popular trail – to 60ft-high **Pfeiffer Falls**, a delicate cascade hidden in the forest, which usually runs from December to May – is an easy 1.4-mile round-trip.

PFEIFFER BEACH   Beach

(www.fs.usda.gov; per vehicle $5; ☉9am-8pm; 🐾) This phenomenal, crescent-shaped and dog-friendly beach is known for its huge double rock formation, through which waves crash with life-affirming power. It's often windy, and the surf is too dangerous for swimming. But dig down into the wet sand – it's purple! That's because manganese garnet washes down from the craggy hillsides above.

To get here from Hwy 1, make a sharp right onto Sycamore Canyon Rd, marked by a small yellow sign that says 'narrow road' at the top. It's about half a mile south of Big Sur Station, or 2 miles south of Pfeiffer Big Sur State Park. From the turnoff, it's two more narrow, twisting miles (RVs and trailers prohibited) down to the beach.

HENRY MILLER LIBRARY   Arts Center

(☎831-667-2574; www.henrymiller.org; admission by donation; ☉11am-6pm Wed-Mon; @ 🛜) 'It was here in Big Sur I first learned to say Amen!' wrote Henry Miller, a Big Sur denizen for 17 years. More of a living memorial, alt-cultural venue and bookstore, this community gathering spot was never Miller's home. The house belonged to Miller's friend, painter Emil White, until his death and is now run by a nonprofit group. Inside are copies of all of Miller's written works, many of his paintings and a collection of Big Sur and Beat Generation material, including copies of the top 100 books Miller said most influenced him. Stop by to browse and hang out on the

Driving Hwy 1

Driving this narrow two-lane highway through Big Sur and beyond is very slow going. Allow about three hours to cover the distance between the Monterey Peninsula and San Luis Obispo, much more if you want to explore the coast. Traveling after dark can be risky and more to the point, it's futile, since you'll miss out on the seascapes. Watch out for cyclists and always use signposted roadside pullouts to let faster-moving traffic pass.

front deck. It's about half a mile south of Nepenthe restaurant.

JULIA PFEIFFER BURNS STATE PARK   Park

(☎831-667-2315; www.parks.ca.gov; per vehicle $10) Named for another Big Sur pioneer, this park hugs both sides of Hwy 1. The big attraction is California's only coastal waterfall, **McWay Falls**, which drops 80ft straight into the sea – or onto the beach, depending on the tide. This is *the* classic Big Sur postcard shot, with tree-topped rocks jutting above a golden, crescent-shaped beach next to swirling blue pools and crashing white surf. To reach this spectacular viewpoint, take the short Overlook Trail west from the parking lot and cross underneath Hwy 1 via a tunnel. From trailside benches, you might spot migrating gray whales between mid-December and mid-April.

The park entrance is on the east side of Hwy 1, about 8 miles south of Nepenthe restaurant.

🛏 Sleeping

GLEN OAKS MOTEL   Motel $$$

(☎831-667-2105; www.glenoaksbigsur.com; Hwy 1; d $175-350; 🛜) At this 1950s redwood-

RICHARD CUMMINS/LONELY PLANET IMAGES ©

and-adobe motor lodge, rustic rooms and cabins seem effortlessly chic. Dramatically transformed by ecoconscious design, these snug romantic hideaways all have gas fireplaces. The woodsy studio cottage has a kitchenette and walk-in shower built for two, or retreat to the one-bedroom house equipped with a full kitchen.

TREEBONES RESORT   Yurts $$$
(☎ 877-424-4787; www.treebonesresort.com; 71895 Hwy 1; d $170-285; ⚐ ♿) Don't let the word 'resort' throw you. Yes, they've got an ocean-view hot tub, heated pool and massage treatments available. But noisy yurts with polished pine floors, quilt-covered beds, sink vanities and redwood decks are actually like 'glamping,' with little privacy. Bathrooms and showers are a short stroll away. Rates include a make-your-own waffle breakfast. Look for the signposted turnoff a mile north of Gorda.

BIG SUR CAMPGROUND & CABINS   Cabins, Campground $$
(☎ 831-667-2322; www.bigsurcamp.com; 47000 Hwy 1; cabins $90-345, tent/RV sites from $40/50; ♿ ⚐) Right on the Big Sur River and shaded by redwoods, cozy house-keeping cabins come with full kitchens

and fireplaces, while canvas-sided tent cabins are dog-friendly (pet fee $15). The riverside campground is especially popular with RVs. There are hot showers, a coin-op laundry, playground and general store. ❧

DEETJEN'S BIG SUR INN   Lodge $$
(☎ 831-667-2377; www.deetjens.com; 48865 Hwy 1; d $90-250) Nestled among redwoods and wisteria, this creekside conglomeration of rustic, thin-walled rooms and cottages was built by Norwegian immigrant Helmuth Deetjen in the 1930s. Some rooms are warmed by wood-burning fireplaces, while cheaper ones share bathrooms.

 Eating

RESTAURANT AT VENTANA   Californian $$$
(☎ 831-667-4242; www.ventanainn.com; 48123 Hwy 1; lunch mains $10-18, dinner mains $29-38; ⏱ 11:30am-9pm; ☎) The old truism about the better the views, the worse the food just doesn't seem to apply here. The resort's ocean-view terrace restaurant and cocktail bar is hands down the hap-

piest place for foodies anywhere along Hwy 1. Dig into tender bison steaks with truffled mac 'n cheese, curried chicken salad or roasted vegetable pastas flavored with herbs grown in the garden right outside.

NEPENTHE & CAFÉ
KEVAH
Californian $$$

📞831-667-2345; www.nepenthebigsur.com 48510 Hwy 1; cafe mains $11-17, restaurant mains $15-39; ⊘restaurant 11:30am-10pm, cafe 9am-4pm; 🚻) Nepenthe comes from a Greek word meaning 'isle of no sorrow,' and indeed, it's hard to feel blue while sitting by the fire pit on this clifftop terrace. Just-OK California bistro cuisine (try the renowned Ambrosia burger) takes a backseat to the views and Nepenthe's history – Orson Welles and Rita Hayworth briefly owned a cabin here in the 1940s. Downstairs, Café Kevah serves light, casual brunches and has head-spinning ocean views from its own outdoor patio (closed in winter and bad weather).

BIG SUR BAKERY &
RESTAURANT
Californian $$$

(📞831-667-0520; www.bigsurbakery.com; 47540 Hwy 1; snacks & drinks from $4, mains $14-36; ⊘bakery from 8am daily, restaurant 11am-2:30pm Tue-Fri, 10:30am-2:30pm Sat & Sun, plus from 5:30pm Tue-Sat) Behind the Shell station, this warmly lit, funky house has seasonally changing menus; wood-fired pizzas share space with more refined dishes like butter-braised halibut. Fronted by a pretty patio, the bakery pours Big Sur's priciest espresso. Expect long waits and standoffish service.

Point Piedras Blancas

Many lighthouses still stand along California's coast, but few offer such a historically evocative seascape. Federally designated an outstanding natural area, the jutting, windblown grounds of this 1875 **lightstation** (📞805-927-7361; www.piedrasblancas.org; tour adult/child 6-17yr $10/5; ⊘tour schedules vary) – one of the tallest on the West Coast – have been laboriously replanted with native flora. Picturesquely,

everything looks much the way it did when the first lighthouse keepers helped ships find safe harbor at the whaling station at San Simeon Bay. Guided tours currently meet at 9:45am on Tuesdays, Thursdays and Saturdays at the old Piedras Blancas Motel, about 1.5 miles north of the lightstation.

San Luis Obispo

Almost halfway between LA and San Francisco, San Luis Obispo is the classic stopover point for road trippers. With no must-see attractions, SLO might not seem to warrant much of your time. That said, this lively yet low-key town has an enviably high quality of life – in fact, talk-show diva Oprah once deemed it America's happiest city. Nestled at the base of the Santa Lucia foothills, SLO is just a grape's throw from thriving Edna Valley wineries, known for their crisp chardonnays and subtle syrahs and pinot noirs.

 Sights

San Luis Obispo Creek, once used to irrigate mission orchards, flows through downtown. Uphill from Higuera St, **Mission Plaza** is a shady oasis with restored adobe buildings and fountains overlooking the creek. Look for the **Moon Tree**, a coast redwood grown from a seed that journeyed onboard Apollo 14's lunar mission.

MISSION SAN LUIS OBISPO DE
TOLOSA
Mission

(www.missionsanluisobispo.org; 751 Palm St; suggested donation $2; ⊘9am-4pm) Those satisfyingly reverberatory bells heard around downtown emanate from this active parish. The fifth California mission, it was established in 1772 and named for a 13th-century French saint. Nicknamed the 'Prince of the Missions,' its modest church has an unusual L-shape and whitewashed walls depicting Stations of the Cross. An adjacent building contains an old-fashioned museum about daily life

BEVERLY & WOODWARD PAYNE ANDERSON/LONELY PLANET IMAGES ©

Don't Miss **Hearst Castle**

Built for William Randolph Hearst (1863–1951), Hearst Castle is a wondrous, historic, over-the-top homage to material excess, perched high on a hill. From the 1920s into the '40s, Hearst and Marion Davies, his longtime mistress, entertained a steady stream of the era's biggest movers and shakers. Invitations were highly coveted, but Hearst had his quirks – he despised drunkenness, and guests were forbidden to speak of death.

Architect Julia Morgan based the main building, Casa Grande, on the design of a Spanish cathedral, and over decades catered to Hearst's every design whim, deftly integrating the spoils of his fabled European shopping sprees. The estate sprawls across acres of lushly landscaped gardens, accentuated by shimmering pools and fountains, statues from ancient Greece and Moorish Spain, and the ruins of what was in Hearst's day the world's largest private zoo (drivers along Hwy 1 can sometimes still spot the zebras).

Much like Hearst's construction budget, the castle will devour as much of your time and money as you let it. To see anything of this state historic monument, you have to take a tour. In peak summer months, show up early enough and you might be able to get a same-day ticket for later that afternoon. For special holiday and evening tours, book at least two weeks in advance.

Before you leave the castle, take a moment to visit the often-overlooked museum area at the back of the visitors center. The center's five-story-high theater shows a 40-minute historical film (admission included with tour tickets) about the castle and Hearst family.

NEED TO KNOW

📞 info 805-927-2020, reservations 800-444-4445; www.hearstcastle.org; tours adult/child from $25/12; ⊙ daily, hr vary

during the Chumash tribal and Spanish colonial periods.

BUBBLEGUM ALLEY Quirky
(off 700 block of Higuera St) SLO's weirdest sight is colorfully plastered with thousands of wads of ABC ('already been chewed') gum. Watch where you step!

Festivals & Events

SAN LUIS OBISPO FARMERS MARKET Food, Culture
(www.downtownslo.com; ⊘6-9pm Thu) The county's biggest and best weekly farmers market turns downtown's Higuera St into a giant street party, with smokin' barbecues, overflowing fruit and veggie stands, live music of all stripes and free sidewalk entertainment, from salvation peddlers to wackadoodle political activists. It's one of the liveliest evenings out anywhere along the Central Coast.

Sleeping

PEACH TREE INN Motel $$
(☎805-543-3170, 800-227-6396; www.peach treeinn.com; 2001 Monterey St; r incl breakfast $79-200; ❄@⌐) The folksy, nothingfancy motel rooms here are inviting, especially those right by the creek or with rocking chairs on wooden porches overlooking grassy lawns, eucalyptus trees and rose gardens. A hearty breakfast features homemade breads.

Eating

🖉**BIG SKY CAFÉ** Californian $$
(www.bigskycafe.com; 1121 Broad St; mains $6-22; ⊘7am-9pm Mon-Wed, 7am-10pm Thu & Fri, 8am-10pm Sat, 8am-9pm Sun; ⌐) Big Sky is a big room, and still the wait can be long – its tagline is 'analog food for a digital world.' Vegetarians have almost as many options as carnivores, and many of the ingredients are sourced locally. Big-plate dinners can be bland, but breakfast (until 1pm daily) gets top marks.

SPLASH CAFE Cafe $
(www.splashbakery.com; 1491 Monterey St; dishes $3-10; ⊘7am-8:30pm Sun-Thu, to 9:30pm Fri & Sat; ⌐) Fresh soups and salads, sandwiches on house-made bread and tempting bakery treats are reason enough to kick back inside this airy uptown cafe, not far from motel row. The organic, handmade Sweet Earth Chocolates shop is nearby.

SANTA BARBARA

Frankly put, this area is damn pleasant to putter around. Just a 90-minute drive

What the…?

'Oh, my!' is one of the more printable exclamations overheard from visitors at the **Madonna Inn** (☎805-543-3000, 800-543-9666; www.madonnainn.com; 100 Madonna Rd; r $179-449; ❄⌨), a garish confection visible from Hwy 101. You'd expect outrageous kitsch like this in Las Vegas, not SLO, but here it is, in all its campy extravagance. Japanese tourists, vacationing Midwesterners and hipster, ironyloving urbanites all adore the 110 themed rooms – including Yosemite Rock, Caveman and hot-pink Floral Fantasy. Check out photos of the different rooms online, or wander the halls and spy into the ones being cleaned. The urinal in the men's room is a bizarre waterfall. But the most irresistible reason to stop here? Old-fashioned cookies from the storybook-esque bakery.

north of Los Angeles, tucked between mountains and the Pacific, Santa Barbara basks smugly in its near-perfection. Founded by a Spanish mission, the city's signature red-tile roofs, white stucco buildings and Mediterranean vibe have long given credence to its claim to the title of the 'American Riviera.' Santa Barbara is blessed with almost freakishly good weather, and no one can deny the appeal of those beaches that line the city tip to toe either. Just ignore those pesky oil derricks out to sea.

Sights

MISSION SANTA BARBARA Mission
(www.sbmission.org; 2201 Laguna St; adult/child 6-15yr $5/1; ⏰9am-4:30pm) Reigning from a hilltop above town, the 'Queen of the Missions' became the 10th California mission on the feast day of Saint Barbara in 1786. Occupied by Catholic priests ever since,

the mission escaped Mexico's policy of forced secularization. Today it functions as a Franciscan friary, parish church and historical museum. The 1820 stone church has Chumash artwork and beautiful cloisters; its imposing Doric facade, an homage to a chapel in ancient Rome, is topped by twin bell towers. Behind the church is an extensive cemetery – look for skull carvings over the door leading outside – with 4000 Chumash graves and the elaborate mausoleums of early settlers.

FREE SANTA BARBARA COUNTY COURTHOUSE Historic Building
(1100 Anacapa St; ⏰8:30am-4:45pm Mon-Fri, 10am-4:45pm Sat & Sun) Built in Spanish-Moorish Revival style, it's an absurdly beautiful place to be on trial. The magnificent 1929 courthouse features hand-painted ceilings, wrought-iron chandeliers and tiles from Tunisia and Spain. Step inside the hushed 2nd-floor mural room depicting Spanish colonial history, then

Left: Outdoor dining, Santa Barbara; **Below:** Mural room, Santa Barbara County Courthouse

(LEFT) HANAN ISACHAR/LONELY PLANET IMAGES ©; (BELOW) WITOLD SKRYPCZAK/LONELY PLANET IMAGES ©

climb the 85ft clocktower for arch-framed panoramas of the city, ocean and mountains. Docent-led tours are usually offered at 2pm daily and 10:30am on Monday, Tuesday, Wednesday and Friday.

SANTA BARBARA MARITIME MUSEUM
Museum

(www.sbmm.org; 113 Harbor Way; adult/child 1-5yr/youth 6-17yr $7/2/4, all free 3rd Thu of the month; ⊙10am-5pm Thu-Tue Sep-May, to 6pm Jun-Aug; 👬) Even li'l cap'ns will get a kick out of this museum by the yacht harbor. A two-level exhibition hall celebrates Santa Barbara's briny history with historical artifacts and memorabilia, hands-on and virtual-reality exhibits, and a small theater for documentary videos.

STEARNS WHARF
Landmark

(www.stearnswharf.org) At its southern end, State St runs into Stearns Wharf, once co-owned by tough-guy actor Jimmy Cagney. Built in 1872, it's the West Coast's oldest continuously operating wooden pier. There's 90 minutes of free parking with validation from any shop or restaurant, but it's more fun to walk atop the very bumpy wooden slats.

 **Beaches**

The long, sandy stretch between Stearns Wharf and Montecito is **East Beach**, Santa Barbara's largest and most crowded. At its far end, near the Biltmore hotel, Armani swimsuits and Gucci sunglasses abound at chic, but narrow **Butterfly Beach**.

Between Stearns Wharf and the harbor, **West Beach** is popular with tourists. There **Los Baños del Mar** (☎805-966-6110; 401 Shoreline Dr; admission $6; ⊙call for hr; 👬), a municipal heated outdoor pool complex, is good for recreational and lap swimming, plus a kids' wading pool. West of the harbor, **Leadbetter Beach**

Downtown Santa Barbara

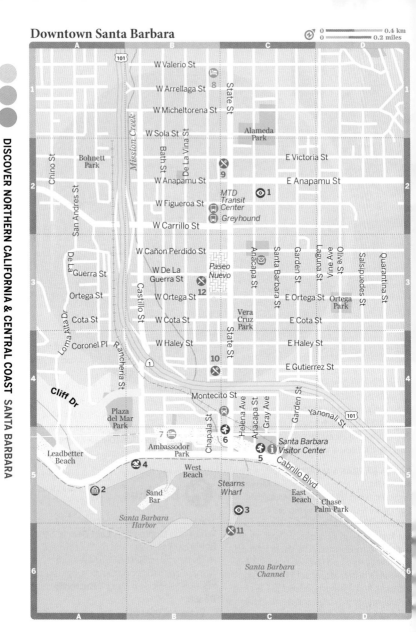

is the spot for beginning surfers and windsurfers. Climbing the stairs on the west end takes you to **Shoreline Park**, with picnic tables and awesome kite-flying conditions.

Further west, near the junction of Cliff Dr and Las Positas Rd, family-friendly **Arroyo Burro (Hendry's) Beach** has free parking and a restaurant and bar. Above the beach is the **Douglas Family**

Downtown Santa Barbara

⊙ Sights
1 Santa Barbara County
   Courthouse.....................................C2
2 Santa Barbara Maritime
   Museum A5
3 Ty Warner Sea Center.....................C5

⊕ Activities, Courses & Tours
4 Los Baños del Mar B5
5 Wheel Fun C5
6 Wheel Fun C5

⊜ Sleeping
7 Harbor House Inn............................B5
8 James House....................................B1

⊗ Eating
9 Bouchon...C2
10 D'Angelo Pastry & Bread B4
11 Santa Barbara Shellfish
   Company...C6
12 Silvergreens....................................B3

Preserve, offering cliffside romps for dogs.

Outside town off Hwy 101 you'll find even more spacious, family-friendly **state beaches** (☎805-958-1033; www.parks.ca.gov; per car $10; ⊙sunrise-sunset), including **Carpinteria State Beach**, about 12 miles southeast of Santa Barbara, and **Refugio & El Capitán State Beaches**, over 20 miles west in Goleta.

 **Activities**

A paved recreational path stretches for 3 miles along the waterfront between Leadbetter Beach and Andrée Clark Bird Refuge, passing Stearns Wharf. **Santa Barbara Bicycle Coalition** (www.sbbike.org) offers free cycling tour maps online.

WHEEL FUN   Cycling
(www.wheelfunrentals.com; ⊙8am-8pm) Cabrillo (23 E Cabrillo Blvd); State St (22 State St) Rents beach cruisers, hybrid mountain bikes and cheesy pedal-powered surreys with the fringe on top (local kids like to bomb 'em with water balloons!).

 Sleeping

Prepare for sticker shock: basic motel rooms by the beach command over $200 in summer. Don't show up without reservations, especially on weekends. Cheaper motels and hotels cluster along upper State St and Hwy 101 between Goleta and Carpinteria.

**INN OF THE SPANISH
GARDEN**   Boutique Hotel $$$
(☎805-564-4700, 866-564-4700; http://span ishgardeninn.com; 915 Garden St; d incl breakfast $259-519; ❄@🛜☀) At this elegant Spanish revival–style downtown hotel, two-dozen romantic rooms and suites have balconies and patios overlooking a gracious fountain courtyard. Beds have luxurious linens, bathrooms boast deep soaking tubs and concierge service is top-notch.

JAMES HOUSE   B&B $$$
(☎805-569-5853; www.jameshousesantabar bara.com; 1632 Chapala St; r incl breakfast $190-240; 🛜) For a traditional B&B experience, revel in this stately Queen Anne Victorian run by a charmingly hospitable owner. All of the antique-filled rooms are sheer elegance, with lofty ceilings, some fireplaces and none of that shabby-chic look. Full sit-down breakfast served.

HARBOR HOUSE INN   Motel $$
(☎805-962-9745, 888-474-6789; www.harbor houseinn.com; 104 Bath St; r $129-335; 🛜🐾) All of these brightly lit studios inside a converted motel have hardwood floors, small kitchens and a cheery design scheme. Rates include a welcome basket of breakfast goodies, a DVD library and three-speed bikes to borrow. Pet fee $15.

 Eating

BOUCHON   French $$$
(☎805-730-1160; www.bouchonsantabarbara .com; 9 W Victoria St; mains $28-36; ⊙5:30-9pm Sun-Thu, to 10pm Fri & Sat) Flavorful French

cooking with a seasonal California influence is on the menu at convivial Bouchon (meaning 'wine cork'). Locally grown farm produce and ranched meats marry beautifully with more than 30 regional wines by the glass. Lovebirds, book a table on the candlelit patio.

SANTA BARBARA SHELLFISH COMPANY
Seafood $$

(www.sbfishhouse.com; 230 Stearns Wharf; dishes $5-19; ⊙11am-9pm) 'From sea to skillet to plate' best describes this end-of-the-wharf crab shack that's more of a counter joint. Great lobster bisque, ocean views and the same location for 25 years.

SILVERGREENS
Healthy $$

(www.silvergreens.com; 791 Chapala St; dishes $4-10; ⊙7:30am-10pm Mon-Fri, 11am-10pm Sun; 👶🍴) Who says fast food can't be fresh and tasty? With the tag line 'Eat smart, live well,' this sun-drenched cafe makes nutritionally sound (check the calorie counts on your receipt) salads, soups, sandwiches and breakfast burritos.

D'ANGELO PASTRY & BREAD
Cafe $

(25 W Gutierrez St; dishes $2-8; ⊙7am-2pm) This retrolicious downtown bakery with

shiny-silver sidewalk bistro tables is a perfect quick breakfast or brunch spot, whether for a buttery croissant and rich espresso or Iron Chef Cat Cora's favorite 'Eggs Rose.'

🔒 Shopping

Downtown's **State St** is packed with shops, from vintage clothing to brand-name boutiques; cheapskates stick to lower State St, while trust-fund babies head uptown. For indie shops, dive into the **Funk Zone**, east of State St, just south of Hwy 101.

ⓘ Getting There & Away

If you use public transportation to get to Santa Barbara, you can get valuable hotel discounts, plus get a nice swag bag of coupons for various activities and attractions, all courtesy of **Santa Barbara Car Free** (www.santabarbaracarfree .org).

Santa Barbara Airbus (☏805-964-7759, 800-423-1618; www.sbairbus.com) Shuttles between Los Angeles International Airport (LAX) and Santa Barbara (one way/round trip $48/90, 2½ to three hours, eight daily).

Santa Barbara Wine Country

Oak-dotted hillsides, winding country lanes, rows of sweetly heavy grapevines stretching as far as the eye can see – it's hard not to gush about the Santa Maria and Santa Ynez Valleys.

With more than 100 wineries spread out across the landscape, it can seem daunting at first. But the wine country's five small towns – Buellton, Solvang, Santa Ynez, Ballard and Los Olivos – are all clustered within 10 miles of one another, so it's easy to stop, shop and eat whenever and wherever you happen to feel like it.

The pastoral **Foxen Canyon Wine Trail** (www.foxencanyonwinetrail.com) runs north from Hwy 154, just west of Los Olivos, into the rural Santa Maria Valley. The **Santa Rita Hills Wine Trail** (www.santaritahillswinetrail.com) shines brightly when it comes to ecoconscious farming practices and top-notch pinot noir. Country tasting rooms line a scenic loop west of Hwy 101 via Santa Rosa Rd and Hwy 246. In the **Santa Ynez Valley** you'll find dozens of wineries inside the triangle of Hwys 154, 246 and 101, including in downtown Los Olivos and Solvang.

Santa Barbara for Children

Museum of Natural History (www.sbnature.org; 2559 Puesta del Sol; adult/child 3-12yr/youth 13-17yr $11/7/8; ☺10am-5pm) Stuffed wildlife mounts, glittering gems and a pitch-dark planetarium captivate kids' imaginations.

Arroyo Burro (Hendry's) Beach (p193) Wide sandy beach, away from the tourist crowds, popular with local families.

Ty Warner Sea Center (www.sbnature.org/seacenter; 211 Stearns Wharf; adult/child 2-12yr/youth 13-17yr $8/5/7; ☺10am-5pm; 👪) Gawk at a gray-whale skeleton, touch tide-pool critters and crawl through a 1500-gallon surge tank.

Santa Barbara Maritime Museum (p193) Peer through a periscope, reel in a virtual fish or check out the gorgeous model ships.

Amtrak (www.amtrak.com; 209 State St) A stop on the daily Seattle–LA *Coast Starlight*. Regional *Pacific Surfliner* trains head south to LA ($25, three hours, six daily) and San Diego ($35, six hours, four daily), or north to San Luis Obispo ($29, 2¾ hours, twice daily).

Napa & Sonoma Wine Country

America's premier viticulture region has earned its reputation as being among the world's best. Despite hype about Wine Country style, it is from the land that all Wine Country lore springs. Rolling hills, dotted with century-old oaks, turn the color of lion's fur under the summer sun. Swaths of vineyards carpet hillsides as far as the eye can see. Where they end, lush redwood forests follow serpentine rivers to the ocean.

There are over 600 wineries in Napa and Sonoma Counties, but it's quality, not quantity, that sets the region apart – especially in Napa, which competes with France and doubles as an outpost of San Francisco's top-end culinary scene. Sonoma prides itself on agricultural diversity, with goat-cheese farms, you-pick-'em orchards and roadside fruit stands – plan to get lost on back roads. As you picnic atop sun-dappled hillsides, grab a hunk of earth and appreciate firsthand the thing that has the greatest meaning in Wine Country.

Cycling through vineyards, Napa Valley (p212)

Napa General Store (p216)

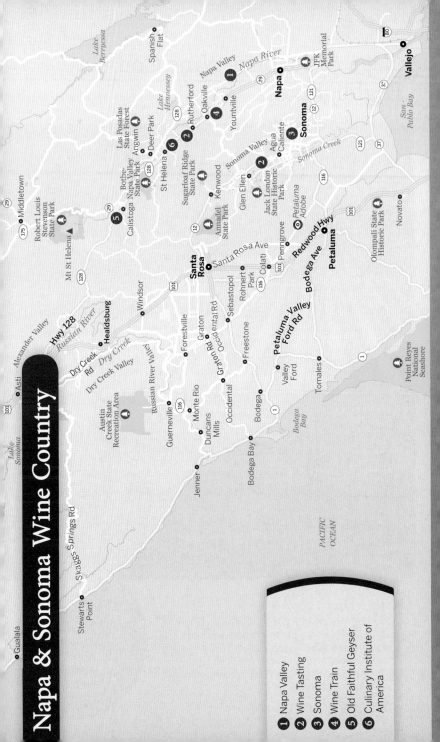

Napa & Sonoma Wine Country

1 Napa Valley
2 Wine Tasting
3 Sonoma
4 Wine Train
5 Old Faithful Geyser
6 Culinary Institute of America

Napa & Sonoma Wine Country Highlights

① Napa Valley

With world-class wineries (over 400 in total), luxurious mud-bath spas, top-tier restaurants and pastoral farmlands of precious vines, Napa Valley (p212) packs it in and flaunts it all. California's fabled *terroir* produces some of world's best bottles yet still harbors lots of natural attractions for families.

Need to Know

BEST TIME TO VISIT Spring and fall, but prices rise for the fall 'crush' **TRANSPORTATION** Heavy traffic on summer weekends **RESTAURANTS** Book ahead for top tables **For more, see p212**

Napa Valley Don't Miss List

BY DALIA CEJA, CEJA VINEYARDS

1 INDIAN SPRINGS

This is the perfect place to relax either as a couple or with a group of friends. I've been going to this Calistoga spa since I was seven. You can take a bath in mud infused with lavender and chamomile, and afterwards take a dip in the Olympic-size natural mineral pool. On a chilly fall day, swimming in the pool – the temperature reaches about 100°F at one end – is my number-one favorite thing to do.

2 DOWNTOWN NAPA

Two places I like downtown are **Betty's Girl** (p216), for custom designs made from vintage dresses, and the 'bubbles and beats' nights at the new **1313 Main wine bar** (www.1313main.com; 1313 Main St).

3 HOT-AIR BALLOON RIDES

Seeing Napa Valley by balloon (p219) is amazing. Even people who are afraid of heights enjoy it because the ride is so still and calm. A champagne breakfast usually comes with it, and depending on the wind most rides generally fly over Yountville, Oakville and Napa. The guides give a history of the geography, and the appellations look like different colored patches. It's best to go in the fall when it looks like a sunset in the fields against a crystal blue sky.

4 OXBOW PUBLIC MARKET

For foodies, coming to this market (p215) is like being a kid in a candy store. There's a spice area with over 300 varieties, artisanal coffee, gourmet Mexican tacos, a tasting area for cheese merchants – all within one big warehouse. On Saturday, a farmers market sets up in the old Copia parking lot outside, and you can buy seasonal produce and prepared meals at food trucks.

5 BICYCLE AND KAYAK TOURS

There are great excursions on offer with bikes and kayaks for adventurous and outdoorsy people. The cycling routes used don't have much traffic, and you can wine taste by bike and then go river kayaking the same day (p211).

Wine Tasting

Don't even think about leaving before you try a chardonnay (remember this is the one that beat the French in 1976; 'steely' chardonnays aged in steel tanks are the latest rage); rosé (ranging from watermelon-ripe pinks to sultry and smoky); pinot noir (hints of rose petals, redcurrant, and 'forest floor' flavors such as moss and black truffles); zinfandel (juicy blackberry and hints of dark chocolate or black pepper); and cabernet sauvignon (Napa's specialty).

Historic Sonoma

California history buffs should make sure to take a stroll around Sonoma Plaza and Sonoma State Historic Park (p228) for vestiges of the 1846 revolution against Mexico, when some American settlers tanked up on liquid courage, declared independence in the town of Sonoma. Tour the military barracks, now a museum, as well as the Mission San Francisco Solano de Sonoma. Vallejo Home (p229), Sonoma State Historic Park

Wine Train

Spend three hours in luxury as you're whisked from Napa to St Helena on the vintage Pullman cars of the Napa Valley Wine Train (p211). Dine on a gourmet multicourse lunch or dinner with wine pairings as you click-clack through the towns and vineyards of Yountville, Oakville and Rutherford, stopping for a tasting along the way. For a twist, try a special full-moon tour or a murder-mystery dinner excursion.

Old Faithful Geyser

Calistoga's hot-spring resorts may have tapped the earth's subterranean flow, but there's nothing like seeing a furious jolt of boiling water burst 60ft to the sky (p222). Bring the whole family to witness this twice-an-hour spectacle, a very visible demonstration of geothermal power. Just missed the frothy show? While away your time at the on-site petting zoo until the next eruption.

Culinary Institute of America at Greystone

A must-see for foodies, the CIA (p219) will boggle your mind with tasty options beyond its celebrated Wine Spectator Greystone Restaurant. Not only does it offer cooking demonstrations, but also wine-flight lessons, olive-oil tastings, multiday boot camps and chocolate sampling. Home chefs should budget time to ogle the more than 1000 cookbook titles at its shop.

Napa & Sonoma Wine Country's Best...

Winery Picnic Spots

○ **Casa Nuestra** (p218) Relax beneath weeping willows.

○ **Gundlach-Bundschu** (p226) One of Sonoma Valley's oldest and loveliest estate vineyards.

○ **Tres Sabores** (p213) Make an appointment for a tour and then linger under the olive trees.

○ **Hall** (p218) Wines by the glass under the mulberry trees.

○ **Kaz** (p227) Kids love the Play-Doh, playground and grape juice.

Car-free Transportation

○ **Balloon** (p219) Soar above the rolling hills and vineyard valleys.

○ **Bicycle** (p211) Explore quiet roads and wineries using your own pedal power.

○ **Ferry** (p210) Cruise in via Vallejo from San Francisco.

○ **Wine Train** (p211) Coast the countryside in a vintage Pullman dining car.

○ **Hiking** (p224) Hike the volcanic cone of Mt St Helena at Robert Louis Stevenson State Park.

Places for Kids

○ **Safari West** (p224) Take an expedition through a free-roaming exotic animal reserve.

○ **Traintown** (p229) Steam-engine rides, a carousel and a Ferris wheel.

○ **Old Faithful Geyser** (p222) Hourly water jets to the sky, plus a fun petting zoo.

○ **Indian Springs Resort** (p223) An old-school resort with a toasty spring-fed swimming pool and outdoor games.

○ **Benziger** (p227) Open-air tram ride and peacocks.

Romantic Wine Country

- **Poetry Inn** (p217) Private balconies, wood-burning fireplaces and indoor-outdoor showers.

- **Spa treatments** (p221) Spoil yourselves with a couples massage or mud bath for two.

- **Madrona Manor** (p235) Victorian mansion restaurant with a garden-view veranda.

- **Carneros Inn** (p214) Chic cottages with fireplaces, giant tubs and alfresco showers, plus a hilltop pool.

ADVANCE PLANNING

- **Two months before** Try to book a table at French Laundry (p218).

- **From several weeks to a few days before** Make tasting appointments at wineries that require them.

RESOURCES

- **Healdsburg** (www.healdsburg.org) Chamber of Commerce and Visitors Bureau.

- **Napa Valley** (www.legendarynapavalley.com) Napa Valley tourism information, spa deals and wine-tasting passes.

- **Russian River** (www.russianriver.com) Russian River Chamber of Commerce and Visitor Center.

- **Sonoma Valley** (www.sonomavalley.com) Site of the Sonoma Valley Visitors Bureau.

- **Press Democrat** (www.pressdemocrat.com) Daily regional newspaper, based in Santa Rosa.

- **Outlet Shopping** (www.premiumoutlets.com) Max out your credit cards on last season's close-outs.

GETTING AROUND

- **Car** Needed for extensive winery-hopping, unless you stay in major hub towns such as Napa or Sonoma, or book a limousine.

- **Bicycle** Visit wineries via quiet back roads, independently or on tours.

- **Bus** Sonoma County Transit and Golden Gate Transit buses operate.

- **Air** Alaska Air has regional services to the Sonoma County Airport (www.sonomacounty airport.org) in Santa Rosa.

- **Airport shuttle** Shuttles run from the San Francisco and Oakland Airports to Napa, and connect those airports to the Santa Rosa airport.

BE FOREWARNED

- **Visiting wineries** Some wineries accept visitors only by appointment.

- **Traffic** Expect heavy traffic on summer weekends.

- **Don't drink and drive** The curvy roads are dangerous, and police monitor traffic, especially on Napa's Hwy 29.

- **The 'crush'** Lodging prices skyrocket during the fall harvest.

Left: Wine tasting, Gundlach-Bundschu;
Above: Onboard the Napa Valley Wine Train

Napa & Sonoma Wine Country Itineraries

California's top wine country features rolling hills, farm-to-table restaurants and plush spas and resorts. And there are hundreds of tasting rooms ensconced in million-dollar estates and quirky barnyards.

DRY CREEK VALLEY **5**

OLD FAITHFUL GEYSER

HEALDSBURG **3**

2

1 CALISTOGA

ALEXANDER VALLEY

6

3 ST HELENA

4 YOUNTVILLE

JACK LONDON STATE HISTORIC PARK

SONOMA VALLEY

3

2

5 NAPA

1 SONOMA

CALISTOGA TO NAPA

Of Wine & Water

Base yourself in the classic Napa Valley resort town of **(1) Calistoga** for a bit of pampering and stress reduction. Book a mud treatment, and spend the rest of the day lazing around a hot-springs-fed swimming pool. If you prune quickly, set off to witness **(2) Old Faithful Geyser**, which shoots 60ft to 100ft into the sky a bit short of every hour; the kids can go wild in a petting zoo as you await the next scheduled eruption. The following day, prepare your taste buds for the epicurean ambrosia to come with a wine-tasting class at the Culinary Institute of America in **(3) St Helena**, and spruce up last season's wardrobe with

a few items from the town's many boutiques. Book an afternoon limo tour to some well-chosen Napa Valley wineries then, for your evening meal, partake of the excellent local French cuisine as you dine in gourmet-thick **(4) Yountville**. In the morning, depart for **(5) Napa** to sample the Oxbow Public Market's foodie delights, taste flights at the downtown Vintners' Collective, and tour the sculpture garden just west of town at di Rosa.

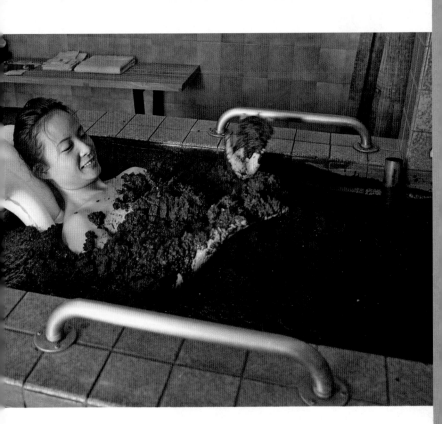

SONOMA TO HEALDSBURG
Rooted in History

Bear west and book two nights in or nearby the town of **(1) Sonoma**. Laid out by Mexican General Vallejo in 1834, the plaza in Sonoma contains Mission-revival buildings dating from the local revolution, and remains the heart of a lively downtown lined with hotels, restaurants and shops. Beyond the plaza, have a gander at the madcap works in the town's avant-garde landscape garden. Pull together a picnic including local cheeses and pass the next day touring wineries throughout the **(2) Sonoma Valley**. Literary buffs should make a stop at the **(3) Jack London State Historic Park**, which contains the final resting spot for the creator of *The Call of the Wild*.

Spend the following two nights in **(4) Healdsburg**, taking a cooking class and then sampling some of the gourmet highlights in the gastronomic capital of Sonoma County. Sign up for a bicycle tour and set off on another wine-tasting hurrah through the **(5) Dry Creek Valley**, working off last night's dinner by pedaling the pretty country lanes. On your final day, head north to the **(6) Alexander Valley** and dip your paddles in for a refreshing canoe trip down the Russian River.

Mudbath, Calistoga (p221)
JERRY ALEXANDER/LONELY PLANET IMAGES ©

Discover Napa & Sonoma Wine Country

At a Glance

○ **Napa Valley** (p212) Awash in cabernet, upscale shopping and top-end restaurants.

○ **Calistoga** (p221) Napa Valley's renowned spa town has hot springs and mud baths.

○ **Sonoma Valley** (p225) The folksier side of Wine Country boasts wineries and 19th-century historical sights.

○ **Healdsburg & the Russian River** (p232) The gastronomic capital of Sonoma County.

ℹ Getting There & Away

From San Francisco, public transportation gets you to the valleys, but it's insufficient for vineyard-hopping. For public-transit information, dial ☎511 from Bay Area telephones, or look online at www.transit.511.org.

Both valleys are 90 minutes' drive from San Francisco. Napa, the farther inland, has over 400 wineries and attracts the most visitors (expect heavy traffic summer weekends). Sonoma County has 260 wineries, 40 in Sonoma Valley, which is less commercial and less congested than Napa. If you have time to visit only one, choose Sonoma for ease.

BUS Evans Transportation (☎707-255-1559; www.evanstransportation.com) Shuttles ($29) to Napa from San Francisco and Oakland Airports.

Golden Gate Transit (☎415-923-2000; www.goldengate.org) Bus 70/80 from San Francisco to Petaluma ($9.25) and Santa Rosa ($10.25); board at 1st and Mission Sts. Connect with Sonoma County Transit buses (p211).

Greyhound (☎800-231-2222; www.greyhound.com) San Francisco to Santa Rosa ($22 to $30) and Vallejo ($17 to $23); transfer for local buses.

Napa Valley Vine (☎800-696-6443, 707-251-2800; www.nctpa.net) Operates bus 10 from the Vallejo Ferry Terminal and Vallejo Transit bus station, via Napa, to Calistoga ($2.90).

Sonoma County Airport Express (☎707-837-8700, 800-327-2024; www.airportexpressinc.com) Shuttles ($34) between Sonoma County Airport (Santa Rosa) and San Francisco and Oakland Airports.

FERRY Baylink Ferry (☎877-643-3779; www.baylinkferry.com) Downtown San Francisco to Vallejo (adult/child $13/6.50, 60 minutes); connect with Napa Valley Vine bus 10.

Cabernet sauvignon grapes
JERRY ALEXANDER/LONELY PLANET IMAGES ©

TRAIN Amtrak (☎800-872-7245; www.amtrak
.com) trains travel to Martinez (south of Vallejo),
with connecting buses to Napa (45 minutes),
Santa Rosa (1¼ hours) and Healdsburg (1¾
hours).

BART trains (☎415 989-2278; www.bart.gov)
run from San Francisco to El Cerrito del Norte
(30 minutes, $4.05). Transfer to **Vallejo Transit**
(☎707-648-4666; www.vallejotransit.com) for
Vallejo ($5, 30 minutes), then take Napa Valley
Vine buses to Napa and Calistoga.

ⓘ Getting Around

You'll need a car to winery-hop. Alternatively visit
tasting rooms in downtown Napa or downtown
Sonoma.

BICYCLE Touring Wine Country by bicycle is
unforgettable. Stick to back roads. We most
love pastoral West Dry Creek Rd, northwest of
Healdsburg, in Sonoma County. Through Sonoma
Valley, take Arnold Dr instead of Hwy 12; through
Napa Valley, take the Silverado Trail instead of
Hwy 29.

Cycling between wineries isn't demanding –
the valleys are mostly flat – but crossing between
Napa and Sonoma Valleys is intense, particularly
via steep Oakville Grade and Trinity Rd (between
Oakville and Glen Ellen).

PUBLIC TRANSPORTATION Napa Valley Vine
(☎800-696-6443, 707-251-2800; www.nctpa

.net) Bus 10 from downtown Napa to Calistoga
(1¼ hours, $2.15).

Sonoma County Transit (☎707-576-7433, 800-
345-7433; www.sctransit.com) Buses from Santa
Rosa to Petaluma ($2.35, 70 minutes), Sonoma
($2.90, 1¼ hours) and western Sonoma County,
including Russian River Valley towns ($2.90, 30
minutes).

TRAIN A cushy, if touristy, way to see Wine
Country, the **Napa Valley Wine Train** (Map p213;
☎707-253-2111, 800-427-4124; www.winetrain
.com; adult/child from $89/55) offers three-hour
daily trips in vintage Pullman dining cars, from
Napa to St Helena and back, with an optional
winery tour. Trains depart from McKinstry St near
1st St.

Tours

BICYCLE Guided tours start around $90 per day
including bikes, tastings and lunch. Daily rentals
cost $25 to $85; make reservations.

Getaway Adventures (☎707-568-3040, 800-
499-2453; www.getawayadventures.com) Great
guided tours, some combined with kayaking,
of Napa, Sonoma, Calistoga, Healdsburg and
Russian River. Single- and multi-day trips.

Napa Valley Adventure Tours (☎707-259-1833,
877-548-6877; www.napavalleyadventuretours

Napa or Sonoma?

Napa and Sonoma valleys run parallel, a few miles apart, separated by the
narrow, imposing Mayacamas Mountains. The two couldn't be more different.
It's easy to mock aggressively sophisticated Napa, its monuments to ego, trophy
homes and trophy wives, $1000-a-night inns, $40+ tastings and wine-snob
visitors, but Napa makes some of the world's best wines. Constrained by its
geography, it stretches along a single valley, so it's easy to visit. Drawbacks are
high prices and heavy traffic, but there are 400 nearly side-by-side wineries. And
the valley is gorgeous.

Sonoma County is much more down-to-earth and politically left leaning.
You'll see lots more rusted-out pick-ups. Though becoming gentrified, Sonoma
lacks Napa's chic factor (Healdsburg notwithstanding), and locals like it that
way. The wines are more approachable, but the county's 260 wineries are spread
out (see boxed text, p227). If you're here on a weekend, head to Sonoma (County
or Valley), which gets less traffic, but on a weekday, see Napa, too. Ideally
schedule two to four days: one for each valley, and one or two additional for
western Sonoma County.

.com; Oxbow Public Market, 610 1st St, Napa)
Guides tours between wineries, off-road trips,
hiking and kayaking. Daily rentals.

Sonoma Valley Cyclery (Map p228; ☎707-935-3377; www.sonomacyclery.com; 20093 Broadway,
Sonoma) Daily rentals; Sonoma Valley tours.

LIMOUSINE Beau Wine Tours (☎707-938-8001, 800-387-2328; www.beauwinetours.com)
Winery tours in sedans and stretch limos;
charges $60 to $95 per hour (three-hour
minimum weekdays, six hours weekends).

Magnum Tours (☎707-753-0088; www.mag
numwinetours.com) Sedans and specialty
limousines from $65 to $125 per hour
(four-hour minimum, five hours Saturdays).
Exceptional service.

NAPA VALLEY

The birthplace of modern-day Wine
Country is famous for regal cabernet
sauvignons, château-like wineries and
fabulous food. Napa Valley attracts more
than four million visitors a year, each
expecting to be wined, dined, soaked in
hot-springs spas and tucked between
crisp linens.

Darioush winery

Napa Valley Wineries

Cab is king in Napa. No varietal captures
imaginations like the fruit of the cabernet
sauvignon vine – Bordeaux is the French
equivalent – and no wine fetches a higher
price. Other heat-loving varietals, such as
sangiovese and merlot, also thrive here.

DARIOUSH   Winery
(☎707-257-2345; www.darioush.com; 4240
Silverado Trail; tastings $18-35; ⊙10:30am-5pm)
Like a modern-day Persian palace, Darioush ranks high on the fabulosity scale,
with towering columns, Le Corbusier
furniture, Persian rugs and travertine
walls. Though known for cabernet,
Darioush also bottles chardonnay, merlot
and shiraz, all made with 100% of their
respective varietals. Call about wine-and-
cheese pairings. Bottles cost $40 to $80.

CEJA   Winery
(☎707-226-6445; www.cejavineyards.com;
1248 First St; tasting $10; ⊙11am-6pm Sun-
Wed, 11m-8pm Thu-Sat; ⊛) Ceja was founded by former vineyard workers, who
now craft superb pinot noir and unusual
blends, including a great pinot-syrah-
cabernet for $20. The tasting room

Napa Valley

Napa Valley

◎ Sights
1	Casa Nuestra	B2
2	Ceja	B7
3	Culinary Institute of America at Greystone	B3
4	Darioush	B6
5	Di Rosa Art & Nature Preserve	A7
6	Frog's Leap	B4
7	Hall	B3
8	Napa Valley Wine Train Depot	B7
9	Old Faithful Geyser	A1
10	Oxbow Public Market	B7
11	Petrified Forest	A1
12	Schramsberg	A2
13	Silverado Museum	B3
14	Tres Sabores	B4

◎ Activities, Courses & Tours
15	Calistoga Spa Hot Springs	B1
	Spa Solage	(see 25)

◎ Sleeping
16	Carneros Inn	A7
17	El Bonita Motel	B3
18	John Muir Inn	B6
19	Poetry Inn	B5

◎ Eating
20	Étoile	B5
21	Farmstead	B3
22	Gott's Roadside	B3
23	Mustards Grill	B5
	Oxbow Public Market	(see 10)
24	Restaurant at Meadowood	B3
25	Solbar	A1

stays open late, and features interesting art, including Maceo Montoya's mural celebrating winemaking's roots. Bottles cost $20 to $50.

⬛ TRES SABORES   Winery
(☏707-967-8027; www.tressabores.com; 1620 South Whitehall Lane, St Helena; tour & tasting $20; ⏱by appointment; 🐾)

At the valley's westernmost edge, where sloping vineyards meet wooded hillsides, Tres Sabores is a portal to old Napa – no fancy tasting room, no snobbery, just great wine in a spectacular setting. Bucking the cabernet custom, Tres Sabores crafts elegantly structured, Burgundian-style zinfandel, and spritely sauvignon

blanc, which the *New York Times* dubbed a Top 10. Guinea fowl and sheep control pests on the 35-acre estate, while golden labs chase butterflies through gnarled old vines. Reservations essential, and include a tour. Afterward, linger at olive-shaded picnic tables and drink in gorgeous valley views. Bottles cost $22 to $80.

FROG'S LEAP — Winery

(707-963-4704, 800-959-4704; www.frogs leap.com; 8815 Conn Creek Rd; tours & tastings $20, by appointment;) Meandering paths wind through magical gardens and fruit-bearing orchards – pick peaches in July – surrounding an 1884 barn and farmstead with cats and chickens. But more than anything, it's the vibe that's wonderful: casual and down-to-earth, with a major emphasis on *fun*. Sauvignon blanc is its best-known wine, but the merlot merits your attention. There's also a dry, restrained cabernet, atypical in Napa. All wines are organic. Appointments are required. Bottles will set you back $18 to $42.

VINTNERS' COLLECTIVE — Tasting Room

(707-255-7150; www.vintnerscollective.com; 1245 Main St; Napa tasting $25; 11am-6pm) Ditch the car and chill in downtown Napa at this super-cool tasting bar – inside a former 19th-century brothel – that represents 20 high-end boutique wineries that are too small to have their own tasting rooms.

Booking Appointments

Because of strict county zoning laws, many Napa wineries cannot legally receive drop-in visitors; unless you've come strictly to buy, you'll have to call ahead. This is *not* the case with all wineries. We recommend booking one appointment and planning your day around it.

SCHRAMSBERG — Winery

(707-942-4558; www.schramsberg.com; 1400 Schramsberg Rd; tastings $45; by appointment) Napa's second-oldest winery, Schramsberg makes some of California's best brut sparkling wines, and in 1972 was the first domestic wine served at the White House. Blanc de blancs is the signature. The appointment-only tasting and tour (book well ahead) is expensive, but you'll sample all the *tête de cuvées*, not just the low-end wines. Tours include a walk through the caves; bring a sweater. It's located off Peterson Dr. Bottles cost $22 to $100.

Napa

The city of Napa anchors the valley, but the real work happens up-valley in the prettier towns of St Helena, Yountville and Calistoga – the latter more famous for water than wine.

Sights

DI ROSA — Gallery

(707-226-5991; www.dirosaart.org; 5200 Carneros Hwy 121; gallery 9:30am-3pm Wed-Fri, by appointment Sat) West of downtown, scrap-metal sheep graze Carneros vineyards at 217-acre di Rosa, a stunning collection of Northern California art, displayed indoors in galleries and outdoors in sculpture gardens. Reservations are recommended for tours.

Sleeping

CARNEROS INN — Resort $$$

(707-299-4900; www.thecarnerosinn.com; 4048 Sonoma Hwy; r Mon-Fri $485-570, Sat & Sun $650-900;) Carneros Inn's snappy aesthetic and retro small town agricultural theme shatters the predictable Wine Country mold. The semidetached, corrugated-metal cottages look like itinerant housing, but inside they're snappy and chic, with cherry-wood floors, ultrasuede headboards, wood-burning fireplaces, heated-tile bathroom floors, giant tubs and indoor-outdoor showers.

Don't Miss Oxbow Public Market

Graze your way through this gourmet market and plug into the Northern California food scene. Look for Hog Island oysters (six for $15); comfort cooking at celeb-chef Todd Humphries' Kitchen Door (mains $13 to $20); Pica Pica's Venezuelan cornbread sandwiches ($8); standout Cal-Mexican at Casa (tacos $4 to $8); pastries at Ca'Momi ($1.50); and Three Twins certified-organic ice cream ($3.65 single cone). Tuesday is locals night, with many discounts. Tuesday and Saturday mornings, there's a farmers market. Friday nights bring live music. Some stalls remain open till 9pm, even on Sundays, but many close earlier.

NEED TO KNOW

Map p213; www.oxbowpublicmarket.com; 610 & 644 First St, Napa; ⊙9am-7pm Mon-Sat, 10am-5pm Sun; 🖋🚻

Splurge on a vineyard-view room. Linger by day at the hilltop swimming pool, and by night at the bar's outdoor fireplaces. There are two excellent on site restaurants to enjoy.

NAPA RIVER INN　　　　　Hotel **$$$**
(☏707-251-8500, 877-251-8500; www.napariver inn.com; 500 Main St; r incl breakfast $229-349; ✳@🛜🐾) Beside the river, in the 1884 Hatt Building, the inn has upper-midrange rooms in three satellite buildings, ranging from Victoriana to modern. Walkable to restaurants and bars. Dogs get special treatment.

JOHN MUIR INN　　　　　Hotel **$$**
(☏707-257-7220, 800-522-8999; www.johnmuir napa.com; 1998 Trower Ave; r incl breakfast Mon-Fri $130-155, Sat & Sun $170-240; ✳@🛜🏊) Request a remodeled room at this excellent-value hotel, north of downtown. Some contain kitchenettes ($5 extra). There's a hot tub and the staff offer great service.

🍴 Eating

🌱UBUNTU   Vegetarian $$$
(☎707-251-5656; www.ubuntunapa.com; 1140
Main St, Napa; dishes $14-18; ☉dinner nightly,
lunch Sat & Sun; 🎵) The Michelin-starred,
seasonal, vegetarian menu features art-
fully presented natural wonders from the
biodynamic kitchen garden, satisfying
hearty eaters with four to five inspired
small plates, and ecosavvy drinkers with
100-plus sustainably produced wines.

PEARL RESTAURANT   New American $$
(☎707-224-9161; www.therestaurantpearl.com;
1339 Pearl St; mains $14-19; ☉Tue-Sat 5:30-
9pm; 🐾) Meet locals at this dog-friendly
bistro with red-painted concrete floors,
pinewood tables and open-rafter ceilings.
The winning down-to-earth cooking
includes double-cut pork chops, chicken
verde with polenta, steak tacos and the
specialty, oysters.

ALEXIS BAKING CO   Cafe $
(☎707-258-1827; www.alexisbakingcompany
.com; 1517 3rd St; dishes $6-10; ☉7:30am-3pm
Mon-Fri, 7am-3pm Sat, 8am-2pm Sun; 🎵🎵)
Our fave spot for scrambles, granola,
focaccia-bread sandwiches, big cups of
joe and boxed lunches to go.

🔒 Shopping

BETTY'S GIRL
     Women's Clothing, Vintage
(☎707-254-7560; 1144 Main St) Hollywood
costume designer Kim Northrup fits
women with fabulous vintage cocktail
dresses, altering and shipping for no additional charge.

NAPA GENERAL STORE   Gifts
(☎707-259-0762; www.napageneralstore.com;
540 Main St) Finally, clever Wine Country
souvenirs that are reasonably priced. The
on-site wine bar is convenient for non-
shopping husbands.

Left: Kitchen, French Laundry (p218); **Below:** Bardessono
(LEFT) JERRY ALEXANDER/LONELY PLANET IMAGES ©; (BELOW) STEPHEN SAKS/LONELY PLANET IMAGES ©

DISCOVER NAPA & SONOMA WINE COUNTRY YOUNTVILLE

 Information

Napa Valley Welcome Center (☎707-260-0107; www.legendarynapavalley.com; 600 Main St; ☉9am-5pm) Spa deals, wine-tasting passes and comprehensive winery maps.

Yountville

This one-time stagecoach stop, 9 miles north of Napa, is now a major foodie destination, with more Michelin stars per capita than any other American town. There are some good inns here, but it's deathly boring at night. You stay in Yountville to drink with dinner without having to drive afterward. St Helena and Calistoga make better bases.

 Sleeping

BARDESSONO   Luxury Hotel **$$$**
(☎707-204-6000, 877-932-5333; www.bardessono.com; 6524 Yount St; r $600-800, ste from $800; ❉@🛜☈) The outdoors flows indoors at California's first-ever LEED-platinum-certified green hotel, made of recycled everything, styled in Japanese-led austerity, with neutral tones and hard angles that feel exceptionally urban for farm country. Glam pool deck and on-site spa. Tops for a splurge.

POETRY INN   Inn **$$$**
(☎707-944-0646; www.poetryinn.com; 6380 Silverado Trail; r incl breakfast $650-1400; ❉🛜☈) There's no better view of Napa Valley than from this understatedly chic, three-room inn, high on the hills east of Yountville. Rooms are decorated in Arts and Crafts–inspired style, and have private balconies, wood-burning fireplaces, 1000-thread-count linens and enormous baths with indoor-outdoor showers. Bring a ring.

217

If You Like…
Sustainable Napa Valley Wines

If you like the sustainable practices at Frog's Leap (p214), we think you'll want to visit these other green-leaning Napa Valley wineries.

1 CASA NUESTRA
(Map p213; ☎707-963-5783; www.casanuestra .com; 3451 Silverado Trail, St Helena; tastings $10, refundable with purchase; ⏰by appointment; 🚴🐾) An old-school, 1970s-vintage, mom-and-pop outfit producing unusual blends, interesting varietals and 100% cabernet franc. The vineyards are all organic and the buildings are solar powered. Bottles cost $20 to $55.

2 HALL
(Map p213; ☎707-967-2626; www.hallwines .com; 401 St Helena Hwy, St Helena; tastings $15-25; ⏰10am-5:30pm; 🐾) Hall specializes in cabernet franc, sauvignon blanc, merlot and cabernet sauvignon. There's a cool abstract-sculpture garden, a lovely picnic area shaded by mulberry trees (where you can have wines by the glass), and a LEED (Leadership in Energy and Environmental Design) gold-certified winery – California's first. Tours are $45, including barrel tastings. Bottles cost $22 to $80.

3 CADE
(off Map p213; ☎707-965-2746; www.cade winery.com; 360 Howell Mtn Rd, Angwin; tasting $20; ⏰by appointment) Ascend Mt Veeder for drop-dead vistas, 1800ft above the valley floor, at Napa's oh-so-swank, first-ever organically farmed LEED gold-certified winery. Hawks ride thermals at eye level, as you sample bright sauvignon blanc and luscious cabernet sauvignon that's more Bordelaise in style than Californian.

MAISON FLEURIE　　B&B $$$
(☎707-944-2056, 800-788-0369; www.maison fleurienapa.com; 6529 Yount St; r incl breakfast $145-295; ❄@🛜♨) Rooms at this ivy-covered country inn are in a century-old home and carriage house, decorated in French-provincial style. There's a big breakfast, and afternoon wine and *hors d'oeuvres*. Hot tub.

NAPA VALLEY RAILWAY INN　　Theme Inn $$
(☎707-944-2000; www.napavalleyrailwayinn .com; 6523 Washington St, Yountville; r $125-260; ❄@🛜♨) Sleep in a converted railroad car, part of two short trains parked at a central platform. They've little privacy, but are moderately priced. Bring earplugs.

 Eating

Make reservations or you might not eat.

FRENCH LAUNDRY　Californian $$$
(☎707-944-2380; www.frenchlaundry.com; 6640 Washington St; prix fixe incl service charge $270; ⏰dinner daily, lunch Sat & Sun) The pinnacle of California dining, Thomas Keller's French Laundry is epic, a high-wattage culinary experience on par with the world's best. Book two months ahead at 10am sharp, or log onto OpenTable.com precisely at midnight. Avoid tables before 7pm; first-service seating moves faster than the second – sometimes too fast.

ÉTOILE　　Californian $$$
(☎707-944-8844; www.chandon.com; 1 California Dr; lunch $26-31, dinner $32-36; ⏰11:30am-2:30pm & 6-9pm Thu-Mon) Within Chandon winery, Michelin-starred Étoile's is perfect for a lingering white-tablecloth lunch in the vines; ideal when you want to visit a winery and eat a good meal with minimal driving.

PANINOTECA OTTIMO　　Sandwiches, Cafe $
(☎707-945-1229; www.napastyleottimo cafe.com; 6525 Washington St; dishes $8-10; ⏰10am-6pm Mon-Sat, 10am-5pm Sun) TV-chef Michael Chiarello's cafe makes stellar salads and delish paninis (try the slow-roasted pork) that pair well with his organically produced wines. Tops for picnic supplies.

MUSTARDS GRILL   Californian $$$
(707-944-2424; www.mustardsgrill.com; 7399
St Helena Hwy; mains $22-27; 🚲) The valley's
original roadhouse whips up wood-fired
California comfort food – roasted meats,
lamb shanks, pork chops, hearty salads
and sandwiches. Great crowd-pleaser.

St Helena

You'll know you're arriving when traffic
halts. St Helena (ha-*lee*-na) is the Rodeo
Dr of Napa, with fancy boutiques lining
Main St (Hwy 29). The historic downtown
is good for a stroll, with great window-
shopping, but parking is next-to-impossi-
ble on summer weekends.

The **St Helena Welcome Center**
(707-963-4456, 800-799-6456; www.sthelena
.com; 657 Main St; 🕙9am-5pm Mon-Fri) has
information and lodging assistance.

 **Sights & Activities**

FREE **SILVERADO MUSEUM**   Museum
(707-963-3757; www.silveradomuseum.org;
1490 Library Lane; 🕙noon-4pm Tue-Sat)
Contains a fascinating collection of
Robert Louis Stevenson memorabilia. In
1880, the author – then sick, penniless
and unknown – stayed in an abandoned
bunkhouse at the old Silverado Mine,
on Mt St Helena (p224), with his wife,
Fanny Osbourne; his novel *The Silverado*

Squatters is based on his time there. To
reach Library Lane, turn east off Hwy 29
at the Adams St traffic light and cross the
railroad tracks.

**CULINARY INSTITUTE OF AMERICA AT
GREYSTONE**   Cooking School
(707-967-2320; 2555 Main St; mains $25-29,
cooking demonstration $20; 🕙restaurant
11:30am-9pm, cooking demonstrations 1:30pm
Sat & Sun) An 1889 stone chateau houses
a gadget- and cookbook-filled **culinary
shop**; fine **restaurant**; weekend **cook-
ing demonstrations**; and **wine-tasting
classes** by luminaries in the field, includ-
ing Karen MacNeil, author of *The Wine
Bible*.

 **Sleeping**

EL BONITA MOTEL   Motel $$
(707-963-3216, 800-541-3284; www.el
bonita.com; 195 Main St, St Helena; $119-179;
❄@🛜🏊🐾) Book in advance to secure
a room at this sought-after motel, with
up-to-date rooms (quietest are in back),
attractive grounds, hot tub and sauna.

HOTEL ST HELENA   Historic Hotel $$
(707-963-4388; www.hotelsthelena.net; 1309
Main St; r $125-235, without bath $105-165;
❄🛜) Decorated with period furnish-
ings, this frayed-at-the-edges 1881 hotel
sits right downtown. Rooms are tiny, but

Flying & Ballooning

Wine Country is stunning from the air – a multihued tapestry of undulating
hills, deep valleys and rambling vineyards. Make reservations.

The **Vintage Aircraft Company** (Map p228; 707-938-2444; www.vintageaircraft
.com; 23982 Arnold Dr) flies over Sonoma in a vintage biplane with an awesome
pilot who'll do loop-de-loops on request (add $50). Twenty-minute tours cost
$175/270 for one/two adults.

Napa Valley's signature hot-air balloon flights leave early, around 6am or 7am,
when the air is coolest; they usually include a champagne breakfast on landing.
Adults pay about $200 to $250, and kids $130 to $150. Call **Balloons Above the
Valley** (707-253-2222, 800-464-6824; www.balloonrides.com) or **Napa Valley Balloons**
(707-944-0228, 800-253-2224; www.napavalleyballoons.com), both in Yountville.

If You Like… Splurge-Worthy Restaurants

If you like the culinary delights of French Laundry (p218), make reservations at these top tables in Wine Country.

1 AD HOC

(☏707-944-2487; www.adhocrestaurant.com; 6476 Washington St, Yountville; menu $48; ⏱dinner Wed-Mon, 10:30am-2pm Sun) Another winning formula by Yountville's culinary oligarch, Thomas Keller, Ad Hoc serves the master's favorite American home cooking in four-course family-style menus, with no variations except for dietary restrictions.

2 CYRUS

(☏707-433-3311; www.cyrusrestaurant.com; 29 North St, Healdsburg; fixed-price menu $102-130; ⏱dinner Thu-Mon, lunch Sat) Napa's venerable French Laundry has stiff competition in swanky Cyrus, an ultrachic dining room in the great tradition of the French country auberge. The emphasis is on luxury foods, expertly prepared with a French sensibility and flavored with global spices, as in the signature Thai-marinated lobster. From the caviar cart to the cheese course, a meal at Cyrus is one to remember.

3 RESTAURANT AT MEADOWOOD

(Map p213; ☏707-967-1205; www.meadowood.com; 900 Meadowood Lane, St Helena; 4-/9-course menu $125/225; ⏱5:30pm-10pm Mon-Sat) If you couldn't score reservations at French Laundry, fear not: the clubby Restaurant at Meadowood – the valley's only other Michelin-three-star restaurant – has a more sensibly priced menu, elegant but unfussy forest-view dining room, and lavish haute cuisine that's never too esoteric.

4 JOLÉ

(☏707-942-5938; www.jolerestaurant.com; 1457 Lincoln Ave, Calistoga; mains $15-20; ⏱5-9pm Sun-Thu, 5-10pm Fri & Sat) The earthy and inventive farm-to-table small plates at chef-owned Jolé evolve seasonally, and may include such dishes as local sole with tangy miniature Napa grapes, caramelized brussels sprouts with capers, and organic Baldwin apple strudel with housemade burnt-caramel ice cream. Four courses cost $50.

good value, especially those with shared bathroom. No elevator.

Eating

Make reservations where possible.

GOTT'S ROADSIDE (TAYLOR'S AUTO REFRESHER) Burgers $$

(☏707-963-3486; www.gottsroadside.com; 933 Main St; dishes $8-15; ⏱10:30am-9pm; ♿) Wiggle your toes in the grass and feast on all-natural burgers, Cobb salads and fried calamari at this classic roadside drive-in, whose original name, 'Taylor's Auto Refresher,' is still listed on the roadside sign. Avoid big weekend waits by calling in your order. There's another branch at Oxbow Public Market (p215).

FARMSTEAD New American $$$

(☏707-963-9181; www.farmsteadnapa.com; 738 Main St; mains $16-26; ⏱11:30am-9pm) A cavernous open-truss barn with big leather booths and rocking-chair porch, Farmstead grows many of its own ingredients – including grass-fed beef – for is earthy menu that highlights wood-fired cooking.

Shopping

Main St is lined with high-end boutiques (think $100 socks), but some mom-and-pop shops remain.

WOODHOUSE CHOCOLATES Food

(www.woodhousechocolate.com; 1367 Main St) Woodhouse looks more like Tiffany & Co than a candy shop, with chocolates similarly priced, but they're made in town and their quality is beyond reproach.

NAPA SOAP COMPANY Beauty

(www.napasoap.com; 651 Main St) Hand-crafted ecofriendly bath products, locally produced.

Calistoga

The least gentrified town in Napa Valley feels refreshingly simple, with an old-fashioned main street lined with shops, not boutiques, and diverse characters wandering the sidewalks.

Calistoga is synonymous with the mineral water bearing its name, bottled here since 1924. Its springs and geysers have earned it the nickname the 'hot springs of the West.'

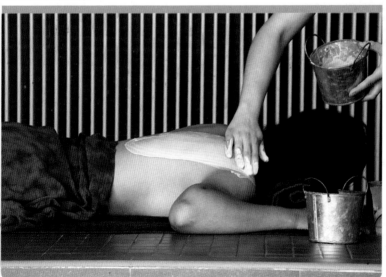 Sights & Activities

Calistoga is famous for hot-spring spas and mud-bath emporiums, where you're buried in hot mud and emerge feeling supple, detoxified and enlivened. (The mud is made with volcanic ash and peat; the higher the ash content, the better the bath.)

Packages take 60 to 90 minutes and cost $70 to $90. You start semi-submerged in hot mud, then soak in hot mineral water. A steam bath and blanket-wrap follow. The treatment can be extended with a massage, increasing the cost to $130 and up.

Baths can be taken solo or, at some spas, as couples. Variations include thin, painted-on clay-mud wraps (called 'fango' baths, good for those uncomfortable sitting in mud), herbal wraps, seaweed baths and various massage treatments. Discount coupons are sometimes available from the visitors center. Book ahead, especially on summer weekends. Reservations essential at all spas.

The following spas in downtown Calistoga offer one-day packages. Some offer discounted spa-lodging packages.

INDIAN SPRINGS
Spa

(☎ 707-942-4913; www.indianspringscalistoga .com; 1712 Lincoln Ave; ⊗8am-9pm) The longest continually operating spa and original Calistoga resort has concrete mud tubs and mines its own ash. Treatments include use of the huge, hot-spring-fed pool. Great cucumber body lotion.

SPA SOLAGE
Spa

(Map p213; ☎ 707-226-0825; www.solagecalisto ga.com; 755 Silverado Trail; ⊗8am-8pm) Chichi, austere, top-end spa, with couples' rooms and a fango-mud bar for DIY paint-on treatments. Also has zero-gravity chairs for blanket wraps, and a clothing-optional pool.

Skin treatment, Spa Solage

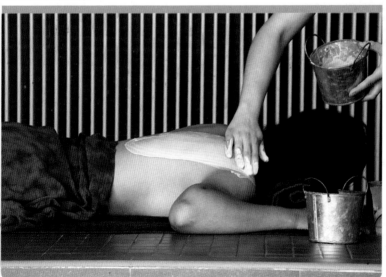

ROGER RESSMEYER/CORBIS ©

Don't Miss Old Faithful Geyser

Calistoga's mini version of Yellowstone's Old Faithful shoots boiling water 60ft to 100ft into the air, every 30 minutes. The vibe is pure roadside Americana, with folksy hand-painted interpretive exhibits, picnicking and a little petting zoo, where you can come nose-to-nose with llamas. It's 2 miles north of town, off Silverado Trail. Look for discount coupons around town.

NEED TO KNOW

Map p213; ☑707-942-6463; www.oldfaithfulgeyser.com; 1299 Tubbs Lane; adult/child $10/free; ⊙9am-6pm summer, to 5pm winter; 👪

CALISTOGA SPA HOT SPRINGS   Spa
(☑707-942-6269, 866-822-5772; www.calisto gaspa.com; 1006 Washington St; ⊙appointments 8:30am-4:30pm Tue-Thu, to 9pm Fri-Mon; 👪) Traditional mud baths and massage at a motel complex with two huge **swimming pools** (⊙10am-9pm) where kids can play while you soak (pool passes $25).

 Sleeping

MOUNTAIN HOME RANCH   Lodge, B&B $$
(☑707-942-6616; www.mountainhomeranch .com; 3400 Mountain Home Ranch Rd;

r $109-119, cabin $119-144, without bath $69; @ 🛜 ≋ 👪 🐾) In continuous operation since 1913, this 340-acre homestead ranch is a flashback to old California. Doubling as a retreat center, the ranch has simple lodge rooms and rustic freestanding cabins, some with kitchens and fireplaces, ideal for families, but you may be here during someone else's family reunion or spiritual quest. No matter. With miles of oak-woodland trails, a hilltop swimming pool, private lake with canoe-ing and fishing, and hike-to warm springs in a magical fault-line canyon, you may hardly notice – and you may never make it to a single winery. Breakfast included, but you'll have to drive 15 minutes to town for dinner.

INDIAN SPRINGS RESORT   Resort $$$

(707-942-4913; www.indianspringscalistoga .com; 1712 Lincoln Ave; motel r $229-299, bungalow $259-349, 2-bedroom bungalow $359-419; ❄️ 🛜 ☀️ 🛝) The definitive old-school Calistoga resort, Indian Springs has bungalows facing a central lawn with palm trees, shuffleboard, bocce, hammocks and Weber grills – not unlike a vintage Florida resort. Some bungalows sleep six. There are also top-end motel-style rooms. Huge hot-springs-fed swimming pool.

DR WILKINSON'S MOTEL & HIDEAWAY COTTAGES   Motel, Cottages $$

(707-942-4102; www.drwilkinson.com; 1507 Lincoln Ave; r $149-255, cottages $165-270; ❄️ 🛜 ☀️) This good-value vintage-1950s motel has well-kept rooms facing a swimming-pool courtyard. There's no hot tub, but there are three pools (one indoors) and mud baths. Doc Wilkinson's also rents simple stand-alone cottages, with kitchens, at the affiliated Hideaway Cottages.

Eating

📝 SOLBAR   Californian $$$

(707-226-0850; www.solagecalistoga.com; 755 Silverado Trail; lunch $15-19, dinner $30-37; 🕖7-11am, 11:30am-3pm, 5:30-9pm) At last Calistoga has a restaurant on par with others down-valley. The ag-chic look is spare, with concrete floors, exposed-wood tables and soaring ceilings. Maximizing seasonal produce, each dish is elegantly composed, some with tongue-in-cheek playfulness – to wit, a first-course fried-green-tomato BLT, with bacon-fat-fried egg, on English muffin. The menu is both light and hearty, so you can mind calories. Reservations are essential.

CALISTOGA INN & BREWERY   American $$

(707-942-4101; www.calistogainn.com; 1250 Lincoln Ave; lunch $9-13, dinner $14-26; 🕖11:30am-3pm & 5:30-9pm) Locals crowd the outdoor beer garden Sundays. Midweek we prefer the country dining room and its big oakwood tables, a homey spot for pot roast and other simple American dishes. There's live music summer weekends.

Sculptures by Robert Arneson and Viola Frey, di Rosa (p214)

Drinking

SOLBAR
Bar

(☎707-226-0850; www.solagecalistoga.com; 755 Silverado Trail) Sip cocktails and wine on cane sofas beside outdoor fireplaces and a palm-lined pool. Wear white.

BRANNAN'S GRILL
Bar

(☎707-942-2233; www.brannansgrill.com; 1374 Lincoln Ave) Calistoga's most handsome restaurant; the mahogany bar is great for martinis and microbrews, especially weekends, when jazz combos sometimes play.

Shopping

WINE GARAGE
Wine

(☎707-942-5332; www.winegarage.net; 1020 Foothill Blvd) Every bottle costs under $25 at this winning wine store, formerly a service station.

CALISTOGA POTTERY
Ceramics

(☎707-942-0216; www.calistogapottery.com; 1001 Foothill Blvd) Winemakers aren't the only artisans in Napa. Watch potters throw vases, bowls and plates, all for sale.

Information

Chamber of Commerce & Visitors Center
(☎707-942-6333, 866-306-5588; www
.calistogavisitors.com; 1133 Washington St;
⏱9am-5pm)

Around Calistoga

FREE ROBERT LOUIS STEVENSON
STATE PARK
Mountain

(☎707-942-4575; www.parks.ca.gov) The long-extinct volcanic cone of Mt St Helena marks the valley's end, 8 miles north of Calistoga. The undeveloped state park on Hwy 29 often gets snow in winter.

It's a strenuous 5-mile climb to the peak's 4343ft summit, but what a view – 200 miles on a clear winter's day. Check conditions before setting out. Also consider 2.2-mile one-way Table Rock Trail (go south from the summit parking area) for drop-dead valley views. Temperatures are best in wildflower season, February to May; fall is prettiest, when the vineyards change colors.

The park includes the site of the Silverado Mine where Stevenson and his wife honeymooned in 1880.

SAFARI WEST
Wildlife Reserve

(☎707-579-2551, 800-616-2695; www.safariwest.com; 3115 Porter Creek Rd; adult/child $68/30; 👪) Giraffes in Wine Country? Whadya know! Safari West covers 400 acres and protects zebras, cheetahs and other exotic animals, which mostly roam free. See them on a guided

Lemurs, Safari West
JUDY BELLAH/LONELY PLANET IMAGES ©

The GIANT
Length 60 ft.
Width 6 ft.

JERRY ALEXANDER/LONELY PLANET IMAGES ©

Don't Miss **Petrified Forest**

Three million years ago, a volcanic eruption at nearby Mt St Helena blew down a stand of redwoods between Calistoga and Santa Rosa. The trees fell in the same direction, away from the blast, and were covered in ash and mud. Over the millennia, the mighty giants' trunks turned to stone; gradually the overlay eroded, exposing them. The first stumps were discovered in 1870. A monument marks Robert Louis Stevenson's 1880 visit. He describes it in *The Silverado Squatters*.

It's 5 miles northwest of town, off Hwy 128. Check online for 10%-off coupons.

NEED TO KNOW
Map p213; ☎707-942-6667; www.petrifiedforest.org; 4100 Petrified Forest Rd; adult/child $10/5; ⊙9am-7pm summer, to 5pm winter

three-hour safari in open-sided jeeps; reservations required. You'll also walk thorough an aviary and lemur condo. The reservations-only cafe serves lunch and dinner. If you're feeling adventurous, stay overnight in nifty canvas-sided **tent cabins** (cabins incl breakfast $200-295), right in the preserve.

SONOMA VALLEY

We have a soft spot for Sonoma's folksy ways. Unlike in fancy Napa, nobody cares if you drive a clunker and vote Green. Locals call it 'Slow-noma.' Anchoring the bucolic 17-mile-long Sonoma Valley, the town of Sonoma makes a great jumping-off point for exploring Wine Country – it's only an hour from San Francisco – and has a marvelous sense of place, with storied 19th-century historical sights surrounding the state's largest town square. If you have more than a day, explore Sonoma's quiet, rustic side along the Russian River Valley (p232) and work your way to the sea.

JERRY ALEXANDER/LONELY PLANET IMAGES ©

Sonoma Valley Wineries

Rolling grass-covered hills rise from 17-mile-long Sonoma Valley. Its 40 wineries get less attention than Napa's, but many are equally good. If you love zinfandel and syrah, you're in for a treat.

Picnicking is allowed at Sonoma wineries. Get maps and discount coupons in the town of Sonoma or, if you're approaching from the south, the **Sonoma Valley Visitors Bureau** (707-935-4747; www.sonomavalley.com; Cornerstone Gardens, 23570 Hwy 121; 10am-4pm) at Cornerstone Gardens (p229).

GUNDLACH-BUNDSCHU   Winery
(707-938-5277; www.gunbun.com; 2000 Denmark St; tastings $10; 11am-4:30pm) One of Sonoma Valley's oldest and prettiest, Gundlach-Bundschu looks like a storybook castle. Founded in 1858 by Bavarian immigrant Jacob Gundlach, it's now at the cutting edge of sustainability. Signature wines are rieslings and gewürztraminers, but 'Gun-Bun' was the first American winery to produce 100% merlot. Tours of the 2000-barrel cave ($20) are available by reservation. Down a winding lane, it's a good bike-to winery, with picnicking,

hiking and a small lake. Bottles cost $22 to $40.

LITTLE VINEYARDS   Winery
(707-996-2750; www.littlevineyards.com; 15188 Sonoma Hwy, Glen Ellen; tastings $5; 11am-4:30pm Thu-Mon;) The name fits at this family-owned small-scale winery, long on atmosphere, with a lazy dog to greet you and a weathered, cigarette-burned tasting bar, which Jack London drank at (before it was moved here). The tiny tasting room is good for shy folks who dislike crowds. If you're new to wine, consider the $20 introductory class (call ahead). Good picnicking on the vineyard-view terrace. The big reds include syrah, petite sirah, zin, cab and several delish blends. Bottles cost $17 to $35. Also rents a cottage in the vines.

BR COHN   Winery
(707-938-4064; www.brcohn.com; 15000 Sonoma Hwy, Glen Ellen; tasting $10, refundable with purchase; 10am-5pm) Picnic like a rock star at always-busy BR Cohn, whose founder managed '70s superband the Doobie Brothers before moving on to make outstanding organic olive oils and fine wines – including excellent caber-

net sauvignon, unusual in Sonoma. In autumn, he throws benefit concerts, amid the olives, by the likes of Skynyrd and the Doobies. Bottles cost $16 to $55.

BENZIGER *Winery*

(☎888-490-2739; www.benziger.com; 1883 London Ranch Rd, Glen Ellen; tasting $10-20, tram tour incl tasting adult/child $15/5; ☉10am-5pm; 👪) If you're new to wine, make Benziger your first stop for Sonoma's best crash course in winemaking. The worthwhile, non-reservable tour includes an open-air tram ride through biodynamic vineyards, and a four-wine tasting. Kids love the peacocks. The large-production wine's OK (head for the reserves); the tour's the thing. Bottles cost $15 to $80.

WELLINGTON *Winery*

(☎707-939-0708; www.wellingtonvineyards .com; 11600 Dunbar Rd, Glen Ellen; tastings $5) Known for port (including a white) and meaty reds, Wellington makes great zinfandel, one from vines planted in 1892.

Wow, what color! The noir de noir is a cult favorite. Alas, servers have vineyard views, while you face the warehouse. Bottles cost $15 to $30.

KAZ *Winery*

(☎707-833-2536; www.kazwinery.com; 233 Adobe Canyon Rd, Kenwood; tastings $5; ☉11am-5pm Fri-Mon; 👪👶) Sonoma's cult favorite, supercool Kaz is about blends: whatever's in the organic vineyards goes into the wine – and they're blended at crush, not during fermentation. Expect lesser-known varietals like alicante bouchet and Lenoir, and a worthwhile cabernet-merlot blend. Kids can sample grape juice, then run around the playground out back, while you sift through LPs and pop your favorites onto the turntable. Crazy fun. Dogs welcome. Bottles cost $20 to $48.

Sonoma & Around

Fancy boutiques may lately be replacing hardware stores, but Sonoma still retains an old-fashioned charm, thanks to the plaza – California's largest town square –

A Wine Country Primer

When people talk about Sonoma, they're referring to the *whole* county, which unlike Napa is huge. It extends all the way from the coast, up the Russian River Valley, into Sonoma Valley and eastward to Napa Valley; in the south it stretches from San Pablo Bay (an extension of San Francisco Bay) to Healdsburg in the north. It's essential to break Sonoma down by district.

West County refers to everything west of Hwy 101 and includes the **Russian River Valley** and the coast. **Sonoma Valley** stretches north–south along Hwy 12. In northern Sonoma County, **Alexander Valley** lies east of Healdsburg, and **Dry Creek Valley** lies north of Healdsburg. In the south, **Carneros** straddles the Sonoma–Napa border, north of San Pablo Bay. Each region has its own particular wines; what grows where depends upon the weather.

Inland valleys get hot; coastal regions stay cool. In West County and Carneros, nighttime fog blankets the vineyards. Burgundy-style wines do best, particularly pinot noir and chardonnay. Further inland, Alexander, Sonoma and much of Dry Creek Valleys (as well as Napa Valley) are fog-protected. Here, Bordeaux-style wines thrive, especially cabernet sauvignon, sauvignon blanc, merlot and other heat-loving varieties. For California's famous cabernets, head to Napa. Zinfandel and Rhône-style varieties, such as syrah and viognier, grow in both regions, warm and cool. In cooler climes, resultant wines are lighter, more elegant; in warmer areas they are heavier and more rustic.

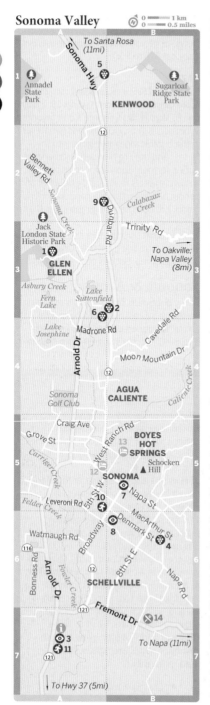

To Santa Rosa
(11mi)

Sonoma Hwy

KENWOOD

Annadel
State
Park

Sugarloaf
Ridge State
Park

Bennett
Valley Rd

Sonoma Creek

Calabazaz
Creek

Dunbar Rd

Trinity Rd

To Oakville;
Napa Valley
(8mi)

Jack
London State
Historic Park

**GLEN
ELLEN**

Asbury Creek

Fern
Lake

Lake
Suttonfield

Lake
Josephine

Madrone Rd

Cavedale Rd

Arnold Dr

Moon Mountain Dr

Caliente Creek

Sonoma
Golf Club

**AGUA
CALIENTE**

Craig Ave

Grove St

West Ranch Rd

**BOYES
HOT
SPRINGS**

Schocken
▲ Hill

Carriger Creek

SONOMA

Napa St

5th St W

Leveroni Rd

MacArthur St

Denmark St

Felder Creek

Watmaugh Rd

Broadway

8th St E

Napa Rd

SCHELLVILLE

Bonuess Rd

Arnold Dr

Fowler Creek

Fremont Dr

To Napa (11mi)

To Hwy 37 (5mi)

Sonoma Valley

⊙ Sights
1	Benziger	A3
2	BR Cohn	B3
3	Cornerstone Gardens	A7
4	Gundlach-Bundschu	B6
5	Kaz	A1
6	Little Vineyards	A3
7	Sonoma Plaza	B5
8	Traintown	B6
9	Wellington	A2

✪ Activities, Courses & Tours
10	Sonoma Valley Cyclery	A5
11	Vintage Aircraft Company	A7

⊜ Sleeping
12	El Pueblo Inn	A5
13	Sonoma Chalet	B5

✖ Eating
14	Fremont Diner	B7

and its surrounding frozen-in-time historic buildings. You can legally drink on the plaza, a rarity in California parks.

 Sights

SONOMA PLAZA   Square
Smack in the center of the plaza, the Mission-revival-style **city hall**, built 1906–08, has identical facades on four sides, reportedly because plaza businesses all demanded City Hall face their direction. At the plaza's northeast corner, the **Bear Flag Monument** marks Sonoma's moment of revolutionary glory. The town shows up for the **farmers market** (⏱5:30-8pm Tue Apr-Oct), where you can sample Sonoma's exquisite produce.

**SONOMA STATE
HISTORIC PARK**   Historic Buildings
(☎707-938-1519; www.parks.ca.gov; adult/child $3/2; ⏱10am-5pm Tue-Sun) The park is comprised of multiple sites. The **Mission San Francisco Solano de Sonoma** (E Spain St), at the plaza's northeast corner, was built in 1823, in part to forestall the Russian coastal colony at Fort Ross from moving inland. The mission was the 21st and final California mission, and the only one

built during the Mexican period (the rest were founded by the Spanish). It marks the northernmost point on El Camino Real. Five of the mission's original rooms remain. The not-to-be-missed chapel dates from 1841.

The adobe **Sonoma Barracks** (E Spain St; ☉daily) was built by Vallejo between 1836 and 1840 to house Mexican troops, but it became the capital of a rogue nation on June 14, 1846, when American settlers, of varying sobriety, surprised the guards and declared an independent 'California Republc' [sic] with a homemade flag featuring a blotchy bear. The US took over the republic a month later, but abandoned the barracks during the Gold Rush, leaving Vallejo to turn then into (what else?) a winery in 1860. Today, displays describe life during the Mexican and American periods.

A half-mile northwest, the lovely **Vallejo Home** (363 3rd St W), otherwise known as Lachryma Montis (Latin for 'Tears of the Mountain'), was built 1851–52 for General Vallejo. It's named for the spring on the property; the Vallejo family later made a handy income piping water to town. The property remained in the family until 1933, when the state of California purchased it, retaining much of its original furnishings. A bike path leads to the house from downtown.

FREE **CORNERSTONE GARDENS** Gardens
(☎707-933-3010; www.cornerstonegardens.com; 23570 Arnold Dr; ☉10am-4pm; ♿) There's nothing traditional about Cornerstone Gardens, which showcase the work of 19 renowned avant-garde landscape designers. We especially love Pamela Burton's 'Earth Walk,' which descends into the ground; and Planet Horticulture's 'Rise,' which exaggerates space. Let the kids run around while you explore top-notch garden shops and gather information from the on site **Sonoma Valley Visitors Bureau** (☎707-935-4747; www.sonomavalley.com; ☉10am-4pm), then refuel at the cafe. Look for the enormous blue chair at road's edge.

TRAINTOWN Amusement Park
(☎707-938-3912; www.traintown.com; 20264 Broadway; ☉10am-5pm daily summer, Fri-Sun only mid-Sep–late May) Little kids adore Traintown, 1 mile south of the plaza. A miniature steam engine makes 20-minute

Vegetable stall, Sonoma Plaza farmers market

loops ($4.75), and there are vintage amusement-park rides ($2.75 per ride), including a carousel and a Ferris wheel.

Sleeping

Off-season rates plummet. Reserve ahead.

SONOMA CHALET B&B, Cottages $$
(☎707-938-3129; www.sonomachalet.com; 18935 5th St W; r without bath $125, with bath $140-180, cottages $190-225; ❄) An old farmstead surrounded by rolling hills, Sonoma Chalet has rooms in a Swiss chalet–style house adorned with little balconies and country-style bric-a-brac. We love the freestanding cottages; Laura's has a wood-burning fireplace. Breakfast is served on a deck overlooking a nature preserve. No air-con in rooms with shared bath. No phones, no internet.

SWISS HOTEL Historic Hotel $$
(☎707-938-2884; www.swisshotelsonoma.com; 18 W Spain St; r incl breakfast Mon-Fri $150-170, Sat & Sun $200-240; ❄ 🛜) It opened in 1905, so you'll forgive the wavy floors. Think knotty pine and wicker. In the morning sip coffee on the shared plaza-view balcony. Downstairs there's a raucous bar and restaurant. No parking lot or elevator.

EL PUEBLO INN Motel $$
(☎707-996-3651, 800-900-8844; www.elpueblo inn.com; 896 W Napa St; r incl breakfast $169-289; ❄🛜@☁👪) One mile west of downtown, family-owned El Pueblo has surprisingly cushy rooms with great beds. The big lawns and the heated pool are perfect for kids; parents appreciate the 24-hour hot tub.

Eating

🍃**FREMONT DINER** American $
(☎707-938-7370; 2698 Fremont Dr/Hwy 121; mains $8-11; ⏰8am-3pm Mon-Fri, 7am-4pm Sat & Sun; 👪) Lines snake out the door weekends at this order-at-the-counter, farm-to-table roadside diner. Snag a table indoors or out and feast on ricotta pancakes with real maple syrup, chicken and waffles, oyster po' boys and finger-licking barbecue. Arrive early to beat the line.

🍃**CAFÉ LA HAYE**
New American $$$
(☎707-935-5994; www.cafelahaye .com; 140 E Napa St; mains $15-25; ⏰5:30-9pm Tue-Sat) One of Sonoma's top tables for earthy New American cooking, made with produce sourced from within 60 miles, La Haye's tiny dining room gets packed cheek-by-jowl and service can border on perfunctory, but the clean simplicity and flavor-packed cooking make it many foodies' first choice. Reserve well ahead.

Jack London State Historic Park
JERRY ALEXANDER/LONELY PLANET IMAGES ©

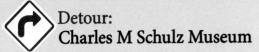

Detour: Charles M Schulz Museum

Charles Schulz, creator of *Peanuts* cartoons, was a long-term Santa Rosa resident. Born in 1922, he published his first drawing in 1937, introduced the world to Snoopy and Charlie Brown in 1950, and produced *Peanuts* cartoons until just before his death in 2000.

At the **museum** (☎707-579-4452; www.schulzmuseum.org; 2301 Hardies Lane, Santa Rosa; adult/child $10/5; ⏰11am-5pm Mon-Fri, 10am-5pm Sat & Sun, closed Tue Sep-May; ♿) in Santa Rosa, a glass wall overlooks a courtyard with a Snoopy labyrinth. Exhibits include *Peanuts*-related art and Schulz's actual studio. Skip Snoopy's Gallery gift shop; the museum has the good stuff.

GIRL & THE FIG

French-Californian $$$

(☎707-938-3634; www.thegirlandthefig.com; 110 W Spain St; lunch mains $10-15, dinner mains $18-26) For a festive evening, book a garden table at this French-provincial bistro. We like the small plates ($11 to $14), especially the steamed mussels with matchstick fries, and duck confit with lentils. Weekday three-course prix-fixe costs $34; add $10 for wine. Stellar cheeses. Reservations essential.

🍷 Drinking

SWISS HOTEL   Bar

(18 W Spain St) Locals and tourists crowd the 1909 Swiss Hotel for afternoon cocktails.

ENOTECA DELLA SANTINA   Wine Bar

(www.enotecadellasantina.com; 127 E Napa St; ⏰2-10pm Wed-Fri, noon-11pm Sat, 4-10pm Tue & Sun) Thirty global vintages by the glass allow you to compare what you're tasting in California with the rest of the world's wines.

🔒 Shopping

VELLA CHEESE CO   Food

(☎707-928-3232; www.vellacheese.com; 315 2nd St E) Known for its dry-jack cheeses (made here since the 1930s), Vella also makes good Mezzo Secco with cocoa powder–dusted rind. Staff will vacuum-pack for shipping.

TIDDLE E WINKS   Toys

(☎7070-939-6993; www.tiddleewinks.com; 115 E Napa St; ♿) Vintage five-and-dime, with classic, mid-20th-century toys.

ⓘ Information

Sonoma Valley Visitors Bureau (☎707-996-1090; www.sonomavalley.com; 453 1st St E; ⏰9am-6pm Jul-Sep, to 5pm Oct-Jun) Arranges accommodations; has a good walking-tour pamphlet and information on events. There's another location at Cornerstone Gardens (p229).

Jack London State Historic Park

Napa has Robert Louis Stevenson, but Sonoma's got Jack London. This 1400-acre **park** (☎707-938-5216; www.jacklondonpark.com; 2400 London Ranch Rd, Glen Ellen; parking $8; ⏰10am-5pm Thu-Mon; ♿) traces the last years of the author's life.

Changing occupations from Oakland fisherman to Alaska gold prospector to Pacific yachtsman – and novelist on the side – London (1876–1916) ultimately took up farming. He bought Beauty Ranch in 1905 and moved there in 1910. With his second wife, Charmian, he lived and wrote in a small cottage while his mansion, Wolf House, was under construction. On the eve of its completion in 1913, it burned

down. The disaster devastated London, and although he toyed with rebuilding, he died before construction got underway. His widow, Charmian, built the House of Happy Walls, which has been preserved as a museum. It's a half-mile walk from there to the remains of Wolf House, passing London's grave along the way. Other paths wind around the farm to the cottage where he lived and worked. Miles of hiking trails (some open to mountain bikes) weave through oak-dotted woodlands, between 600ft and 2300ft elevation. Watch for poison oak. NB: State budget cuts may temporarily close this park; call ahead.

HEALDSBURG & THE RUSSIAN RIVER

Lesser-known West Sonoma County was formerly famous for its apple farms and vacation cottages. Lately vineyards are replacing the orchards, and the Russian River has now taken its place among California's important wine appellations for superb pinot noir.

'The River,' as locals call it, has long been a summertime weekend destination for Northern Californians, who come to canoe, wander country lanes, taste wine, hike redwood forests and live at a lazy pace. In winter the river floods, and nobody's here.

The Russian River begins in the mountains north of Ukiah, in Mendocino County, but the most famous sections lie southwest of Healdsburg, where it cuts a serpentine course toward the sea.

Russian River Area Wineries

Pinot noir does beautifully here, as does chardonnay, which also grows in hotter regions, but prefers the longer 'hang time' of cooler climes.

Russian River Valley

The highest concentration of wineries is along **Westside Rd**, between Guerneville and Healdsburg.

IRON HORSE VINEYARDS
Winery

(☎707-887-1507; www.ironhorsevineyards
.com; 9786 Ross Station Rd, Sebastopol; tastings
$10-20, refundable with purchase; ⊙10am-
4:30pm; 👶) Atop a hill with drop-dead
views over the county, Iron Horse is
known for pinot noir and sparkling wines,
which the White House often pours. The
outdoor tasting room is refreshingly un-
fussy; when you're done with your wine,
pour it in the grass. Located off Hwy 116.
Bottles cost $20 to $85.

PORTER CREEK
Winery

(☎707-433-6321; www.portercreekvineyards
.com; 8735 Westside Rd, Healdsburg; tastings
free; 👶) Inside a vintage 1920s garage,
Porter Creek's tasting bar is a former
bowling-alley lane, plunked atop barrels.
Porter is old-school Northern California and an early pioneer in biodynamic
farming. High-acid, food-friendly pinot
noir and chardonnay are specialties, but
there's silky zinfandel and other Burgun-
dian- and Rhône-style wines, too. Check
out the aviary and yurt. Bottles cost $24
to $65.

DE LA MONTANYA
Winery

(☎707-433-3711; www.dlmwine.com; 2651 Westside Rd at Foreman Lane, Healdsburg; tastings $5,
refundable with purchase; ⊙call ahead Mon-Thu,
11am-4:30pm Fri-Sun; 👶) On weekends,
meet the practical-joker winemaker at
this tiny winery, known for 17 small-batch
varieties made with estate-grown fruit.
Viognier, primitivo, pinot and cabernet
are signatures; the 'summer white' and
gewürztraminer are great back-porch
wines. Apple-shaded picnic area and
bocce ball, too. Bottles $20 to $60.

Healdsburg
Once a sleepy ag town best known for
its Future Farmers of America parade,
Healdsburg has emerged as northern
Sonoma County's culinary capital.

233

Detour:
Dry Creek Valley

Hemmed in by 2000ft-high mountains, Dry Creek Valley is relatively warm, ideal for sauvignon blanc and zinfandel, and in some places cabernet sauvignon. It's west of Hwy 101, between Healdsburg and Lake Sonoma.

Preston Vineyards (☎707-433-3372; www.prestonvineyards.com; 9282 W Dry Creek Rd; tasting $10, refundable with purchase; ⏱11am-4:30pm; 🚲) An early leader in organics, Lou Preston's 19th-century farm feels like old Sonoma County. The signature is citrusy sauvignon blanc, but try the Rhône varietals and small-lot wines: mourvédre, viognier, cinsault and cult-favorite barbera. Bottles cost $24 to $38.

Truett-Hurst (☎707-433-9545; www.truetthurst.com; 5610 Dry Creek Rd; tastings $5, refundable with purchase; ⏱10am-5pm; 👪) Pull up an Adirondack chair and picnic creekside at Truett-Hurst, Dry Creek's newest biodynamic winery. Sample terrific old-vine zins, standout petite sirah and Russian River pinots at the handsome contemporary tasting room, then meander through fragrant butterfly gardens to the creek, where salmon spawn in autumn. Ever-fun weekends, with food-and-wine pairings and **live music** (⏱1-5pm Sat & Sun).

Foodie-scenester restaurants and cafes, wine-tasting rooms and fancy boutiques line Healdsburg Plaza, the town's sun-dappled central square (bordered by Healdsburg Ave and Center, Matheson and Plaza Sts). It's best visited on weekdays – stroll tree-lined streets, sample locavore cooking and savor NorCal flavor. Tasting rooms surround the plaza.

 **Activities**

RIVER'S EDGE KAYAK & CANOE TRIPS
Boating

(☎707-433-7247; www.riversedgekayakand canoe.com; 13840 Healdsburg Ave) Rents hard-sided canoes ($70/$85 per half/full day) and kayaks ($40/$55). Self-guided rentals include shuttle. Guided trips – by reservation – originate upriver in Alexander Valley, and end in town.

RELISH CULINARY SCHOOL
Cooking Course

(☎707-431-9999, 877-759-1004; www.relishcu linary.com; 14 Matheson St; ⏱by appointment) Plug into the locavore food scene with culinary day trips, demo-kitchen classes or winemaker dinners.

🛏 Sleeping

🌿 H2 HOTEL
Hotel $$$

(☎707-431-2202, 707-922-5251; www.h2hotel .com; 219 Healdsburg Ave; r incl breakfast weekday $255-455, weekend $355-555; ❄@🛜☲) Little sister to the Hotel Healdsburg, H2 has the same angular concrete style, but was built LEED-gold-certified from the ground up, with a living roof, reclaimed everything, and fresh-looking rooms with cush organic linens. Tiny pool, free bikes.

GEYSERVILLE INN
Motel $$

(☎707-857-4343, 877-857-4343; www.geyserville inn.com; 21714 Geyserville Ave, Geyserville; r weekday $119-169, weekend $189-249; ❄🛜☲👪) Eight miles north of Healdsburg, this immaculately kept upmarket motel is surrounded by vineyards. Rooms have unexpectedly smart furnishings, like overstuffed side chairs and fluffy feather pillows. Request a remodeled room. Hot tub.

Eating

Healdsburg is the gastronomic capital of Sonoma County. Reservations essential.

MADRONA MANOR
Californian $$$

(☏707-433-4231, 800-258-4003; www.madrona manor.com; 1001 Westside Rd; 4-/5-/6-course menu $73/82/91; ☺6-9pm Wed-Sun) You'd be hard-pressed to find a lovelier place to pop the question than this retro-formal Victorian mansion's garden-view veranda, though there's nothing old-fashioned about the artful Californian haute cuisine, which defines artisinal: the kitchen churns its own butter, each course comes with a different variety of still-warm house-baked bread, lamb and cheese originate down the road, and desserts include ice cream flash-frozen tableside.

SCOPA
Italian $$

(☏707-433-5282; www.scopahealdsburg.com; 109-A Plaza St, Healdsburg; mains $12-26; ☺5:30-10pm Tue-Sun) Space is tight inside this converted barbershop, but it's worth cramming in for perfect thin-crust pizza and rustic Italian home cooking, like Nonna's slow-braised chicken, with sautéed greens, melting into toasty polenta. A lively crowd and good wine prices create a convivial atmosphere, however cramped.

DOWNTOWN BAKERY & CREAMERY
Bakery $

(☏707-431-2719; www.downtownbakery.net; 308a Center St; ☺7am-5:30pm) Healdsburg's finest bakery makes scrumptious pastries.

🍷 Drinking & Entertainment

🥤 FLYING GOAT COFFEE
Cafe

(www.flyinggoatcoffee.com; 324 Center St; ☺7am-6pm) See ya later, Starbucks. Flying Goat is what coffee should be – fair-trade and house-roasted – and locals line up for it every morning.

BEAR REPUBLIC BREWING COMPANY
Brewery

(www.bearrepublic.com; 345 Healdsburg Ave; ☺11:30am-late) Bear Republic features handcrafted award-winning ales, non-award-winning pub grub and live music weekends.

🔒 Shopping

🏷 ARBORETUM
Clothing

(☏707-433-7033; www.arboretumapparel.com; 332 Healdsburg Ave; ☺Wed-Mon) Lending fresh meaning to 'fashion-conscious,' this ecoboutique features fair trade and US designers, with great finds like organic-cotton pants for men and ultra-soft bamboo-fiber cardigans for gals.

🏷 GARDENER
Homewares

(☏707-431-1063; www.thegardener.com; 516 Dry Creek Rd) Garden-shop lovers: don't miss this rural beauty.

🏷 STUDIO BARNDIVA
Gifts, Homewares

(☏707-431-7404; www.studiobarndiva; 237 Center St) Reclaimed ephemera never looked so chic: thousand-dollar *objets d'art*.

ℹ Information

Healdsburg Chamber of Commerce & Visitors Bureau (☏707-433-6935, 800-648-9922; www.healdsburg.org; 217 Healdsburg Ave; ☺9am-5pm Mon-Fri, to 3pm Sat, 10am-2pm Sun) A block south of the plaza.

Yosemite & the Sierra Nevada

An outdoor adventurer's wonderland, the Sierra Nevada is a year-round pageant of snow sports, white-water rafting, hiking, biking, backpacking and rock climbing. Skiers and snowboarders blaze hushed pine-tree slopes, and wilderness-seekers get away from the stresses of modern civilization. With granite mountains watching over high-altitude lakes, the eastern spine of California is a formidable topographical barrier embracing magnificent natural landscapes. And interspersed between its river canyons and 14,000ft peaks are the ghost towns left behind by California's white settlers, and bubbling hot-springs pools. In the foothills, Gold Rush sites take you back to the days of the '49ers.

In the majestic national parks of Yosemite, Sequoia and Kings Canyon, visitors will be humbled by the enduring groves of solemn giant sequoias, the ancient rock formations and valleys, and the omnipresent opportunity to see bears and other wildlife.

Merced River, with El Capitan (p257) in the background **237**
DOUGLAS STEAKLEY/LONELY PLANET IMAGES ©

Yosemite & the Sierra Nevada

Tahoe City

Nevada City

Auburn State Recreation Area

Marshall Gold Discovery State Historic Park **3**

Placerville

Folsom Lake

To Sacramento (5mi)

Lake Tahoe **2**

South Lake Tahoe

El Dorado National Forest

Grover Hot Springs State Park

Markleeville

Bear Valley

Lake Alpine

Murphys

Arnold

Calaveras Big Trees State Park **11**

Stanislaus National Forest

Sonora

Groveland

Modesto

Ebbetts Pass (8730ft) *(closed in winter)*

Sonora Pass (9624ft) *(closed in winter)*

Dodge Ridge

Sierra

Mokelumne River

Stanislaus River

Tuolumne River

Monitor Pass (8314ft) *(closed in winter)*

Topaz Lake

Walker

Humboldt-Toiyabe National Forest

Hoover Wilderness Area

Yosemite National Park **1**

Tioga Pass

Yosemite Valley

El Portal

Briceburg

Bridgeport **6**

Bodie State Historic Park

Mono Lake **5**

Lee Vining

Ansel Adams Wilderness Area

June Lake

Mammoth Mountain (11,053ft)

Mammoth Lakes

Devils Postpile National Monument

Humboldt-Toiyabe National Forest

Inyo National Forest

Benton

Inyo National Forest

Crowley Lake

Inyo National Forest

Ancient Bristlecone Pine Forest

CARSON CITY

Nevada

Walker Lake

0 40 km
0 20 miles

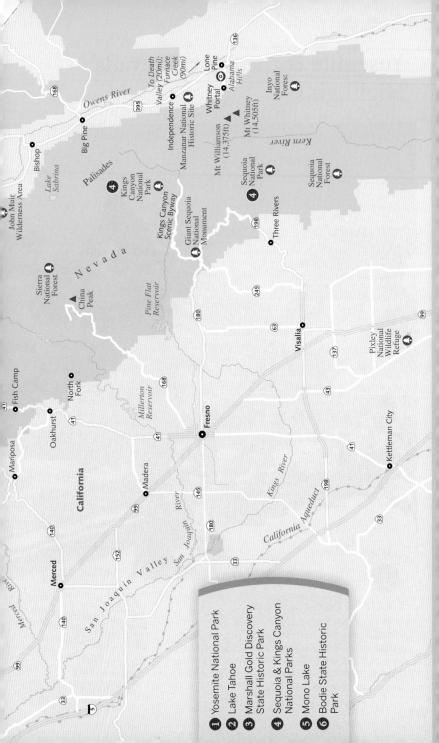

Yosemite & the Sierra Nevada Highlights

① Yosemite National Park

Yosemite (p254) has a way with humans. Its beauty – which can be utterly overwhelming – inspired writers and artists like John Muir and Ansel Adams to produce some of their finest work. It's one of those rare places that touches you, and makes you want to slow down and hurry back. Glacier Point

Need to Know
BEST PHOTO OPS Valley View and Tunnel View PEAK WATERFALL VIEWING May & June TRAVEL TIP Park and use the free Valley shuttle For more, see p254

Yosemite Don't Miss List

BY KARI COBB, YOSEMITE NATIONAL PARK RANGER

1 MARIPOSA GROVE

Mariposa Grove (p258; pictured left) is very accessible to non-hikers because you can drive or shuttle right up to it. The lower grove has some of the biggest trees – including the Grizzly Giant and the Tunnel Tree, which you can walk through – all mixed in with ponderosa pines and cedars. If you're able to hike further, the upper grove is almost entirely sequoias.

2 GLACIER POINT

One of the most iconic viewpoints of Yosemite, Glacier Point (p259) has amazing views of Half Dome, Yosemite Falls, Vernal Fall and Nevada Fall, and you can see into the Tuolumne high country as well as the Clark Range and Red Peak Pass. It's neat to be there in 80 degree weather because you can still see the high country areas covered in snow.

3 TUNNEL VIEW

This Valley viewpoint is at one end of a mile-long tunnel (p255). It's a popular place to take photographs because so many of the Valley's main features are visible. Visitors are able to take in the sights of Bridalveil Fall, Cathedral Rock, Half Dome and El Capitan, all from the parking lot.

4 YOSEMITE FALLS

The flow peaks here around the end of May, though it's usually dry during September and for most of October. The lower fall (p255; upper fall pictured left) is an easy 1-mile loop over the creek bridge to the base. In midsummer when it's 90°F in the Valley, the mist from the waterfall creates its own environment and the fall becomes a great place to cool off because it's 15°F cooler.

5 TENAYA LAKE

The temperature in the Tenaya Lake (p258) area is cooler than the Valley because of the high elevation. On the east side of the lake, there's a fantastic beach with picnic tables that's wonderful on warm summer days. You can eat your lunch and watch the climbers go up nearby Stately Pleasure Dome.

Playtime in Lake Tahoe

Seen from the summit of a powdery white mountain or from a kayak streaming through placid waters, the peak-ringed idyll of Lake Tahoe (p248) rejuvenates and inspires. The largest alpine lake in North America, 'Big Blue' is a year-round outdoor playground that beckons you to experience it on foot, bike or skis, or by boat or car.

Hunt for Gold

So what if it's been over 160 years: maybe there's still an unearthed jackpot to be di covered near the Marshall Gold Discove State Historic Park (p273). Visit the now-quiet epicenter of the Gold Rush days – where prospectors swarmed from across the country and around th world to make their fortunes – and try your own luck panning for gold

RICHARD CUMMINS/LONELY PLANET IMAGES ©

WITOLD SKRYPCZAK/LONELY PLANET IMAGES ©

Sequoia & Kings Canyon National Parks 4

Often eclipsed by the supernova of Yosemite, these parks (p263) encapsulate the best of the Sierra Nevada. Crane your neck between divine granite peaks and North America's deepest canyons, and explore river caves and a never-ending supply of alpine meadows and lakes. Let your jaw hang slack at the shaggy forests of giant sequoias, the biggest trees on earth. Sequoia tree, Sequoia National Park

5 Mono Lake

Brought back from the brink of extinction by local conservationists, this enormous basin (p266) – the second-oldest lake in North America – is truly a sight to ponder. Salty tufa castles rise from subterranean springs, standing watch where mountains meet the desert. Migrating birds feast on clouds of lake flies once relished by local Native American tribes, and bubbly volcanic craters and deep rock fissures buffer the vast blue bowl.

6 Bodie State Historic Park

Hopscotch back in time to the era of the lawless Wild West, and imagine the quick-draw bar-room brawls and frenzied gold strikes of this former boom town (p272), one of the West's most authentic and best-preserved ghost towns. It's now a serene landscape dotted with weather-battered wooden buildings, but in its heyday it was renowned for its opium dens and more than five dozen saloons.

YOSEMITE & THE SIERRA NEVADA HIGHLIGHTS 243

Yosemite & the Sierra Nevada's Best...

Ski Resorts

○ **Squaw Valley** (p248)
The north shore's biggest and most luxurious resort complex.

○ **Mammoth Mountain** (p269) Lots of sunshine and dramatic surrounding peaks, plus the longest season in the state.

○ **Heavenly** (p249) Shred the slopes in both California and Nevada.

○ **Northstar-at-Tahoe** (p248) Another big player on the north shore, and recently revamped.

Time Warps

○ **Bodie State Historic Park** (p272) A well-preserved high-desert ghost town.

○ **Vikingsholm Castle** (p252) Hike in to a 1920s Scandinavian-style mansion on the bay.

○ **Manzanar National Historic Site** (p270) A memorial to one of the darkest events in US history.

○ **Sutter's Fort State Historic Park** (p274) Sacramento's first white settlement.

Flora & Fauna

○ **Mariposa Grove** (p258) Towering redwoods in Yosemite National Park.

○ **Giant Forest** (p265) The largest living trees on earth, in Sequoia National Park.

○ **Tuolumne Meadows** (p258) Summer wildflowers bring dazzling contrast to Yosemite's verdant landscape.

○ **Mono Lake** (p266) Migratory birds roost on the lake's islands in spring and summer.

○ **Stream Profile Chamber** (p266) Lets you explore underwater wildlife in South Lake Tahoe.

Scenic Drives

○ **Hwy 395** (p266) Be wowed by snowy Eastern Sierra mountain views.

○ **Kings Canyon Scenic Byway** (p265) A jaw-dropping descent into a deep rock canyon.

○ **Tioga Road** (p258) View Yosemite's pristine high-country along Hwy 120.

○ **Perimeter of Lake Tahoe** (p248) Take a loop around this blue jewel, ringed by snow-dusted mountains.

ADVANCE PLANNING

○ **Five months before** Reserve a campsite in Yosemite.

○ **Three to four months before** Book hiking permits for Half Dome.

○ **One week before** Buy ski-lift tickets online for discounts at Mammoth Mountain and Heavenly.

RESOURCES

○ **California Department of Transportation** (www.dot.ca.gov) For up-to-date highway conditions in California, including road closures and construction updates.

○ **@YosemiteNPS** (www.twitter.com/yosemitenps) Yosemite's official Twitter feed.

○ **Yosemite Online** (www.yosemite.ca.us) By folks who know Yosemite.

○ **Sacramento Bee** (www.sacbee.com) Sacramento daily paper.

○ **Sierra Web** (www.thesierraweb.com) Area events and links to local visitor information in the Eastern Sierra.

○ **Sierra Wave** (www.sierrawave.net) Eastern Sierra news.

○ **Roadside Heritage** (www.roadsideheritage.org) Free audio downloads about the history and sights along Hwy 395; excellent for road trips.

GETTING AROUND

○ **Air** Larger airports in Sacramento and Reno, Nevada; limited service to Fresno and Mammoth Lakes.

○ **Train** Amtrak runs from the Bay Area to Sacramento and Lake Tahoe, with connections to Yosemite.

○ **Car** The best way to explore off-the-beaten-track destinations.

○ **Bus** Good local and regional transportation options, including free shuttles within Yosemite.

BE FOREWARNED

○ **Road closures** Hwy 120 (across Yosemite) shuts down from about November through May, and heavy snow sometimes closes Hwy 89 near Emerald Bay at Lake Tahoe.

○ **Snow chains** Roads are plowed in winter, but snow chains may be required.

○ **Half Dome permits** This grueling, iconic hike now requires a permit, obtainable online.

Left: Yosemite Falls (p257); **Above:** Hiking, Tuolumne Meadows
(LEFT) EMILY RIDDELL/LONELY PLANET IMAGES ©;
(ABOVE) JOHN MOCK/LONELY PLANET IMAGES ©

Yosemite & the Sierra Nevada Itineraries

Outdoor lovers, this is where you recharge your batteries. Brace yourself for the oxygen-scarce mountain peaks and thundering waterfalls that comprise some of the most stunning natural attractions in the state.

3 DAYS

YOSEMITE VALLEY TO TUOLUMNE MEADOWS

Weekend in Yosemite

Kick off a taste of Yosemite National Park with a stop at the **(1) Tunnel View** lookout. Try to keep the superlatives from tumbling through your lips as you gaze at daredevil waterfalls and ageless monoliths that form the crown jewel of **(2) Yosemite Valley**. From the Valley, lace up your boots and head out to conquer the **(3) Mist Trail**, giving yourself time and lots of scenic breather stops along the way. The following day, drive south to **(4) Wawona**, stopping for breakfast at the historic Wawona Hotel and then taking the shuttle for a gander at the giant sequoias of Mariposa Grove. Then motor to **(5) Glacier Point**, stopping en route for a hike to Dewey Point. Save lunch for when you get to road's end, in full view of Half Dome and the frothy ribbons of white water at Vernal and Nevada Falls. On the third day, head to the high country via the moonscape overlook of **(6) Olmsted Point**, finishing the journey with a ramble through the summertime wildflower carpet at **(7) Tuolumne Meadows**.

Lake Tahoe

NEVADA

OLMSTED POINT
TUOLUMNE MEADOWS
BODIE STATE HISTORIC PARK
MONO LAKE
TUNNEL VIEW
MIST TRAIL
YOSEMITE VALLEY
GLACIER POINT
WAWONA
MAMMOTH LAKES
DEVILS POSTPILE
MANZANAR NATIONAL HISTORIC SITE
ALABAMA HILLS

Top Left: View of El Capitan from Glacier Point (p259);
Top Right: Rock formations, Alabama Hills (p271)

(TOP LEFT) MARK NEWMAN/LONELY PLANET IMAGES ©;
(TOP RIGHT) JOHN ELK III/LONELY PLANET IMAGES ©

5 DAYS

MONO LAKE TO THE ALABAMA HILLS

Awesome Eastern Sierra

From Tuolumne Meadows, continue east up and over Tioga Pass to explore the splendor along the north–south corridor of scenic Hwy 395. A divine apparition of tufa formations poke out of saline **(1) Mono Lake**, where you can kayak or canoe around eerie islands and discreetly spy on nesting birds. Spend a day wandering the high-desert ghost town of **(2) Bodie State Historic Park**, an abandoned Wild West settlement that looks ready for its next gunfight. Drive south along the snowcapped Sierra crest to the high-altitude resort town of **(3) Mammoth Lakes**, and take your pick of outdoor adventures, including hikes to granite-rimmed lakes or careening down its summer mountain-bike park. Don't leave town without a stroll out to witness the curious basalt rock columns of **(4) Devils Postpile**. Continuing south, tour the reconstructed remnants and excellent interpretive museum at the WWII-era concentration camp of **(5) Manzanar National Historic Site**, a desolate Japanese-American detention center shadowed by looming Mt Williamson. End your journey watching the sunset glow off the iconic orange landscape of the **(6) Alabama Hills**, the setting for countless Western movies and TV shows.

Discover Yosemite & the Sierra Nevada

At a Glance

○ **Lake Tahoe** (p248) Year-round outdoor recreation and snow-sports paradise.

○ **Yosemite National Park** (p254) A jaw-dropping valley and one of the country's most iconic parks.

○ **Eastern Sierra** (p266) Fierce mountains, oodles of lakes and dramatic wilderness.

○ **Gold Country** (p271) Relive the Gold Rush in these historical settlements.

LAKE TAHOE

Shimmering in myriad shades of blue and green, Lake Tahoe is the USA's second-deepest lake and, at 6255ft high, it's also one of the highest-elevation lakes in the country. Driving around the lake's spell-binding 72-mile scenic shoreline will give you quite a workout behind the wheel.

The horned peaks surrounding the lake, which straddles the California–Nevada state line, are year-round destinations. Winter brings bundles of snow, perfect for those of all ages to hit the slopes at Tahoe's top-tier ski and snowboard resorts.

Tahoe Ski & Snowboard Resorts

SQUAW VALLEY Skiing, Snowboarding
(☎530-583-6985, 800-403-0206; www.squaw.com; 1960 Squaw Valley Rd, off Hwy 89, Olympic Valley; adult/child under 13yr/teen 13-19yr $88/10/64; ⊙9am-7pm Mon-Thu, to 9pm Fri-Sun) Few ski hounds can resist the siren call of this mega-sized, world-class, see-and-be-seen resort that hosted the 1960 Winter Olympic Games. Hard-core skiers thrill to white-knuckle cornices, chutes and bowls, while beginners practice their turns in a separate area on the up-per mountain.

NORTHSTAR-AT-TAHOE Skiing, Snowboarding
(☎530-562-1010, 800-466-6784; www.north starattahoe.com; 5001 Northstar Dr, off Hwy 267, Truckee; adult/child 5-12yr/youth 13-22yr $92/41/80; ⊙8:30am-4pm; ⊞) An easy 7 miles south of I-80, this hugely popular resort has great intermediate terrain.

Northstar-at-Tahoe
LEE FOSTER/LONELY PLANET IMAGES ©

Advanced and expert skiers can look for tree-skiing challenges on the back of the mountain, reached via a new high-speed lift.

HEAVENLY Skiing, Snowboarding
(☎775-586-7000, 800-432-8365; www.skiheavenly.com; 3860 Saddle Rd, South Lake Tahoe; adult/child 5-12yr/teen 13-19yr $90/50/78; ⏱9am-4pm Mon-Fri, 8:30am-4pm Sat, Sun & holidays) The 'mother' of all Tahoe mountains boasts the most acreage, the longest run (5.5 miles) and the biggest vertical drop around. Follow the sun by skiing on the Nevada side in the morning, moving to the California side in the afternoon.

South Lake Tahoe & Stateline

Highly congested and arguably overdeveloped, South Lake Tahoe is a chock-a-block commercial strip bordering the lake, framed by picture-perfect alpine mountains. At the foot of the world-class Heavenly mountain resort and buzzing from the gambling tables in the casinos just across the border in Stateline, Nevada, Lake Tahoe's south shore draws visitors with a cornucopia of activities and lodging and restaurant options, especially for summer beach access and tons of powdery winter snow.

Sights & Activities

HEAVENLY GONDOLA Gondola, Zip line
(www.skiheavenly.com; Heavenly Village; adult/child 5-12yr/teen 13-19yr from $32/20/26; ⏱10am-5pm Jun-Aug, reduced off-season hr; 👶) Soar to the top of the world as you ride this gondola, which sweeps you from Heavenly Village to some 2.4 miles up the mountain in just 12 minutes. From the observation deck at 9123ft, get gobstopping panoramic views of the entire Tahoe Basin, the Desolation Wilderness and Carson Valley. Then jump on the Tamarack Express chair lift to get all the way to the mountain summit, where the longest zip line in the continental US, **Heavenly Flyer** (per trip $40; ⏱11am-4pm), lets you speed through the air for a heady 3100ft.

Sleeping

DEERFIELD LODGE AT HEAVENLY Boutique Hotel $$$
(☎530-544-3337, 888-757-3337; http://tahoedeerfieldlodge.com; 1200 Ski Run Blvd; r/ste incl breakfast from $219/259; ❄🐾👶) A small boutique hotel close to Heavenly ski resort, Deerfield has a dozen intimate rooms and spacious suites that each have a patio or balcony facing the green courtyard, along with a whirlpool tub, flickering gas fireplace and amusing coat racks crafted from skis and snowboards.

FIRESIDE LODGE Inn $$
(☎530-544-5515; www.tahoefiresidelodge.com; 515 Emerald Bay Rd/Hwy 89; d incl breakfast $119-255; 🐾👪👶) This woodsy cabin B&B wholeheartedly welcomes families, with free bikes and kayaks to borrow and evening s'mores. Kitchenette rooms and suites have river-rock gas fireplaces, cozy patchwork quilts and pioneer-themed touches like wagon wheels or vintage skis. Pet fee $20.

Eating

CAFÉ FIORE Italian $$$
(☎530-541-2908; www.cafefiore.com; 1169 Ski Run Blvd; mains $16-31; ⏱5:30-9pm Sun-Thu, to 9:30pm Fri & Sat) Upscale Italian without pretension, this tiny romantic eatery pairs succulent pasta, seafood and meats with an award-winning 300-vintage wine list. Swoon over the rack of lamb, homemade white-chocolate ice cream and near-perfect garlic bread. Reservations are essential.

BURGER LOUNGE American $
(www.tahoeburgerlounge.com; 717 Emerald Bay Rd/Hwy 89; items $3-6; ⏱11am-8pm, to 9pm Jun-Aug; 👶) You can't miss that giant beer mug standing outside a shingled cabin. Step inside for the south shore's tastiest burgers, including the crazy 'Just a Jiffy' (with peanut butter, bacon and cheddar cheese) or the zingy pesto fries.

DISCOVER YOSEMITE & THE SIERRA NEVADA   SOUTH LAKE TAHOE & STATELINE

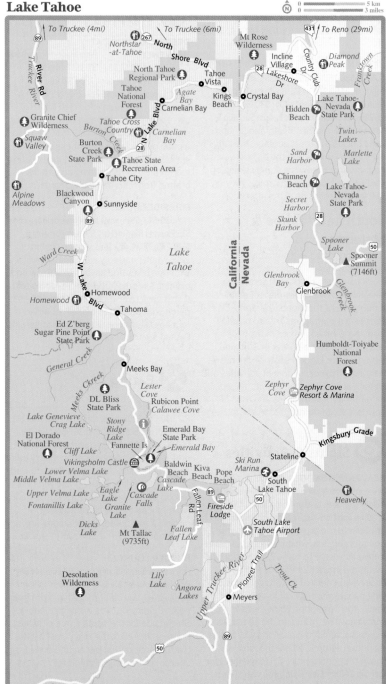

Drinking & Entertainment

BEACON BAR & GRILL   Bar
(www.camprichardson.com; Camp Richardson Resort, 1900 Jameson Beach Rd; ⏱11am-10pm)
Imagine all of Lake Tahoe is your very own front yard when you and your buddies sprawl across this big wraparound wooden deck.

BREWERY AT LAKE TAHOE   Brewpub
(www.brewerylaketahoe.com; 3542 Lake Tahoe Blvd; ⏱from 11am daily, closing time varies) Crazy-popular brewpub pumps its signature Bad Ass Ale into grateful local patrons, who may sniff at bright-eyed out-of-towners. The barbecue is dynamite and a roadside patio opens in summer.

Western Shore

Lake Tahoe's densely forested western shore, between Emerald Bay (p252) and Tahoe City, is idyllic. Hwy 89 sinuously wends past gorgeous state parks with swimming beaches, hiking trails, pine-shaded campgrounds and historic mansions.

Lake Tahoe (p248)

Tahoe City

The north shore's commercial hub, Tahoe City straddles the junction of Hwys 89 and 28, making it almost inevitable that you'll find yourself breezing through here at least once during your 'round-the-lake sojourn.

Sleeping

MOTHER NATURE'S INN   Inn $$
(☎530-581-4278, 800-558-4278; www.mother naturesinn.com; 551 N Lake Blvd; r $60-135; 🐾) Right in town behind Cabin Fever knick-knack boutique, this good-value option offers quiet motel-style rooms with a tidy country look, fridges, eclectic furniture and comfy pillow-top mattresses.

PEPPER TREE INN   Motel $$
(☎530-583-3711, 800-624-8590; www.pepper treetahoe.com; 645 N Lake Blvd; r incl breakfast $90-199; 🛜🏊) The tallest building in town, this somberly painted establishment redeems itself with some bird's-eye lake views. Fairly comfortable modern rooms with that familiar log-cabin decor each have a microwave and mini fridge.

JOHNNY HAGLUND/LONELY PLANET IMAGES ©

WITOLD SKRYPCZAK/LONELY PLANET IMAGES ©

Don't Miss **Emerald Bay State Park**

Sheer granite cliffs and a jagged shoreline hem in glacier-carved Emerald Bay, a teardrop cove that will have you digging for your camera. Its most captivating aspect is the water, which changes from cloverleaf green to light jade depending on the angle of the sun.

You'll spy panoramic pullouts all along Hwy 89, including at **Inspiration Point**, opposite Bayview Campground. Just south, the road shoulder evaporates on both sides of a steep drop-off, revealing a postcard-perfect view of Emerald Bay to the north and Cascade Lake to the south.

The mesmerizing blue-green waters of the bay frame **Fannette Island**. This uninhabited granite speck, Lake Tahoe's only island, holds the vandalized remains of a tiny 1920s teahouse belonging to heiress Lora Knight, who would occasionally motorboat guests to the island from **Vikingsholm Castle** (tours adult/child 6-13yr $8/5; ⊙10am-4pm late May-Sep), her Scandinavian-style mansion on the bay. Completed in 1929, it has trippy design elements aplenty, including sod-covered roofs that sprout wildflowers in late spring.

NEED TO KNOW

☑530-541-3030; www.parks.ca.gov; per car $8; ⊙late May-Sep

✖ Eating & Drinking

DOCKSIDE 700 WINE BAR & GRILL American $$
(☑530-581-0303; www.dockside700.com; 700 N Lake Blvd; breakfast & lunch $5-10, dinner $13-29; ⊙9am-9pm Mon-Fri, 8am-9pm Sat & Sun;

) On a lazy summer afternoon, grab a table on the back deck that overlooks the boats bobbing at Tahoe City Marina. On weekends, barbecue chicken, ribs and steak light a fire under dinner (reservations advised), alongside seafood pastas and pizzas.

RIVER RANCH
LODGE   New American $$$
(☏ 530-583-4264; www.riveranchlodge.com;
Hwy 89 at Alpine Meadows Rd; mains patio &
cafe $8-15, restaurant $18-31; ⊙lunch Jun-Sep,
dinner year-round, call for seasonal hr) This
riverside dining room is a popular stop,
drawing rafters and bikers to its patio for
summer barbecue lunches. Dinner is a
meat-heavy affair, with filet mignon and
roasted duck.

Truckee & Donner Lake
Cradled by mountains and the Tahoe
National Forest, Truckee is a thriving town
steeped in Old West history. Today tour-
ism fills much of the city's coffers, thanks
to a well-preserved historical downtown
and its proximity to Lake Tahoe and no
fewer than six downhill and four cross-
country ski resorts.

 Sights

DONNER MEMORIAL STATE PARK Park
(☏ 530-582-7892; www.parks.ca.gov; per car
$8; ⊙seasonal park hr vary, museum 9am-4pm
year-round) At the eastern end of Donner
Lake, this state-run park occupies one
of the sites where the doomed Don-
ner Party got trapped during the fateful
winter of 1846–47. Though its history is
gruesome, the park is gorgeous and has
a sandy beach, picnic tables hiking trails
and wintertime cross-country skiing and
snowshoeing.

The entry fee includes admission to the
excellent **Emigrant Trail Museum**, which
has fascinating, if admittedly macabre,
historical exhibits and a 25-minute film
re-enacting the Donner Party's horrific
plight. A short trail leads to a memorial at
one family's cabin site.

 **Sleeping**

**CEDAR HOUSE
SPORT HOTEL**   Boutique Hotel $$$
(☏ 530-582-5655, 866-582-5655; www.cedar
housesporthotel.com; 10918 Brockway Rd; r incl
breakfast $170-270; 🛜 🐾) This chic, environ-
mentally conscious contemporary lodge
aims at getting folks out into nature. It
boasts countertops made from recycled
paper, 'rain chains' that redistribute water
from the green roof garden, low-flow
plumbing and in-room recycling. However,
it doesn't skimp on plush robes, sexy
platform beds with pillow-top mattresses,
flat-screen TVs or the outdoor hot tub.

The Doomed Donner Party

In the 19th century, tens of thousands of people migrated west along the
Overland Trail with dreams of a better life in California. Among them was the
ill-fated Donner Party.

By the time the party reached the eastern foot of the Sierra Nevada, near
present-day Reno, morale and food supplies ran dangerously low. To restore their
livestock's energy and reprovision, the emigrants decided to rest here for a few
days. But an exceptionally fierce winter came early, quickly rendering what later
came to be called Donner Pass impassable and forcing the pioneers to build basic
shelter near today's Donner Lake. Snow fell for weeks, reaching a depth of 22ft.

By the time the first rescue party arrived at Donner Lake in late February, the
trapped pioneers were still surviving – barely – on boiled ox hides. But when the
second rescue party, led by the banished James Reed, made it through in March,
evidence of cannibalism was rife. Journals and reports tell of 'half-crazed people
living in filth, with naked, half-eaten bodies strewn about the cabins.'

CLAIR TAPPAAN LODGE
Hostel $

(530-426-3632, 800-629-6775; www.sierra club.org/outings/lodges/ctl; 19940 Donner Pass Rd; dm incl meals per adult $50-60, child under 14yr $25-32;) About a mile west of Sugar Bowl, this cozy Sierra Club–owned rustic mountain lodge puts you near major ski resorts and sleeps up to 140 people in dorms and family rooms. Rates include family-style meals, but you're expected to do small chores and bring your own sleeping bag, towel and swimsuit (for the hot tub!). In winter, go cross-country skiing or snowshoeing, or careen down the sledding hill out back.

✖ Eating & Drinking

MOODY'S BISTRO & LOUNGE
Californian $$$

(530-587-8688; www.moodysbistro.com; 10007 Bridge St; lunch $12-16, dinner $20-34; 11:30am-9:30pm Mon-Thu, 11:30am-10pm Fri, 11am-10pm Sat, 11am-9:30pm Sun) With its sophisticated supper-club looks and live jazz (Thursday to Saturday evenings), this gourmet restaurant in the Truckee Hotel oozes urbane flair. Only the freshest, organic and locally grown ingredients make it into the chef's perfectly pitched concoctions like pork loin with peach BBQ sauce, roasted beets with shaved fennel, or tempura-fried mozzarella with herbs.

SQUEEZE IN
Diner $$

(530-587-9814; www.squeezein.com; 10060 Donner Pass Rd; mains $8-13; 7am-2pm;) Across from the Amtrak station, this favorite dishes up breakfasts big enough to feed a lumberjack. Over 60 varieties of omelets – along with burgers, burritos and big salads – are served in this funky place crammed with silly tchotchkes and colorful handwritten notes on the walls.

YOSEMITE NATIONAL PARK

The jaw-dropping head-turner of America's national parks, and a Unesco World Heritage site, Yosemite (yo-*sem*-it-ee)

Left: Mirror Lake (p258); **Below:** Chipmunks, Glacier Point (p259)

(LEFT) THOMAS WINZ/LONELY PLANET IMAGES ©; (BELOW) JUDY BELLAH/LONELY PLANET IMAGES ©

garners the devotion of all who enter. From the waterfall-striped granite walls buttressing emerald-green Yosemite Valley to the skyscraping giant sequoias catapulting into the air at Mariposa Grove, the place inspires a sense of awe and reverence – four million visitors wend their way to the country's third-oldest national park annually. But lift your eyes above the crowds and you'll feel your heart instantly moved by unrivalled splendors: the haughty profile of Half Dome, the hulking presence of El Capitan, the drenching mists of Yosemite Falls, the gemstone lakes of the high country's subalpine wilderness and Hetch Hetchy's pristine pathways.

History

The Ahwahneechee, a group of Miwok and Paiute peoples, lived in the Yosemite area for around 4000 years before a group of pioneers, most likely led by legendary explorer Joseph Rutherford Walker, came through in 1833. During the Gold Rush era, conflict between the miners and native tribes escalated to the point where a military expedition (the Mariposa Battalion) was dispatched in 1851 to punish the Ahwahneechee, eventually forcing the capitulation of Chief Tenaya and his tribe.

In 1864 President Abraham Lincoln signed the Yosemite Grant, which eventually ceded Yosemite Valley and the Mariposa Grove of Giant Sequoias to California as a state park. This landmark decision paved the way for a national park system, of which Yosemite became a part in 1890, thanks to efforts led by pioneering conservationist John Muir.

 Sights

Yosemite Valley

The park's crown jewel, spectacular meadow-carpeted Yosemite Valley stretches 7 miles long, bisected by the

255

Yosemite National Park

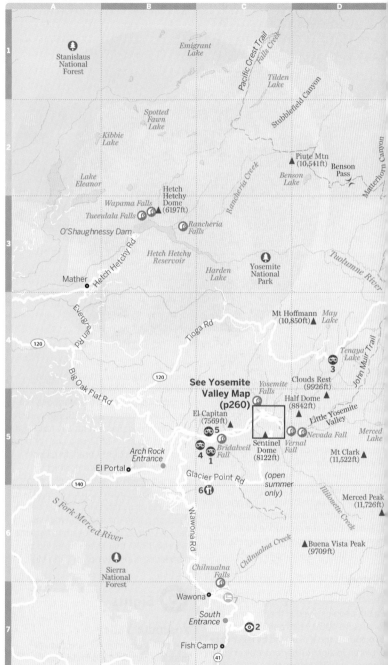

See Yosemite
Valley Map
(p260)

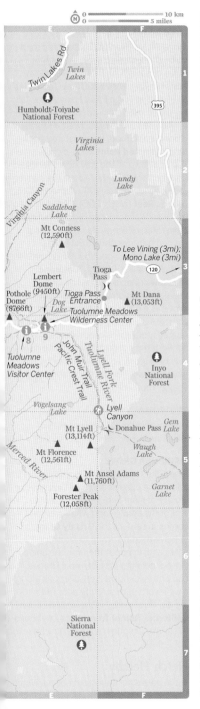

Yosemite National Park

◎ Sights
1 Dewey Pt Lookout.................................C5
2 Mariposa Grove..................................C7
3 Olmsted Pt...D4
4 Tunnel View...C5
5 Valley View...C5

◎ Activities, Courses & Tours
6 Badger Pass Ski Area.........................C6

◎ Sleeping
7 Wawona Hotel.....................................C7

◎ Eating
  Wawona Hotel Dining Room........(see 7)

◎ Information
8 Tuolumne Meadows Visitor
    Center..E4
9 Tuolumne Meadows Wilderness
    Center..E4

rippling Merced River and hemmed in by some of the most majestic chunks of granite anywhere on earth. The most famous are, of course, the monumental 7569ft **El Capitan** (El Cap; Map p256), one of the world's largest monoliths and a magnet for rock climbers, and 8842ft **Half Dome** (Map p256), the park's spiritual centerpiece – its rounded granite pate forms an unmistakable silhouette. You'll have great views of both from **Valley View** (Map p256) on the valley floor, but for the classic photo op head up Hwy 41 to **Tunnel View** (Map p256), which boasts a new viewing area.

Yosemite's waterfalls mesmerize even the most jaded traveler, especially when the spring runoff turns them into thunderous cataracts. Most are reduced to a mere trickle by late summer. **Yosemite Falls** (Map p256) is considered the tallest in North America, dropping 2425ft in three tiers. A slick wheelchair-accessible trail leads to the bottom of this cascade or, if you prefer solitude and different perspectives, you can also clamber up the **Yosemite Falls Trail** (Map p260), which puts you atop the falls after a grueling 3.4 miles. No less impressive is nearby **Bridalveil Fall** (Map p260) and others scattered throughout the valley.

Any aspiring Ansel Adams should lug their camera gear along the 1-mile paved trail to **Mirror Lake** (off Map p260) early or late in the day to catch the ever-shifting reflection of Half Dome in the still waters. The lake all but dries up by late summer.

FREE **YOSEMITE MUSEUM** Museum
(Map p260; ⏰9am-4:30pm or 5pm, closed for lunch) This museum has Miwok and Paiute artifacts, including woven baskets, beaded buckskin dresses and dance capes made from feathers. There's also an **art gallery** with paintings and photographs from the museum's permanent collection. Behind the museum, a self-guided interpretive trail winds past a reconstructed c 1870 **Indian village** with pounding stones, an acorn granary, a ceremonial roundhouse and a conical bark house.

FREE **NATURE CENTER AT HAPPY ISLES** Museum
(Map p260; ⏰9:30am-4pm May-Sep; 👪) A great hands-on nature museum, the Nature Center displays explain the differences between the park's various pinecones, rocks, animal tracks and (everyone's favorite subject) scat.

Mandatory Half Dome Permits

To stem lengthy lines (and increasingly dangerous conditions) on the vertiginous cables of Half Dome, the park now requires that all-day hikers obtain an advance **permit** (☎877-444-6777; www.recreation .gov; per person $1.50) to climb the cables. Permits go on sale four months in advance, and the 300 available per day sell out almost immediately. The process is still in development, so check www.nps. gov/yose/planyourvisit/hdpermits. htm for the latest information.

Tioga Road & Tuolumne Meadows

Tioga Rd (or Hwy 120 E), the only road through the park, travels through 56 miles of superb high country at elevations ranging from 6200ft at Crane Flat to 9945ft at Tioga Pass. Heavy snowfall keeps it closed from about November until May. Beautiful views await after many a bend in the road, the most impressive being **Olmsted Point** (Map p256), where you can gawp all the way down Tenaya Canyon to Half Dome. Above the canyon's east side looms the aptly named 9926ft **Clouds Rest** (Map p256). Continuing east on Tioga Rd soon drops you at **Tenaya Lake** (Map p256), a placid blue basin framed by pines and granite cliffs.

Beyond here, about 55 miles from Yosemite Valley, 8600ft **Tuolumne Meadows** (Map p256) is the largest subalpine meadow in the Sierra. It provides a dazzling contrast to the valley, with its lush open fields, clear blue lakes, ragged granite peaks and domes, and cooler temperatures. If you come during July or August, you'll find a painter's palette of wildflowers decorating the shaggy meadows.

Wawona

Wawona is about 27 miles south of Yosemite Valley.

MARIPOSA GROVE Forest
(Map p256) The main lure in this area of the park is the biggest and most impressive cluster of giant sequoias in Yosemite. The star of the show – and what everyone comes to see – is the **Grizzly Giant**, a behemoth that sprang to life some 2700 years ago, or about the time the ancient Greeks held the first Olympic Games. You can't miss it – it's a half-mile walk along a well-worn path starting near the parking lot. Also nearby is the walk-through **California Tunnel Tree**, which continues to survive despite having its heart hacked out in 1895.

Hetch Hetchy

In the park's northwestern corner, Hetch Hetchy, which is Miwok for 'place of tall

Don't Miss Glacier Point

A lofty 3200ft above the valley floor, 7214ft **Glacier Point** (Map p260) presents one of the park's most eye-popping vistas and practically puts you at eye level with Half Dome. To the left of Half Dome lies U-shaped, glacially carved Tenaya Canyon, while below you'll see Vernal and Nevada Falls. Glacier Point is about an hour's drive from Yosemite Valley via Glacier Point Rd off Hwy 41. Along the road, hiking trails lead to other spectacular viewpoints, such as **Dewey Point** (Map p256) and **Sentinel Dome** (Map p260).

grass,' gets the least amount of traffic yet sports waterfalls and granite cliffs that rival its famous counterparts in Yosemite Valley. The main difference is that Hetch Hetchy Valley is now filled with water, following a long political and environmental battle in the early 20th century.

The 8-mile long **Hetch Hetchy Reservoir** (Map p256), its placid surface reflecting clouds and cliffs, stretches behind O'Shaughnessy Dam, site of a parking lot and trailheads. An easy 5.4-mile (round-trip) trail leads to the spectacular **Tueeulala** (*twee*-lala) and **Wapama Falls** (Map p256), which each plummet more than 1000ft over fractured granite walls on the north shore of the reservoir.

 **Activities**

Hiking

Over 800 miles of hiking trails cater to hikers of all abilities. Take an easy half-mile stroll on the valley floor; venture out all day on a quest for viewpoints, waterfalls and lakes; or go camping in the remote outer reaches of the backcountry.

Some of the park's most popular hikes start right in Yosemite Valley, including to the top of Half Dome (17-mile round-trip), the most famous of all. It follows a section of the **John Muir Trail** and is strenuous, difficult and best tackled in two days with an overnight in Little Yosemite Valley. Reaching the top can only be

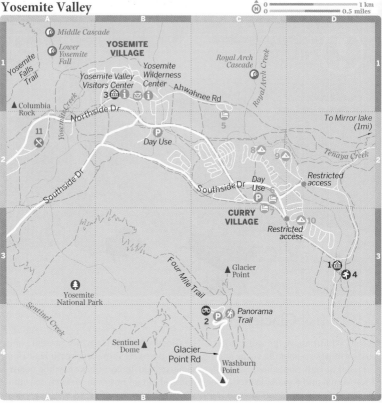

done after rangers have installed fixed cables. Depending on snow conditions, this may occur as early as late May or as late as July, and the cables usually come down in mid-October. To whittle down the cables' notorious human logjams, the park now requires permits for day hikers (see p258), but the route is still nerve-wracking as hikers must 'share the road.' The less ambitious or physically fit will still have a ball following the **Mist Trail** as far as **Vernal Fall** (Map p256; 2.6-mile round-trip), the top of **Nevada Fall** (Map p256; 6.5-mile round-trip) or idyllic **Little Yosemite Valley** (Map p256; 8-mile round-trip).

Rock Climbing

With its sheer spires, polished domes and soaring monoliths, Yosemite is rock-climbing nirvana. The main climbing season runs from April to October.

Swimming

On a hot summer day, nothing beats a dip in the gentle Merced River, though if chilly water doesn't float your boat, you can always pay to play in the outdoor swimming pools at Curry Village and Yosemite Lodge at the Falls (adult/child $5/4).

Rafting

From around late May to July, floating the Merced River from Stoneman Meadow, near Curry Village, to Sentinel Bridge is a leisurely way to soak up Yosemite Valley views. Four-person **raft rentals** (☎209-372-4386; per adult/child over 50lb $26/16) for the 3-mile trip are available from the con-

Yosemite Valley

◎ Sights
1 Nature Center at Happy Isles D3
2 Sentinel Dome....................................... C4
3 Yosemite Museum................................ B1

◆ Activities, Courses & Tours
4 John Muir Trail & Mist Trail
  (Trailhead)..D3

◎ Sleeping
5 Ahwahnee Hotel...................................C2
6 Campground Reservation
  Office C2
7 Curry Village C3
8 Lower Pines Campground...................C2
9 North Pines Campground....................C2
10 Upper Pines Campground..................D3

⊗ Eating
Ahwahnee Dining Room.............. (see 5)
11 Mountain Room Restaurant................A2
Yosemite Lodge Food Court ...... (see 11)

◉ Drinking
Ahwahnee Bar .... (see 5)
Mountain Room Lounge .... (see 11)

cessionaire in Curry Village and include equipment and a shuttle ride back to the rental kiosk.

Winter Sports

The white coat of winter opens up a different set of things to do, as the valley becomes a quiet, frosty world of snow-draped evergreens, ice-coated lakes and vivid vistas of gleaming white mountains sparkling against blue skies.

**BADGER PASS
SKI AREA** Skiing, Snowboarding
(Map p256; ☏209-372-8430; www.badgerpass.com; lift ticket adult/child $42/23; 🚹) Most of the action converges on one of California's oldest ski resorts. The gentle slopes are perfect for families and beginner skiers and snowboarders. It's about 22 miles from the valley on Glacier Point Rd.

Tours

First-timers often appreciate the two-hour **Valley Floor Tour** (per adult/child $25/13;

⊙**year-round**) run by DNC Parks & Resorts, which covers the valley highlights.

For other tour options stop at the tour and activity desks at Yosemite Lodge at the Falls, Curry Village or Yosemite Village, call ☏209-372-4386 or check www.yosemitepark.com.

Sleeping

Competition for campsites is fierce from May to September, when arriving without a reservation and hoping for the best is tantamount to getting someone to lug your Barcalounger up Half Dome. Even first-come, first-served campgrounds tend to fill by noon, especially on weekends and around holidays. **Reservations** (☏877-444-6777, 518-885-3639; www.recreation.gov) become available from 7am PST on the 15th of every month in one-month blocks, and often sell out within minutes.

Opening dates for seasonal campgrounds vary according to the weather.

All noncamping reservations within the park are handled by **DNC Parks & Resorts** (☏801-559-4884; www.yosemitepark.com) and can be made up to 366 days in advance; reservations are absolutely critical from May to early September.

Yosemite Valley

AHWAHNEE HOTEL Historic Hotel $$$
(Map p260; r from $449; ❄ @ 🛜 🐾) The crème de la crème of Yosemite's lodging, this sumptuous historic property dazzles with soaring ceilings, Turkish kilims lining the hallways and atmospheric lounges with mammoth stone fireplaces. It's the gold standard for upscale lodges, though if you're not blessed with bullion, you can still soak up the ambience during after-noon tea, a drink in the bar or a gourmet meal.

CURRY VILLAGE Cabins $$
(Map p260; tent cabins $112-120, cabins without/with bath $127/168; 🐾) Founded in 1899 as a summer camp, Curry has hundreds of units squished tightly together beneath towering evergreens. The canvas cabins

are basically glorified tents, so for more comfort, quiet and privacy get one of the cozy wood cabins, which have bed-spreads, drapes and vintage posters.

Wawona

WAWONA HOTEL　　Historic Hotel **$$**
(Map p256; Wawona; r without/with bath incl breakfast $147/217; ⏰mid-Mar–Dec; 🛜🏊👪) This National Historic Landmark, dating from 1879, is a collection of six graceful, whitewashed New England–style build-ings flanked by wide porches. The 104 rooms – with no phone or TV – come with Victorian–style furniture and other period items, and about half the rooms share bathrooms, with nice robes provided for the walk there.

 # Eating

**MOUNTAIN ROOM
RESTAURANT**　　Steakhouse **$$**
(Map p260; 📞209-372-1281; Yosemite Lodge; mains $17-35; ⏰5:30-9:30pm, shorter hr winter

hours; 🍴👪) With a killer view of Yosemite Falls, the window tables at this casual and elegant contemporary steakhouse are a hot commodity. The chefs at the lodge whip up the best meals in the park, with flat-iron steak and locally caught moun-tain trout wooing diners under a rotating display of nature photographs. Reserva-tions accepted only for groups larger than eight, and casual dress is okay.

**🖋AHWAHNEE DINING
ROOM**　　Californian **$$$**
(Map p260; 📞209-372-1489; Ahwahnee Hotel; mains breakfast $7-16, lunch $16-23, dinner $26-46; ⏰7-10:30am, 11:30am-3pm & 5:30-9pm) The formal ambience (mind your manners) may not be for everybody, but few would not be awed by the sumptuous decor, soaring beamed ceiling and palatial chan-deliers. The menu is constantly in flux, but most dishes have perfect pitch and are beautifully presented. There's a dress code at dinner, but otherwise shorts and sneakers are okay. Reservations highly recommended for brunch and dinner.

**🖋WAWONA HOTEL
DINING ROOM**　　American **$$**
(Map p256; Wawona Hotel; breakfast & lunch $11-15, dinner $19-30; ⏰7:30-10am, 11:30am-1:30pm & 5:30-9pm Easter-Dec; 🍴👪) Beautiful sequoia-painted lamps light this old-fashioned white-tablecloth dining room, and the Victorian detail makes it an enchanting place to have an upscale (though somewhat over-priced) meal.

**YOSEMITE
LODGE FOOD
COURT**　　Cafeteria **$**
(Map p260; Yosemite Lodge; mains $7-12; ⏰6:30am-8:30pm Sun-Thu, to 9pm Fri & Sat; 🍴) This self-service restaurant has several tummy-filling stations serving pastas,

Suspension bridge, Kings Canyon National Park (p264)
JOHN MOCK/LONELY PLANET IMAGES ©

burgers, pizza and sandwiches, either made to order or served from beneath heat lamps.

🍷 Drinking

MOUNTAIN ROOM LOUNGE Bar
(Map p260; Yosemite Lodge, Yosemite Valley)
Catch up on the latest sports news while knocking back draft brews at this large bar that buzzes in wintertime. Order a s'mores kit (graham crackers, chocolate squares and marshmallows) to roast in the open-pit fireplace. Kids are welcome until 9pm.

AHWAHNEE BAR Bar
(Map p260; Ahwahnee Hotel, Yosemite Valley)
The perfect way to experience the Ahwahnee without dipping too deep into your pockets; settle in for a drink at this cozy bar, complete with pianist.

ℹ Information

Yosemite's entrance fee is $20 per vehicle or $10 for those on bicycle or foot and is valid for seven consecutive days.

For recorded park information, campground availability, and road and weather conditions, call ☎209-372-0200.

Yosemite National Park (www.nps.gov/yose) Official Yosemite National Park Service site with the most comprehensive and current information.

Yosemite Valley Visitor Center (Map p260; ☎209-372-0299; Yosemite Village; ⊙9am-7:30pm summer, shorter hr year-round)

ℹ Getting There & Away

Yosemite is one of the few national parks that can be easily reached by public transportation. Greyhound buses and Amtrak trains serve Merced, west of the park, where they are met by buses operated by Yosemite Area Regional Transportation System (YARTS; ☎209-388-9589, 877-989-2787; www.yarts.com), and you can buy Amtrak tickets that include the YARTS segment all the way into the park.

In summer, another YARTS route runs from Mammoth Lakes along Hwy 395 to Yosemite Valley via Hwy 120.

ℹ Getting Around

Bicycle

Bicycling is an ideal way to take in Yosemite Valley. You can rent a wide-handled cruiser (per hour/day $10/28) or a bike with an attached child trailer (per hour/day $16.50/54) at Yosemite Lodge at the Falls or Curry Village.

Car

Glacier Point and Tioga Rds are closed in winter.

Public Transportation

The free, air-conditioned Yosemite Valley Shuttle Bus is a comfortable and efficient way of traveling around the park. Buses operate year-round at frequent intervals and stop at 21 numbered locations, including parking lots, campgrounds, trailheads and lodges.

SEQUOIA & KINGS CANYON

The twin parks of Sequoia and Kings Canyon dazzle with superlatives, though they're often overshadowed by Yosemite, their smaller neighbor to the north (a three-hour drive away). With towering forests of giant sequoias containing some of the largest trees in the world, and the mighty Kings River careening through the depths of Kings Canyon, one of the deepest chasms in the country, the parks are lesser-visited jewels where it's easier to find quiet and solitude. Throw in opportunities for cave spelunking, rock climbing and backcountry hiking through granite-carved Sierra landscapes, and backdoor access to Mt Whitney – the tallest peak in the lower 48 states – and you have all the ingredients for two of the best parks in the country.

The two parks, though distinct, are operated as one unit with a single admission (valid for seven consecutive days) of $20 per carload. For 24-hour recorded information, including road conditions, call ☎559-565-3341 or visit www.nps.gov/seki, the parks' comprehensive website.

Kings Canyon National Park

With a dramatic cleft deeper than the Grand Canyon, Kings Canyon offers true adventure to those who crave seemingly endless trails, rushing streams and gargantuan rock formations.

Sights & Activities

General Grant Grove

This sequoia grove is nothing short of magnificent. The paved half-mile **General Grant Tree Trail** is an interpretive walk that visits a number of mature sequoias, including the 27-story **General Grant Tree**. This giant holds triple honors as the world's third-largest living tree, a memorial to US soldiers killed in war, and as the nation's Christmas tree. The nearby **Fallen Monarch**, a massive, fire-hollowed trunk that you can walk through, has been a cabin, hotel, saloon and stables for US Cavalry horses.

Cedar Grove & Roads End

Pretty spots around here include **Roaring River Falls**, where water whips down a sculpted rock channel before tumbling into a churning pool, and the 1.5-mile **Zumwalt Meadow Loop**, an easy nature trail around a verdant green meadow bordered by river and granite canyon.

Sleeping & Eating

JOHN MUIR LODGE   Lodge $$
(☎559-335-5500, 866-522-6966; www.sequoia -kingscanyon.com; Grant Grove Village, off Generals Hwy; r $69-190) An atmospheric wooden building hung with historical black-and-white photographs, this year-round hotel is a place to lay your head and still feel like you're in the forest. Wide porches have wooden rocking chairs, and homespun, if thin-walled, rooms contain rough-hewn wood furniture and patchwork bedspreads (no TVs).

GRANT GROVE CABINS   Cabins $$
(☎559-335-5500, 866-522-6966; www.sequoia -kingscanyon.com; Grant Grove Village, off Generals Hwy; cabins $65-140) Set amid towering sugar pines, around 50 cabins range from decrepit tent-top shacks (open from early June until early September) to rustic but

Giant sequoia trees, Sequoia National Park

JOHN ELK III/LONELY PLANET IMAGES ©

Scenic Drive: Kings Canyon Scenic Byway (Highway 180)

The 31-mile roller coaster road connecting Grant Grove and Cedar Grove ranks among the most dazzling in all of California.

The road soon begins its jaw-dropping descent into the canyon, snaking past chiseled rock walls, some tinged by green moss and red iron minerals, others decorated by waterfalls. Turnouts provide superb views, especially at **Junction View**.

Eventually the road runs parallel with the gushing Kings River, its thunderous roar ricocheting off granite cliffs soaring as high as 8000ft, making Kings Canyon even deeper than the Grand Canyon. Stop at **Boyden Cavern** (☎888-965-8243; www.boydencavern.com; tours adult/child from $13/8; ☺10am-5pm late May-Sep, 11am-4pm late Apr-late May & Oct–mid-Nov) for a tour of its whimsical formations. About 5 miles further east, **Grizzly Falls** can be torrential or drizzly, depending on the time of year.

comfortable heated duplexes (a few are wheelchair-accessible) with electricity, private bathrooms and double beds.

GRANT GROVE RESTAURANT American $$
(Grant Grove Village, off Generals Hwy; mains $7-16; ☺7-10:30am, 11am-4pm & 5-9pm late May-early Sep, reduced hr early Sep-late May; 🛜🚻) More of a diner, this is where most visitors to Grant Grove Village chow down, and there can be a wait at times. There's a breakfast buffet, lunch sandwiches and filling full dinners.

ⓘ Information

Kings Canyon Visitor Center (☎559-565-4307; ☺8am-7pm early Jul-late Aug, variable hr otherwise) In Grant Grove Village. Has exhibits, maps and wilderness permits.

ⓘ Getting There & Around

The road to Cedar Grove Village is only open from around April or May until the first snowfall.

Sequoia National Park

Picture unzipping your tent flap and crawling out into a 'front yard' of trees as high as a 20-story building and as old as the Bible. Brew some coffee as you plan your day in this extraordinary park with its soul-sustaining forests and gigantic peaks soaring above 12,000ft.

Sights & Activities

Giant Forest

Named by John Muir in 1875, this area is the top destination in the parks, about 2 miles south of Lodgepole Village. By volume the largest living tree on earth, the massive **General Sherman Tree** rockets 275ft to the sky. Pay your respects via a short descent from the Wolverton Rd parking lot, or join the **Congress Trail**, a paved 2-mile pathway that takes in General Sherman and other notable named trees, including the **Washington Tree**, the world's second-biggest sequoia, and the see-through **Telescope Tree**.

FREE GIANT FOREST MUSEUM Museum
(☎559-565-4480; ☺9am-7pm summer, to 5pm or 6pm spring & fall, to 4pm winter) For a primer on the intriguing ecology, fire cycle and history of the 'big trees', drop in at this excellent museum.

Open in the warmer months, Crescent Meadow Rd heads east from the Giant

If You Like...
Kids' Activities

If you like the Nature Center at Happy Isles (p258), check out these other family-friendly excursions.

1 STREAM PROFILE CHAMBER
(530-543-2674; trailhead at USFS Taylor Creek Visitor Center, off Hwy 89; admission free; 8am-4:30pm late May–mid-Jun & Oct, to 5:30pm mid-Jun–Sep) Outside of South Lake Tahoe, this submerged glass structure in a teeming creek lets you check out what plants and fish live below the waterline. Come for the Kokanee salmon run in October, when the brilliant red beauties arrive to spawn.

2 BEETLE ROCK EDUCATION CENTER
(559-565-4480; admission free; 1-4pm late Jun–mid-Aug; 🚸) In Sequoia National Park, bugs, bones and artificial animal scat are just some of the cool things children get to play with at this bright and cheerful cabin with activity stations galore. Scan bugs with digital microscopes, touch a taxidermied bobcat, put on a puppet show and paint ecology posters. Binoculars lure youngsters out back for spotting animals.

3 CURRY VILLAGE ICE RINK
(per session adult/child $8/6, rental skates $3; Nov-Mar) Take a spin on Yosemite's outdoor rink, where you'll be skating under the watchful eye of Half Dome.

Forest Museum for 3 miles to **Crescent Meadow**, a relaxing picnic spot, especially in spring when it's ablaze with wildflowers. The road passes **Moro Rock**, a landmark granite dome whose top can be reached via a quarter-mile carved staircase for views of the Great Western Divide, a chain of mountains running north–south through Sequoia National Park.

Sleeping & Eating

WUKSACHI LODGE   Hotel $$$

(559-565-4070, 866-807-3598; www.visit sequoia.com; 64740 Wuksachi Way, off Gener-

als Hwy; r $90-335; 🛜) Built in 1999, the Wuksachi Lodge is the most upscale lodging and dining option in the park. But don't get too excited – the wood-paneled atrium lobby has an inviting stone fireplace and forest views, but charmless motel-style rooms with oak furniture and thin walls have an institutional feel.

Information

Lodgepole Visitor Center (559-565-4436; 9am-4:30pm mid-Apr–mid-May, from 8am mid-May–late Jun & early Sep–mid-Oct, 7am-6pm late Jun-early Sep) Maps, information, exhibits, Crystal Cave tickets and wilderness permits.

EASTERN SIERRA

Cloud-dappled hills and sun-streaked mountaintops dabbed with snow typify the landscape of the Eastern Sierra, where slashing peaks – many over 14,000ft – rush abruptly upward from the arid expanses of the Great Basin and Mojave deserts. It's a dramatic juxtaposition that makes for a potent cocktail of scenery. Pine forests, lush meadows, ice-blue lakes, simmering hot springs and glacier-gouged canyons are some of the beautiful sights you'll find.

The Eastern Sierra Scenic Byway, officially known as Hwy 395, runs the entire length of the range. Note that in winter, when traffic thins, many facilities are closed.

Mono Lake

North America's second-oldest lake is a quiet and mysterious expanse of deep blue water, whose glassy surface reflects jagged Sierra peaks, young volcanic cones and the unearthly tufa (*too*-fah) towers that make the lake so distinctive. Jutting from the water like drip sand castles, tufas form when calcium bubbles up from subterranean springs and combines with carbonate in the alkaline lake waters.

The brackish water teems with buzzing alkali flies and brine shrimp, both considered delicacies by dozens of migratory bird species that return here year after year, including about 85% of the state's nesting population of California gulls, which takes over the lake's volcanic islands from April to August.

 Sights & Activities

SOUTH TUFA RESERVE   Nature Reserve
(office 760-647-6331; entry adult/child $3/ free) Tufa spires ring the lake, but the biggest grove is on the south rim with a mile-long interpretive trail. Ask about ranger-led tours at the Mono Basin Scenic Area Visitors Center. To get to the reserve, head south from Lee Vining on Hwy 395 for 6 miles, then east on Hwy 120 for 5 miles to the dirt road leading to a parking lot.

NAVY BEACH   Beach
The best place for swimming is at Navy Beach, just east of the reserve. It's also the best place to put in canoes or kayaks. From late June to early September, the **Mono Lake Committee** (760-647-6595; www.monolake.org/visit/canoe; tours $25; 8am, 9:30am & 11am Sat & Sun) operates one-hour canoe tours around the tufas.

Half-day kayak tours along the shore or out to Paoha Island are also offered by **Caldera Kayaks** (760-934-1691; www.cal derakayak.com; tours $75; mid-May–mid-Oct). Both require reservations.

 Sleeping & Eating

EL MONO MOTEL   Motel $
(760-647-6310; www.elmonomotel.com; 51 Hwy 395; r $69-99; May-Oct;) Grab a board game or soak up some mountain sunshine in this friendly flower-ringed place attached to an excellent cafe. In operation since 1927, and often booked solid, each of its 11 simple rooms (a few share bathrooms) is unique, decorated with vibrant and colorful art and fabrics.

HISTORIC MONO INN   Californian $$$
(760-647-6581; www.monoinn.com; 55620 Hwy 395; dinner mains $8-25; 11am-9pm May-Dec) A restored 1922 lodge owned by the family of photographer Ansel Adams, this is now an elegant lakefront restaurant with outstanding California comfort food, fabulous wine and views to match. Browse the 1000-volume cookbook

Mono Lake

FEAERGUS COONEY/LONELY PLANET IMAGES ©

HOWARD STAPLETON/ALAMY ©

Don't Miss **Crystal Cave**

Discovered in 1918 by two fishermen, Crystal Cave was carved by an underground river and has formations estimated to be 10,000 years old. Stalactites hang like daggers from the ceiling, and milky white marble formations take the shape of ethereal curtains, domes, columns and shields.

Tickets are *only* sold at the Lodgepole and Foothills visitors centers and *not* at the cave. Allow about one hour to get to the cave entrance, which is a half-mile walk from the parking lot at the end of a twisty 7-mile road; the turnoff is about 3 miles south of the Giant Forest. Bring a sweater or light jacket, as it's a huddle-for-warmth 48°F inside.

NEED TO KNOW

☎559-565-3759; www.sequoiahistory.org; Crystal Cave Rd; adult/child/senior $13/7/12;
⏱tours 10:30am-4:30pm mid-May–late Oct

---

collection upstairs, and stop in for music on the creekside terrace. It's located about 5 miles north of Lee Vining. Reservations recommended.

WHOA NELLIE DELI Deli $$
(www.whoanelliedeli.com; near junction of Hwys 120 & 395; mains $8-19; ⏱7am-9pm mid-Apr–Oct) Great food in a gas station? Come on... No, really, you gotta try this amazing kitchen where chef Matt 'Tioga' Toomey feeds delicious fish tacos, wild buffalo meatloaf and other tasty morsels to locals and clued-in passersby.

ⓘ Information

Mono Basin National Forest Scenic Area Visitors Center (☎760-647-3044; www.monolake.org/visit/vc; Hwy 395; ⏱8am-5pm mid-Apr–Nov) Half a mile north of Lee Vining.

Mammoth Lakes

This is a small mountain resort town endowed with larger-than-life scenery – active outdoorsy folks worship at the base of its dizzying 11,053ft Mammoth

Mountain. Everlasting powder clings to these slopes, and when the snow finally fades, the area's an outdoor wonderland of mountain-bike trails, excellent fishing, endless alpine hiking and blissful hidden spots for hot-spring soaking.

eas, both laced with fabulous trails leading to shimmering lakes, rugged peaks and hidden canyons. Major trailheads leave from the Mammoth Lakes Basin, Reds Meadow and Agnew Meadows; the latter two are accessible only by shuttle (see the boxed text, p273).

 Activities

Skiing & Snowboarding

MAMMOTH MOUNTAIN Skiing
(☎760-934-2571, 800-626-6684, 24hr snow report 888-766-9778; www.mammothmountain .com; lift tickets adult/senior & child $92/46) This is a skiers' and snowboarders' dream resort, where sunny skies, a reliably long season (usually from November to June) and over 3500 acres of fantastic tree-line and open-bowl skiing are a potent cocktail.

Mountain-Biking

MAMMOTH MOUNTAIN BIKE PARK Mountain-Biking
(☎800-626-6684; www.mammothmountain .com; day pass adult/child $43/22; ⊙9am-4:30pm Jun-Sep) Come summer, Mammoth Mountain morphs into the massive Mammoth Mountain Bike Park, with more than 80 miles of well-kept single-track trails. Several other trails traverse the surrounding forest.

But you don't need wheels (or a medic) to ride the vertiginous **gondola** (adult/ senior $23/12) to the apex of the mountain, where there's a cafe and an interpretive center with scopes pointing towards the nearby peaks.

Hiking

Mammoth Lakes rubs up against the Ansel Adams Wilderness and John Muir Wilderness ar-

Sleeping

TAMARACK LODGE & RESORT Resort $$
(☎760-934-2442, 800-626-6684; www.tama racklodge.com; lodge r $99-169, cabins $169-599; @ 🛜 🐾) Kind people run this charming year-round resort on the shore of Lower Twin Lake. In business since 1924, the cozy lodge includes a fireplace, bar, excellent restaurant, 11 rustic rooms and 35 cabins. The cabins range from very simple to simply deluxe, and come with full kitchen, private bathroom, porch and wood-burning stove.

AUSTRIA HOF LODGE Lodge $$
(☎760-934-2764; www.austriahof.com; 924 Canyon Blvd; r incl breakfast $130-215; 🛜)

Mammoth sculpture, Mammoth Mountain
JOHN ELK III/LONELY PLANET IMAGES ©

Close to Canyon Lodge, rooms here have modern knotty pine furniture, thick down duvets and DVD players. Ski lockers and a sundeck hot tub make winter stays here even sweeter.

 Eating

LAKEFRONT
RESTAURANT Californian, French $$$
(☏760-934-3534; www.tamaracklodge.com
/lakefront-restaurant; Lakes Loop Rd, Twin Lakes;
mains $28-38; ☽5-9:30pm year-round, plus
11am-2pm summer, closed Tue & Wed in fall &
spring) The Tamarack Lodge has an intimate and romantic dining room overlooking Twin Lakes. The chef crafts French-Californian specialties like elk medallions au poivre and heirloom tomatoes with Basque cheese, and the staff are superbly friendly. Reservations recommended.

GOOD LIFE CAFE Californian $
(www.mammothgoodlifecafe.com; Mammoth Mall,
126 Old Mammoth Rd; mains $8-10; ☽6:30am-
3pm; ☒) Healthy food, generously filled veggie wraps and big bowls of salad make this a perennially popular place. The front patio is blissful for a long brunch on a warm day.

① Getting There & Away

Mammoth's updated airport Mammoth Yosemite (MMH) has a daily nonstop flight to San Francisco, operating winter through to spring on United (www.united.com). Alaska Airlines (www.alaska air.com) runs a similar seasonal (and cheaper) San Jose flight and year-round service to Los Angeles.

Manzanar National Historic Site

A stark wooden guard tower alerts drivers to one of the darkest chapters in US history, which unfolded on a barren and windy sweep of land some 5 miles south of Independence. Little remains of the infamous war concentration camp, a dusty square mile where more than 10,000 people of Japanese ancestry were cor-

ralled during WWII following the attack on Pearl Harbor. The camp's lone remaining building, the former high-school auditorium, houses a superb **interpretive center** (☎760-878-2194; www.nps.gov/manz; ⏱9am-4:30pm Nov-Mar, to 5:30pm Apr-Oct).

Watch the 20-minute documentary, then explore the thought-provoking exhibits chronicling the stories of the families that languished here yet built a vibrant community. Afterwards, take a self-guided 3.2-mile driving tour around the grounds, which includes a recreated mess hall and barracks, vestiges of buildings and gardens, as well as the haunting camp cemetery.

Alabama Hills

In Lone Pine, the warm colors and rounded contours of the Alabama Hills stand in contrast to the jagged snowy Sierras just behind. The setting for count-less ride-'em-out movies and the popular *Lone Ranger* TV series, the stunning orange rock formations are a beautiful place to experience sunrise or sunset. A number of graceful rock arches are within easy hiking distance of the roads. Head west on Whitney Portal Rd and either turn left at Tuttle Creek Rd, after a half-mile, or north on Movie Rd, after about 3 miles.

GOLD COUNTRY

Gold Country is where it all began – the drowsy hill towns and oak-lined byways of today's quiet road trip belie the wild chaos of California's founding. Shortly after a sparkle caught James Marshall's eye in 1848, the rush for gold brought a stampede of 300,000 '49ers to the Sierra foothills. Today, fading historical markers tell tales of bloodlust and banditry, while the surviving boomtowns survive on antiques, ice cream, wine and Gold Rush ephemera.

271

Don't Miss **Bodie State Historic Park**

For a time warp back to the Gold Rush era, swing by Bodie, one of the West's most authentic and best-preserved ghost towns. Gold was first discovered here in 1859, and within 20 years the place grew from a rough mining camp to an even rougher boomtown with a population of 10,000 and a reputation for unbridled lawlessness. Fights and murders took place almost daily, the violence no doubt fueled by liquor dispensed in the town's 65 saloons, some of which did double duty as brothels, gambling halls or opium dens. The hills disgorged some $35 million worth of gold and silver in the 1870s and '80s, but when production plummeted, so did the population, and eventually the town was abandoned to the elements.

About 200 weather-beaten buildings still sit frozen in time in this cold, barren and windswept valley heaped with tailing piles. The former Miners' Union Hall now houses a **museum** and **visitors center**. Rangers conduct free general tours.

Bodie is about 13 miles east of Hwy 395 via Rte 270; the last 3 miles are unpaved. Although the park is open year-round, the road is usually closed in winter and early spring, so you'd have to don snowshoes or cross-country skis to get there.

NEED TO KNOW

Bodie State Historic Park (📞760-647-6445; www.parks.ca.gov/bodie; Hwy 270; adult/child $7/5; 🕙9am-6pm Jun-Aug, to 3pm Sep-May); visitors center (🕙9am-one hr before park closes)

Nevada City

Maybe it's all those prayer flags, or new-agey Zen goodies that clutter the sandalwood-scented gift shops, but, like a yogi in the lotus position, Nevada City is all about *balance*. The city has the requisite Victorian Gold Rush tourist attractions – an elegantly restored town center, an informative local history museum, girlishly decorated bed-and-breakfasts by the dozen – and a proud contemporary

Detour:
Devils Postpile

The surreal volcanic formation of **Devils Postpile National Monument** is a fascinating attraction. The 60ft curtains of near-vertical, six-sided basalt columns formed when rivers of molten lava slowed, cooled and cracked with perplexing symmetry. This honeycomb design is best appreciated from atop the columns, reached by a short trail. The columns are an easy, half-mile hike from the **Devils Postpile Ranger Station** (📞760-934-2289; www.nps.gov/depo; 🕐9am-5pm summer).

The road here is only accessible from about June until September, weather permitting, but is closed to private vehicles unless you are camping, have lodge reservations or are disabled (in which case you must pay a $10 per car fee). Otherwise you must use a mandatory **shuttle bus** (per adult/child $7/4).

identity, with a small but thriving independent arts and culture scene.

🛏 Sleeping & Eating

🏨 OUTSIDE INN   Motel $
(📞530-265-2233; www.outsideinn.com; 575 E Broad St, Nevada City; r $75-150; ❄🔇🏊👪) The best option for active explorers, this is an exceptionally friendly and fun motel, with 14 individually named and decorated rooms and a staff that loves the outdoors. Some rooms have a patio overlooking a small creek; all of them have nice quilts, access to BBQ grills and excellent information about hiking in the area.

🍴 NEW MOON CAFÉ   Californian $$
(www.thenewmooncafe.com; 230 York St; mains $13-20; 🕐11:30-2pm Tue-Fri & 5pm-8:30pm Tue-Sun) Pure elegance, Peter Selaya's regularly changing menu keeps an organic, local bent. If you visit during the peak of the summer keep to the aquatic theme by trying the wild, line-caught fish or seared duck, prepared with a French-Asian fusion.

Marshall Gold Discovery State Historic Park

Compared to the stampede of gun-toting, hill-blasting, hell-raising settlers that populate tall tales along Hwy 49, the **Marshall Gold Discovery State Historic Park** (per car $5; 🕐8am-7pm; 🔇) is a place of bucolic tranquillity, with two tragic heroes in John Sutter and James Marshall. Sutter, who had a fort in Sacramento, partnered with Marshall to build a sawmill on a swift stretch of the American River in 1847. It was Marshall who discovered gold here on January 24, 1848, and though the men tried to keep their findings secret, it eventually brought a chaotic rush of prospectors from around the world. In one of the great tragic ironies of the Gold Rush, the men who made this discovery died nearly penniless.

The park's quiet charms are mostly experienced outdoors, strolling past the carefully reconstructed mill and taking in the grounds. There's also a humble **Visitor Information Center & Museum** (📞530-622-3470; Bridge St; 🕐10am-4pm Tue-Sun) with a tidy shop where you can buy kitsch from the frontier days.

Panning for gold is popular – you can pay $7 to pan for a quick training session and 45 minutes of gold panning, or pan for free if you have your own.

Sacramento

Square in the middle of the sweltering valley, Sacramento's downtown is couched by the confluence of two cool rivers – the American and the Sacramento – and its streets are shushed by the leaves of huge oaks.

If You Like...
Water Fun

If you like exploring Mono Lake's waters (p267), you might enjoy these other aquatic adventures.

1 LAKE TAHOE CRUISES
(☎800-238-2463; www.zephyrcove.com; 2hr cruise adult/child from $45/15; 👪) Two paddle wheelers ply Lake Tahoe's 'big blue' year-round with a variety of cruises, including a narrated two-hour daytime trip to Emerald Bay. The *Tahoe Queen* leaves from Ski Run Marina in town, while the MS *Dixie II* is based at Zephyr Cove Marina on the eastern shore in Nevada.

2 AUBURN STATE RECREATION AREA
(☎530-885-4527; www.parks.ca.gov) Steel yourself for a face full of spray as you raft the churning gorges of the American River. Adrenaline seekers can top up with a bracing dose of springtime white water, while lazy-day paddlers can drift along and float with more mellow currents.

3 SWIMMING AT MUIR ROCK
A short walk from Roads End in Kings Canyon (p263), this large flat river boulder is where John Muir often gave talks during Sierra Club field trips. The rock now bears his name, and the lazy river setting abounds with gleeful swimmers in summer.

Sights

FREE CALIFORNIA STATE CAPITOL   Historic Building
(☎916-324-0333; cnr 10th & L Sts; ⊙9am-5pm) The California State Capitol is Sacramento's most recognizable structure. Built in the late 19th century, it underwent major reconstruction in the 1970s, and its marble halls offer a cool place for a stroll. It could be argued that the 40 acres of garden surrounding the dome, **Capitol Park**, are better than the building itself.

SUTTER'S FORT STATE HISTORIC PARK   Historic Site
(www.parks.ca.gov/suttersfort; cnr 27th & L Sts; adult/child $5/3; ⊙10am-5pm) Originally built by John Sutter, the park was once the only trace of white settlement for hundreds of miles – hard to tell by the housing developments that surround the park today. California history buffs should carve out a couple hours to stroll within its walls, where original furniture, equipment and a working ironsmith are straight out of the 1850s.

CALIFORNIA STATE RAILROAD MUSEUM   Museum
(www.californiastaterailroadmuseum.org; 125 I St; adult/child 6-17yr $9/4; ⊙10am-5pm) At Old Sac's north end is this excellent museum, the largest of its kind in the US. It has an impressive collection of railcars, locomotives, toy models and memorabilia, and a fully outfitted Pullman sleeper and vintage diner cars to induce joy in railroad enthusiasts. Tickets include entrance to the restored **Central Pacific Passenger Depot**, across the plaza from the museum entrance. On weekends from April to September, you can board a steam-powered passenger train from the depot (adult/child $10/5) for a 40-minute jaunt along the riverfront.

 Sleeping & Eating

CITIZEN HOTEL   Boutique Hotel $$
(☎916-492-4460; 926 J St; r $159, suites from $215; 📶) With an elegant, ultra-hip upgrade by the Joie de Vivre group, the long-vacant Citizen has suddenly become one of the coolest stays in this part of the state. Rooms are lovely with luxurious linen, bold patterned fabrics and stations for your iPod. The little touches make a big impression too: vintage political cartoons adorn the walls, loaner bikes and a nightly wine reception. There's an upscale farm-to-table restaurant on the ground floor (a daily menu of seasonal mains starts around $25).

Detour:
Calaveras Big Trees State Park

This **park** (📞209-795-2334; per vehicle $6) is home to giant sequoia redwood trees. Reaching as high as 325ft and with trunk diameters up to 33ft, these leftovers from the Mesozoic era are thought to weigh upwards of 3000 tons, or close to 20 blue whales.

The redwood giants are distributed in two large groves, one of which is easily seen from the **North Grove Big Trees Trail**, a 1.5-mile self-guided loop, near the entrance, where the air is fresh with pine and rich soil. A 4-mile trail that branches off from the self-guided loop climbs out of the North Grove, crosses a ridge and descends 1500ft to the Stanislaus River.

DELTA KING　　　　　Riverboat **$$**
(📞916-444-5464, 800-825-5464; www.delta king.com; 100 Front St; r $113-163; ❄@📶) If you stay near Old Town, you can't beat the experience of sleeping aboard the *Delta King*, a docked 1927 paddle-wheeler that lights up like a Christmas tree at night.

LA BONNE SOUPE CAFE　Sandwiches **$**
(www.labonnesoupe.com; 920 8th St; $8-10; 🕙11am-3pm Mon-Fri) Chef Daniel Pont as-sembles his divine sandwiches with such loving, affectionate care that the line of downtown lunchers snakes out the door. If you're in a hurry, skip it; Pont's humble lunch counter is focused on quality that predates drive-through haste. And the creamy soups made from scratch prove the restaurant's name is a painful under-statement.

San Diego & the Deserts

There's a certain arrogance that comes with living on the SoCal coast. It's a breezy confidence that springs from the assumption that your life is just, well, *better* than everyone else's. But as far as coastal snobs go, San Diegans are the ones we like the most. Whether it's a battle-tested docent sharing stories on the USS *Midway* or a no-worries surf diva helping you catch a wave, folks here are willing to share the good life.

Inland, a different kind of beauty beckons. There's something undeniably artistic in the way the landscape unfolds in the California desert: weathered volcanic peaks, 'singing' sand dunes, mountains shimmering in rainbow hues, and hot, natural, mineral water spurting forth to feed palm oases and soothe aching muscles in stylish spas. Through it all threads iconic Route 66. No matter what your trail through the desert, it might creep into your consciousness and never fully leave.

Fifth Ave, San Diego
WITOLD SKRYPCZAK/LONELY PLANET IMAGES ©

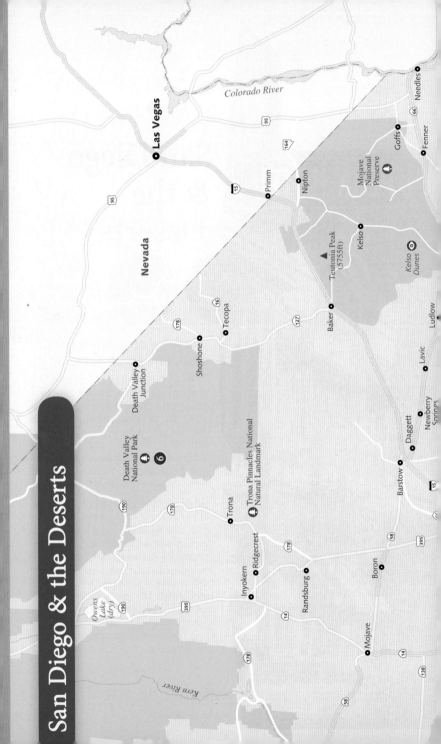

San Diego & the Deserts

Las Vegas

Colorado River

Nevada

Needles

66

Fenner

Goffs

Nipton

Mojave National Preserve

Primm

15

95

164

95

Teutonia Peak (5755ft)

Kelso

Kelso Dunes

Ludlow

Tecopa

16

178

122

Baker

Shoshone

Death Valley Junction

Lavic

Newberry Springs

Daggett

Death Valley National Park 6

Barstow

15

190

178

Trona Pinnacles National Natural Landmark

Trona

Inyokern

Ridgecrest

178

Randsburg

58

395

Boron

Owens Lake (dry)

190

395

14

Mojave

178

58

14

Kern River

138

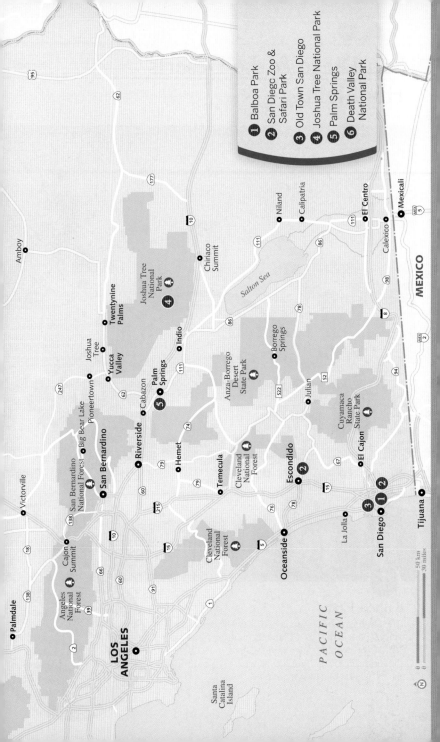

San Diego & the Deserts Highlights

① Balboa Park

The rumors are true: Balboa Park is the largest urban cultural park in the US. It's famous for its picturesque El Prado promenade, lined with theaters, museums and formal gardens. The 1200-acre park is also an ideal place to watch San Diegans at play.

Need to Know

WHEN TO VISIT Mornings are busy with school groups; museums close Mondays **MAPS & INFO** Stop at the Information Center to plan your day **FREE DAYS** Some museums are free Tuesdays **For more, see p291**

Balboa Park Don't Miss List

CARRIE TAYLOE, SAN DIEGO
TOURISM PROFESSIONAL & REGIONAL
DIRECTOR AT SMART DESTINATIONS

1 SAN DIEGO ZOO
No visit to Balboa Park is complete without a stop at the **San Diego Zoo** (p296). One of the best views of the city is by way of the zoo's Skyfari Aerial Tram. Go in the afternoon when the crowds have thinned out. And don't forget to bring something warm – most days you'll need a sweater because of the wind.

2 REUBEN H FLEET SCIENCE CENTER
This **science center** (p293) is very family-friendly. Expect tons of interactive and educational activities for little adventurers. The new IMAX theatre is excellent.

3 LITTLE JAPAN
Go to the Japanese-style **Tea Pavilion** (p302) for lunch. Try the Moroccan green mint tea and soba noodles, then finish off with homemade *mochi* (a sweet, glutinous rice cake). If you are lucky enough to visit in the spring, don't miss the Cherry Blossom Festival at the **Japanese Friendship Garden** (p292).

4 SEASONAL FESTIVALS
In summer, come for the **Twilight in the Park** concert series in the **Spreckels Organ Pavilion** (p293). My family loves **December Nights** in Balboa Park, a huge festival with free museum admissions, performances and international food sampling at the House of Pacific Relations. Huge crowds, but it's worth it!

5 ROMANCE IN THE PARK
For a great date night, walk through the park at dusk, then head over to **Prado** (p302) for dinner – my husband and I love the Kobe beef sushi rolls and spiced ahi dishes. Finish your evening under the stars with a show at the **Old Globe Theatre** (p305).

San Diego Zoo & Safari Park

Explore the animal kingdom at the world-famous San Diego Zoo (p296), set on 100 beautifully landscaped acres in northern Balboa Park. It's home to more than 3000 finned, furry and feathered creatures – more than 800 species are represented. At the affiliated Safari Park (p298), a 1800-acre open-range zoo just outside the city, herds of giraffes, zebras, rhinos and other animals roam the valley floor.

Old Town San Diego

Established in the late 18th century, this settlement of wood and adobe buildings was once the city's center of commerce and culture. Today, the Old Town State Historic Park (p294) offers a taste of southern California history – guided tours take visitors past an antique dentist's office, the tinsmith, an early court house and Wells Fargo Bank, the adobe home of an early commandant, even an old brick house that's officially 'haunted.'

Joshua Tree National Park

Straddling the transition zone between the Colorado Desert and the higher, cooler Mojave Desert, Joshua Tree National Park (p313) is known for its stunning wildflowers, varied cacti (like ocotillos, whose octopus-like tentacles shoot out crimson flowers in spring), and, of course, its famous Joshua trees. The park's mystical desert vistas and lush oases charm hikers and mountain-bikers throughout the year.

Palm Springs

In the 1950s and '60s, Palm Springs was the swinging getaway of Sinatra, Elvis and dozens of other stars who partied the night away. Today, you can rub shoulders with the local hipsters and elderly folk, hike palm-oasis canyons, soak in hot springs and shop for modern art. A ride on the Palm Springs Aerial Tramway (p307) is a great way to take it all in.

Death Valley National Park

The largest national park in the continental USA, Death Valley National Park (p317) spans more than 5000 sq miles. Though the name is foreboding, this crazy-quilted geological playground is full of life – you'll find giant sand dunes, mosaic marbled canyons, extinct volcanic craters, palm-shaded oases and dozens of rare wildlife species that exist nowhere else in the world.

San Diego & the Deserts' Best...

Sandy Landscapes

◦ **Death Valley National Park** (p317) Famous for 'singing' sand dunes and surreal desert vistas.

◦ **Coronado** (p295) Go barefoot on the white, butter-soft sand in front of the Hotel del Coronado.

◦ **Palm Springs** (p306) Natural hot springs and a retro-cool resort town in the middle of a hot desert.

◦ **La Jolla** (p297) This picturesque shoreline is dotted with sunbathing sea lions.

Microbreweries & Wine Bars

◦ **Stone Brewing Company** (p305) Try the Stone Barley Wine.

◦ **Lost Abbey** (p305) Go for the Lost and Found Abbey Ale.

◦ **Wine Steals** (p304) Have a flight of California reds.

◦ **AleSmith** (p305) Sample the potent Old Numbskull at your own risk.

◦ **George's at the Cove** (p303) The wine list is second only to the spectacular views.

Historic Sites

◦ **Old Town State Historic Park** (p294) San Diego's original settlement.

◦ **Mission Basilica San Diego de Alcalá** (p294) Founded in 1773 by Padre Junípero Serra.

◦ **Elvis Honeymoon Hideaway** (p312) The King's Palm Springs love nest.

◦ **Hotel del Coronado** (p295) *Some Like It Hot* was filmed here in 1959.

◦ **Whaley House** (p294) The Victorian house is 'officially' haunted.

Hikes

o **Tahquitz Canyon** (p309)
Trails go past waterfalls and rock art.

o **Indian Canyons** (p309)
Cuts through the Agua Caliente Indian Reservation.

o **Mosaic Canyon** (p318)
Multicolored rock walls delight hikers and climbers alike.

o **Kelso Dunes** (p316) The Mojave's famous 'singing' sand dunes.

o **Telescope Peak** (p319)
Death Valley's most challenging summit.

Need to Know

ADVANCE PLANNING

o **Two months before**
Look up festivals and events around the areas you're visiting; some may be worth planning your stay around.

o **One month before**
Look online for discount tickets and promotions to expensive attractions like SeaWorld and the San Diego Zoo Safari Park.

o **Two weeks before**
Break in your boots for all of the hiking you'll do around Death Valley and Joshua Tree.

RESOURCES

o **www.sandiego.org** The official San Diego traveler's resource.

o **www.hiking-in-ps.com**
Hiking information for the Palm Springs area, including Joshua Tree.

o **www.visitpalmsprings .com** Online visitor's guide to the Palm Springs area.

o **www.nps.gov/deva**
Death Valley resources and information.

GETTING AROUND

o **Car** The obvious choice for Route 66, Death Valley and Joshua Tree.

o **Train** The Pacific Surfliner route runs north from San Diego; the ride to Los Angeles is wonderfully scenic.

o **Walking** Downtown San Diego and downtown Palm Springs are very walkable.

o **Bus** Public transportation is easy within San Diego, but be aware that the longer-haul bus to Palm Springs isn't such a pleasant ride.

BE FOREWARNED

o **Deathly temperatures**
It's way too hot to hike in Death Valley National Park during summer; don't even think about it.

o **Museum closures** Most museums in San Diego's Balboa Park are closed on Mondays.

o **Renting a car** Southern California is very much a driver's destination. Shop around for the best deals online before starting your trip.

o **In-demand campsites**
If you're dying to camp in any of California's national parks, especially popular ones like Joshua Tree, you'll need to reserve a site well in advance.

t: Hotel del Coronado; **Above:** Beach, La Jolla

San Diego & the Deserts Itineraries

Don't miss Death Valley and Joshua Tree; Palm Springs serves as a midtrip oasis. In San Diego, the most appealing attractions – wild animals, beach paths and science centers – aren't just for kids.

3 DAYS

SAN DIEGO ZOO SAFARI PARK TO SEAWORLD
San Diego Fun

The southern quarter of California is a dream for youngsters. A must-see for kids (and adults) is the **(1) San Diego Zoo Safari Park**, a game-changer on the zoo market, where the animals roam free and the people are fenced off. For a relaxing late afternoon or sunset, get some fresh air at **(2) Mission Beach**, where younger kids will beg for a ride on the antique roller coaster at Belmont Park and older kids will enjoy cycling or in-line skating on the beach paths.

Alternate the wild-animal activity and exercise with a quieter day by stopping at the **(3) New Children's Museum**, where parents will dig the modern-art vibe, and the nap-time-and-apple-juice-set will love the hands-on exhibits. In the afternoon, head to the **(4) Reuben H Fleet Science Center** in Balboa Park. The interactive science center, with a new IMAX theater, is as fun for parents as it is for children. Get a good night's sleep before venturing on to the pièce de résistance, **(5) SeaWorld**, where trained orcas, splashy water rides, marine-animal shows and cotton candy make for a child's dream day.

DEATH VALLEY
NATIONAL PARK 6

Nevada

MOJAVE NATIONAL
PRESERVE 5

CALIFORNIA ROUTE 4
66 MUSEUM

JOSHUA TREE 1
NATIONAL PARK

3 2 PALM SPRINGS

PALM
SPRINGS
AERIAL TRAMWAY

MISSION
BEACH 1 SAN DIEGO ZOO SAFARI PARK

5 SEAWORLD

2 4 REUBEN H FLEET
3 SCIENCE CENTER

NEW
CHILDREN'S
MUSEUM   MEXICO

Top Left: Surf and skate store, Mission Beach (p302);
Top Right: Death Valley National Park (p317)

(TOP LEFT) RICHARD CUMMINS/LONELY PLANET IMAGES ©;
(TOP RIGHT) WITOLD SKRYPCZAK/LONELY PLANET IMAGES ©

5 DAYS

JOSHUA TREE TO DEATH VALLEY
Desert Road Trip

There's no reason you have to rough it for a week just because you're visiting a pair of national parks – just make Palm Springs your glamorous pit stop. Begin in **(1) Joshua Tree National Park**, where you can hop around smooth, big-shouldered boulders in the Hidden Valley and take artistic photographs of the legendary tree that inspired a U2 album. Shake the dirt off your hiking boots and head west to **(2) Palm Springs** for a day and night of art-gallery-hopping, cocktails, shopping, perhaps even a visit to Elvis Presley's one-time love nest. Don't miss a ride aboard the **(3) Palm Springs Aerial Tramway** – it's a rare opportunity to ascend through five distinct life zones in fewer than 15 minutes.

Fill up your tank and grab a large cup of coffee: your drive north to Death Valley will take half a day. If you're not in a particular hurry, detour to the **(4) California Route 66 Museum** in Victorville to revel in the mythology of the Mother Road or head east at Barstow to catch a glimpse of the spectacular volcanic cinder cones, desert tortoises, jackrabbits and coyotes of **(5) Mojave National Preserve**. Finish your trip amid the eerie desert landscapes and Old West–style ghost towns of **(6) Death Valley National Park**.

Discover San Diego & the Deserts

At a Glance

○ **San Diego** (p288) This laid-back SoCal capital features museums and lively beach communities.

○ **Palm Springs** (p306) Retro-chic desert oasis known for hot springs, galleries and shopping.

○ **Joshua Tree National Park** (p313) This dynamic, boulder-strewn landscape is home to the legendary Joshua tree.

○ **Route 66** (p316) A joyride down this famous highway offers a taste of classic Americana.

○ **Death Valley National Park** (p317) Trippy desertscapes and rock formations in an arid playground.

Gaslamp Quarter, San Diego
RICHARD CUMMINS/LONELY PLANET IMAGES ©

SAN DIEGO

 Sights

California's second-largest city and America's eighth largest, San Diego doesn't seduce like San Francisco or thrill like LA, but life here is so persistently pleasant, what with 70 miles of coastline and the nation's most enviable climate, you won't care much. Small wonder that San Diegans promote their hometown as 'America's Finest City.'

The area around 5th Ave, once known as The Stingaree, used to be a notorious red-light district. These days, the Gaslamp Quarter is enjoying a second, post-Petco wave of revitalization and growth. Restored buildings (built between the 1870s and the 1920s) have become home to restaurants, bars, galleries, shops and theaters. The 16-acre area south of Broadway between 4th and 6th Aves is designated a National Historic District.

Downtown

Just south of Broadway, running along 5th Ave, is the historic **Gaslamp Quarter**, the primary hub for shopping, dining and entertainment.

WILLIAM HEATH DAVIS HOUSE   Historic building
(Map p292; ☏ 619-233-4692; www.gaslamp quarter.org; 410 Island Ave; adult/senior $5/4; ⊙10am-6pm Tue-Sat, 9am-3pm Sun) For a taste of local history, peruse the exhibits inside this museum; the saltbox house was the one-time home of William Heath Davis, the man credited with starting the

development of modern San Diego. Upstairs, look for the hidden Prohibition-era still. Self-guided tours are available and the foundation also offers guided walking tours (adult/senior and student $10/8; 11am Saturday) of the quarter.

SAN DIEGO CHINESE HISTORICAL MUSEUM
Museum

(Map p292; ☎619-338-9888; www.sdchm.org; 404 3rd Ave; admission $2; ☺10:30am-4pm Tue-Sat, from noon Sun) This was the heart of San Diego's former Chinatown. Exhibits include a former warlord's 40-piece wood-carved bed – assembled without nails – as well as the ornate, ultratiny slippers worn by women with bound feet.

MUSEUM OF CONTEMPORARY ART
Museum

(Map p292; ☎858-454-3541; www.mcasd.org; 1001 & 1100 Kettner Blvd; adult/student/senior $10/free/5; ☺11am-5pm Thu-Tue, to 7pm 3rd Thu each month, with free admission 5-7pm) This modern-art museum emphasizes minimalist and pop art, conceptual works and cross-border art. The original branch, open since the 1960s, is in La Jolla (p297).

NEW CHILDREN'S MUSEUM
Museum

(Map p292; ☎619-233-8792; www.thinkplaycreate.org; 200 W Island Ave; adult & child/ senior/child under 1yr $10/5/free; ☺10am-4pm Mon, Tue, Fri & Sat, to 6pm Thu, noon-4pm Sun) Part art studio, part children's museum, and part modern-art gallery, the museum displays artist-created exhibits that encourage kids of all ages to think about art, react to it, and create it.

Little Italy

Like any 'Little Italy' worth its salt, San Diego's version offers friendly pizzerias with red-and-white checkered tablecloths, unpretentious espresso bars, mom-and-pop delis, and family-friendly businesses.

You'll find the busiest patio tables on the eastern side of **India Street** (Map p292), a prime spot for a glass of Chianti.

Embarcadero

MARITIME MUSEUM
Museum

(Map p292; ☎619-234-9153; www.sdmaritime .com; 1492 N Harbor Dr; adult/child/senior $14/8/11; ☺9am-8pm, to 9pm late May-early Sep; ✋) The 100ft masts of the square-rigger tall ship *Star of India* – one of seven open to the public here – make this museum easy to find. Built on the Isle of Man and launched in 1863, the restored ship plied the England–India trade route, carried immigrants to New Zealand, became a trading ship based in Hawaii and worked the Alaskan salmon fisheries. Nowadays it's taken out once a year, making it the oldest active ship in the world.

For the highest wow-per-square-foot factor, squeeze into the museum's B-39 Soviet attack submarine. Metered parking and $10 day lots are nearby.

USS MIDWAY MUSEUM
Museum

(Map p292; ☎619-544-9600; www.midway .org; Navy Pier; adult/child/senior & student $18/10/15; ☺10am-5pm; ✋) Commissioned in 1945, the ship is the Navy's longest-serving aircraft carrier, seeing action in Vietnam and the first Gulf War. An engaging self-guided audio tour – filled with first person accounts from former crewmen – takes visitors on a maze-like climb through the engine room, the brig, the

Go San Diego Card

If you're planning on doing significant sightseeing in San Diego, it's wise to pick up the **Go San Diego Card** (☎866-628-9032; www .smartdestinations.com; adult/child 1-day $69/58, 2-day $99/87, 3-day $174/134). Depending on the pass purchased, cardholders have steeply discounted entry into their choice of 50 of the city's top attractions, including the San Diego Zoo and Safari Park, the Midway Aircraft Carrier Museum, the Air and Space Museum, Legoland and Knott's Berry Farm.

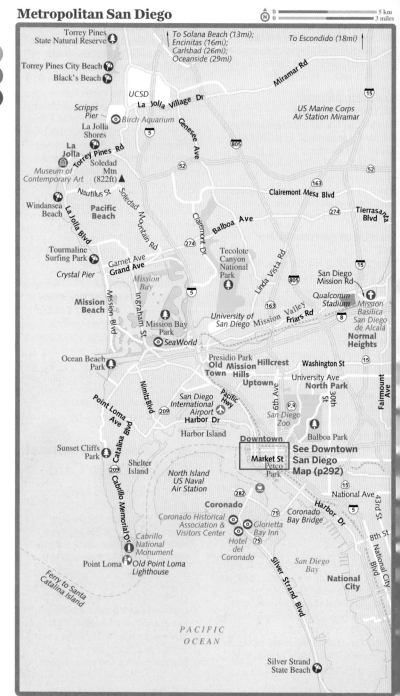

galley and the 4-acre flight deck, where an impressive lineup of fighter jets – including an F-14 Tomcat – await up-close inspection. Parking costs $5 to $7.

Balboa Park

The park stretches over an impressive 1200 acres, preening on prime real estate just minutes from Hillcrest, downtown, the beaches and Mission Valley.

El Prado is the park's main pedestrian thoroughfare, surrounded on both sides by romantic Spanish colonial-style buildings originally constructed for the 1915–16 Panama-California Exposition.

For a good park map, stop by the **Balboa Park Information Center** (☎619-239-0512; www.balboapark.org; 1549 El Prado; ☺9:30am-4:30pm) in the House of Hospitality. Helpful staff here sell the **Passport to Balboa Park** (single entry to 14 park museums for 1 week adult/child $45/24) and the **Stay-for-the-Day Pass** (your choice of 5 museums in day for $35).

CALIFORNIA BUILDING & MUSEUM OF MAN
Museum

From the west, El Prado passes under an archway and into an area called the California Quadrangle, with the **Museum of Man** (☎619-239-2001; www.museumofman .org; Plaza de California; adult/child 3-12yr/child 13-17yr/senior $12.50/5/8/10; ☺10am-4:30pm) on its northern side. This was the main entrance for the 1915 exposition, and the building was said to be inspired by the churrigueresque church of Tepotzotlán near Mexico City. Inside, the museum specializes in anthropology, with a focus on Native American cultures, particularly those in the American Southwest.

SAN DIEGO NATURAL HISTORY MUSEUM
Museum

(☎619-232-3821; www.sdnhm.org; 1788 El Prado; adult/child/senior $17/11/15; ☺10am-5pm; ♿) Seventy-five million years of SoCal fossils are the subject of one of the museum's newer permanent exhibits, Fossil Mysteries, which opened at the museum in 2006. Ongoing and upcoming exhibits cover climate change in polar regions and the ancient bond between horses and humans.

SAN DIEGO AIR & SPACE MUSEUM
Museum

(☎619-234-8291; www.sandiegoairandspace .org; 2001 Pan American Plaza; adult/child/

San Diego Air & Space Museum

RICHARD CUMMINS/LONELY PLANET IMAGES ©

291

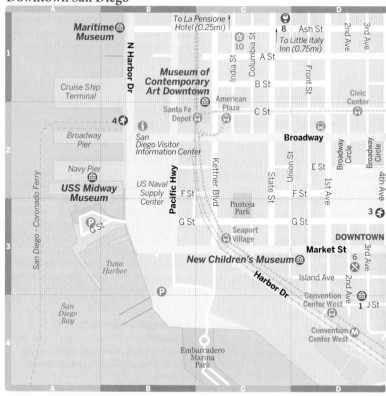

student & senior $16.50/6/13.50; ⊙10am-5:30pm Jun-Aug, to 4:30pm Sep-May) One look at the banged-up silver pod inside the rotunda of this museum, at the end of Pan American Plaza, and you'll be glad you chose not to become an astronaut. Exhibits here trace the history of aviation, providing close-up views of planes with dangerous names – Flying Tiger, Cobra and Skyhawk – plus a few reproductions.

SAN DIEGO MUSEUM OF ART   Museum
(☏619-232-7931; www.sdmart.org; 1450 El Prado, Plaza de Panama; adult/child/senior $12/4.50/9; ⊙10am-5pm Tue-Sat, noon-5pm Sun, to 9pm Thu Jun-Sep) The permanent collection holds a number of paintings by European masters (a few of the Spanish old masters are represented by sculptures on the building's facade), as well as noteworthy American landscape paintings and a

fine collection of Asian art. The **Sculpture Garden** has pieces by Alexander Calder and Henry Moore.

TIMKEN MUSEUM OF ART   Museum
(☏619-239-5548; www.timkenmuseum.org; 1500 El Prado; admission free; ⊙10am-4:30pm Tue-Sat, from 1:30pm Sun) The Timken is special because its simple exterior stands in bold contrast to the park's ubiquitous Spanish colonial style. It's also free. Paintings are from the Putnam Foundation collection and include works by Europeans Rembrandt, Rubens, El Greco, Cézanne and Pissarro, and Americans John Singleton Copley and Eastman Johnson.

BALBOA PARK GARDENS   Gardens
The **Alcazar Garden**, a formal Spanish-style garden, is tucked in a courtyard across from the Old Globe, south of El

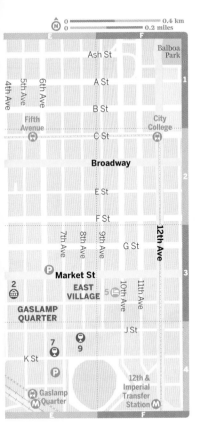

Downtown San Diego

◎ Top Sights
Maritime Museum B1
Museum of Contemporary Art
Downtown... C1
New Children's Museum..................... D3
USS Midway Museum A2

◎ Sights
1 San Diego Chinese Historical
Museum D4
2 William Heath Davis House E3

✈ Activities, Courses & Tours
3 Another Side of San Diego D3
4 San Diego Harbor Excursion.............. B2

⊖ Sleeping
5 Hotel Indigo F3

✗ Eating
6 Café 222 .... D3

◗ Drinking
7 Altitude Sky Lounge E4
8 Extraordinary Desserts...................... C1
9 Wine Steals East Village..................... E4

✪ Entertainment
10 Anthology.. C1

Prado, while the **Palm Canyon**, which has more than 50 species of palms, is a short stroll south. For a tranquil stroll or a bit of meditation, the **Japanese Friendship Garden** (☏619-232-2721; www.niwa.org; adult/student & senior $4/3; ☺10am-4pm Tue-Sun, to 5pm in summer), just north of Spreckels Organ Pavilion, is a convenient retreat.

SPRECKELS ORGAN
PAVILION   Landmark
South of Plaza de Panama, an extravagantly curved colonnade provides shelter for one of the world's largest outdoor organs. Donated by the Spreckels family, of sugar fortune and fame, the pipe organ – which has more than 4500 pipes – came with the stipulation that San Diego must always have an official organist. Free concerts are held at 2pm every Sunday.

REUBEN H FLEET SCIENCE
CENTER   Museum
(☏619-238-1233; www.rhfleet.org; 1875 El Prado; adult/child & senior $10/8.75; ☺10am-varies; ⛄) The exhibits at this hands-on science center include the energy-focused So Watt! and the galaxy-minded Origins in Space, where colorful Hubble images of colliding galaxies are particularly mesmerizing.

Old Town

In 1769 Padre Junípero Serra and Gaspar de Portola established the first Spanish settlement in California on Presidio Hill, overlooking the valley of the San Diego River.

Today, this area below Presidio Hill is called Old Town, and it presents life as it was between 1821 and 1872. Although it is neither very old (most of the buildings are reconstructions), nor exactly a town (more like a leafy suburb), it's a more-or-less faithful copy of San Diego's original

nucleus, offering a pedestrian plaza surrounded by historic buildings, shops, a number of restaurants and cafes, and a good opportunity to explore San Diego's early days.

OLD TOWN STATE HISTORIC PARK VISITOR CENTER   Museum
(📞619-220-5422; www.parks.ca.gov; Robinson-Rose House, 4002 Wallace St; ⏰10am-5pm; P) It houses memorabilia and books about the era as well as a diorama depicting the pueblo in 1872. If you're really interested in the historical background, take a guided tour, which leaves from the visitors center at 11am and 2pm.

WHALEY HOUSE   Historical Building
(📞619-297-7511; www.whaleyhouse.org; 2476 San Diego Ave; adult/child/senior $6/4/5; ⏰10am-9:30pm Jun-Aug, 10am-5pm Mon & Tue, 10am-9:30pm Thu-Sat Sep-May) We can't guarantee what you'll see at this lovely Victorian home (and the city's oldest brick building), two blocks northeast of the Old Town perimeter. What's intriguing

is that the house was *officially* certified as haunted by the US Department of Commerce.

MISSION BASILICA SAN DIEGO DE ALCALÁ   Mission
(Map p290; 📞619-281-8449; www.missionsandiego.com; 10818 San Diego Mission Rd; adult/child/student & senior $3/1/2; ⏰9am-4:45pm) Though the first California mission was established on Presidio Hill near Old Town, Padre Junípero Serra decided in 1773 to move upriver several miles, closer to a better water supply and more arable land. Extensive reconstruction began in 1931, and the pretty white church and the buildings you see now are the result of the thorough restoration.

The mission is two blocks north of I-8 via the Mission Gorge Rd exit just east of I-15.

Hillcrest

Just up from the northwestern corner of Balboa Park, you hit **Hillcrest** (Map p290), the heart of Uptown. It's San Diego's most bohemian district, with a decidedly urban

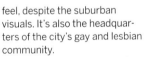

Left: Beach, Coronado; **Below:** Sculpture, Mission Basilica San Diego de Alcalá

(LEFT) IAN DAGNALL/ALAMY ©; (BELOW) RICHARD CUMMINS/LONELY PLANET IMAGES ©

feel, despite the suburban visuals. It's also the headquarters of the city's gay and lesbian community.

For a tour, begin at the **Hillcrest Gateway**, which arches over University Ave at 5th Ave. On 5th Ave between University Ave and Washington St is the multiplex **Landmark Hillcrest Cinemas** and lots of restaurants and shops. Then head south on 5th Ave to find a variety of cafes, friendly gay bars, vintage clothing shops and independent bookstores, many with a good selection of nonmainstream publications.

Coronado

In February 1888, the Hotel del Coronado (at the time the largest hotel west of the Mississippi) welcomed its very first guests. Today, the hotel and its stunning surroundings are the primary reasons to visit this well-manicured community.

The city of **Coronado** (Map p290) is now connected to the mainland by the graceful 2.12-mile Coronado Bay Bridge (opened in 1969), as well as by a narrow spit of sand known as the Silver Strand, which runs south to Imperial Beach and connects Coronado to the mainland.

The **Coronado Visitors Center** (Map p290; ☎619-437-8788; www.coronado visitorcenter.com; 1100 Orange Ave; ⊙9am-5pm Mon-Fri, 10am-5pm Sat & Sun) conducts a walking tour ($12), starting from the **Glorietta Bay Inn** (Map p290; 1630 Glorietta Blvd), near Silver Strand Blvd, at 11am Tuesday, Thursday and Saturday.

The **Coronado Historical Assocation** (Map p290; ☎619-437-8788; ⊙10:30am Tue & Fri, 2pm Sat & Sun, tour $15), housed in the same space as the visitors center, runs 90-minute tours of the historic Hotel del Coronado. Reserve ahead.

HOTEL DEL CORONADO   Historic Building
(Map p290; 1500 Orange Ave) This iconic hotel, familiar today with its whitewashed exterior, red conical towers, cupolas and

GERALD FRENCH/CORBIS ©

Don't Miss San Diego Zoo

If it slithers, crawls, stomps, swims, leaps or flies, chances are you'll find it in this world-famous zoo in northern Balboa Park. Since its opening in 1916, the zoo has also pioneered ways to house and display animals that mimic their natural habitat, leading to a revolution in zoo design and, so the argument goes, to happier animals.

Today, the zoo is home to thousands of animals representing 800-plus species in a beautifully landscaped setting. Perennial favorite **Polar Bear Plunge** (just remodeled) wows crowds with up-close, underwater views of the bears through thick glass walls. Other hot spots are **Elephant Odyssey** and **Panda Canyon**, where a live narrator shares facts about pandas at the outdoor viewing area here and, more importantly, keeps the line moving.

Arboreal orangutans and siamangs peacefully coexist in the **Lost Forest**. Don't miss the vast **Scripps Aviary** and **Owens Rain Forest Aviary**, where carefully placed feeders (and remarkably fearless birds) allow for close-up viewing. The koalas in the **Outback** have proved so popular that Australians may be surprised to find them an unofficial symbol of San Diego. At **Discovery Outpost**, youngsters can pet small critters and watch animal shows.

Arrive early, when the animals are most active. There's a large, free parking lot off Park Blvd that starts filling fast right at opening time. Bus 7 will get you there from downtown.

NEED TO KNOW

Map p290; ☏619-231-1515; www.sandiegozoo.org; 2920 Zoo Dr; adult/child with guided bus tour & aerial tram ride $40/30; ☺ from 9am, closing times vary; 👪

balconies, sprang from the vision of two of the jackrabbit hunters, Elisha Babcock and HL Story, who bought the island for $110,000. They cooked up the idea of building a grand hotel as a gimmick to en-tice people to buy parcels of land on the island. The hotel had its grand opening, with 399 completed rooms, in February 1888 (although work on the property continued for two more years).

Guests have included 11 US presidents and world royalty – pictures are displayed in the history gallery downstairs from the lobby. The Hotel, affectionately known as The Del, achieved its widest exposure in the 1959 movie *Some Like It Hot,* which earned its lasting association with Marilyn Monroe.

CORONADO FERRY Ferry
(☏ 619-234-4111; www.sdhe.com; 1 way $4.25; ☺ 9am-10pm) Hourly ferry shuttles between the Broadway Pier on the Embarcadero to the Coronado Ferry Landing at the foot of First Street, where **Bikes & Beyond** (☏ 619-435-7180; rental per 1-2 hr $25; ☺ 9am-8pm, call for seasonal hr) rents bicycles.

Point Loma
CABRILLO NATIONAL MONUMENT
Monument
(Map p290; ☏ 619-557-5450; www.nps.gov /cabr; per car $5, per person $3; ☺ 9am-5pm; P) Historically, this is the spot where Portuguese conquistador Juan Rodríguez Cabrillo landed in 1542 – making him the first European to step on the United States' western shores. The 1854 **Old Point Loma Lighthouse**, atop the point, is furnished with typical lighthouse furniture from the 1880s.

La Jolla Village & the Coast
For a camera-worthy stroll, take the half-mile bluff-top path that winds above the shoreline a few blocks west of the Village. Near the path's western end is the **Children's Pool**, off Coast Dr near Jenner Blvd. Here, a jetty funded by Ellen Browning Scripps protects the beach from big waves. Originally intended to give La Jolla's youth a safe place to frolic, the Children's Pool beach is

now populated by sea lions, which you can view up close as they lounge on the shore.

A short walk north leads to picnic tables and grills plus views of **La Jolla Cove** just below the path. This gem of a beach provides access to some of the best snorkeling around; it's also popular with rough-water swimmers.

MUSEUM OF CONTEMPORARY ART Museum
(MCASD; Map p290; ☏ 858-454-3541; www .mcasd.org; 700 Prospect St; adult/student/senior $10/free/5; ☺ 11am-5pm Thu-Tue, to 7pm 3rd Thu each month, with free admission 5-7pm) The La Jolla branch of the small but excellent museum shows world-class exhibitions that rotate every six months. Overall, MCASD holds more than 4000 works of art created after 1950 in its collection.

SAN DIEGO-LA JOLLA UNDERWATER PARK ECOLOGICAL RESERVE Diving, Snorkeling
Look for the white buoys offshore from Point La Jolla north to Scripps Pier that

Museum of Contemporary Art
RICHARD CUMMINS/LONELY PLANET IMAGES ©

Detour:
San Diego Zoo Safari Park

How close can you get to the animals at this 1800-acre **open-range zoo** (☏760-747-8702; www.sandiegozoo.org; 15500 San Pasqual Valley Rd, Escondido; admission incl tram adult/child $40/30; ☺from 9am, closing times vary; ♿) just 30 miles northeast of downtown? Consider this sign near the Lowlands Gorilla Habitat: 'In gorilla society prolonged eye contact is not only impolite, but it's considered a threat. Please respect the social signals of our gorillas and do not stare at them directly.' Seems we're so close we need to be reminded of our manners. But the sign is indicative of the experience here, where protecting and preserving wild animals and their habitats – while educating guests in a soft-handed manner – is the primary goal.

For a minisafari, hop aboard The Journey into Africa biodiesel tram for a drive through the world's second-largest continent. Sit on the left-hand side for slightly better views of the rhinos, giraffes, ostriches and other herbivores (by law, predators can't share space with prey).

The park is in Escondido. Take the freeway to the Via Rancho Parkway exit, turn right and continue to San Pasqual Rd. Turn right and follow signs to the park. Parking costs $10.

mark this protected zone with a variety of marine life, kelp forests, reefs and canyons.

CAVE STORE — Cave
(☏858-459-0746; www.cavestore.com; 1325 Coast Blvd; adult/child $4/3; ☺10am-5pm) For a spooky mini-adventure, continue walking north on Coast Blvd. Here, 145 wooden steps descend a dank, man-made tunnel (completed in 1905) to the largest of the caves, Sunny Jim Cave.

La Jolla Shores

(Map p290) Called 'the Shores,' this area northeast of La Jolla Cove is where La Jolla's cliffs meet the wide, sandy beaches that stretch north to Del Mar.

BIRCH AQUARIUM — Aquarium
(Map p290; ☏858-534-3474; http://aquarium.ucsd.edu; 2300 Exhibition Way; adult/child/student & senior $12/8.50/9; ☺9am-5pm; P ♿) Divers feed leopard sharks, garibaldi, sea bass and eels in the 70,000-gallon kelp tank during half-hour shows; check the website for times. The 13,000-gallon shark tank holds white-tip and black-tip reef sharks and others native to tropical reef habitats.

TORREY PINES STATE NATURAL RESERVE — Wildlife Reserve
(Map p290; ☏858-755-2063; www.torreypine.org; 12600 N Torrey Pines Rd; car $10; ☺8am-dusk) Birders, whale-watchers, hikers and those seeking great coastal views will want to amble through this tree-studded reserve that preserves the last mainland stands of the Torrey pine (*Pinus torreyana*), a species adapted to sparse rainfall and sandy, stony soils that's only found here and on Santa Rosa Island in Channel Islands National Park.

Admission is free if you enter on foot.

 Activities

PACIFIC BEACH SURF SCHOOL — Surfing
(☏858-373-1138; www.pacificbeachsurfschool.com; 4150 Mission Blvd, Suite 161; private/semi-private lessons per person $80/65) Learn to hang 10 at surf school or just rent a board and wet suit (half-day $25) at San Diego's oldest surf shop.

OEX DIVE & KAYAK — Water Sports
(☏858-454-6195; www.oexcalifornia.com; 2243/2132 Avenida de la Playa, La Jolla)

For gear or instruction, including spearfishing seminars and stand-up paddleboard lessons, head to this one-stop resource.

FAMILY KAYAK Kayaking
(619-282-3520; www.familykayak.com) Ocean kayaking is a good way to see sea life and explore cliffs and caves that are inaccessible from land.

 Tours

ANOTHER SIDE OF SAN DIEGO Walking, Boat
(Map p292; 619-239-2111; www.anothersideof sandiegotours.com; 300 G St) This highly rated tour company does Segway tours of Balboa park, horseback riding on the beach and Gaslamp food tours.

OLD TOWN TROLLEY TOURS Trolley
(619-298-8687; www.trolleytours.com; adult/ child $34/17) Not to be confused with the Metropolitan Transit System's rail trolleys, these open-air, hop-on-hop-off buses loop to the main attractions in and around downtown and in Coronado.

SAN DIEGO HARBOR EXCURSION Boat
(Map p292; 619-234-4111; www.sdhe.com; 1050 N Harbor Dr; adult/child from $22/11) A variety of bay and harbor cruises.

 **Sleeping**

Downtown

LA PENSIONE HOTEL Boutique Hotel $
(off Map p292; 800-232-4683; www.lapen sionehotel.com; 606 W Date St; r $100; P ❄ 🛜) At this four-story Little Italy hotel, rooms are built around a frescoed courtyard – a pleasant place to sip coffee from the adjacent cafe. Thanks to extensive renovations in 2010, the hotel looks fresh and stylish, even if rooms are on the small side.

LITTLE ITALY INN B&B $$
(off Map p292; 619-230-1600; www.littleitaly hotel.com; 505 W Grape St; incl breakfast r with shared/private bath $89/109, 2-room apt from $149; 🛜) If you can't get enough of Little Italy's charm, this pretty B&B is an ideal place to hang your hat. The 23-room Victorian-style inn boasts comfortable beds, cozy bathrobes in each room, a casual European-style breakfast and wine socials on weekend evenings.

Del Mar, San Diego

DAVID TOMLINSON/LONELY PLANET IMAGES ©

Don't Miss **SeaWorld**

Along with the zoo, SeaWorld is one of San Diego's most popular attractions, and Shamu has become an unofficial mascot for the city itself (not to be a spoilsport, but for the record, several killer whales here perform under the name Shamu). SeaWorld has a shamelessly commercial feel, but it's undoubtedly entertaining and even educational.

SeaWorld's claim to fame is its live shows, which feature trained dolphins, seals, sea lions and killer whales. Current hits are **Blue Horizons**, a bird and dolphin extravaganza, and **One Ocean**, featuring Shamu and his killer-whale amigos leaping, diving and gliding.

In **Penguin Encounter**, you'll smell the 250 tuxedoed show-offs before you see them. Nearby, dozens of sharks glide overhead as you walk through a 57ft acrylic tube at **Shark Encounter**. Species include reef sharks and sand tiger sharks, some impressively large.

The park is easy to find by car – take SeaWorld Dr off I-5 less than a mile north of where it intersects with I-8. Take bus 9 from downtown. Tickets sales end 90 minutes before closing time.

NEED TO KNOW

Map p290; ☎800-257-4268, 619-226-3901; www.seaworld.com/seaworld/ca; 500 SeaWorld Dr; adult/child 3-9yr $70/62; ☼9am-10pm Jul–mid-Aug, to 11pm Fri-Sun, shorter hr rest of year; ♿

HOTEL INDIGO Boutique Hotel **$$**
(Map p292; ☎619-727-4000; www.hotelsandiego downtown.com; 509 9th Ave; r from $146; P❄@☎♨🐾) The first LEED-certified hotel in San Diego, Hotel Indigo is smartly designed and ecofriendly. The design is contemporary but colorful; guest rooms feature huge floor-to-ceiling windows, spa-style baths and large flat-screen TVs. Parking is $35.

Coronado

HOTEL DEL CORONADO
Luxury/Historic Hotel **$$$**
(Map p290; ☎619-435-6611, 800-468-3533; www.hoteldel.com; 1500 Orange Ave; r from $325;

[P] [❄] [@] [🛜] [☂]) The 120-year old hotel combines tradition (p295), luxury and access to the city's most stunning beach. Amenities include two pools, a full-service spa, fitness center, shops, restaurants and manicured grounds. Parking is another $25.

Ocean Beach & Point Loma

INN AT SUNSET CLIFFS Hotel $$
([📞] 619-222-7901, 866-786-2543; www.innat sunsetcliffs.com; 1370 Sunset Cliffs Blvd, Point Loma; r from $175; [P] [❄] [@] [🛜] [☂]) Hear the surf crashing onto the rocky shore at this breezy charmer wrapped around a flower-bedecked courtyard. Newly renovated rooms are light-filled but on the small side; recent efforts to decrease the hotel's water and plastic consumption have made the place greener.

Mission Bay & Pacific Beach

CRYSTAL PIER HOTEL Quirky, Historic Hotel $$$
(Map p290; [📞] 800-748-5894; www.crystalpier .com; 4500 Ocean Blvd; d cottage from $300, 3-night minimum; [P] [🛜]) White clapboard cottages with flower boxes and blue shutters are the draw at this popular hotel,

and not just because they're picturesque. The cottages – dating from 1936 – are special because they sit atop the pier itself, offering one-of-a-kind views of coast and sea. Book well in advance for summer reservations.

La Jolla

LA VALENCIA Historic Hotel $$$
([📞] 858-454-0771, 800-451-0772; www.lavalen cia.com; 1132 Prospect St, La Jolla; r $285-515, ste $695; [P] [❄] [@] [🛜] [☂]) For Old Hollywood charm, book a room at this pink 1926 Mediterranean-style palace. Even if you can't afford to sleep with the ghosts of Depression-era Hollywood, have a drink in **La Sala**, the elegant Spanish-revival lounge. Parking is $32.

 Eating

Downtown & Embarcadero

CAFÉ 222 Breakfast $
(Map p292; [📞] 619-236-9902; www.cafe222.com; 222 Island Ave; mains $7-11; [🕐] 7am-1:45pm; [♿]) This small, airy breakfast spot is renowned for pumpkin waffles, orange

Birch Aquarium (p298)

If You Like...
Beach Communities

If you feel at home among the surfers and sun-worshippers of La Jolla and Coronado, kick off your flip-flops at a few of San Diego's other beachfront neighborhoods.

1 MISSION BEACH
Home to a retro, family-style amusement park, **Belmont Park** (☎858-488-1549; www.belmontpark.com; admission free, rides $2-6, unlimited rides adult/child $27/16; ⏰from 11am; Ⓟ), since 1925. The classic wooden **Giant Dipper roller coaster** (per person $6; ⏰from 11am) might just shake the teeth right out of your mouth. Continue onto Pacific Beach (PB) via the beachfront boardwalk, **Ocean Front Walk**.

2 PACIFIC BEACH
Along **Garnet Ave**, hordes of twentysomethings toss back brews and gobble cheap tacos. At the ocean end, **Crystal Pier** is worth a look. Built in the 1920s, it's home to San Diego's quirkiest hotel, the Crystal Pier Hotel, which consists of a cluster of Cape Cod–style cottages built out over the waves.

3 OCEAN BEACH
In bohemian Ocean Beach you can get tattooed, shop for antiques and walk into a restaurant barefoot. Newport Ave is the main drag, filled with surf shops, bars, music stores, java joints and used-clothing stores. The street ends a block from the half-mile-long **Ocean Beach Pier**; just north is the central beach scene, with volleyball courts and sunset barbecues.

pecan pancakes and farm-fresh egg scramblers.

C LEVEL   Seafood $$
(☎619-298-6802; www.islandprime.com; 880 Harbor Island Dr; mains $14-30; ⏰11am-late) The food is as aesthetically pleasing as the view from this Harbor Island patio lounge with sweeping vistas of the bay and downtown. Here, carefully crafted

salads, sandwiches and light seafood fare are winning rave reviews. The Social Hour (3:30pm to 5:30pm Monday to Friday) offers $5 'bites and libations.'

Balboa Park

PRADO   Mediterranean, American $$
(☎619-557-9441; www.pradobalboa.com; 1549 El Prado; mains lunch $10-15, dinner $21-34; ⏰11:30am-3pm Mon-Fri & from 5pm Tue-Sun, 11am-3pm Sat & Sun; ⏰) This classic lunch spot in the museum district of Balboa Park serves up fresh Mediterranean cuisine such as steamed mussels, shrimp paella and grilled portobello sandwiches. Breezy outdoor seating and the Mexican-tiled interior are equally inviting; happy-hour food and drink specials (4pm to 6pm Tuesday to Friday) are a steal.

TEA PAVILION   Asian $
(2215 Pan American Way; mains $5-10; ⏰10am-5pm, later in summer) Enjoy a quick and spicy noodle bowl – or a simple cup of tea – under an umbrella at this low-key eatery next to the Japanese Garden.

Old Town

OLD TOWN MEXICAN CAFÉ   Mexican $
(☎619-297-4330; www.oldtownmexcafe.com; 2489 San Diego Ave; mains $4-15; ⏰7am-2am; ⏰) Watch the staff turn out fresh tortillas in the window while waiting for a table. Besides breakfast (great *chilaquiles* – soft tortilla chips covered with mole), there's *pozole* (spicy pork stew), avocado tacos and margaritas at the festive central bar.

Hillcrest & Mission Hills

Check out the Hillcrest **farmers market** (3960 Normal & Lincoln Sts; ⏰9am-2pm Sun) if you're here on a Sunday.

BREAD & CIE   Bakery $
(www.breadandciecatering.com; 350 University Ave; mains $6-10; ⏰7am-7pm Mon-Fri, to 6pm Sat, 9am-6pm Sun; ⏰) A delightful sensory overload of aromatic fresh bread, chattering locals and pastry-filled trays awaits inside this bustling Hillcrest crossroads.

KOUS KOUS

Moroccan **$$**

(www.kouskousrestaurant.com; 3940 4th Ave; mains $14-20; ⊙5pm-late; 🖋) Entering this otherworldly Moroccan eatery is like stepping onto another continent: the dining room is seductively illuminated by glowing lanterns, dinner guests sit on jewel-toned cushions drinking exotic cocktails, and the aroma of ginger, nutmeg and foreign spices hangs in the air.

Coronado

CORONADO BREWING COMPANY

Pub **$$**

(www.coronadobrewingcompany.com; 170 Orange Ave; mains $10-22; ⊙10:30am-late) The delicious house brew (the Pilsner-style Coronado Golden) goes well with the pizzas, pastas, sandwiches and fries at this good-for-your-soul, bad-for-your-diet bar and grill near the ferry.

1500 OCEAN

Seafood **$$$**

(Map p290; 📞619-522-8490; www.dine1500 ocean.com; Hotel del Coronado, 1500 Orange Ave; mains $18-45; ⊙5:30-9pm Tue-Thu, to 10pm Fri-Sun) Bright marigolds border the veranda at the Del's most romantic restaurant, adding a cheerful splash of color to palm-framed views of the sea. Come here to impress someone, celebrate or simply revel in your good fortune over duck confit or seared scallops.

Ocean Beach

HODAD'S

Burgers **$**

(www.hodadies.com; 5010 Newport Ave, Ocean Beach; burgers $4-9; ⊙5am-10pm) If there was a glossy magazine called *Beach Bum Living*, then legendary Hodad's, with its surfboards- and-license-plates decor, communal wooden tables and baskets of burgers and fries, would score the very first cover. Many say the succulent burgers are the best in town.

Mission Bay & Pacific Beach

THE MISSION

Breakfast, Latin American **$**

(3795 Mission Blvd; dishes $7-11; ⊙7am-3pm; 🖋🎏) Savor the famously delicious coffee or homemade cinnamon bread for breakfast – or kick back with Chino-Latino lunch specialties that include ginger sesame wraps and rosemary potatoes with salsa and eggs.

🖋 JRDN

Seafood, Californian **$$$**

(www.jrdn.com; Tower 23, 723 Felspar St; mains breakfast $10-18, lunch $9-18, dinner $23-46; ⊙7-11am Mon-Fri, 9am-4pm Sat & Sun, 5-10pm daily) Sustainably farmed meats and seafood join local veggies for a plate-topping farmers market at chic, vowel-disdaining JRDN, where you can choose futuristic decor indoors or ocean views outdoors.

La Jolla

GEORGE'S AT THE COVE

Modern American **$$**

(📞858-454-4244; www.georgesatthecove.com; 1250 Prospect St; mains $11-48; ⊙11am-11pm)

Giant Dipper, Belmont Park
RICHARD CUMMINS/LONELY PLANET IMAGES ©

Crystal Pier, Pacific Beach (p302)

RICHARD CUMMINS/LONELY PLANET IMAGES ©

Chef Trey Foshee's Euro-Cal cuisine is as dramatic as this eatery's oceanfront location. George's has graced just about every list of top restaurants in California. Three venues allow you to enjoy it at different price points: **George's Bar** (lunch mains $9-16), **Ocean Terrace** (lunch mains $11-18) and **George's California Modern** (dinner mains $28-48). Walk-ins welcome at the bar, but reservations are recommended for the latter two.

 Drinking

WINE STEALS   Wine Bar
(☎ 619-295-1188; www.winestealssd.com; 1243 University Ave, Hillcrest) Laid-back wine tastings (go for a flight or choose a bottle off the rack in the back), live music, gourmet pizzas and cheese platters bring in a nightly crowd to this low-lit wine bar. Look for two newer branches in San Diego, **Wine Steals East Village** (Map p292; 793/5 J Street, Downtown) and **Lounge-Point Loma** (2970 Truxtun Rd, Point Loma).

CAFE 1134   Cafe
(1134 Orange Ave, Coronado; mains $8-10; ⊙9am-7pm) This cool coffee shop on Coronado's

main drag offers more than your morning fix: think delicious Greek-style egg scramblers, grilled panini, spinach salads, high-end teas and a wine and beer list.

STARLITE   Cocktail Bar
(www.starlitesandiego.com; 3175 India St, Mission Hills) Slightly out of the way – don't worry, the drive is worthwhile – is this hipster cocktail haven with top-notch house creations and a lively central bar. The list changes frequently: just try anything made with ginger beer.

LIVING ROOM COFFEEHOUSE   Coffee Shop
(www.livingroomcafe.com; 1010 Prospect St, La Jolla; ⊙6am-midnight) This popular cafe serves spinach salads, quiche lorraine, and apricot strudel and has a great central position in the heart of the Village. There's a **second location** (2541 San Diego Ave) in Old Town and several others around town.

EXTRAORDINARY DESSERTS   Cafe
(☎ 619-294-2132; www.extraordinarydesserts.com; 2929 5th Ave, Hillcrest; ⊙8:30am-11pm Mon-Thu, to midnight Fri, 10am-midnight Sat, 10am-11pm Sun; 👪) For those with a sweet tooth, Karen Krasne's treasure trove of

stylishly decadent pastries – fruit-topped tarts, chunky cookies, creamy chocolate cheesecake and unforgettable bread pudding, to name a few – is heaven. There's a **second location** (Map p292; 1430 Union St) with a full bar in Little Italy.

ALTITUDE SKY LOUNGE　Cocktail Bar
(Map p292; www.altitudeskylounge.com; 660 K St) The Marriott's rooftop bar is our favorite. It may have the de rigueur fire pits and sleek decor, but unlike other open-air lounges, the vibe is friendly, not hipper-than-thou.

 **Entertainment**

CINEMA UNDER THE STARS　Cinema
(619-295-4221; www.topspresents.com; 4040 Goldfinch St, Mission Hills; 🎎) Catch classic films, both new and old – from *An Affair to Remember* to the latest Harry Potter installment – at this family-friendly outdoor theater.

ANTHOLOGY　Live Music
(Map p292; 619-595-0300; www.anthologysd .com; 1337 India St; cover free-$60) Near Little Italy, Anthology presents live jazz, blues and Indie music in a swank supper-club setting, from both up-and-comers and big-name performers.

CASBAH　Live Music
(619-232-4355; www.casbahmusic.com; 2501 Kettner Blvd; cover free-$20) Liz Phair, Alanis Morissette and the Smashing Pumpkins all rocked this funky Casbah on their way up the charts; catch local acts and headliners like Bon Iver.

LA JOLLA PLAYHOUSE　Theater
(619-550-1010; www.lajollaplayhouse.com; UCSD, 2910 La Jolla Village Dr) Classic and contemporary plays.

OLD GLOBE THEATRE　Theater
(619-234-5623; www.theoldglobe.org; Balboa Park) Three venues stage Shakespeare, classics and contemporary plays.

 **Shopping**

Local fashionistas head to La Jolla, shoppers in search of colorful housewares like the museum stores at Balboa Park and the Mexican artisan stands of Old Town, hipsters hit the secondhand clothing racks in Hillcrest and Ocean Beach. Surf shops and bikini boutiques dot the coast.

BAZAAR DEL MUNDO SHOPS　Homewares, Handicrafts
(www.bazaardelmundo.com; 4133 Taylor St, Old Town) Housed in a romantic hacienda-

San Diego Microbreweries

San Diegans take their craft beers seriously – even at a dive bar, you might overhear local guys talking about hops and cask conditioning. Various microbreweries on the city outskirts specialize in India Pale Ale (IPA) and Belgian-style brews; the following venues are beer-enthusiast favorites.

Stone Brewing Company (760-471-4999; www.stonebrew.com; 1999 Citracado Pkwy, Escondido; 🕙11am-9pm) Take a free tour before a guided tasting of Oaked Arrogant Bastard Ale and Stone Barley Wine.

Lost Abbey (800-918-6816; www.lostabbey.com; 155 Mata Way #104, San Marcos; 🕙1-6pm Wed-Thu, 3-9pm Fri, noon-6pm Sat & Sun) More than 20 brews ($1 per taste) are on tap in the tasting room – try Lost and Found Abbey Ale.

AleSmith (858-549-9888; www.alesmith.com; 9368 Cabot Dr; 🕙2-7pm Thu & Fri, noon-6pm Sat, noon-4pm Sun) Wee Heavy and the potent Old Numbskull ($1 per taste) are the stand-out brews.

style building in Old Town, these lively shops specialize in high-quality Latin American artisan wares, folk art, Mexican jewelry and home accessories.

🌿 UNITED NATIONS INTERNATIONAL GIFT SHOP   Homewares, Handicrafts
(United Nations Bldg, 2171 Pan American Plaza, Balboa Park) Fair-trade gifts and housewares from Africa and Latin America.

PANGAEA OUTPOST   Market
(www.pangaeaoutpost.com; 909 Garnet Ave, Pacific Beach) This indoor marketplace features 70 miniboutiques and craft stores – think surf-baby tanks, hand-painted wine glasses and Oaxacan figurines.

ℹ Information

Tourist Information

San Diego Visitor Information Centers
(☎619-236-1212, 800-350-6205; www.sandiego .org) Downtown **(Map p292; cnr W Broadway & Harbor Dr;** ⏰9am-5pm Jun-Sep, 9am-4pm Oct-May); La Jolla **(7966 Herschel Ave;** ⏰11am-5pm, **possible longer hr Jun-Sep & Sat & Sun)** The downtown location is designed for international visitors.

ℹ Getting There & Away

Air

San Diego International Airport-Lindbergh Field (SAN; Map p290; ☎619-231-2100; www .san.org; 3225 N Harbor Dr) Because of the limited length of runways, most flights into this airport are domestic.

Bus

Greyhound (Map p292; ☎619-515-1100; www .greyhound.com; 120 W Broadway, Downtown) Serves San Diego from cities all over North America. There are hourly direct buses to Los Angeles (one way/round-trip $19/31, two to three hours).

Train

Amtrak (☎800-872-7245; www.amtrak.com) Runs the *Pacific Surfliner* several times daily

to Los Angeles ($36, three hours) and Santa Barbara ($41, 5½ hours) from the Santa Fe Depot (Map p292; 1055 Kettner Blvd, Downtown). Amtrak and Metrolink (☎800-371-5465; www .metrolinktrains.com) commuter trains connect Anaheim to San Diego ($27, two hours).

ℹ Getting Around

To/From the Airport
Bus 992 ('the Flyer,' $2.25) operates at 10- to 15-minute intervals between the airport and Downtown, with stops along Broadway. A taxi fare to Downtown from the airport is $10 to $15.

Boat
San Diego Harbor Excursion operates a water taxi (☎619-235-8294; www.sdhe.com; per person one way $7; ⏰9am-9pm Sun-Thu, to 11pm Fri & Sat) serving Harbor Island, Shelter Island, Downtown and Coronado.

Trolley
Blue Line trolleys head south to San Ysidro (last stop, just before Tijuana, Mexico) and north to Old Town Transit Center. The Green Line runs east through Mission Valley, past Fashion Valley to Qualcomm Stadium and Mission San Diego de Alcala. The Orange Line connects the Convention Center and Seaport Village with downtown.

A one-way trolley route costs $2.50; buy tickets at vending machines on station platforms.

PALM SPRINGS
In the 1950s and '60s, Palm Springs, some 100 miles east of LA, was the swinging getaway of Sinatra, Elvis and dozens of other stars, partying the night away in midcentury-modern estate homes. In today's PS, elderly denizens mix amicably with younger hipsters and an active gay and lesbian community.

The best day to be in Palm Springs is Thursday, when Palm Canyon Dr morphs into a fun street fair with farmers market, food vendors, live music and arts and handicrafts booths. Called **Villagefest**, the weekly partly is held from 6pm to 10pm (from 7pm June to September) between Amado and Baristo Rds and brings out locals and visitors in droves.

NIK WHEELER/ALAMY ©

◎ Sights

PALM SPRINGS AERIAL
TRAMWAY   Cable Car

(☏760-325-1449; www.pstramway.com; 1 Tram Way; round-trip adult/child $24/17; ⊘10am-8pm Mon-Fri, 8am-8pm Sat & Sun, last tram down 9:45pm; 👪) North of downtown, this rotating cable car is a highlight of any Palm Springs trip. It climbs nearly 6000 vertical feet through five different vegetation zones, from the Sonoran desert floor to the San Jacinto Mountains, in less than 15 minutes. It's 30°F to 40°F cooler at the top, so bring warm clothing.

The turnoff for the tram is about 3 miles north of downtown Palm Springs.

PALM SPRINGS ART MUSEUM   Museum

(☏760-322-4800; www.psmuseum.org; 101 Museum Dr; adult/child $12.50/5, 4-8pm Thu free; ⊘10am-5pm Tue, Wed & Fri-Sun, noon-8pm Thu) This art beacon is a good place for keeping tabs on the evolution of American painting, sculpture, photography and glass art over the past century or so. Alongside well-curated temporary exhibitions, the permanent collection is especially strong when it comes to modern painting and sculpture and includes works by Henry Moore, Ed Ruscha, Mark di Suvero and other heavy hitters.

LIVING DESERT   Zoo

(☏760-346-5694; www.livingdesert.org; 47900 Portola Ave; adult/child $14.25/7.75; ⊘8am-1:30pm (last entry 1pm) Jun-Sep, 9am-5pm (last entry 4pm) Oct-May; 👪) This amazing, wide-open zoo, located in Palm Desert, shows off a variety of desert plants and animals, along with exhibits on desert geology and Native American culture. It's educational fun and worth the 30-minute drive down-valley. Highlights include a walk-through wildlife hospital and an African-themed village with a fair-trade market and storytelling grove.

CABOT'S PUEBLO MUSEUM   Museum

(☏760-329-7610; www.cabotsmuseum.org; 67616 E Desert Ave, at Miracle Hill; tour adult/child $10/8; ⊘tours 9:30am, 10:30am, 11:30am, 1:30pm & 2:30pm Tue-Sun Oct-May, 9:30am Jun-Sep) Cabot Yerxa, a wealthy East Coaster who traded high society for desert solitude, hand-built this rambling 1913 adobe in Desert Hot Springs from reclaimed and found objects, including telephone poles and wagon parts. Today

307

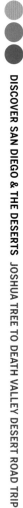

Palm Springs

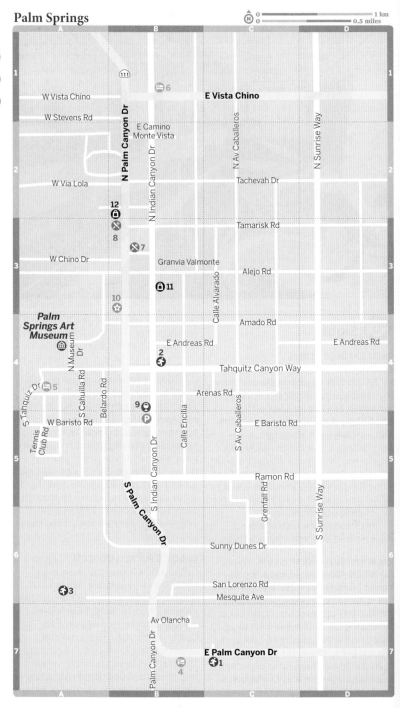

Palm Springs

◎ **Top Sights**
Palm Springs Art Museum A4

✪ **Activities, Courses & Tours**
1 Feel Good Spa at Ace Hotel &
   Swim Club.....................................C7
2 Spa Resort Casino...............................B4
   Spa Terre at Riviera Palm
   Springs ....(see 6)
3 Tahquitz Canyon................................A6

🛏 **Sleeping**
4 Caliente Tropics..................................B7
5 Orbit In...A4
6 Riviera Palm Springs B1

🍴 **Eating**
7 Cheeky's...B3
8 Trio...B3

🍷 **Drinking**
   Birba ....(see 7)
9 Shanghai Red's B4

🎭 **Entertainment**
10 Azul...B3

🛍 **Shopping**
11 Angel View B3
12 Trina Turk B2

it's a quirky museum displaying Native American basketry and pottery, as well as a photo collection from Cabot's turn-of-the-century travels to Alaska.

Activities

TAHQUITZ CANYON   Hiking
(☎ 760-416-7044; www.tahquitzcanyon.com; 500 W Mesquite Ave; adult/child $12.50/6; ⏱7:30am-5pm daily Oct-Jun, Fri-Sun Jul-Sep, last entry 3:30pm) A historic and sacred centerpiece for the Agua Caliente people, this canyon featured in the 1937 Frank Capra movie *Lost Horizon*.

The visitors center has natural and cultural history exhibits and also shows a video about the legend of Tahquitz, a shaman of the Cahuilla people. Rangers lead educational 2-mile, 2½-hour hikes that visit a seasonal 60ft-high waterfall, an ancient irrigation system and rock art.

INDIAN CANYONS   Hiking
(☎ 760-323-6018; www.indian-canyons.com; adult/child $9/5, guided hikes $3/2; ⏱8am-5pm daily Oct-Jun, Fri-Sun Jul-Sep) Streams flowing from the San Jacinto Mountains sustain a rich variety of plants in oases around Palm Springs. Home to Native American communities for hundreds of years and now part of the Agua Caliente Indian Reservation, these canyons, shaded by fan palms and surrounded by towering cliffs, are a delight for hikers.

Tours

The visitors center has brochures for self-guided tours, including public art and historic sites (free), modernism ($5) and stars' homes ($5).

BEST OF THE BEST TOURS   General
(☎ 760-320-1365; www.thebestofthebesttours .com; tours from $25) Extensive program includes windmill tours and bus tours of celebrity homes.

DESERT ADVENTURES   General
(☎ 760-340-2345; www.red-jeep.com; 90min/3hr tours $85/125) Four-wheel-drive tours of the Joshua Tree backcountry and the San Andreas Fault.

HISTORIC WALKING TOURS   Walking
(☎ 760-323-8297; www.pshistoricalsociety.org; tour $10; ⏱10am Thu & Sat) Just what it says. Organized by the Palm Springs Historical Society.

Sleeping

**RIVIERA PALM
SPRINGS**   Luxury Hotel $$$
(☎ 760-327-8311; www.psriviera.com; 1600 Indian Canyon Dr; r $240-260, ste $290-540; ❄@🛜🏊) If you're lusting for luxury, check into this famous Rat Pack playground that just emerged from a big-bucks renovation and is sparkling brighter than ever. Expect the full range of fancy mod cons amid luscious gardens and cute '60s accents like shag rugs, classily campy crystal chandeliers and Warhol art.

CALIENTE TROPICS Motel $

(☎760-327-1391; www.calientetropics.com; 411 E Palm Canyon Dr; d $66-111; ❄ 🛜 🏊 ♿ 🐾) Elvis once frolicked poolside at this premier budget pick, a nicely kept 1950s tiki-style motor lodge. Drift off to dreamland on quality mattresses in rooms that are spacious and dressed in warm colors.

ORBIT IN Boutique Hotel $$

(☎760-323-3585; www.orbitin.com; 562 W Arenas Rd; d incl breakfast $149-259; ❄ 🛜 🏊) Swing back to the '50s – pinkie raised and all – during the 'Orbitini' happy hour at this fabulously retro property, with high-end Mid-Century Modern furniture (Eames, Noguchi et al) in rooms set around a quiet saline pool with a Jacuzzi and fire pit.

 Eating

TRIO Modern American $$

(☎760-864-8746; www.triopalmsprings.com; 707 N Palm Canyon Dr; mains $13-28; 🕐4-10pm)

The winning formula in this '60s modernist space: updated American comfort food (awesome Yankee pot roast!), eye-catching artwork and picture windows. The $19 'early bird' three-course dinner (served 4pm to 6pm) is a steal.

CHEEKY'S Modern American $$

(☎760-327-7595; www.cheekysps.com; 622 N Palm Canyon Dr; mains $6-13; 🕐8am-2pm Wed-Mon; 🐾) Waits can be long and service only so-so, but the farm-to-table menu dazzles with witty inventiveness. Dishes change weekly, but custardy scrambled eggs, arugula pesto frittata and bacon bar 'flights' keep making appearances.

 **Drinking**

BIRBA Bar

(www.birbaps.com; 622 N Palm Canyon Dr; 🕐6-11pm Wed-Fri, from 9:30am Sat & Sun) It's cocktails and pizza at this fabulous indoor-outdoor space where floor-to-ceiling sliding glass doors separate the

Left: Snowcapped mountains, Palm Springs; **Below:** Joshua tree

(LEFT) MELVIN SURDIN/ALAMY ©; (BELOW) DAVID TOMLINSON/LONELY PLANET IMAGES ©

long marble bar from a hedge-fringed patio with sunken fire pits.

SHANGHAI RED'S   Bar

(www.fishermans.com/shanghaireds.php; 235 S Indian Canyon Dr; ⏰5pm-late) Part of Fisherman's Market & Grill, this joint has a busy courtyard, an inter-generational crowd and live blues on Friday and Saturday nights.

⭐ Entertainment

AZUL   Music

(☎760-325-5533; www.azultapaslounge .com; 369 N Palm Canyon Dr; mains $11-24; ⏰11am-late) Popular with gays and their friends, the Azul restaurant has almost nightly entertainment in its piano bar, plus the wickedly funny **Judy Show** (www .thejudyshow.com; incl dinner $35) on Sundays, starring impersonator Michael Holmes as Judy Garland, Mae West and other campy legends of yore.

🛍 Shopping

TRINA TURK   Clothing

(www.trinaturk.com; 891 N Palm Canyon Dr) Trina makes form-flattering 'California-chic' fashions that are beautifully presented amid shag carpeting and floral foil wallpaper in her original boutique in a 1960s Albert Frey building.

ANGEL VIEW   Vintage

(www.angelview.org; 462 N Indian Canyon Dr; ⏰9am-6pm Mon-Sat, 10am-5pm Sun) At this well-established thrift store, today's hipsters can shop for clothes and accessories as cool as when they were first worn a generation or two ago.

ℹ Information

Palm Springs Official Visitors Center (☎760-778-8418; www.visitpalmsprings.com; 2901 N Palm Canyon Dr; ⏰9am-5pm) This well-stocked

311

LEIGH GREEN/ALAMY ©

Don't Miss Elvis' Love Nest

One of the most spectacular Mid-Century Modern houses in Palm Springs was designed in the early 1960s by local developer Robert Alexander for his wife Helene. It consists of four circular rooms built on three levels, accented with glass and stone throughout. *Look* Magazine called it the 'House of Tomorrow' and featured it in an eight-page spread, making the Alexanders national celebrities. Sadly the entire family died in a plane crash in 1965, but the estate gained even greater fame a year later when Elvis Presley moved in. On May 1, 1967 he carried his new bride Priscilla over the threshold to begin their honeymoon. The **Elvis Honeymoon Hideaway** has been authentically restored and can be rented for events and visited on daily tours. Tickets are sold over the phone and online.

NEED TO KNOW

☎760-322-1192; www.elvishoneymoon.com; 1350 Ladera Circle; tours daily by appointment per person $25

and well-staffed visitors center is 3 miles north of downtown, in a 1965 Albert Frey–designed gas station at the tramway turnoff.

ⓘ Getting There & Away

Air

A 10-minute drive northeast of downtown, Palm Springs International Airport (www.palm springsairport.com; 3400 E Tahquitz Canyon Way) is served year-round by Alaska, Allegiant,

American, Delta, Horizon, United, US Airways and Westjet, and seasonally by Sun Country.

Car & Motorcycle

From LA, the trip to Palm Springs and the Coachella Valley takes about two to three hours via I-10.

Train

Amtrak serves the unstaffed and kinda-creepy – it's deserted and in the middle of nowhere – North Palm Springs Station, 5 miles north of downtown

Palm Springs. *Sunset Limited* trains run to/from LA ($37, 2½ hours) on Sunday, Wednesday and Friday; trains are often late.

ⓘ Getting Around

To/From the Airport

Many area hotels provide free airport transfers. Otherwise a taxi to downtown Palm Springs costs about $12.

Car & Motorcycle

Though you can walk to most sights in downtown Palm Springs, you'll need a car to get around the valley. Major rental-car companies have airport desks.

JOSHUA TREE NATIONAL PARK

Taking a page from a Dr Seuss book, the whimsical Joshua trees (actually tree-sized yuccas) welcome visitors to this 794,000-acre park at the convergence of the Colorado and Mojave Deserts.

Hikers seek out hidden, shady, desert-fan-palm oases fed by natural springs and small streams, while mountain bikers are hypnotized by the desert vistas seen from dirt 4WD roads.

The mystical quality of this stark, boulder-strewn landscape has inspired many artists, most famously the band U2, which named its 1987 album *The Joshua Tree*.

◉ Sights & Activities

HIDDEN VALLEY   Outdoors
Some 8 miles south of the West Entrance, this whimsically dramatic cluster of rocks is a rock climbers' mecca, but just about anyone can enjoy a clamber on the giant boulders. An easy 1-mile trail loops through it and back to the parking lot and picnic area.

KEYS VIEW   Lookout
From Park Blvd, it's an easy 20-minute drive up to Keys View (5185ft), where breathtaking views take in the entire Coachella Valley and extend as far as the Salton Sea and – on a good day – Mexico. Looming in front of you are Mt San Jacinto (10,834ft) and Mt San Gorgonio (11,500ft), two of Southern California's highest peaks, while down below you can spot a section of the San Andreas Fault.

DESERT QUEEN RANCH   Historic Site
(☏reservations 760-367-5555; tour adult/child $5/2.50; ☉tours 10am & 1pm daily year-round, 7pm Tue & Thu-Sat Oct-May) Anyone interested in local history and lore should take the 90-minute guided tour of this ranch

Top Spas

Get your stressed-out self to these pampering shrines to work out the kinks and turn your body into a glowing lump of tranquility.

Feel Good Spa at Ace Hotel & Swim Club (Map p308; ☏760-329-8791; www.acehotel.com/palmsprings/spa; 701 E Palm Canyon Dr) At Palm Springs' newest hipster spa you can get a treatment inside a yurt.

Spa Resort Casino (Map p308; ☏760-778-1772; www.sparesortcasino.com; 100 N Indian Canyon Dr) Try a five-step 'taking of the waters' course through the valley's original hot springs.

Spa Terre at Riviera Palm Springs (Map p308; ☏760-778-6690; www.psriviera.com; 1600 N Indian Canyon Dr) The ultimate in swanky pampering, with Watsu pool and exotic spa rituals.

that's also known as Keys Ranch after its builder, Russian immigrant William Keys. He built a homestead here on 160 acres in 1917 and over the next 60 years turned it into a full working ranch, school, store and workshop.

The ranch is about 2 miles northeast of Hidden Valley Campground, up a dirt road. Drive as far as the locked gate where your guide will meet you.

Hiking

Staff at the visitors centers can help you match your time and fitness level to the perfect trail. Distances given are round-trip.

49 Palms Oasis Escape the crowds on this 3-mile up-and-down trail starting near Indian Cove.

Barker Dam A 1.1-mile loop that passes a little lake and a rock incised with Native American petroglyphs; starts at Barker Dam parking lot.

Lost Horse Mine A strenuous 4-mile climb that visits the remains of an authentic Old West silver and gold mine, in operation until 1931.

Lost Palms Oasis Reach this remote canyon filled with desert fan palms on a fairly flat 7.2-mile trek starting from Cottonwood Spring.

Boulder walking, Barker Dam

Cycling

Village Bicycle (760-808 4557; Hallee Rd; 10am-6pm Mon-Fri, 9am-9pm Sat, 9am-2pm Sun), behind Sam's in Joshua Tree, rents basic mountain bikes for $45 per day.

Popular riding routes include challenging **Pinkham Canyon Rd**, starting from the Cottonwood visitors center, and the long-distance **Black Eagle Mine Rd**, which starts 6.5 miles further north.

Rock Climbing

JT's rocks are famous for their rough, high-friction surfaces, and from boulders to cracks to multipitch faces, there are more than 8000 established routes, many right off the main road.

Shops catering to climbers with quality gear, advice and tours include the following:

Joshua Tree Outfitters (760-366-1848; www.joshuatreeoutfitters.com; 61707 Twentynine Palms Hwy, Joshua Tree; usually 9am-5pm)

Nomad Ventures (760-366-4684; www .nomadventures.com; 61795 Twentynine Palms Hwy, Joshua Tree; 8am-6pm Mon-Thu, to 8pm

TYLER ROEMER/LONELY PLANET IMAGES

Fri & Sat, to 7pm Sun Oct-Apr, 9am-7pm daily
May-Sep)

🛏 Sleeping

Inside the park there are only camp-grounds but there are plenty of lodging options along Hwy 62.

HICKSVILLE TRAILER
PALACE   Motel $$
(☏310-584-1086; www.hicksville.com; r $75-200; ❄🐾🏊👪) Fancy sleeping among glowing wigs, in a haunted house, or in a horse stall? Check in at Hicksville, where 'rooms' are eight outlandishly decorated vintage trailers set around a kidney-shaped saltwater swimming pool.

DESERT LILY   B&B $$
(☏760-366-4676; www.thedesertlily.com; Joshua Tree Highlands; s/d incl breakfast $140/155; ⊗closed Jul & Aug; @🖥) The charming Carrie presides over this three-room adobe retreat with Old West–meets-Southwest decor. Days start with scrumptious breakfasts and there's always a tray of fresh cookies in the common area anchored by a fireplace.

🍴 Eating

📍RICOCHET
GOURMET   International $
(www.ricochetjoshuatree.com; 61705 Twentynine Palms Hwy, Joshua Tree; mains $8-15; ⊗7am-5pm Mon-Sat, 8am-5pm Sun; 🖥👪) At this neighborhood-adored cafe-cum-deli, the menu bounces from breakfast frittatas to curry chicken salad and fragrant soups, all of them homemade with organic and seasonal ingredients.

📍RESTAURANT AT
29 PALMS INN   American $$
(☏760-367-3505, www.29palmsinn.com; 73950 Inn Ave, Twentynine Palms; mains lunch $7.50-10, dinner $9-21; 🖥) This well-respected restaurant has its own organic garden and

❤ If You Like…
Scenic Drives

If you catch your thrills by hitting the open road across dramatic desertscapes and motoring up to Keys View, fill up your tank and try one of these unforgettable car journeys:

1 GEOLOGY TOUR RD
East of Hidden Valley, travelers with 4WD vehicles or mountain bikes can take this 18-mile field trip down into and around Pleasant Valley, where the forces of erosion, earthquakes and ancient volcanoes have played out in stunning splendor.

2 COVINGTON FLATS
Joshua trees grow throughout the northern park, including right along Park Blvd, but some of the biggest trees are found in this area accessed via La Contenta Rd, south off Hwy 62 between the towns of Yucca Valley and Joshua Tree. For photogenic views, follow the dirt road 3.8 miles up the Eureka Peak (5516ft) from the picnic area.

3 PINTO BASIN RD
To see the natural transition from the high Mojave Desert to the low Colorado Desert, wind along down to Cottonwood Spring, a 30-mile drive from Hidden Valley. Stop at **Cholla Cactus Garden**, where a quarter-mile loop leads around waving ocotillo plants and jumping 'teddy bear' cholla.

does burgers and salads at lunchtime and grilled meats and toothsome pastas for dinner.

🍷 Drinking & Entertainment

JOSHUA TREE SALOON   Bar
(http://thejoshuatreesaloon.com; 61835 Twentynine Palms Hwy, Joshua Tree; mains $9-17; ⊗8am-late; 🖥) This watering hole with jukebox, pool tables and cowboy flair serves bar food along with rib-sticking burgers and steaks. Most people come here for the nightly entertainment, such

315

Detour:
Mojave National Preserve

If you're on a quest for the 'middle of nowhere,' you'll find it in the wilderness of the **Mojave National Preserve** (Map p278; ☑760-252-6100; www.nps.gov/moja; admission free), a 1.6-million-acre jumble of sand dunes, Joshua trees, volcanic cinder cones and habitats for bighorn sheep, desert tortoises, jackrabbits and coyotes.

as open-mike Tuesdays, karaoke Wednesdays and DJ Fridays. Over 21 only.

ℹ Information

Joshua Tree National Park (☑760-367-5500; www.nps.gov/jotr) is flanked by I-10 in the south and by Hwy 62 (Twentynine Palms Hwy) in the north. Entry permits ($15 per vehicle) are valid for seven days and come with a map and the seasonally updated *Joshua Tree Guide*.

Tourist Information

Black Rock Park Nature Center (9800 Black Rock Canyon Rd, south of Hwy 62; ⊙8am-4pm Sat-Thu, noon-8pm Fri Oct-May) At the Black Rock Campground.

Cottonwood Visitor Center (Cottonwood Spring Rd, north of I-10; ⊙9am-3pm) Just inside the park's south entrance.

Joshua Tree Park Visitor Center (Park Blvd, Joshua Tree; ⊙8am-5pm) Outside the west entrance.

Oasis Park Visitor Center (National Park Blvd, at Utah Trail, Twentynine Palms; ⊙8am-5pm) Outside the north entrance.

ℹ Getting There & Around

Rent a car in Palm Springs or LA. From LA, the trip takes about 2½ to three hours via I-10 and Hwy 62.

From Palm Springs it takes about an hour to reach the park's west (preferable) or south entrances.

ROUTE 66

Completed in 1926, iconic Route 66 connected Chicago and Los Angeles across the heartland of America. What novelist John Steinbeck called the 'Mother Road' came into its own during the Depression, when thousands of migrants escaped the Dust Bowl by slogging westward in beat-up old jalopies painted with 'California or Bust' signs, *Grapes of Wrath* style.

Los Angeles to Barstow

Route 66 kicks off in Santa Monica, at the intersection of Ocean Ave and Santa Monica Blvd. Follow the latter through Beverly Hills and West Hollywood, turn right on Sunset Blvd and pick up the 110 Fwy north to Pasadena. Take exit 31B and drive south on Fair Oaks Ave for an egg cream at the **Fair Oaks Pharmacy** (☑626-799-1414; www.fairoakspharmacy.net; 1526 Mission St, South Pasadena; mains $4.50-10; ⊙9am-9pm Mon-Sat, 10am-7pm Sun; 🚻), a nostalgic soda fountain from 1915.

Continue east on Colorado Blvd to Colorado Pl and **Santa Anita Park** (☑626-574-7223, tour reservations 626-574-6677; www.santaanita.com; 285 W Huntington Dr, Arcadia; ⊙racing 26 Dec-20 Apr), where the Marx Brothers' *A Day at the Races* was filmed and legendary thoroughbred Seabiscuit ran.

Colorado Pl turns into Huntington Dr E, which you'll follow to 2nd Ave, where you turn north, then east on Foothill Blvd. This older alignment of Route 66 follows Foothill Blvd through Monrovia, where the 1925 Mayan Revival–style architecture of the allegedly haunted **Aztec Hotel** (311 W Foothill Blvd, Monrovia) is worth a look.

Continue east on W Foothill Blvd, then jog south on S Myrtle Ave and hook a left on E Huntington Dr through Duarte, which puts on a **Route 66 parade** (http://duarteroute66parade.com) every September, with boisterous marching bands, old-fashioned carnival games and a classic-car show.

Cruising on through Fontana, birthplace of the notorious Hells Angels biker club, you'll see the now-boarded-up **Giant Orange** (15395 Foothill Blvd, Fontana), a 1920s juice stand of the kind that was once a fixture alongside SoCal's citrus groves.

Foothill Blvd continues on to Rialto where you'll find the **Wigwam Motel** (☏ 909-875-3005; www.wigwammotel.com; 2728 W Foothill Blvd, San Bernardino; r $65-82; ✳ 🛜 🏊), whose kooky concrete faux tipis date from 1949. Get back onto I-15 and drive up to the Cajon Pass. At the top, take the Oak Hill Rd exit (No 138) to the **Summit Inn Cafe** (☏ 760-949-8688; 5960 Mariposa Rd, Oak Hills; mains $5-12; ⏱ 6am-8pm Mon-Thu, to 9pm Fri & Sat), a 1950s roadside diner with antique gas pumps, a retro jukebox and a lunch counter that serves ostrich burgers and date shakes.

Get back on I-15 and drive downhill to Victorville, exiting at 7th St and driving past the San Bernardino County Fairgrounds, home of the Route 66 Raceway. Follow 7th St to D St and turn left for the excellent **California Route 66 Museum** (www.califrt66museum.org; 16825 South D St, Victorville; donations welcome; ⏱ 10am-4pm Mon & Thu-Sat, 11am-3pm Sun), inside the old Red Rooster Cafe opposite the train station.

Follow South D St north under I-15 where it turns into the National Trails Hwy. Beloved by Harley bikers, this rural stretch to Barstow is like a scavenger hunt for Mother Road ruins, such as antique filling stations and tumbledown motor courts.

DEATH VALLEY NATIONAL PARK

The name itself evokes all that is harsh, hot and hellish – a punishing, barren and lifeless place of Old Testament severity. Yet closer inspection reveals that in Death Valley nature is putting on a truly spectacular show: singing sand dunes, water-sculpted canyons, boulders moving across the desert floor, extinct volcanic craters, palm-shaded oases and plenty of endemic wildlife. This is a land of superlatives, holding the US records for hottest temperature (134°F, or 57°C), lowest point (Badwater, 282ft below sea level) and largest national park outside Alaska (over 5000 sq miles).

Sand dunes near Stovepipe Wells (p318)

WITOLD SKRYPCZAK/LONELY PLANET IMAGES ©

Sights

Furnace Creek

Furnace Creek is Death Valley's commercial hub, with a general store, park visitors center, gas station, post office, ATM, internet access, golf course, lodging and restaurants.

FREE **Borax Museum** (🕐9am-9pm Oct-May, variable in summer) is great for finding out what all the fuss about borax was about. It also has a great collection of pioneer-era stagecoaches and wagons out back. A short drive north, an interpretive trail follows in the footsteps of late-19th-century Chinese laborers and through the adobe ruins of **Harmony Borax Works**, where you can take a side trip through twisting **Mustard Canyon**.

South of Furnace Creek

If possible start out early in the morning to drive up to **Zabriskie Point** for spectacular valley views across golden badlands eroded into waves, pleats and gullies. Escape the heat by continuing on to **Dante's View** at 5475ft, where you can simultaneously see the highest (Mt Whitney) and lowest (Badwater) points in the contiguous USA. The drive there takes about 1½ to two hours round-trip.

Badwater itself, a foreboding landscape of crinkly salt flats, is a 17-mile drive south of Furnace Creek. Here you can walk out onto a boardwalk above a constantly evaporating bed of salty, mineralized water that's otherworldly in its beauty. Along the way, you may want to check out narrow **Golden Canyon**, easily explored on a 2-mile round-trip walk, and **Devil's Golf Course**, where salt has piled up into saw-toothed miniature mountains. A 9-mile one-way scenic loop along **Artists Drive** is best done in the late afternoon when exposed minerals and volcanic ash make the hills erupt in fireworks of color.

Stovepipe Wells & Around

Stovepipe Wells, about 26 miles northwest of Furnace Creek, was Death Valley's original 1920s tourist resort. Today it has a small store, gas station, ATM, motel, campground and bar. En route, look for the roadside pull-off where you can walk out onto the powdery, Sahara-

Mosaic Canyon

DISCOVER SAN DIEGO & THE DESERTS DEATH VALLEY NATIONAL PARK

like **sand dunes**. Across the road, look for the **Devil's Cornfield**, full of arrow weed clumps. Some 2.5 miles southwest of Stovepipe Wells, a 3-mile gravel side road leads to **Mosaic Canyon**, where you can hike and scramble along the smooth multi-hued rock walls. Colors are sharpest at midday.

Along Emigrant Canyon Rd

Some 6 miles southwest of Stovepipe Wells, Emigrant Canyon Rd veers off Hwy 190 and travels south to the park's higher elevations. En route you'll pass the turnoff to **Skidoo**, a mining ghost town where the silent movie *Greed* was filmed in 1923. It's an 8-mile trip on a graded gravel road suitable only for high-clearance vehicles to get to the ruins and jaw-dropping Sierra Nevada views.

Further south Emigrant Canyon Rd passes the turnoff for the 7-mile dirt road leading past the **Eureka Mines** to the vertiginous **Aguereberry Point** (high-clearance vehicles only), where you'll have fantastic views into the valley and out to the colorful Funeral Mountains from a lofty 6433ft. The best time to visit is in the late afternoon.

Emigrant Canyon Rd now climbs steeply over Emigrant Pass and through Wildrose Canyon to reach the **charcoal kilns**, a lineup of large, stone, beehive-shaped structures historically used by miners to make fuel for smelting silver and lead ore. The landscape is subalpine, with forests of piñon pine and juniper; it can be covered with snow, even in spring.

Panamint Springs

About 30 miles west of Stovepipe Wells, on the edge of the park, Panamint Springs is a tiny enclave with a motel, campground, pricey gas station and small store. Several often overlooked but wonderful hidden gems are easily accessed from here. **Father Crowley Point**, for instance, peers deep into Rainbow Canyon, created by lava flows and scattered with colorful volcanic cinders.

Activities

FARABEE'S JEEP RENTALS   Driving Tour

(☎760-786-9872; www.deathvalleyjeeprentals.com; 2-/4-door Jeep incl 200 miles $175/195; ☻mid-Sep–mid-May) If you don't have a 4WD but would like to explore the park's backcountry, you can rent a Jeep from this outfit, provided you're over 25 years old, have a valid driver's license, credit card and proof of insurance.

FURNACE CREEK CYCLERY   Mountain-Biking

(☎760-786-3372, ext 372; bike hire 1/24hr $10/49; ☻year-round) Another way to get off the asphalt is by renting a mountain bike from the Cyclery at Furnace Creek Ranch. Cycling is allowed on all established paved and dirt roads, but never on trails. Ask at the visitors center for recommended routes.

Hiking

Avoid hiking in summer, except on higher-elevation mountain trails, which may be snowed in during winter.

On Hwy 190, just north of Beatty Cutoff Rd, is the half-mile **Salt Creek Interpretive Trail**; in late winter or early spring, rare pupfish splash in the stream alongside the boardwalk. A few miles south of Furnace Creek is **Golden Canyon**, where a self-guided interpretive trail winds for a mile up to the now-oxidized iron cliffs of **Red Cathedral**.

The park's most demanding summit is **Telescope Peak** (11,049ft), with views that plummet down to the desert floor, which is as far below as two Grand Canyons deep! The 14-mile round-trip climbs 3000ft above Mahogany Flat, off upper Wildrose Canyon Rd.

Sleeping

In-park lodging is pricey and often booked solid in springtime but there are several gateway towns with cheaper lodging.

HOLGER LEUE/LONELY PLANET IMAGES ©

STOVEPIPE WELLS VILLAGE Motel **$$**
(📞760-786-2387; www.escapetodeathvalley
.com; Hwy 190, Stovepipe Wells Village; RV sites
with hookups $31, r $80-155; ✳🛜🏊👪)
Newly spruced-up rooms feature quality
linens beneath cheerful Native Ameri-
can–patterned bedspreads as well as
coffeemakers. The small pool is cool
and the cowboy-style restaurant (mains
$5 to $25) delivers three square meals
a day.

FURNACE CREEK RANCH Resort **$$**
(📞760-786-2345; www.furnacecreekresort.com;
Hwy 190, Furnace Creek; cabins $130-162, r $162-
213; ✳🛜🏊👪) Tailor-made for families,
this rambling resort has been subjected
to a vigorous facelift, resulting in spiffy
rooms swathed in desert colors, updated
bathrooms, new furniture and French
doors leading to porches with comfortable patio furniture.

 Eating & Drinking

Furnace Creek and Stovepipe Wells have
general stores stocking basic groceries
and camping supplies.

TOLL ROAD RESTAURANT American **$$**
(Stovepipe Wells Village, Hwy 190; full breakfast
buffet $12, dinner $12-25; ⏰7-9:30am & 7-10pm
mid-May–mid-Oct, 7-10am & 5-9pm mid-Oct–mid-
May; 🛜👪) Above-par cowboy cooking
happens at this ranch house which gets
Old West flair from a rustic fireplace and
rickety wooden chairs and tables. Food,
including late-night snacks, is also served
next door at the **Badwater Saloon** (⏰from
11am) along with cold draft beer and Sky-
nyrd on the jukebox.

FURNACE CREEK INN International **$$$**
(📞760-786-2345; mains lunch $13-17, dinner $24-
38; ⏰7:30-10:30am, noon-2:30pm & 5:30-9:30pm
mid-Oct–mid-May) Views of the Panamint
Mountains are stellar from this formal dining room with a dress code (no shorts or
T-shirts, jeans OK), where the menu draws
inspiration from continental, southwestern
and Mexican cuisine. The nicest place for
sunset cocktails is the outdoor patio.

ℹ Information

Entry permits ($20 per vehicle) are valid for
seven days and sold at self-service pay stations
throughout the park. For a free map and
newspaper, show your receipt at the visitors center

Furnace Creek visitors center (☎760-786-3200; www.nps.gov/deva; Hwy 190, Furnace Creek; ◷8am-5pm) Under construction at press time, the renovated main visitors center should have reopened by the time you're reading this.

ⓘ Getting There & Away

Gas is expensive in the park, so fill up your tank beforehand.

Furnace Creek can be reached via Baker (115 miles, two to 2½ hours), Beatty (45 miles, one to 1½ hours), Las Vegas (via Hwy 160, 120 miles, 2½ to three hours), Lone Pine (105 miles, two hours), Los Angeles (300 miles, five to 5½ hours) and Ridgecrest (via Trona, 120 miles, 2½ to three hours).

Disneyland & Orange County

Once upon a time, long before the *Real Housewives* threw lavish pool parties and the rich teens of MTV's *Laguna Beach* screamed at each other on our TV screens, Orange County's public image was defined by an innocent animated mouse.

Even in his wildest imagination, Walt Disney couldn't have known that Mickey would one day share the spotlight with Botoxed socialites and rich kids driving Porsches along the sunny Pacific Coast Hwy. But Walt might have imagined the bigger picture – those same catfighting teens are now adults and will be bringing their little ones to Disneyland soon.

These seemingly conflicting cultures, plus a growing population of Vietnamese and Latino immigrants seeking the American dream, form the county's diverse population of more than three million. And while there's truth to the televised stereotypes, look closer – there are also deep pockets of individuality and open-mindedness keeping the OC real.

Marina, Newport Beach (p345)

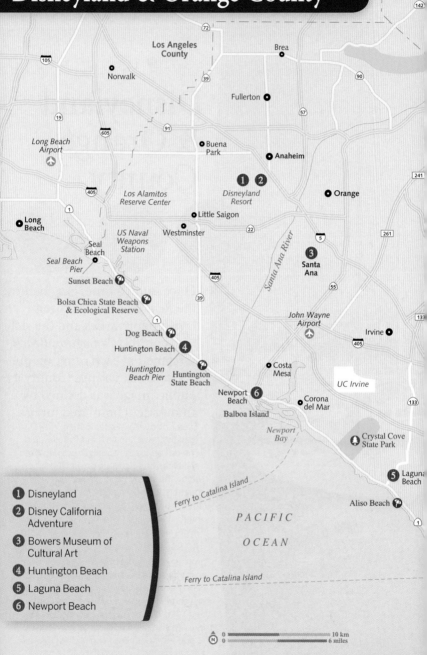

Disneyland & Orange County

Los Angeles County

Diamond

142

72

Brea

Norwalk

90

Fullerton

105

19

605

91

57

Long Beach Airport

Buena Park

Anaheim

241

405

1

2

Disneyland Resort

Orange

Los Alamitos Reserve Center

Little Saigon

1

Long Beach

Westminster

22

261

5

US Naval Weapons Station

Santa Ana River

3

Santa Ana

Seal Beach

Seal Beach Pier

55

Sunset Beach

405

John Wayne Airport

133

Bolsa Chica State Beach & Ecological Reserve

39

Irvine

1

405

Dog Beach

Huntington Beach

4

UC Irvine

Huntington Beach Pier

Huntington State Beach

Costa Mesa

Newport Beach

6

Corona del Mar

133

Balboa Island

Newport Bay

Crystal Cove State Park

5

Laguna Beach

1. Disneyland
2. Disney California Adventure
3. Bowers Museum of Cultural Art
4. Huntington Beach
5. Laguna Beach
6. Newport Beach

Ferry to Catalina Island

Aliso Beach

1

PACIFIC

OCEAN

Ferry to Catalina Island

N
0   10 km
0   6 miles

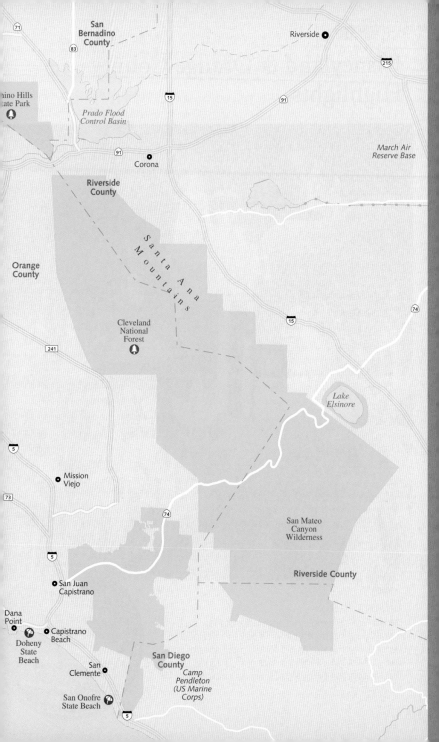

Disneyland & Orange County Highlights

① Disneyland

Disneyland, also known as 'the Happiest Place on Earth' is Walt's original theme park. Inside this 'imagineered' hyperreality, the streets are always clean, the employees – called Cast Members – are always upbeat, and there's a parade every day of the year. It's a Small World, Disneyland

Need to Know

GETTING AROUND Disney's monorail, trams and trains are great for families **RUSH HOUR** The busiest time is 11am to 4pm **TICKETS** Buy online to save time and money **For more, see p334**

Disneyland Don't Miss List

BY LISA ROBERTSON, FORMER DISNEYLAND CAST MEMBER & AUTHOR OF BABES IN DISNEYLAND

1 DISNEYLAND RAILROAD

A trip to Disneyland offers guests the chance to do something they cannot do in any other Disney park: walk in Walt Disney's footsteps. Walt created his Magic Kingdom with great passion and detail. Take the grand tour of the park onboard the **Disneyland Railroad** (p334). The train provides a great overview for those looking to get a quick orientation to the park's layout and size; it stops in New Orleans Square, Mickey's Toontown, and Tomorrowland before returning to Main Street station.

2 PIRATES OF THE CARIBBEAN

The **Pirates of the Caribbean** (p335; pictured left) attraction is a favorite: it completely immerses guests into pirate battles and sends them down two flumes. A lot of people don't realize that this ride was really famous before the well-known movie franchise.

3 OLD-FASHIONED ATTRACTIONS

Open on crowded days and during summer months, **Davy Crockett's Explorer Canoes** (p335) is the only attraction in the park that's not on a track – these canoes are 'man powered.' It's a lot of fun on a hot day.

4 WALT'S VISION

Check out one of the attractions Walt carefully planned with his 'Imagineers', like the **Jungle Cruise** (p335) in Adventureland. Disneyland is the tangible result of one man's dream. It offers families the opportunity to come together and leave the world behind. No TV, no work, no errands to run – just a chance to focus on one another and live out some of life's fantasies and adventures.

5 SKIPPING THE LINES

Make the most of your time at the park by using Disney's **Fastpass system** (p343), a virtual queuing system that holds your place in line – and single-rider lines. Families should ask about the the 'Rider Swap' program, which allows parents to take turns going on turbulent rides or waiting on the sidelines with younger children.

Disney California Adventure

'The other park,' Disney California Adventure (p337), opened in 2001, is an ode to California geography, history and culture – or at least a sanitized, G-rated version of it. DCA covers more acres than Disneyland, features more modern rides and attractions, and is usually less crowded than the original park. Major improvements are underway – look for Cars Land, the park's exciting new themed section.

2

3

Bowers Museum of Cultural Art

The perpetual sunshine, crowded beaches and kids wearing Mickey Mouse ears might have you craving a taste of higher culture. The small but highly respected Bowers Museum of Cultural Art (p348) is just the ticket, with an excellent permanent collection of pre-Columbian, Native American, and Oceanic art, plus world-class special exhibits that bring the art crowds down from Los Angeles.

Huntington Beach

In Surf City, USA (a name taken from Jan and Dean's 1963 pop hit by the same name), the classic SoCal pastime is big business – buyers from major retailers come here to see what surfers are wearing so they can market the look. Just look around at the skateboarders, dog walkers, cyclists, beach-volleyball enthusiasts, and party animals – Huntington Beach (p344) is the quintessential place to celebrate the coastal lifestyle.

Laguna Beach

If you've ever wanted to step into a painting, a sunset stroll through Laguna Beach (p348) might be the next best thing. The hidden coves, romantic cliffs, azure waves and waterfront parks aren't the only draw. Arts festivals and gallery nights imbue the city with an artistic sensibility you won't find elsewhere in SoCal. The locals, though wealthy, are live-and-let-live – there's a palpable artistic *joie de vivre* in the air.

Newport Beach

Orange County's ritziest beach community is known for beautiful, moneyed people and a particularly lovely environment: Newport Beach (p345) surrounds a pretty natural harbor that's one of the largest for pleasure craft in the US. At almost any hour of the day, you'll see a steady stream of cyclists, joggers and skaters on paved beach paths that extend as far as the eye can see.

Disneyland & Orange County's Best...

Theme Park Attractions

○ **Indiana Jones Adventure** (p335) An exciting archaeological adventure at Disneyland.

○ **Space Mountain** (p335) Disneyland's thrillingly futuristic in-the-dark roller coaster.

○ **Twilight Zone Tower of Terror** (p338) Drop 13 stories down an elevator chute at DCA.

○ **Pirates of the Caribbean** (p335) An eerie 17-minute-long cruise past pirate ships and cannon fights.

Fine Dining

○ **Napa Rose** (p341) Wine and dine inside Disney's Grand Californian Hotel.

○ **Catal Restaurant & Uva Bar** (p341 and p342) Cal-Mediterranean dishes and 40 wines by the glass; surprisingly sophisticated for Downtown Disney.

○ **French 75 Bistro & Champagne Bar** (p348) Splurge on French cuisine and bubbly in Laguna Beach.

○ **Mr Stox** (p342) Have steak or rack of lamb in Anaheim's country-club-style institution.

Vintage Landmarks

○ **Balboa Fun Zone** (p346) The postcard-pretty Ferris wheel dates from 1936.

○ **Main Street, USA** (p334) Walt modeled Disneyland's entryway on his childhood town.

○ **Ruby's Crystal Cove Shake Shack** (p347) Antique wooden milkshake stand with ocean views.

○ **Huntington Beach Pier** (p344) The All-American wooden pier, built in 1904, is on the US National Register of Historic Places.

Beach Moments

○ **Watch the surfers** (p344) Watch professional surfers from the Huntington Beach pier.

○ **Explore hidden coves** (p348) Find your own patch of sand via Laguna Beach's side streets.

○ **Check out the Wedge** (p346) Marvel at giant waves – and brave knee-boarders and bodysurfers – in Newport Beach.

○ **Bike along the beach** (p344) Rental stands are everywhere in Huntington Beach.

Need to Know

ADVANCE PLANNING

For Disneyland:

○ **One month before** Make area hotel reservations or book a Disneyland vacation package.

○ **One week before** Check the parks' opening hours and entertainment schedules online. Make dining reservations for sit-down restaurants. Print out your tickets or passes at home to avoid lines at the park.

○ **The night before** Pack sunscreen, sunglasses, a jacket, and extra batteries and memory cards for digital and video cameras. Make sure your electronic devices (including cameras and phones) are fully charged.

RESOURCES

○ **Mouse Wait** (www.mousewait.com) This free iPhone app offers up-to-the-minute info on ride wait times and what's happening in the parks.

○ **Walt Disney Travel Company** (www.disneytravel.com) Many say they've saved money booking their vacation packages here.

○ **The OC Forever Summer** (www.visittheoc.com) Orange County's official tourism website.

BE FOREWARNED

○ **Chilly waters** Don't let the sunshine fool you – the Pacific is cold. Surfers often wear wet suits even in summertime.

○ **Limited attractions** If you visit off-season, some of Disneyland's attractions, shows and fireworks may not be running – check the website to avoid disappointment.

○ **Necessary reservations** If you show up without reservations to any of Disney's sit-down restaurants, you might not be able to get a table.

○ **Trouble in paradise** Some kids' rides – including Mr Toad's Wild Ride – can be surprisingly scary. Tell your kids that if they get lost, they should contact the nearest Disney staff, who will escort them to a 'lost children' center (on Disneyland's Main Street USA or at DCA's Pacific Wharf).

Left: Ruby's Crystal Cove Shake Shack;
Above: Balboa Fun Zone
(LEFT) ANGUS OBORN/LONELY PLANET IMAGES ©;
(ABOVE) RICHARD CUMMINS/LONELY PLANET IMAGES ©

Disneyland & Orange County Itineraries

*To see both Disney parks, plan for three full days,
allowing short breaks to avoid Mickey overload. With
a few more days, combine a trip to Disneyland with
visits to a few of Orange County's idyllic beaches.*

**DISNEYLAND RESORT &
DISNEY CALIFORNIA ADVENTURE**

HUNTINGTON BEACH 2

NEWPORT BEACH 3

BALBOA ISLAND 4

LAGUNA BEACH 5

PACIFIC OCEAN

3 DAYS

DISNEYLAND TO DISNEY CALIFORNIA ADVENTURE

Best of Disneyland

Three days is about the right amount
of time to fully appreciate both parks:
Disneyland and the adjacent Disney
California Adventure. On day one, arrive
at **(1) Disneyland** as early as possible.
Stroll down Main Street, USA, stopping for
coffee and pastries while taking in views of
Sleeping Beauty Castle. Enter Tomorrowland and get in line to ride Space Mountain.
Traveling with kids? Head to Fantasyland
for the classic It's a Small World, then race
down the Matterhorn Bobsleds or take tots
to Mickey's Toontown. Head back to the
hotel for a break during the park's busiest
afternoon hours.

Later, or on day two, grab a Fastpass for
Indiana Jones Adventure and Pirates of the
Caribbean before dining in New Orleans
Square. Plummet down Splash Mountain,
then visit the Haunted Mansion before the
fireworks and Fantasmic! shows begin.
At **(2) Disney California Adventure**,
take a virtual hang-gliding ride on Soarin'
Over California before trying out the brand-
new Little Mermaid – Ariel's Undersea
Adventure ride and Ferris wheel. Then
explore Cars Land. After dark, drop by the
Twilight Zone Tower of Terror and catch the
World of Color light and water show.

DISNEYLAND TO LAGUNA BEACH
Disney Meets the Beach

5 DAYS

You can get your Disney fix and still have time to revel in the relaxed SoCal beach scene. Start with a day or two at **(1) Disneyland**. After wandering down Main Street, USA, stop for a classic photo op at Sleeping Beauty Castle. Don't miss a ride on thrilling Space Mountain. You'll need a Fastpass – or a good deal of patience waiting in line – to get onto Indiana Jones Adventure and Pirates of the Caribbean. Other essential attractions include the classic It's a Small world, and the eerie – but not too scary for kids – Haunted Mansion. Catch the fireworks at the day's end.

Next, head for the beach, starting with nearby Surf City, USA – **(2) Huntington Beach**. Catch a surf competition, go for fish tacos and margaritas at happy hour on Main St, or just rent a bike and pedal along the beach paths. Continue south to ritzy **(3) Newport Beach**. Take the ferry to **(4) Balboa Island** for boutique shopping, ice cream and pretty views. Finish in the artsy beach 'village' of **(5) Laguna Beach** to gallery hop and explore hidden beach coves.

Beachfront, Balboa Island (p346)

Discover Disneyland & Orange County

At a Glance

○ **Disneyland & Disney California Adventure** (p334) 'The happiest place on earth' – Walt's original theme park.

○ **Huntington Beach** (p344) Otherwise known as Surf City, USA.

○ **Newport Beach** (p345) Glamorous yachts and beautiful beaches.

○ **Laguna Beach** (p348) Bohemian-chic art enclave by the sea.

DISNEYLAND & ANAHEIM

Sights & Activities

You can see either Disneyland or Disney California Adventure in a day, but going on all the rides requires at least two days (three if visiting both parks), as waits for top attractions can be an hour or more.

DISNEYLAND   Amusement Park

Upon entering **Disneyland** (☏714-781-4565/4400; www.disneyland.com; 1313 Harbor Blvd, Anaheim; 1-day pass Disneyland Park or DCA adult/child 3-9yr $80/74, both parks $105/99; 👫), you're funneled onto Main Street, USA.

MAIN STREET, USA
Fashioned after Walt's hometown of Marceline, MO, bustling Main Street, USA resembles a classic turn-of-the-20th-century all-American town.

Nearby there's a station for the **Disneyland Railroad**, a steam train that loops the park and stops at four different locations.

Main St ends in the **Central Plaza**, the hub of the park from which the eight different lands (such as Frontierland and Tomorrowland) can be reached. **Sleeping Beauty Castle** lords over the plaza, its towers and turrets fashioned after Neuschwanstein, a Bavarian castle owned by Mad King Ludwig.

TOMORROWLAND
What did the future look like to Disney's 1950s imagineers? Visiting Tomorrowland suggests a space-age community where

Fountain, Disneyland
RICHARD CUMMINS/LONELY PLANET IMAGES ©

monorails and rockets are the primary forms of transportation.

The retro high-tech **monorail** glides to a stop in Tomorrowland, its rubber tires traveling a 13-minute, 2.5-mile round-trip route to Downtown Disney. Right away, kiddies will want to shoot laser beams on **Buzz Lightyear's Astro Blaster** adventure. Then jump aboard the **Finding Nemo Submarine Voyage**.

Space Mountain, Tomorrowland's signature attraction and one of the USA's best roller coasters, hurtles you into complete darkness at frightening speed.

Another classic is **Captain EO**, a short 3D sci-fi film starring a young Michael Jackson. Look for Anjelica Huston in a delightful cameo.

FANTASYLAND
Behind Sleeping Beauty Castle, Fantasyland is filled with the characters of classic children's stories – it's also your best bet for meeting princesses and other characters in costume. If you only see one attraction in Fantasyland, visit **It's a Small World**, a boat ride past hundreds of creepy animatronic children from different cultures, now joined by Disney characters, all singing the annoying theme song in an astounding variety of languages. Another classic, the **Matterhorn Bobsleds** is a steel-frame roller coaster that mimics a bobsled ride down a mountain.

Fans of old-school attractions will also get a kick out of the *Wind in the Willows*–inspired **Mr Toad's Wild Ride**, a loopy jaunt in an open-air jalopy through London. Younger kids love whirling around the **Mad Tea Party** teacup ride and the **King Arthur Carrousel**, then cavorting with characters in nearby **Mickey's Toontown**, a topsy-turvy minimetropolis where kiddos can traipse through Mickey's and Minnie's houses.

FRONTIERLAND
In the wake of the successful *Pirates of the Caribbean* movies, Tom Sawyer Island – the only attraction in the park personally designed by Uncle Walt – was re-imagined as **Pirate's Lair on Tom Sawyer Island** and now honors Tom in name only. After a raft ride to the island, wander among roving pirates, cannibal cages, ghostly apparitions and buried treasure. Or just cruise around the island on the 18th-century replica **Sailing Ship Columbia** or the **Mark Twain Riverboat**, a Mississippi-style paddle wheeler. The rest of Frontierland gives a nod to the rip-roarin' Old West with a shooting gallery and the **Big Thunder Mountain Railroad**, a mining-themed roller coaster.

ADVENTURELAND
Adventureland loosely derives its style from Southeast Asia and Africa. The hands-down highlight is the jungle-themed **Indiana Jones Adventure**. Enormous Humvee-type vehicles lurch and jerk their way through the wild for spine-tingling encounters with creepy crawlies and scary skulls in re-creations of stunts from the famous film trilogy.

Cool down with a **Jungle Cruise** where exotic animatronic animals from the Amazon, Ganges, Nile and Irrawaddy Rivers jump out and challenge your boat's skipper.

NEW ORLEANS SQUARE
Chicory coffee, jazz bands, wrought-iron balconies, mint juleps and beignets – must be New Orleans. (It's Walt Disney's version, of course, so the drinks are alcohol-free and the beignets are shaped like Mickey Mouse.) **Pirates of the Caribbean**, the longest ride in Disneyland (17 minutes) and the inspiration for the movies, opened in 1967 and was the first addition to the original park. Today, you'll float through the subterranean haunts of tawdry pirates where artificial skeletons perch atop mounds of booty, cannons shoot across the water, wenches are up for auction and the mechanical Jack Sparrow character is creepily lifelike. At the **Haunted Mansion**, '999 happy haunts' – spirits and goblins, shades and ghosts – evanesce while you ride the Doom Buggy through web-covered graveyards of dancing skeletons.

CRITTER COUNTRY
Tucked behind the Haunted Mansion, Critter Country's main attraction is **Splash**

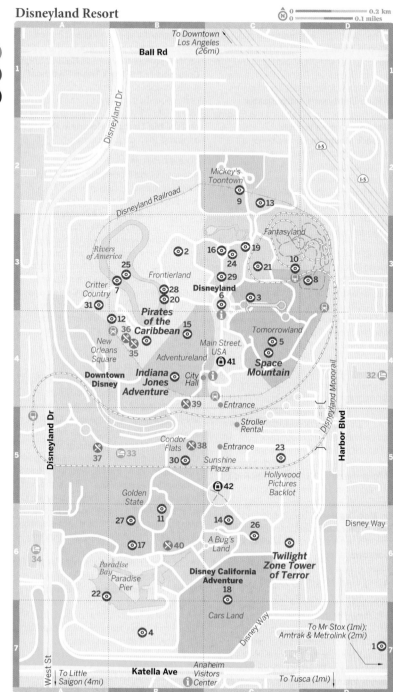

Disneyland Resort

◉ Top Sights
Indiana Jones Adventure	B4
Pirates of the Caribbean	B4
Space Mountain	C4
Twilight Zone Tower of Terror	C6

◉ Sights
1	Anaheim GardenWalk	D7
2	Big Thunder Mountain Railroad	B3
3	Buzz Lightyear's Astro Blaster	C3
4	California Screamin'	B7
5	Captain EO	C4
6	Central Plaza	C3
7	Davy Crockett's Explorer Canoes	B3
8	Disneyland Monorail	D3
9	Disneyland Railroad Station	C2
10	Finding Nemo Submarine Voyage	C3
11	Grizzly River Run	B6
12	Haunted Mansion	B4
13	It's a Small World	C2
14	It's Tough to Be a Bug	C6
15	Jungle Cruise	B4
16	King Arthur Carousel	C3
17	Little Mermaid – Ariel's Undersea Adventure	B6
18	Luigi's Flying Tires	C6
19	Mad Tea Party	C3
20	Mark Twain Riverboat	B3
	Mater's Junkyard Jamboree	(see 18)
21	Matterhorn Bobsleds	C3
22	Mickey's Fun Wheel	A6
23	Monsters, Inc: Mike & Sulley to the Rescue!	C5
24	Mr Toad's Wild Ride	C3
25	Pirate's Lair on Tom Sawyer Island	B3
26	Princess Dot Puddle Park	C6
	Radiator Springs Racers	(see 18)
27	Redwood Creek Challenge Trail	B6
28	Sailing Ship Columbia	B3
29	Sleeping Beauty Castle	C3
30	Soarin' over California	B5
31	Splash Mountain	A3

◉ Sleeping
32	Carousel Inn & Suites	D4
33	Disney's Grand Californian Hotel & Spa	B5
34	Disney's Paradise Pier Hotel	A6

◉ Eating
35	Blue Bayou	B4
36	Café Orleans	B4
37	Catal Restaurant	A5
38	La Brea Bakery	B5
	Napa Rose	(see 33)
39	Picnic Area	B4
40	Wine Country Trattoria	B6

◉ Drinking
Golden Vine Winery	(see 40)
Nava Rose Lounge	(see 33)
Uva Bar	(see 37)

◉ Shopping
41	Emporium	C4
42	Greetings from California	C5

Mountain, a flume ride that transports you through the story of Brer Rabbit and Brer Bear, based on the controversial 1946 film *Song of the South*. Nearby on the Rivers of America, you can paddle **Davy Crockett's Explorer Canoes** on summer weekends.

DISNEY CALIFORNIA ADVENTURE   Amusement Park
'The other park,' **Disney California Adventure** (DCA; ☎714-781-4565/4400; www .disneyland.com; 1313 Harbor Blvd, Anaheim; 1-day pass Disneyland Park or DCA adult/child 3-9yr $80/74, both parks $105/99; ⊕), is located just across the plaza from Disneyland's monument to fantasy and make-believe.

DCA has been undergoing a $1.1 billion building spree that's set to finish in 2012.

Some of the new attractions have already rolled out, like the epic **World of Color** water show and the **Little Mermaid – Ariel's Undersea Adventure** ride, while others, like **Cars Land** (based on the Disney Pixar classic), are hotly anticipated.

SUNSHINE PLAZA
The entrance to DCA was designed to look like an old-fashioned painted-collage postcard. After passing under the Golden Gate Bridge, you'll arrive at Sunshine Plaza, where a 50ft-tall sun made of gold titanium 'shines' all the time (heliostats direct the rays of the real sun onto the Disney sun). According to the plans, in 2012, Sunshine Plaza will be replaced by an homage to a 1920s Los Angeles streetscape, complete

with a red trolley running down the street into what will be renamed 'Hollywoodland.'

HOLLYWOOD PICTURES BACKLOT
With its soundstages, movable props and studio store, Hollywood Pictures Backlot is designed to look like the backlot of a Tinseltown studio.

The big attraction, however, is the **Twilight Zone Tower of Terror**, a 13-story drop down an elevator chute situated in a haunted hotel – which eerily resembles the historic Hollywood Roosevelt Hotel in Los Angeles. From the upper floors of the tower, you'll have views of the Santa Ana Mountains, if only for a few heart-pounding seconds. Less brave children can navigate a taxicab through 'Monstropolis' on the **Monsters, Inc: Mike & Sulley to the Rescue!** ride heading back toward the street's beginning.

Changes are ahead, but not all have been announced to the public; this area is being reimagineered as part of 'Hollywoodland' in 2012.

A BUG'S LAND
Attractions here, which were designed in conjunction with Pixar Studios' film *A Bug's Life* in mind, include the 3D **It's Tough to Be a Bug!** – kids will love putting on a pair of 'bug eyes.' **Princess Dot Puddle Park**, where guests can splash around and enjoy the spray of sprinklers and drenching fountains, is a relief on a sweltering summer's day.

GOLDEN STATE
Golden State is home to one of DCA's coolest attractions, **Soarin' over California**, a virtual hang-gliding ride, which uses Omnimax technology that lets you float over landmarks such as the Golden Gate Bridge, Yosemite Falls, Lake Tahoe and Malibu. **Grizzly River Run** takes you 'rafting' down a faux Sierra Nevada river; you *will* get wet so try it on a warm day.

Nearby, kids can tackle the **Redwood Creek Challenge Trail,** with its 'Big Sir' redwoods, wooden towers and lookouts, and rock slide and climbing traverses.

PARADISE PIER
The brand-new attraction here is the **Little Mermaid – Ariel's Undersea Adventure** ride, in which guests board giant clam shells and descend below the waves (so to speak, with the help of elaborate special effects) into a colorful underwater world.

The state-of-the-art **California Screamin'** roller coaster resembles an old wooden coaster, but it's got a smooth-as-silk steel track: it feels like you're being shot out of a cannon. Want a bird's-eye view of the park? Head to **Mickey's Fun Wheel**, a 15-story Ferris wheel where gondolas pitch and yaw (unless you've requested one of the stationary ones).

CARS LAND
Look for this brand-new area of DCA, designed around the popular Pixar movie *Cars* and expected to open sometime in 2012. Take a tractor ride through **Mater's Junkyard Jamboree**, steer your bumper car through **Luigi's Flying Tires** or ride with the wacky **Radiator Springs Racers**. Route 66–themed gift shops and diners will take on that special glow of nostalgia underneath neon lights in the evening.

DOWNTOWN DISNEY
This quarter-mile-long pedestrian mall feels longer than it is, mostly because it's packed with stores, restaurants, entertainment venues and, in summer, people.

Is It a Small World After All?

Pay attention to the cool optical illusion along Main Street, USA. As you look from the entrance up the street toward Sleeping Beauty Castle, everything seems far away and larger-than-life. When you're at the castle looking back, everything seems closer and smaller. This technique is known as forced perspective, a trick used on Hollywood sets where buildings are constructed at a decreasing scale to create an illusion of height or depth. Welcome to Disneyland.

Don't Miss Disney Fireworks & Parades

Disneyland's **Magical**, the fireworks spectacular above Sleeping Beauty Castle, happens nightly around 9:30pm in summer; for the rest of the year, check the online schedule to find out when and where evening fireworks are happening. In winter, artificial snow falls on Main Street, USA after the fireworks.

At the **Princess Fantasy Faire** in Fantasyland, your little princesses and knights can join the Royal Court and meet some Disney princesses.

Fantasmic!, an outdoor extravaganza on Disneyland's Rivers of America, may be the best show of all, with its full-size ships, lasers and pyrotechnics.

Disney California Adventure (DCA) has one major advantage over the original Disneyland Park – the live entertainment here is more varied and often more impressive. The premier show is **World of Color**, a dazzling nighttime display of lasers, lights and animation projected over Paradise Bay.

During the day, don't miss the **Pixar Play Parade**, led by race car Lightning McQueen from *Cars* and featuring energetic appearances by characters from other animated movies like *Monsters, Inc, The Incredibles, Ratatouille, Finding Nemo* and *Toy Story*.

Also popular is Disney's **Aladdin – A Musical Spectacular**, a 40-minute one-act musical extravaganza based on the movie of the same name. Teens will prefer the nearby **ElecTRONica**, a street party–style show with live DJs, lasers, martial artists and dancing.

Verify all show times once you arrive in the parks.

 **Sleeping**

For the full Disney experience, splurge and stay right at the **resort** (☎ reservations 714-956-6425; www.disneyland.com).

DISNEY'S GRAND CALIFORNIAN HOTEL & SPA   Luxury Hotel **$$$** (☎ 714-635-2300; http://disneyland.disney .go.com/grand-californian-hotel; 1600 S Disney-land Dr; d $384-445; ❄ ⌂ ≋ ⋔) Along the promenade of Downtown Disney, you'll

see the entrance to this splurgeworthy craftsman-style hotel offering family-friendly scavenger hunts, swimming pools bordered by private cabanas and its own entrance to DCA.

DISNEY'S PARADISE PIER HOTEL
Hotel $$

(☎714-999-0990; www.disneyland.com; 1717 S Disneyland Dr; r $290-370; @ 🛜 ≋ 👬) From some rooms at Paradise Pier, you can see fireworks and DCA's fabulous World of Color show – a major perk for those traveling with small children with early bedtimes. Sunbursts, surfboards and a giant superslide are all on deck at the Paradise Pier Hotel, the cheapest, but maybe the most fun, of the Disney hotel trio.

🌿 CAROUSEL INN & SUITES
Hotel $$

(☎714-758-0444; www.carouselinnandsuites .com; 1530 S Harbor Blvd; r $139-239; ❄ 🛜 ≋ 👬) Recently remodeled, this four-story hotel makes an effort to look stylish, with upgraded furniture and pots

of flowers hanging from the wrought-iron railings of its exterior corridors. The rooftop pool has great views of Disneyland fireworks.

Eating

There are dozens of dining options inside the theme parks; it's part of the fun to hit the walk-up food stands for treats like huge dill pickles, turkey legs and sugar-dusted churros.

Disneyland

BLUE BAYOU
Cajun $$$

(☎714-781-3463; New Orleans Sq; lunch $22-40; ⏱11:30am-park closure) Surrounded by the 'bayou' inside Pirates of the Caribbean, this place is famous for its Monte Cristo sandwiches at lunch and Creole and Cajun specialties at dinner. Whatever the time of day, you'll feel like you're dining outside under the stars, the ride's boats floating peacefully by.

CAFÉ
ORLEANS Southern **$**
(New Orleans Sq; mains $11-20; ⊙11am-
park closure) Jambalaya and virgin mint
juleps served cafeteria-style. Have lunch
under the pavilion while listening to live
music.

Disney California Adventure
WINE COUNTRY TRATTORIA Italian **$$**
(Golden Vine Winery, Golden State; mains $12-25;
⊙11am-6pm) DCA's best place for a relax-
ing sit-down lunch serves wonderfully
appetizing Italian pasta, salads, gourmet
sandwiches and wines by the glass.

Downtown Disney
LA BREA BAKERY Bakery, Café **$**
(1556 Disneyland Drive; breakfast $5-20;
⊙8am-11pm) This branch of one of LA's top
bakeries serves up great sandwiches and
salads. Express items under $10.

NAPA ROSE Californian **$$$**
(☎714-781-3463; Disney's Grand Californian
Hotel & Spa, 1600 S Disneyland Dr; mains $32-
45; ⊙5:30-10pm) Disney's – and one of
the OC's – finest restaurants occupies a
soaring Arts and Crafts–style dining room
overlooking DCA's Grizzly Peak. There's a
special emphasis on pairing native ingredients with native wines.

CATAL
RESTAURANT Californian, Italian **$$$**
(☎714-774-4442; www.patinagroup.com/catal;
1580 S Disneyland Dr; breakfast $9-14, dinner
$23-38; ⊙8am-10pm; ⊞) The chef cooks
up a fusion of Californian and Mediter-
ranean cuisines (squid-ink pasta with
lobster, grilled ahi with curry sauce) at
this airy two-story restaurant decorated
in a sunny Mediterranean-Provençal style
with exposed beams and lemon-colored
walls.

Anaheim
The 2008 opening of **Anaheim Garden-
Walk** (☎714-635-7400; www.anaheimgarden
walk.com; 321 W Katella Ave), an outdoor mall

Detour: Little Saigon

If you head a few miles southwest of Disneyland, you'll drive into the city of Westminster near the junction of I-405 and Hwy 22. Home to a large Vietnamese population, here the community has carved out its own vibrant commercial district around the intersection of Bolsa and Brookhurst Aves. At its heart is the **Asian Garden Mall** (www.asiangardenmall.com; 9200 Bolsa Ave), a behemoth of a structure packed with 400 ethnic boutiques, including herbalists and jade jewelers. On weekend evenings in summer, there's a night market from 7pm to midnight with vendors, food and live entertainment. The mini food court offers a variety of noodle and vegetable dishes and the *pho ga* (chicken noodle soup) is superb.

on Katella Ave one block east of Harbor Blvd, brought a welcome influx of sit-down eateries within walking distance of the park. Other nearby options are listed here.

TUSCA Californian, Italian $$
(www.tusca.com; Hyatt Regency Orange County, 11999 Harbor Blvd, Garden Grove; mains $11-24; ⏱6:30am-2pm & 5-10pm) Tusca's crispy handmade pizzas and seasonally inspired pastas prepared by a northern Italian chef (with herbs and veggies grown on the hotel's rooftop) justify the detour.

MR STOX Californian $$
(☏714-634-2994; www.mrstox.com; 1105 E Katella Ave; lunch $12-20, dinner $20-42; ⏱11:30am-2:30pm Mon-Fri, 5:30pm-10pm Mon-Sat, to 9pm Sun) For country-club ambience, settle into one of the oval booths and savor some of Anaheim's best California Cuisine. Mains include prime rib, duck and rack of lamb, plus a fair number of seafood and vegetarian options.

🍷 Drinking & Entertainment

Disneyland Resort

You can't buy any alcohol in Disneyland, but you can at DCA, Downtown Disney and Disney's trio of resort hotels.

UVA BAR Wine Bar
(www.patinagroup.com/catal; 1580 S Disneyland Dr; ⏱11am-10pm; 👪) Named after the Italian word for grape, this bar resembling a Paris metro station is Downtown Disney's best outdoor spot to tipple wine, nibble Cal-Mediterranean tapas and people-watch.

GOLDEN VINE WINERY Wine Bar
(Golden State; ⏱11am-park closure) This centrally located terrace is a great place for relaxing and regrouping in DCA. Nearby at Pacific Wharf, walk-up window **Rita's Baja Blenders** whips up frozen cocktails.

NAPA ROSE LOUNGE Wine Bar
(Disney's Grand Californian Hotel & Spa, 1600 S Disneyland Dr; ⏱5:30-10pm) Raise a glass to Napa as you nosh on pizzettas, artisan cheese plates and Scharffen Berger chocolate truffle cake.

🛍 Shopping

Disneyland & Disney California Adventure

Every section of the Disney parks has its own shopping options tailored to its own particular themes – Davy Crockett, New Orleans, the Old West, Route 66 or a seaside amusement park. The biggest theme-park stores – Disneyland's **Emporium** (Main Street, USA) and DCA's **Greetings from California** – have a mind-boggling variety of souvenirs, clothing and Disneyana, from T-shirts to mouse ears.

ℹ️ Information

Fastpass & Single Riders

With a bit of preplanning, you can significantly cut your wait time for popular attractions. One option is using the Fastpass system. At the Fastpass ticket machine (located near the entrance to the ride) insert your ticket. You'll receive a slip of paper showing a window of time for boarding the ride. Show up within that window and join the Fastpass line.

If you're traveling solo, ask the greeter at the entrance to the ride if there's a single-rider line; you can often head to the front of the queue.

Stroller Rental

You can rent a stroller for $15 per day ($25 for two strollers) outside the main entrance of Disneyland.

Tickets & Opening Hours

Both parks are open 365 days a year, but park hours depend on the marketing department's projected attendance numbers. You can access the current calendar (☎recorded info 714-781-4565, live assistance 714-781-7290; www.disneyland.com) by phone or online.

One-day admission to either Disneyland or DCA costs $80 for adults and $74 for children aged three to nine. To visit both parks in one day costs $105/99 per adult/child. Multiday Park Hopper Tickets cost $173/161 for two days, $214/198 for three days, $234/216 for four days and $246/226 for five days.

Tourist Information

Anaheim Visitors Center (☎714-765-8888; www .anaheimoc.org; 800 W Katella Ave; ☺8am-5pm Mon-Fri) Just south of DCA at the Anaheim Convention Center.

Central Plaza Information Board (☎714-781-4565; Main Street, USA, Disneyland Park) One of several information centers in the theme parks.

ℹ️ Getting There & Away

Air

Southern California Gray Line/Coach America (☎714-978-8855; www.graylineanaheim.com) runs the Disneyland Resort Express between LAX and Disneyland-area hotels at least hourly (one way/round-trip to LAX $20/30). It also serves John Wayne Airport (SNA) in Santa Ana ($15/25).

Bus

Frequent departures are available with **Greyhound** (☎714-999-1256; 100 W Winston Rd) to and from downtown LA ($8 to $15, about one hour) and to San Diego ($14 to $27, 2½ hours).

Car

Disneyland Resort is just off I-5 on Harbor Blvd, about 30 miles south of downtown LA.

All-day parking costs $15. Enter the 'Mickey & Friends' parking structure from southbound

Little Saigon, Westminster
LEE FOSTER/LONELY PLANET IMAGES ©

Disneyland Dr at Ball Rd. Take the tram to reach the parks; follow the signs.

The parking lots for Downtown Disney are reserved for shoppers and have a different rate structure: the first three hours are free, with an additional two more free hours if you have a validation from a table-service restaurant or the movie theater. After that it's $6 per hour, up to $30 a day.

Train

If you're arriving by train, you'll stop at the depot (2150 E Katella Ave) next to Angel Stadium, a quick shuttle or taxi ride east of Disneyland. Amtrak (☏714-385-1448; www.amtrak.com) and Metrolink (☏800-371-5465; www.metrolinktrains.com) commuter trains connect Anaheim to LA's Union Station ($14, 50 minutes) and San Diego ($27, two hours).

ⓘ Getting Around

Bus

The bus company Anaheim Resort Transit (ART; ☏714-563-5287, 888-364-2787; www.rideart.org) provides frequent service between Disneyland and hotels in the immediate area, saving headaches of parking and walking. An all-day pass costs $4 per adult and $1 per child aged three to nine.

Many hotels and motels have free shuttles to Disneyland and other area attractions; ask before booking.

Monorail

Take the monorail from Tomorrowland to the Disneyland Hotel, across from Downtown Disney, and save about 20 minutes of walking time. It's free if you've bought a park admission ticket.

ORANGE COUNTY BEACHES

Huntington Beach

In June 2011, the mayor of Huntington Beach (HB) presented the 'key to the city' to surfing legend Kelly Slater – an event that tells you everything you need to know about this beach community.

In late July, the city hosts the US Open of Surfing (www.usopenofsurfing.com), a six-star competition drawing more than 600 surfers, 400,000 spectators and a minivillage of concerts, motocross demos and skater jams.

◉ Sights & Activities

Surfing in Huntington Beach is competitive; control your longboard or draw the ire of territorial locals. Surf north of the pier. If you just want to watch surfers in action, walk down to **Huntington City Beach** at the foot of the pier. Just south is **Huntington State Beach**, the place to build a beach bonfire. Romp with your dog in the surf at **Dog Beach**, northwest of Goldenwest St.

INTERNATIONAL SURFING MUSEUM   Museum

(☏714-960-3483; www.surfingmuseum.org; 411 Olive Ave; suggested donation $2; ☉noon-5pm Mon & Wed-Fri, to 9pm Tue, 11am-6pm Sat & Sun) A small but interesting collection of surf-related memorabilia can be found at this museum just off Main St. Exhibits chronicle the sport's history with photos, surfboards and surf music.

⬥ BOLSA CHICA STATE ECOLOGICAL RESERVE   Nature Reserve

(☏714-846-1114; ☉sunrise-sunset) Just north of HB, PCH looks out onto Bolsa Chica State Ecological Reserve. At first glance it may look rather desolate (especially with the few small oil wells scattered about), but this restored salt marsh is an environmental success story teeming with bird life – according to reports, 321 of Orange County's 420 bird species have been spotted here in the past decade. A 1.5-mile loop trail starts from the parking lot on PCH.

🛏 Sleeping

SHOREBREAK HOTEL Luxury Hotel $$$

(☏714-861-4470; www.shorebreakhotel.com; 500 Pacific Coast Hwy; r from $224; ❄@🛜🐾) Stunning and sleek, the brand-new Shorebreak – the latest from Joie de Vivre, the popular California boutique hotel chain – is the hands-down winner for the coolest place to stay near the water. There's an airy patio with several fire pits, a state-of-the-art fitness center, an evening wine reception for guests, and 157 rooms with flat-screen TVs and decks or balconies (some face the sea).

Eating & Drinking

SUGAR SHACK Breakfast $
(www.hbsugarshack.com; 2131/2 Main St; mains $5-10; ☺6am-4pm Mon, Tue & Thu, to 8pm Wed, to 5pm Fri-Sun) The sidewalk patio is the place to sit at this Main St stalwart for some of HB's best people-watching. And if you're here really early, you might catch surfer dudes donning their wet suits.

CHRONIC TACOS Mexican $
(www.eatchronictacos.com; 328 11th St; mains under $8; ☺8am-9pm) For surfer haute cuisine, mosey into this sticker-covered shack and request a made-to-order Fatty Taco, then settle in for one of the best Mexican meals around.

DUKE'S American $$
(www.dukeshuntington.com; 317 Pacific Coast Hwy; lunch $9-15, dinner $20-30; ☺noon-10pm Tue-Sat, 5-10pm Mon; ♿) It's definitely touristy, but this Hawaiian-themed restaurant – named after surfing legend Duke Kahanamoku – is also fun and offers up some of the best views around. If you're just in the mood for drinks, try the Barefoot Bar downstairs.

BEACHFRONT 301 American $$
(www.beachfront301.com; 301 Main St; mains $8-18; ☺10am-late; ♿) This laid-back bar and grill is renowned for its happy hour (all day Monday and 3pm to 9pm Tuesday through Friday) with bargain food and drink specials. Offerings include $3 Baja-style chicken tacos and onion rings; $5 will buy you a veggie pizza, Santa Fe chicken wrap or double cheeseburger.

ℹ Information

Huntington Beach Convention and Visitors Bureau (☎714-969-3492; www.surfcityusa.com;

If You Like...
Kid-Friendly Attractions

If you (or, ahem, your kids) can't get enough of the wholesome, family-oriented attractions at Disneyland, pile the family into the car and try out a few of these.

1 KNOTT'S BERRY FARM
(☎714-220-5200; www.knotts.com; 8039 Beach Blvd, Buena Park; adult/child 3-11yr & senior $57/25; ☺from 10am, closing hr vary; ♿) This Old West–themed park offers shows and thrill rides, like the Xcelerator, blasting to 82mph in only 2.3 seconds, and GhostRider, one of the tallest wooden roller coasters in the world.

2 NEWPORT HARBOR NAUTICAL MUSEUM
(☎949-675-8915; www.nhnm.org; Balboa Fun Zone, 600 E Bay Ave; adult/child $4/2; ☺11am-6pm Sun-Thu, to 7pm Sat) This lively nautical museum has a kid-friendly wing with a 'Touch Tank' where visitors can interact with sea creatures (sea stars, bat stars, sea urchins) found in the region's tidepools.

3 OCEAN INSTITUTE
(☎949-496-2274; www.ocean-institute.org; 24200 Dana Pt Harbor Dr; adult/child $6.50/4.50, extra for cruises; ☺10am-3pm Sat & Sun; ♿) South of Newport Beach in Dana Point, this kid-oriented museum includes replicas of historic tall ships, maritime-related exhibits and and a Pyrate Adventure Sail – with a cast of pirates – on the 118ft *Spirit of Dana Point* ship.

Suite 208, 301 Main St; ☺9am-5pm Mon-Fri) provides tourist maps and other information.

Newport Beach & Around
The upscale suburb of Newport is as famous for its ritzy homes ($15 million, anyone?) as it is for its surprisingly relaxed beach. The 6-mile-long Balboa Peninsula has two piers – **Newport Pier** and **Balboa Pier** – stretches of white sandy beach and a renowned body surfing spot at the end: the Wedge.

Detour: Costa Mesa

Locals make frequent pilgrimmages to the land-locked suburb of Costa Mesa to do some serious credit-card damage at **South Coast Plaza** (📞800-782-8888; www .southcoastplaza.com; 3333 Bristol St). This sprawling shopping complex is home to 300 luxury stores. Boutiques such as Chanel and Rolex do their part to keep the numbers high.

The **Lab** (📞714-966-6660; www.thelab.com; 2930 Bristol St; 🕙10:30am-9pm Mon-Sat, 11am-6pm Sun) is an ivy-covered, outdoor 'anti-mall' where indie shoppers can sift through vintage clothing, trendy styles and eclectic tennis shoes.

Sights & Activities

BALBOA FUN ZONE Amusement Park
(www.thebalboafunzone.com; 603 E Bay Ave; 🕙11am-9pm Sun-Thu, to 10pm Fri & Sat) Opposite the Balboa Pier on the harbor side of the peninsula. Visitors can hop aboard the iconic Ferris wheel (you'll catch great views of the sea from the top) or take a spin on the carousel, which has been around since 1936.

WEDGE Surfing
At the very tip of the peninsula, by the West Jetty, the Wedge is a bodysurfing and knee-boarding spot famous for its perfectly hollow waves that can get up to 30ft high.

BALBOA ISLAND Island
In the middle of the harbor sits the island that time forgot. The 1.5-mile promenade that circles the island makes a terrific car-free stroll or jog. Near the Ferris wheel on the harbor side, the **Balboa Island Ferry** (www.balboaislandferry.com; 410 S Bayfront; adult/child/car & driver $1/0.50/2; 🕙6:30am-midnight), shuttles passengers across the bay. The ferry lands at Agate Ave, about 11 blocks west of Marine Ave, which is lined with swimwear boutiques, Italian trattorias and cocktail bars.

CRYSTAL COVE STATE PARK Park
(📞949-494-3539; www.crystalcovestatepark .com; Pacific Coast Hwy; 🕙6am-sunset) Once you get past the parking lots ($15), it's easy

to forget you're in a crowded metropolitan area at this state park, where visitors are treated to 2000 acres of undeveloped woodlands and 3.5 miles of coastline.

NEWPORT BAY ECOLOGICAL RESERVE Nature Reserve
Inland from the harbor, where runoff from the San Bernardino Mountains meets the sea, the brackish water of the Newport Bay Ecological Reserve supports more than 200 species of birds. For guided tours with naturalists and weekend kayak tours of the Back Bay (from $20 per person) contact the **Newport Bay Naturalists & Friends** (📞949-640-6746; www .newportbay.org).

Sleeping

NEWPORT CHANNEL INN Motel $$
(📞800-255-8614; www.newportchannelinn.com; 6030 W Coast Hwy; r $109-200; ❄🐾) Cyclists love this two-story motel's proximity to the beach bike path, which is just across the street. Other perks include large rooms, a big common sundeck and genuinely friendly owners.

BAY SHORES PENINSULA HOTEL Hotel $$
(📞949-675-3463, 800-222-6675; www.thebest inn.com; 1800 W Balboa Blvd; d $179-300; ❄@🐾) This three-story hotel has a fun, beach-minded hospitality that makes the surfing lifestyle seem accessible – even

if you're a middle-aged landlubber who's never touched a board in your life.

Eating

BLUEWATER GRILL   Seafood $$
(www.bluewatergrill.com; 630 Lido Park Dr; mains $8-30; ⏱11am-10pm Mon-Thu, to 11pm Fri & Sat, 10am-10pm Sun) This casual yet elegant New England–style seafood eatery, occupying a quiet spot on the edge of the bay, is a hit with locals thanks to spacious patio seating, raw-oyster bar, fresh grilled swordfish and the famous house clam chowder.

SABATINO'S SAUSAGE COMPANY   Italian $$
(www.sabatinoschicagosausage.com; 251 Shipyard Way; mains $10-27; ⏱11am-10pm Mon-Fri, from 8:30am Sat & Sun) Famous for Sicilian-style sausage – you'll see a stream of locals coming in to buy it at the central deli counter – Sabatino's also turns out savory seafood stews and pasta tossed with fresh clams and mussels.

SOL GRILL   Seafood, American $
(www.solgrill.com; 110 McFadden Pl; mains $5-25; ⏱5-10pm Tue-Sun; 🚌) This down-to-earth

bar and eatery, specializing in ahi chowder, lobster ravioli and fruity sangria, has brightly painted walls and an unpretentious atmosphere.

Drinking

RUBY'S CRYSTAL COVE SHAKE SHACK   Cafe, Juice Bar
(☎949-464-0100; 7703 E Coast Hwy; shakes under $5; ⏱10am-sunset) This been-here-forever wooden milkshake stand is now owned by the Ruby's Diner chain, but the shakes and the ocean view are just as good as ever.

ALTA COFFEE WAREHOUSE   Coffee Shop
(www.altacoffeeshop.com; 506 31st St; ⏱7am-11pm Sun-Thu, to midnight Fri & Sat) Regulars hang their mug on the wall at this cozy coffee shop housed in an inviting bungalow. Try the iced toffee coffee or come for a lunchtime salad on the patio.

Getting Around

OCTA (☎714-560-6282; www.octa.net) bus 71 stops at the corner of PCH and Hwy 55, and goes

Laguna Beach (p348)

PAUL KENNEDY/LONELY PLANET IMAGES ©

Detour:
Bowers Museum of Cultural Art

The **Bowers** (📞714-567-3600; www.bowers.org; 2002 N Main St; permanent collection adult/child $12/9; ⏱10am-4pm Tue-Sun) may be small, but the place draws major crowds with its tantalizing, high-quality special exhibits; at the time of writing, offerings included 'The Art and Craft of the American Whaler' and a collection of Chinese objects borrowed from the Shanghai Museum. This Mission-style museum also has a rich permanent collection of pre-Columbian, African, Oceanic and Native American art. Special exhibits may require separate tickets, which have cost as much as $27 per adult; the museum is free on the first Sunday of each month.

south to Palm St beside the Balboa Pier. Check current schedules at www.octa.net.

The local fare is $1.50 per trip, cash only. It can be purchased from OCTA fare boxes or the bus driver – you'll need exact change.

Laguna Beach

Orange County's most relaxed beach town has just about everything you'd want in a casual seaside vacation – great shopping, cliff-top restaurants, myriad art galleries, romantic inns and palm trees.

Sights & Activities

LAGUNA ART MUSEUM   Museum
(📞949-494-8971; www.lagunaartmuseum.org; 307 Cliff Dr; adult/child under 12yr/student $12/ free/10; ⏱11am-5pm, later in summer) This breezy museum has changing exhibits, usually featuring one or two California artists, plus a permanent collection heavy on California landscapes, vintage photographs and works by early Laguna artists.

 Beaches

At the western end of Broadway, **Main Beach** has benches, tables, restrooms and volleyball and basketball courts. It's also the best beach for swimming.

Just northwest of Main Beach, follow the path to the grassy, bluff-top **Heisler Park** for sweeping views of the craggy coves and deep blue sea. Drop down

below the park to **Diver's Cove**, a deep, protected inlet popular with snorkelers and, of course, divers.

Tours

FIRST THURSDAYS ART WALK   Walking
(📞949-683-6871; www.firstthursdaysartwalk .com; admission free) On the first Thursday of the month, downtown gets festive during these walks, which includes 40 local galleries and the Laguna Art Museum from 6pm to 9pm.

Sleeping

🌿 **CASA LAGUNA INN**   B&B $$$
(📞800-233-0449; www.casalaguna.com; 2510 S Coast Hwy; r from $300; ❄@🛜❄🐾) Laguna's B&B gem is built around a historic 1920s Mission-revival house surrounded by lush, manicured, mature plantings. Rooms are inside former artists' bungalows built in the 1930s and '40s; all have delicious beds, some have Jacuzzi tubs.

Eating

FRENCH 75 BISTRO & CHAMPAGNE BAR   French $$
(📞949-494-8444; www.french75.net; 1464 S Coast Hwy; mains $19-35; ⏱4:30-11pm) Fantastic coq au vin, chocolate souffle, and icy

champagne cocktails (half-price at the bar everyday from 4:30pm to 6:30pm) are the main draws at this refined but friendly bistro.

THE STAND　　　　　　Vegan **$**
(238 Thalia St; mains $6-12; ⊙7am-7pm; 🖋) This tiny tribute to vegan cuisine reflects what's best about Laguna living – it's friendly, unassuming and filled with indie spirit. The long menu includes hummus-and-guac sandwiches, sunflower-sprout salads and bean-and-rice burritos.

🍷 Drinking & Entertainment

K'YA BISTRO BAR　　　Cocktail Bar
(www.kyabistro.com; 1287 S Coast Hwy) This chic rooftop bar does killer cocktails (strawberry balsamic martini, anyone?) and tasty small plates. Perched atop the La Casa del Camino Hotel, the bar is noteworthy for its beautiful coastal views and friendly vibe.

LAS BRISAS　　　　　Cocktail Bar
(📞949-497-5434; www.lasbrisaslaguna beach.com; 361 Cliff Dr) Locals roll their eyes at the mere mention of this tourist-heavy spot, but out-of-towners flock here for a good reason: the blufftop view of the beach.

ℹ Information

Laguna Beach Visitors Center (📞949-497-9229; www.lagunabeachinfo.org; 381 Forest Ave; ⊙10am-4pm Mon-Fri) The staff at this visitors center is very helpful, and one wall here is filled with maps, brochures, bus schedules and coupons.

ℹ Getting There & Around

To reach Laguna Beach from the I-405, take Hwy 133 (Laguna Canyon Rd) southwest. Laguna is

❤ If You Like… Small Towns

If the relaxed vibe and slow pace of 'the Village' in Laguna Beach (p348) is your thing, check out these picturesque SoCal towns.

1 **ORANGE**
(www.cityoforange.org) For a pleasant dose of small-town life complete with a wide selection of family-owned restaurants and shops, head to Old Towne Orange. Built around a pretty plaza at the intersection of Chapman Ave and Glassell Sts, it has the most concentrated collection of antiques shops in Orange County. It's located northeast of Newport Beach off CA-55.

2 **SEAL BEACH**
(www.sealbeachca.gov) In the pageant for charming small towns, Seal Beach enjoys unfair advantages over the competition: 1.5 miles of pristine beach glittering like an already won crown, plus a three-block Main St lined with locally owned restaurants, mom-and-pop stores and indie coffee houses. North of Huntington Beach.

3 **CORONA DEL MAR**
(www.visitnewportbeach.com) This ritzy bedroom community, perched on the privileged eastern bluffs of the Newport Channel, has some of the best coastal views in SoCal. It also includes a high-end stretch of Pacific Coast Hwy, with trendy shops and restaurants, and the lovely Corona del Mar State Beach.

served by **OCTA** (📞714-560-6282; www.octa .net) bus 1, which runs along the coast from Long Beach to San Clemente.

Laguna Beach Transit (www.lagunabeachcity .net; 375 Broadway) has its central bus depot on Broadway, just north of the visitors center in the heart of the Village. For tourists, the most important route is the one that runs along PCH.

California
In Focus

California Today   352
Growing pains are par for the course in California, a creative social experiment and multicultural mosaic.

History   354
From Native Americans, Spanish missions and Manifest Destiny to 20th-century technology booms, earthquakes and race discrimination, here's how California evolved.

Family Travel   362
Where to go and what to bring if your traveling companions are in diapers, high school, or somewhere in between.

Way of Life   366
Bust the myths and stereotypes, uncover the realities and find out just what makes Californians tick.

The Arts   369
Be entranced by California's soulful side and a New World of architecture, art and sound.

California Cuisine   373
Feast at local farmers markets and food trucks while tippling sun-kissed vintages and sampling ground-breaking microbrews.

Beaches & Outdoor Activities   378
Get the scoop on digging your toes in the sand and the myriad ways to play in the Golden State.

Land & Wildlife   383
Meet the state's iconic wildlife and find out what makes California really shake, rattle 'n' roll.

Vineyard, Napa Valley (p212)
PHOTOGRAPHER: WES WALKER/LONELY PLANET IMAGES ©

California Today

Huntington Beach (p344), Orange County

> Tolerance for other people's beliefs, be they conservative, liberal or just plain wacky, is the social glue.

belief systems
(% of population)

36 Protestant **31** Catholic **•3** Jewish **30** Other

if California were 100 people

40 would be Caucasian
38 would be Latino
13 would be Asian American
6 would be African American
3 would be other

population per sq mile

† ≈ 80 people

USA   California   Los Angeles

California Dreamin' vs Reality

Even if you've seen it in movies or on TV, California still comes as a shock to the system. Venice Beach skateboarders, Santa Cruz hippies, Marin County wild-mushroom hunters, Rodeo Drive–pillaging trophy wives and Silicon Valley millionaires aren't on different channels; they all live here, where tolerance for other people's beliefs, be they conservative, liberal or just plain wacky, is the social glue.

Recently, the most divisive political hot-potato topic has been same-sex marriage, and the proposed constitutional amendment to ban it, which remains tied up in legal battles. Medical marijuana is old news for Californians, who approved a state proposition allowing its use back in 1996 – although the proliferation of marijuana clubs and rumors of Mexican cartel intervention have raised eyebrows lately.

MICAH WRIGHT/LONELY PLANET IMAGES ©

as ex-Governor Arnold Schwarzenegger sometimes did. That said, the state's current budget crisis has resulted in deep cuts in environmental protections, as well as social services and education.

Fast Companies

California's technological innovations need no introduction by anyone. Perhaps you've heard of PCs, iPods, Google and the internet? The home of Silicon Valley and a burgeoning biotech industry, Northern California is giving Southern California's gargantuan entertainment industry a run for its money as the state's main economic engine.

Slow Food

You may notice Californians tend to proselytize about their food and idolize homegrown chefs like rock stars. After a few bites, you may begin to understand their obsession. Mulling over menus also means taking a stand on issues close to many Californian's hearts: organic and non-GMO crops, veganism, grass-fed versus grain-fed meat, biodynamic vineyards, fair-trade coffee, and the importance of buying local food. It's no accident that the term 'locavore' – meaning people who eat food grown locally – was invented here.

New World Religions

California made national headlines in the 1960s with gurus from India, in the '70s with Jim Jones' People's Temple and Erhard Seminars Training, the '90s with Heaven's Gate doomsday UFO cult in San Diego, and in 2011 when Oakland radio minister Harold Camping proselytized that the Rapture was about to happen. Around since 1954, the controversial Church of Scientology is still seeking acceptance, with celebrity proponents from movie-star Tom Cruise to musician Beck.

Roots of Environmentalism

There's no denying that California's culture of conspicuous consumption is exported via Hollywood flicks and reality TV. But since the 1960s, Californians have trailblazed another way by choosing more sustainable foods and low-impact lifestyles, preserving old-growth forests, declaring nuclear-free zones, pushing for environmentally progressive legislation and establishing the USA's biggest market for hybrid vehicles.

It was Californians who originally helped kick-start the world's conservation movement in the midst of the 19th-century industrial revolution, with laws curbing industrial dumping, swaths of prime real estate set aside as urban green space, and pristine wilderness protected by national and state parks. Today, even conservative California politicians prioritize environmental issues on their agendas,

History

Paiute people in traditional clothing

Beckoning from the edge of the continent, California has witnessed a steady stream of people drawn to its natural resources and culture of cutting-edge ideas. Successively inhabited and developed by Native American tribes, European explorers and missionaries, white land-hungry settlers and frenzied gold miners, the Golden State is also the birthplace of the 1960s countercultural movement and ground zero for computer technology and innovation.

The First Peoples

Immigration is hardly a new phenomenon here, since people have been migrating to California for millennia. Archaeological sites indicate this geographic region was first inhabited soon after people migrated across the long-gone land bridge from Asia during an ice age at least 20,000 years ago. Many archaeological sites have yielded evidence, from large middens of seashells along the beaches to campfire

25,000–10,000 BC
Earliest known humans cross over the Bering Strait from Asia.

sites on the Channel Islands, that people have been living along this coast for around 8000 years.

Archaeological evidence paints a clear picture of the diversity of indigenous peoples living here at the time of first European contact. Native peoples spoke over 60 different languages and numbered as many as 300,000. They mostly lived in small groups, often migrating with the seasons from the coast into the mountains. Acorn meal was their dietary staple, supplemented by small, wild game and seafood.

A New World for Europeans

Following the conquest of Mexico in the early 16th century, the Spanish turned their attention toward exploring the edges of their new empire. In 1542 the Spanish crown engaged Juan Rodríguez Cabrillo, a Portuguese explorer and retired conquistador, to lead an expedition up the West Coast to find the fabled golden land beyond Mexico's west coast.

When Cabrillo sailed into San Diego Bay in 1542, he and his crew became the first Europeans to see mainland California. Staring back at them from shore were the Kumeyaay – to learn more about this coastal tribe, visit San Diego's Museum of Man. Cabrillo's ships sat out a storm in the harbor, then sailed northward. They made a stop at the Channel Islands where, in 1543, Cabrillo fell ill, died and was buried. The expedition continued as far as Oregon, but returned with no evidence of a sea route to the Atlantic, a city of gold or islands of spice. The unimpressed Spanish authorities forgot about California for the next 50 years.

The English privateer Sir Francis Drake sailed up the California coast in 1579. He missed the entrance to San Francisco Bay, but pulled in near what is now called Point Reyes to repair his ship, which was bursting with the weight of plundered Spanish silver. He claimed the land for Queen Elizabeth, named it Nova Albion (New England) and left for other adventures, starting with journeying north up the Pacific Coast to Alaska.

The Mission Period

Around the 1760s, as Russian ships came to California's coast in search of sea-otter pelts, and British trappers and explorers spread throughout the West, King Carlos III of

The Best...
Places for Ancient History

1 La Brea Tar Pits (p68)

2 Redwood trees (p151)

3 Petroglyphs at Lava Beds National Monument (p173)

4 Petrified Forest (p225)

5 Devils Postpile (p273)

IN FOCUS HISTORY

6000 BC
Date of earliest petroglyphs (rock art) found at Lava Beds National Monument near Mt Shasta.

1542
Juan Rodríguez Cabrillo becomes the first European to 'discover' California.

1579
English explorer Sir Francis Drake stops by Marin County.

Spain grew worried that these other newcomers might pose a threat to Spain's claim. Conveniently for the king, the Catholic Church was anxious to start missionary work among the indigenous peoples, so church and state combined forces to found missions inside presidios (military posts).

Ostensibly, the presidios' purpose was to protect the missions and deter foreign intruders. The idea was to have Native American converts live inside the missions, learn trade and agricultural skills, and ultimately establish pueblos (small towns). But these garrisons created more threats than they deterred, as the soldiers aroused local hostility by raiding Native American camps to sexually assault and kidnap women. Not only were the presidios militarily weak, but their weaknesses were well known to Russia and Britain, and didn't strengthen Spain's claims to California.

Ultimately, the mission period was pretty much a failure. The Spanish population remained small; the missions achieved little more than mere survival; foreign intruders were not greatly deterred; and more Native Americans died than were converted. Most of California's missions are still standing today, though a few are in ruins. Of California's original chain of 21 missions, the earliest were founded by peripatetic Franciscan priest Junípero Serra.

From Mexico to Manifest Destiny

When Mexico gained independence from Spain in 1821, many of the new nation's people looked to California to satisfy their thirst for private land. By the mid-1830s the Spanish missions had been secularized, with a series of Mexican governors doling out hundreds of free land grants, or ranchos, that were largely given over to rearing livestock to supply a profitable trade in hide and tallow. The new landowners, called rancheros or Californios, quickly prospered and became the social, cultural and political heavyweights of Alta (Upper) California.

American explorers, trappers, traders, whalers, settlers and opportunists showed increasing interest in California, seizing on prospects that the rancheros ignored. Some of the Americans who started businesses converted to Catholicism, married locals and assimilated into Californio society. Impressed by California's potential wealth and hoping to fulfill the promise of Manifest Destiny (the USA's imperialist doctrine to extend its borders from coast to coast), US President Andrew Jackson sent an emissary to offer the financially strapped Mexican government $500,000 for California in 1835. Though American settlers were by then showing up by the hundreds, especially in Northern California, Jackson's emissary was tersely rejected.

In 1836 Texas had seceded from Mexico and declared itself an independent republic. On May 11, 1846, the US declared war on Mexico, following disputes over the former's annexation of Texas. By July, US naval units occupied every port on the California coast, including Monterey, the capital of Alta California. When US troops captured Mexico City in September 1847, ending the war, the Mexican government had little choice but to cede much of its northern territory to the US. The Treaty of Guadalupe Hidalgo, signed

1769

Padre Junípero Serra establishes the first of 21 missions along the 650-mile El Camino Real. Street sign, El Camino Real, Monterey

STEPHEN SAKS/LONELY PLANET IMAGES ©

1821

Mexico wins independence from Spain, taking over rule of Alta (Upper) California after Spain's 52-year reign.

on February 2, 1848, turned over what is now California, Nevada, Utah and parts of Arizona, New Mexico, Colorado and Wyoming to the US. Two years later, California was admitted as the 31st state of the USA.

There's Gold in Them Thar Hills

By remarkable coincidence, gold was discovered at Sutter's Creek, about 120 miles northeast of San Francisco, little more than a week before the signing of the Treaty of Guadalupe Hidalgo that ended the Mexican–American War. By 1849, surging rivers of wagon trains were creaking into California filled with miners, pioneers, savvy entrepreneurs, outlaws and prostitutes, all seeking their fortunes.

Population growth and overnight wealth stimulated every aspect of California life, from agriculture and banking to construction and journalism. But mining damaged the land: hills were stripped bare, erosion wiped out vegetation, streams silted up and mercury washed down rivers into San Francisco Bay. San Francisco became a hotbed of gambling, prostitution, drink and chicanery, giving rise to its moniker 'the Barbary Coast,' whose last vestiges live on today in the strip joints in San Francisco's North Beach neighborhood.

The Best... California Mission Buildings

1 Mission Santa Barbara (p192)

2 Mission San Francisco Solano de Sonoma (p228)

3 Mission San Luis Obispo de Tolosa (p189)

4 Mission Basilica San Diego de Alcalá (p294)

Development, Discrimination & Natural Resources

Opening the floodgates to massive migration into the West, the transcontinental railroad drastically shortened the trip from New York to San Francisco from two months to five days, profitably linking markets on both coasts. Los Angeles was not connected to the transcontinental railroad until 1876, when Southern Pacific Railroad laid tracks from San Francisco south to the fledgling city.

By this time, rampant speculation had raised land prices in California to levels no farmer or immigrant could afford; the railroad brought in products that undersold goods made in California; and some 15,000 Chinese laborers – no longer needed for railroad construction – flooded the labor market. A period of unrest ensued, which culminated in anti-Chinese discrimination and the federal 1882 Chinese Exclusion Act, banning Chinese immigration. The act was not repealed until 1943.

Much of the land granted to the railroads was sold in big lots to speculators who also acquired, with the help of corrupt politicians and administrators, a lot of the farmland intended for new settlers. A major share of the state's agricultural land thus became

1840s
Chinese immigrants are recruited to build the growing railroad business.

1846
The Mexican–American War begins; drunk Californians in Sonoma declare independence, which lasts for 22 days.

1849
The Gold Rush continues; San Francisco gains 10 times the population and 100 times the bars.

The Best... Places to Experience the Gold Rush

1 Bodie State Historic Park (p272)

2 Sonoma (p227)

3 Marshall Gold Discovery State Historic Park (p273)

4 San Francisco's North Beach (p118)

5 Sutter's Fort State Historic Park (p274)

consolidated as large holdings in the hands of a few city-based landlords, establishing the pattern (which continues to this day) of industrial-scale 'agribusiness' rather than small family farms. These big businesses were well placed to provide the substantial investment and the political connections required to bring irrigation water to the farmland. They also solidified an ongoing need for cheap farm labor.

In the absence of coal, iron ore or abundant water, heavy industry developed slowly in California, though the 1892 discovery of oil in central Los Angeles by Edward Doheny stimulated the development of petroleum processing and chemical industries. By the year 1900, California was producing 4 million barrels of oil per year and the population of LA had doubled to over 100,000 people.

While bucolic Southern California was urbanizing, Northern Californians who had witnessed devastation from mining and logging firsthand were forming the nation's first conservation movement. Naturalist John Muir founded the Sierra Club in 1892 and campaigned for the federal government to establish the first national park in Yosemite. However, dams and pipelines continued to be built to support communities in SoCal deserts and coastal cities – including the Hetch Hetchy Reservoir in Yosemite, which supplies the Bay Area with water today, and aqueducts from the Sierra Nevada to slake the thirst of Los Angeles. In drought-prone California, tensions still regularly come to a boil between developers and conservationists, and NorCal drinking-water hoarders and SoCal lawn-water splurgers.

Growing into the 20th Century

The population, wealth and importance of California increased dramatically throughout the 20th century. The great San Francisco earthquake and fire of 1906 decimated the city, but it was barely a hiccup in the state's development. The revolutionary years in Mexico, from 1910 to 1921, caused a huge influx of immigrants from south of the border, reestablishing Latino communities that had been smothered by Anglo dominance. Meanwhile, SoCal's oil industry boomed in the 1920s and Hollywood entered its so-called 'Golden Age,' which lasted through the 1950s.

The Great Depression saw another wave of immigrants, this time from the impoverished Great Plains states of the Dust Bowl. Outbreaks of social and labor

1892
John Muir founds the Sierra Club after helping establish Yosemite as a national park.

1906
A 7.9 earthquake and resulting fire destroys much of San Francisco.

1928
The Jazz Singer is released as the first feature-length 'talkie'; worldwide demand for films grows Hollywood.

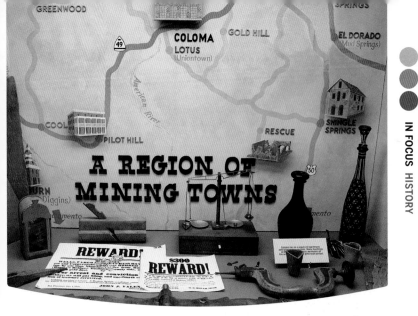

unrest led to the rapid growth of the Democratic Party in California, as well as trade unions for blue-collar workers. Many of the Depression-era public works projects sponsored by the federal government had lasting benefits, from San Francisco's Bay Bridge to the restoration of historic missions statewide, notably Mission La Purísima Concepción near Santa Barbara.

WWII had a major impact on California. Women were co-opted into wartime factory work and proved themselves in a range of traditionally male jobs. Anti-Asian sentiments resurfaced, many Japanese Americans were interned and more Mexicans crossed the border to fill labor shortages. Some military servicepeople who passed through California liked the place so much that they returned to settle after the war. In the postwar decade, the state's population jumped by 40%, reaching 13 million by 1955.

Radicals, Trendsetters & Technology

Unconstrained by tradition, Californians have long been leaders in new attitudes and social movements. During the affluent postwar years of the 1950s, the Beat movement in San Francisco's North Beach railed against the banality and conformity of suburban life, instead choosing bohemian coffeehouses for jazz, poetry and pot.

Exhibit, Marshall Gold Discovery State Historic Park (p273)

PHOTOGRAPHER: RICHARD CUMMINS/LONELY PLANET IMAGES ©

1939
Hewlett-Packard is formed in Dave Packard's garage in Palo Alto.

1962
César Chávez organizes migrant laborers into what will eventually become the United Farm Workers.

1967
San Francisco's Summer of Love kicks off the hippie movement.

The Best... History Museums

1 California State Railroad Museum (p274)

2 San Diego Natural History Museum (p291)

3 Emigrant Trail Museum (p253)

4 Grammy Museum (p63)

5 Museum of the American West (p67)

6 Manzanar National Historic Site (p270)

When the postwar baby boomers came of age, many took up where the Beat generation left off, heeding 1960s countercultural icon Timothy Leary's counsel to 'turn on, tune in and drop out.' Their revolt climaxed in San Francisco's Haight-Ashbury during the 1967 'Summer of Love.' Sex, drugs and rock 'n' roll ruled the day. With the foundation for social revolution already laid, gay liberation exploded in San Francisco in the '70s. Today San Francisco remains one of the world's most exuberantly gay cities – just take a stroll through the Castro.

In the 1980s and '90s, California catapulted to the forefront of the healthy lifestyle, with more aerobics classes and self-actualization workshops than you could shake a shaman's stick at. In-line skating, snowboarding and mountain-biking rose to fame here first.

Geeking Out

As digital technology continually reinvents our world view, California has also led the world in developing computer technology. In the 1950s, Stanford University needed to raise money to finance postwar growth, so it built an industrial park and leased space to high-tech companies like Hewlett-Packard, which formed the nucleus of Northern California's Silicon Valley.

When Silicon Valley introduced the first personal computer in 1968, advertisements breathlessly gushed that Hewlett-Packard's 'light' (40lb) machine could 'take on roots of a fifth-degree polynomial, Bessel functions, elliptic integrals and regression analysis' – all for just $4900 (about $29,000 today). Consumers didn't know quite what to do with computers, but in his 1969 *Whole Earth Catalog,* author (and former CIA LSD tester) Stewart Brand explained that the technology governments used to run countries could empower ordinary people. Hoping to bring computer power to the people, 21-year-old Steve Jobs and 26-year-old Steve Wozniak introduced the Apple II, with unfathomable memory (4KB of RAM) and microprocessor speed (1MHz), at the 1977 West Coast Computer Faire. But the question remained: what would ordinary people do with all that computing power?

By the mid-1990s, an entire dot-com industry of online start-ups boomed in Silicon Valley, and suddenly people were getting their mail, news, politics, pet food and, yes, sex online. In the fat years of the late 1990s, companies nationwide jumped on the dot-

1978

San Francisco elects the nation's first openly gay politician, Harvey Milk (assassinated later that year).

1989

The Bay Area is hit by the 7.1 Loma Prieta earthquake during the World Series. Earthquake damage in 1989, San Francisco

DAVID RYAN/LONELY PLANET IMAGES ©

com bandwagon following the exponential growth of the web, and many reaped huge overnight profits.

Boom & Bankruptcy

When dot-com profits weren't forthcoming, venture funding dried up and fortunes in stock options disappeared on one nasty Nasdaq-plummeting day: March 10, 2000. No place in America was more affected by the demise of the dot-coms in 2000 than California. Overnight, 26-year-old vice-presidents and Bay Area service-sector employees alike found themselves jobless. But as online users continued to look for useful information, and for one another, in those billions of web pages, search engines and social media boomed.

In 2008, the unraveling subprime mortgage-lending crisis triggered a US stock-market crash and caused the entire nation to sink into a recession. Massive unemployment devastated California, once the world's sixth-largest economy. By 2009 the state was so broke that it issued IOU slips to creditors. Struggling to make ends meet, California began a series of vilified cost-cutting measures that included steep tuition hikes at public universities and proposed service cutbacks in many of its 250 state parks.

2004
The most anticipated IPO in history, Google shares start at $85 (eventually peaking above $700).

2008
Californians pass Proposition 8, against same-sex marriage. Courts ruled it unconstitutional; appeals are pending.

2013
America's Cup to be held in San Francisco.

Family Travel

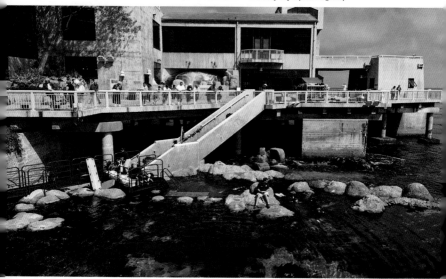

Monterey Bay Aquarium (p180)

STEPHEN SAKS/LONELY PLANET IMAG

California is a tailor-made destination for traveling with kids. In addition to Southern California's theme parks, there are thousands of places to explore. Sunny skies lend themselves to outdoor activities including swimming, snorkeling, bicycling, kayaking, hiking and horseback riding. In winter, when it's cold and rainy or snowing outside, or even during summer when fog hugs the coast, you'll find museums and indoor entertainment galore.

California with Kids

Children's discounts are widely available for everything from museum admission and movie tickets to bus fares and motel stays. The definition of a 'child' varies – in some places anyone under 18 is eligible while at others the cutoff is age six. At amusement parks, some rides may have minimum-height requirements, so let younger kids know about this in advance to avoid disappointment and tears.

It's perfectly fine to bring kids, even toddlers, along to casual restaurants, which often have high chairs. Many diners and family restaurants break out paper place mats and crayons for drawing. Ask about cheaper children's menus too. At theme parks, pack a cooler in the car and have a picnic in the parking lot to avoid ballpark prices. On the road, many larger supermarkets have wholesome, ready-to-eat takeout dishes.

Baby food, infant formula, soy and cow's milk, disposable diapers (nappies) and other necessities are widely available in drugstores and supermarkets. Most women are discreet about breastfeeding in public. Many public toilets have a baby-changing table and gender-neutral private 'family' bathrooms may be available at airports, museums etc.

Children's Highlights

It's easy to keep kids entertained no matter where you travel in California. Throughout this book, look for family attractions and other fun activities, all marked with the child-friendly icon (👪). At national and state parks, be sure to ask at visitors centers about ranger-led activities and self-guided 'Junior Ranger' programs, in which kids earn themselves a badge after completing an activity.

Theme Parks

o **Disneyland & Disney California Adventure** All ages of kids, even teens and the eternally young at heart, adore the 'Magic Kingdom.'

o **Knott's Berry Farm** SoCal's original thrills-a-minute theme park.

o **Universal Studios Hollywood** Movie-themed action rides, special-effects shows and a tram tour of a working studio backlot.

Aquariums & Zoos

o **Monterey Bay Aquarium** Get acquainted with the denizens of the deep next door to the Central Coast's biggest marine sanctuary.

o **San Diego Zoo & Safari Park** Journey around the world and go on safari outdoors at California's best and biggest zoo.

o **Aquarium of the Pacific** Long Beach's high-tech aquarium houses critters from balmy Baja California to the chilly north Pacific, including a shark lagoon.

o **SeaWorld** Penguins, sharks and Shamu in San Diego. Need we say more?

Need to Know

o **Changing facilities** Available in most public locations, such as malls and rest stops.

o **Cots** Many hotels offer cots for kids for a nominal fee or at no cost.

o **Diapers (nappies)** Readily available at grocery stores and even most convenience stores.

o **Health** California retains a very high standard of health and clean facilities.

o **High chairs** Almost ubiquitous in casual restaurants; call ahead at upscale places.

o **Strollers** Available to rent at Disneyland and SeaWorld.

o **Transportation** On buses, parents hold children on laps. Car seats are required for children under six.

Beaches

○ **Los Angeles** Carnival fun at Santa Monica Pier, Manhattan Beach's waterfront volleyball courts or Malibu's perfect beaches just beyond.

○ **Orange County** Newport Beach with its kiddie-sized Balboa Pier rides, Laguna Beach's miles of million-dollar sands, Huntington Beach (aka 'Surf City USA') and old-fashioned Seal Beach.

○ **San Diego** Head over to Coronado's idyllic Silver Strand, play in Mission Bay by SeaWorld, lap up La Jolla and kick back in surf-style North County beach towns.

○ **Central Coast** Laze on Santa Barbara's unmatched beaches, then roll all the way north to Santa Cruz's famous boardwalk and pier.

○ **Lake Tahoe** In summer, it's California's favorite high-altitude beach escape: a sparkling diamond tucked in the craggy Sierra Nevada mountains.

Parks

○ **Yosemite National Park** Get a juicy slice of Sierra Nevada scenery, with gushing waterfalls, alpine lakes, and glacier-carved valleys and peaks.

○ **Redwood National and State Parks** On the misty North Coast, a string of nature preserves protect magnificent wildlife, beaches and the planet's tallest trees.

○ **Lassen Volcanic National Park** Off-the-beaten-path destination in the Northern Mountains, with otherworldly volcanic scenery, and lakeside camping and cabins.

○ **Griffith Park** Bigger than NYC's Central Park, this LA green space has tons of fun for younger kids, from miniature train rides and a merry-go-round to planetarium shows.

Museums

○ **San Francisco** The Bay Area is a mind-bending classroom for kids, especially at the hands-on Exploratorium and ecofriendly California Academy of Sciences.

○ **Los Angeles** See stars (the real ones) at the Griffith Observatory, and dinosaur bones at the Page Museum at the La Brea Tar Pits.

○ **San Diego** Balboa Park is jam-packed with museums like the Reuben H Fleet Science Center (and a world-famous zoo, too), or take younger kids downtown to the engaging New Children's Museum.

Planning

Accommodations

Motels and hotels typically have rooms with two beds or an extra sofa bed, ideal for families. They also may have rollaway beds or cots that can be brought into the room, typically for a surcharge. Some offer 'kids stay free' promotions, although this may apply only if no extra bedding is required. Some B&Bs don't allow children; ask when booking.

Resorts may have drop-off day camps for kids or on-call babysitting services. At other hotels, the front-desk staff or concierge might help you make arrangements. Be sure to ask whether babysitters are licensed and bonded, what they charge per hour per child, whether there's a minimum fee and if they charge extra for transportation and meals.

Transportation

Airlines usually allow infants (up to age two) to fly for free. Children receive substantial discounts on Amtrak trains and Greyhound buses. In cars, any child under age six or weighing less than 60lb must be buckled up in the back seat in a child or infant safety seat. Most car-rental agencies rent these seats for about $10 per day or $50 per trip, but you must specifically book them in advance. Rest stops on freeways are few and far between, and gas stations and fast-food bathrooms are frequently icky. However, you're not usually too far from a shopping mall, which generally has well-kept restrooms.

What to Pack

Sunscreen. Lots of sunscreen.

And bringing sunscreen will remind you to bring hats, bathing suits, flip-flops and goggles. If you like beach umbrellas and sand chairs, pails and shovels, you'll probably want to bring or buy your own at local supermarkets and drugstores. At many beaches, you can rent bicycles and all kinds of water-sports gear (eg snorkel sets).

For outdoor vacations, bring broken-in hiking shoes and your own camping equipment. Outdoors gear can be purchased or sometimes rented from outdoor outfitters and specialty shops.

The Best... Attractions for Kids

1 Exploratorium (p103)

2 Monterey Bay Aquarium (p180)

3 Disneyland (p334)

4 San Diego Zoo (p296)

5 Yosemite National Park (p254)

6 Santa Cruz Beach Boardwalk (p176)

IN FOCUS FAMILY TRAVEL

Way of Life

Barbecue, San Luis Obispo Farmers Market (p191)

LEE FOSTER/LONELY PLANET IMAGES

The rest of America shakes its head in wonder at California, never quite sure how to categorize it. It's best not to try, since the Golden State is forever reinventing itself. Remember, this is the place that gave the world both hippies and Ronald Reagan.

Regional Identity

It's best to think of California as two states: Southern California (SoCal) and Northern California (NorCal). Although nobody can agree on exactly where to draw the line between the two, it falls somewhere between San Francisco, with its liberal-minded hipsters, and Los Angeles, the glitzy but tarnished 'City of Angels.'

In any case, believe everything you've ever heard about Californians, so long as you realize the stereotypes are always exaggerated. Sure, blonde surfers shout 'Dude!' across San Diego beaches, hippies and Rastafarians gather for drum circles in San Francisco's Golden Gate Park, and tree huggers toke on joints in the North Coast woods but, all in all, it's hard to peg the population.

In the Bay Area, the politics are liberal and the people open-minded, with a strong live-and-let-live ethic and an often passionate devotion to the outdoors. The hard-to-classify Central Coast, with its smaller pockets of population, starts near wacky, left-of-center Santa Cruz and stretches all the way south to surreally beautiful, sexily posh Santa Barbara. Composed of dozens of independent cities, LA is impossible to generalize about, but one thing is for sure: almost everybody drives.

Between LA and San Diego lies Orange County, aka 'the OC,' where beautifully bronzed, buff bodies soak up rays on the sands. The politics 'behind the Orange Curtain' are notably conservative and extend south to San Diego, partly due to its sizable military population.

Lifestyle

If you're like most Californians, you practically live in your car. Californians commute an average of 30 minutes each way to work. But Californians have zoomed ahead of the national energy-use curve in their smog-checked cars, buying more hybrid and fuel-efficient cars than any other state.

Eight of the 10 most expensive US housing markets are in California and, in the most expensive area, suburban La Jolla, the average house price is $1.875 million. Almost half of all Californians reside in cities, but much of the remaining population lives in the suburbs, where the cost of living is just as high, if not higher. Marin County outside San Francisco is currently the costliest place to live in the US. Yet California cities (especially San Francisco and San Diego) consistently top national quality-of-life indexes.

Homelessness is not part of the California dream, but it's a reality for at least 160,000 Californians. Also standing in line at homeless shelters are the working poor, unable to cover medical care and high rent on minimum-wage salaries. Some California cities have criminalized loitering, panhandling and even sitting on sidewalks.

Population & Multiculturalism

With 37 million residents, California is the most populous US state: one in every nine Americans lives here. It's also one of the fastest growing states, with three of America's 10 biggest cities (Los Angeles, San Diego and San Jose) and over 350,000 newcomers every year.

Its racial makeup continues to shift: Hispanic, Latino and Asian populations steadily increase while the Caucasian (non-Hispanic) population declines. At least one in four

Marriage: Equal Rights for All

Forty thousand Californians were already registered as domestic partners when, in 2004, San Francisco Mayor Gavin Newsom issued marriage licenses to same-sex couples in defiance of a California same-sex marriage ban. Four thousand same-sex couples promptly got hitched. The state ban was nixed by California courts in June 2008, but then a proposition passed in November 2008 to amend the state's constitution to prohibit same-sex marriage. Civil-rights activists are challenging the constitutionality of the proposition, but meanwhile California's reputation as a haven of GLBT (gay/lesbian/bisexual/transgender) tolerance is lagging behind a half-dozen other states that have already legalized same-sex marriage.

The Best...
Places to
Soak up the
Sun & Scene

1 Crissy Field (p104)

2 Runyon Canyon (p73)

3 Balboa Park (p291)

4 Tennessee Valley Trail (p139)

5 San Luis Obispo Farmers Market (p191)

California residents is foreign-born and 40% speak a language other than English (primarily Spanish) at home.

One of every four immigrants to the USA lands in California, with the largest segment coming from Mexico. Most legal immigrants to California are sponsored by family members who already live here. In addition, an estimated two million undocumented immigrants currently live in California.

Sports

California has more professional sports teams than any other state, and loyalties to local football (NFL), basketball (NBA) and major-league baseball (MLB) teams run deep. For proof that Californians do get excited about sports, go ahead and just try to find tickets for an Oakland Raiders or San Diego Chargers football, San Francisco Giants baseball, Los Angeles Lakers basketball or Los Angeles Kings hockey game before they sell out.

The regular season for major-league baseball runs from April to September, soccer from April to October, women's basketball (WNBA) from late May to mid-September, NFL from September to early January, ice hockey (NHL) from October to March and NBA from November to April.

The Arts

Atrium of the San Francisco Museum of Modern Art (p105)

SABRINA DALBESIO/LONELY PLANET IMAGES ©

California supports thriving music and arts scenes that aren't afraid to be completely independent, even outlandish at times. And thanks to the movie industry, perhaps no other city can claim the pop-cultural influence that Los Angeles exerts worldwide. Meanwhile, writers and musicians have been seeking inspiration in gritty LA and bohemian San Francisco for decades. Southern California in particular has proved to be fertile ground for new architectural styles.

Film & TV

California's major export – film – is a powerful presence in the lives of not only Americans but people around the world. Images of California are distributed far beyond its borders, ultimately reflecting back upon the state itself. With increasing regularity, Hollywood films feature California as both a setting and a topic and, in some cases, almost as a character.

Today, the high cost of filming in LA has sent location scouts beyond the San Fernando Valley (where most movie and TV studios are found) and north of the border to Canada, where they're welcomed with open arms in 'Hollywood North.' A few production companies are still based in the Bay Area, including Pixar Animation Studios, Francis Ford Coppola's American Zoetrope and George Lucas' Industrial Light & Magic, made up of high-tech gurus who produce computer-generated special effects for Hollywood blockbusters.

The first TV station began broadcasting in Los Angeles in 1931. Through the next decades, iconic images of LA were beamed into living rooms across the US in shows such as *Dragnet* (1950s); *The Beverly Hillbillies* (1960s); *The Brady Bunch* (1970s); *LA Law* (1980s); *Baywatch, Melrose Place* and *The Fresh Prince of Bel-Air* (1990s); and teen 'dramedies' (drama-comedies) *Beverly Hills, 90210* (1990s), which made that LA zip code into a status symbol, and *The OC* (2000s), set in Newport Beach, Orange County. If you're a fan of reality TV, you'll spot Southern California starring in everything from *Top Chef* to *The Real Housewives of Orange County* and MTV's *Laguna Beach* and *The Hills,* about rich, gorgeous twentysomethings cavorting in SoCal. Get a sneak peek of new TV shows by joining a live studio audience in LA.

Literature

Californians read more than movie scripts: they make up the largest market for books in the US, and they read more than the national average. Skewing the curve is bookish San Francisco, with more writers, playwrights and book purchases per capita than any other US city.

The West Coast has long drawn artists and writers, and today California's resident literary community is as strong as ever with such talent as Alice Walker, Pulitzer Prize–winning author of *The Color Purple* (1982); progressive feminist poet Adrienne Rich; Chilean American novelist Isabel Allende; Amy Tan, author of such popular fiction as *The Joy Luck Club* (1989); Maxine Hong Kingston, coeditor of the landmark anthology *The Literature of California* (2000); Dave Eggers, the hipster behind *McSweeney's* quarterly literary journal; and Michael Chabon, author of the Pulitzer Prize–winning *The Amazing Adventures of Kavalier and Clay* (2000).

Few writers nail California culture as well as Joan Didion. She's best known for her collection of essays, *Slouching Towards Bethlehem* (1968), which takes a caustic look at 1960s flower power and Haight-Ashbury. Tom Wolfe also put '60s San Francisco in perspective with *The Electric Kool-Aid Acid Test* (1968), which follows Ken Kesey's band of Merry Pranksters, who began their acid-laced 'magic bus' journey near Santa Cruz. Charles Bukowski's semiautobiographical novel *Post Office* (1971) captures LA's down-and-out Downtown. Richard Vasquez' *Chicano* (1971) takes a dramatic look at LA's Latino barrio.

California on Celluloid

Here are our top picks for classic California flicks:

○ *The Maltese Falcon* (1941) John Huston directs Humphrey Bogart as Sam Spade, the classic San Francisco private eye.

○ *Sunset Boulevard* (1950) Billy Wilder's classic stars Gloria Swanson and William Holden in a bonfire of Hollywood vanities.

○ *Vertigo* (1958) The Golden Gate Bridge dazzles and dizzies in Alfred Hitchcock's noir thriller starring Jimmy Stewart and Kim Novak.

○ *Chinatown* (1974) Roman Polanski's gripping version of the early-20th-century water wars that made and nearly broke LA.

○ *LA Story* (1991) Steve Martin lovingly wrote this hilarious, though dated, parody of nearly every aspect of LA life, from enemas to earthquakes.

Back in the 1930s, San Francisco and LA became the capitals of the pulp detective novel, which was often made into a classic noir film. Dashiell Hammett (*The Maltese Falcon*, 1930) made San Francisco's fog a sinister character. The king of hard-boiled crime writers was Raymond Chandler (*The Big Sleep*, 1939), who thinly disguised Santa Monica as shadowy Bay City. A renaissance of noir crime fiction has been masterminded by James Ellroy (*LA Confidential*, 1990) and Walter Mosley (*Devil in a Blue Dress*, 1990), whose Easy Rawlins detective novels are set in LA's South Central.

Music

From smoky jazz clubs that once filled San Francisco's North Beach to hard-edged West Coast rap and hip-hop born in South Central LA, California music has rocked the world. Much of the US recording industry is based in Los Angeles, and SoCal's film and TV industries have proven powerful talent incubators. But today's troubled pop princesses and airbrushed boy bands are only here thanks to the tuneful revolutions of the decades of innovation that came before, from country folk to urban rap.

In the 1960s, Jim Morrison and The Doors busted onto the Sunset Strip, and San Francisco launched the psychedelic-rock revolution with big-name acts such as the Grateful Dead and Janis Joplin. The late '70s and early '80s saw the birth of California's own brand of punk, including the LA-based bands X and Black Flag, and the Dead Kennedys in San Francisco. In the 1980s, the funk-punk sound of the Red Hot Chili Peppers exploded out of LA and avant-garde rocker Frank Zappa's 1982 single *Valley Girl* taught the rest of America to say 'Omigo-o-od!' like an LA teenager.

By the 1990s alternative rock acts like Beck and Weezer had gained national presence. Los Lobos was king of the Latino bands, an honor that has since passed to Ozomatli. Another key '90s band was the ska-punk-alt-rock No Doubt, of Orange County. Berkeley revived punk in the '90s with Grammy Award–winning Green Day. In the late 1990s, the Bay Area birthed underground artists like E-40 and the 'hyphy movement,' a reaction against the increasing commercialization of hip-hop. LA today is the hotbed for West Coast rap and hip-hop.

Architecture

California's architecture, a fruitful jumble of styles, is as diverse as the state's population. The late-18th and early-19th centuries saw the construction of Spanish colonial missions built with materials that were on hand: adobe, limestone and grass. And during the mid-19th-century Gold Rush, California's nouveau riche started constructing grand mansions. Victorian architecture, especially the showy Queen Anne style, is most prevalent in NorCal cities such as San Francisco.

Simplicity was the hallmark of the Arts and Crafts style, a reaction against the mass production of the industrial revolution. Modernism has characteristics such as boxlike building shapes, open floor plans, plain facades and abundant glass, and was adapted to residential houses that reflected SoCal's see-and-be-seen culture. More recently, postmodernism sought to reemphasize the structural form of the building and the

The Best... Big-City Art Museums

1 San Francisco Museum of Modern Art (SFMOMA; p105)

2 Getty Center, Los Angeles (p75)

3 Los Angeles County Museum of Art (LACMA; p72)

4 MH de Young Memorial Museum, San Francisco (p106)

space around it; examples in LA include Richard Meier's Getty Center and Frank Gehry's Walt Disney Concert Hall.

Visual Arts

With the invention of photography, the improbable truth of California's landscape and its inhabitants was revealed. San Francisco native Ansel Adams' sublime photographs documented the majesty of Yosemite, and Berkeley-based Dorothea Lange turned her unflinching lens on the plight of California migrant workers in the Great Depression and Japanese Americans forced to enter internment camps in WWII.

After WWII, pristine, poolside SoCal aesthetics competed with San Francisco's love of rough-and-readymade 1950s Beat collage, 1960s psychedelic Fillmore posters, earthy '70s funk and beautiful-mess punk, and '80s graffiti and skate culture.

Today, the California contemporary art scene brings all these influences together with muralist-led social commentary, cutting-edge technology and an obsessive dedication to craft. To see California art at its most exciting and experimental, don't miss the alternative gallery scene in Culver City and the converted warehouses of LA's Chinatown. In San Francisco, check out the indie art spaces in the Mission District and laboratory-like galleries and museums in South of market's (SoMa) Yerba Buena Arts District.

California Cuisine

Meatloaf sandwich

JERRY ALEXANDER/LONELY PLANET IMAGES ©

If you don't kiss the ground when you set foot in California, you might once you've tried the food. As you graze the Golden State from surfer-worthy fish tacos to foraged-ingredient tasting menus, you'll often have cause to compliment the chef – but they're quick to share the compliment with local producers. What's come to represent California cuisine need not be fancy. It's all about the ingredients.

If not for the hundreds of cultures and nationalities that have immigrated to California over the past 200 years, Californians might never eat. Fusion dominates menus these days, from kimchi tacos to vegan soul food. Like actors' credits in a film, you'll find that California menus often list by name the many cheesemakers, wineries, farms, ranches and fisheries that provide the stellar ingredients.

Regional Cuisine

Los Angeles

Most of California's produce is grown in the hot, irrigated Central Valley, south of the Bay Area, but road-tripping foodies tend to bolt through this sunny stretch lined with fast-food speed traps to reach Los Angeles in time for dinner. Authenticity-trippers know exactly

The Best... Farmers Markets

1 LA's Original Farmers Market (p81)

2 Oxbow Public Market, Napa (p215)

3 Ferry Plaza Farmers Market, San Francisco (p102)

4 Santa Monica (p81)

5 Hillcrest, San Diego (p303)

where to go, however: directly to Koreatown for tender *kalbi* (marinated barbecued beef short ribs) and strong *soju* (barley spirits), East LA for tacos *al pastor* (tacos with marinated fried pork) and margaritas on the rocks, and Little Tokyo for sashimi faceted like diamonds and palate-purifying *junmai* sake.

San Francisco

When San Francisco ballooned into a Gold Rush boom-town of 25,000 in 1850 there was only one woman per 100 men – but there were hundreds of eateries, ranging from ubiquitous Chinese noodle shops to struck-it-rich French fine dining. The first Italian restaurant in the USA opened in San Francisco's North Beach in 1886, serving the ever-popular cioppino (Dungeness crab stew).

Even 160 years after that boom went bust, there's still one restaurant for every 28 San Franciscans – that's 10 times more than any other North American city. All that competition keeps chefs innovating and prices lower than you'd find for equivalent dining experiences elsewhere. Chinese, Mexican, French and Italian restaurants remain perennial local favorites, along with more recent San Francisco crazes for sushi, tandoori and pho (Vietnamese noodles). San Francisco has more award-winning chefs per capita than any other US city (sorry, New York). Today the busiest SF tourist attraction is no longer the Golden Gate Bridge, but the local, sustainable, seasonal bounty at the San Francisco Ferry Plaza Farmers Market.

The Bay Area & Northern California

Just as influential (or more) as San Francisco, the Bay Area and Northern California have changed the way the world looks at food. California cuisine was perfected in Berkeley at Alice Waters' iconic Chez Panisse. World-renowned food writer and expert Michael Pollan is a journalism professor at nearby UC Berkeley.

Scratch any food trend's surface and you'll likely find it happening in the Bay Area and Northern California. Marin County, one of the wealthiest in the USA, can afford to make sustainable and organic food a priority.

Wine Country

George Yount (of Yountville fame) was the first Napa resident to plant a few grape vines in the 1830s, and before the arrival of the 20th century, there were already almost 150 wineries in the region. The climate and soil were a perfect mix for agriculture, and the natural hot springs around Calistoga brought tourists in from San Francisco. Even before Prohibition, the Wine Country was cemented as a destination for folks with a taste for the good life.

By the 1930s Sonoma was supplying some excellent jack cheese to accompany the local wine. But local chefs have kept the food scene evolving. Chef Thomas Keller transformed Yountville's saloon-turned-restaurant French Laundry into an international foodie landmark in 1994, showcasing local produce and casual elegance in multicourse feasts. Other chefs eager to make their names and fortunes among free-spending wine tasters flocked to the area. If you'd like to learn a thing or two about cooking, you can sign up for day or weekend courses, or a full-time chef training program at the Culinary Institute of America in St Helena.

Drinks

Powerful drink explains a lot about California. Mission vineyards planted in the 18th century gave Californians a taste for wine, which led settlers to declare an independent 'Bear Flag Republic' in the Mexican settlement of Sonoma one drunken night in 1846 (it lasted a month). The Gold Rush brought a rush on the bar: by 1850, San Francisco had 500 saloons shilling hooch. Today California's traditions of wine, beer and cocktails are converging in saloon revivals, wine-bar trends, and microbrewery booms – and for the morning after, specialty coffee roasters.

Wine

Up until the 1830s, mission communion wine was considered fine for Sundays and minor revolutions, but by this time, Californians were importing premium varietals. When imported French wine was slow to arrive via Australia during the Gold Rush, two Czech brothers named Korbel started making their own bubbly in 1882, and today their winery is the biggest US distributor of sparkling wines. Drinkers began switching to the local stuff from Sonoma and Napa Valleys, and by the end of the century, vintages from California Wine Country were quietly winning medals at Paris expositions. Some California vines survived federal scrutiny during Prohibition, on the grounds that the grapes were needed for sacramental wines back east – a bootlegging bonanza that kept West Coast speakeasies well supplied, and saved old vinestock from being torn out by authorities.

California had an established reputation for mass-market plonk and bottled wine spritzers by 1976, when upstart wineries in Napa Valley and the Santa Cruz Mountains suddenly gained international status. Stag's Leap Wine Cellars cabernet sauvignon, Chateau Montelena chardonnay, and Ridge Monte Bello cabernet sauvignon beat venerable French wines to take top honors at a landmark blind tasting by international critics now known as the Judgment of Paris. The tasting was repeated 30 years later, with Stag's Leap and Ridge again taking top honors (Montelena had sold out its original vintage).

Sonoma, Napa, the Santa Cruz area and Mendocino county continue to produce the state's most illustrious vintages. With an exceptional combination of coastal fog, sunny valleys, rocky hillsides and volcanic soils, the Napa and Sonoma Valleys together

Food Trucks

Weekday lunches may last only 30 minutes for Californians, and every minute counts. Californians torn between gourmet sit-down meals and enjoying sunshine outdoors no longer have to make a choice: food trucks deliver gourmet options to office hubs, from rotisserie chicken salads to clamshell buns packed with roast duck and fresh mango.

To find out when trucks are coming to a curb near you, search for 'food truck' and your location on **Twitter**. Come prepared with cash and sunblock: most trucks are cash only, and queues for popular trucks can take 10 to 20 minutes. Look for prominently displayed permits as your guarantee of proper food preparation, refrigeration and regulated working conditions.

The Best... California Brews

1 Anderson Valley Brewery (Mendocino) Boont Amber Ale

2 Uncommon Brewers (Santa Cruz) Baltic Porter

3 Anchor Steam (San Francisco) Christmas Ale

4 Bear Republic (Healdsburg) Racer 5 IPA

5 Sierra Nevada (Chico) Pale Ale

mimic wine-growing regions across France and Italy. Precious bottom-land sells for up to $20,000 an acre in skinny, 30-mile-long Napa, where many wineries understandably stick to established, marketable chardonnay and cabernet sauvignon. Neighboring Sonoma and Mendocino have complex microclimates, with morning fog cover to protect the thin-skinned, prized pinot noir grape.

But California's risk-taking attitude prevails even on prestigious Napa, Sonoma and Mendocino turf, with unconventional red blends and freak-factor pinots with 'forest floor' flavors claiming top honors in the industry.

Today, sustainable winemaking processes have become widespread across California, establishing the Lodi Rules for green winemaking (see www.lodi wine.com) and pursuing Demeter certification for biodynamic wines (http://demeter-usa.org). California's renegade winemakers are now experimenting with natural-process winemaking methods such as wild-yeast fermentation, bringing the thrill of the unexpected to tasting rooms across the state. While you're visiting, you may notice owl boxes for pest management, sheep for weed control, and solar panels atop LEED-certified winery buildings – all increasingly standard features of California's environmentally savvy wineries.

Beer

Drinking snobbery is often reversed in California: wine drinkers are always game for a glass of something local and tasty, while beer drinkers fuss over their monk-brewed triple Belgians and debate relative hoppiness levels. California beer-drinkers are spoiled for choice: according to the Brewers' Association, California has twice as many breweries as any other state. You won't get attitude for ordering beer with fancy food here – many California sommeliers are happy to suggest beer pairings with your meal, and some spiffy NorCal saloons offer tasting plates specifically to accompany beer.

For quality small-batch brews you won't find elsewhere, seek out microbreweries – any self-respecting Californian city has at least one craft brewery or brewpub of note. But for instant relief on scorching summer days, craft beers are widely available at California corner stores in bottles and cans, in six-packs and singles. California's craft breweries are increasingly canning craft beer to make their beer cheaper, greener, and more widely distributed across California, while preserving the classic satisfaction of popping the tab on a cold one on a hot California beach day.

Spirits

Tonight you're gonna party like it's 1899. Before picking up their shakers at night, local bartenders have spent days dusting off 19th-century recipes. The highest honorific for a California bartender these days isn't mixologist (too technical) or artisan (too medieval), but 'drink historian.' Gone are the mad-scientist's mixology beakers of two years ago: California bartenders are now judged by their absinthe fountains and displays of swizzle sticks from long-defunct ocean liners. Just don't be surprised if your anachronistic cocktail comes served in a cordial glass, punch bowl or Mason jar, instead of a tumbler, highball or martini glass. All that authenticity-tripping over happy

hour may sound self-conscious, but after strong pours at California's vintage saloons and revived speakeasies, consciousness is hardly an issue.

Coffee

When California couples break up, the thorniest issue is: who gets to keep the cafe? Californians are fiercely loyal to specific roasts and baristas, and most first internet dates meet on neutral coffee grounds. Berkeley's Peet's Coffee kicked off this specialty coffee craze for espresso drinks made with single-origin beans in 1966, and in the 1971 supplied beans to an offshoot known as Starbucks. Santa Cruz was another early adopter of specialty coffee roasting and drinking in 1978 – like Berkeley, it's a college town – and Santa Cruz Coffee became one of the first US roasters and cafes to offer certified fair trade coffee beans.

Braised fillet of Arctic black cod
PHOTOGRAPHER: BRENT WINEBRENNER/LONELY PLANET IMAGES ©

Beaches & Outdoor Activities

Waxing surfboards, La Jolla (p297)

ANTHONY PIDGEON/LONELY PLANET IMAG

Californians know they're spoiled silly with spectacular natural riches, so they express their gratitude by taking every chance to hit the trails, hop onto the saddle or grab a paddle. Now it's your turn: go kayaking under sea arches and along rocky coastlines, spot a whale breaching off the bow of your boat or make your California dreamin' come true with a surfing lesson.

Swimming

If lazing on the beach and taking quick dips in the Pacific is what you've got in mind, look to Southern California (SoCal). With miles and miles of wide, sandy beaches, you won't find it hard to get wet and wild, especially between Santa Barbara and San Diego. Once you get far enough south, let's say Santa Barbara, the beaches become golden and sandy, and the weather and the waters turn balmy. By the time you hit Los Angeles, Orange County (aka 'the OC') and San Diego, you'll find SoCal beach culture in full swing – at least during summer. SoCal beaches can be chilly and too stormy for swimming in winter. Ocean temperatures become tolerable by May or June, peaking in July and August.

Northern California waters are unbearably cold year-round, with a dangerously high swell in places and rocky beaches that often make swimming uninviting. Diehards should bring or rent a wetsuit!

The biggest hazards along the coast are riptides and dangerous ocean currents. Popular beaches have lifeguards, but can still be dangerous places to swim. Obey all posted warning signs and ask about local conditions before venturing out. If you get caught in a riptide, which pulls you away from shore, don't fight it or you'll get exhausted and drown. Instead, swim parallel to the shoreline and, once the current stops pulling you out, swim back to shore.

Surfing

Surf's up! Are you down? Even if you never set foot on a board – and we, like, totally recommend that you do, dude – there's no denying the influence of surfing on every aspect of Californian beach life. Invented by Pacific Islanders, surfing first washed ashore in 1907, when business tycoon Henry Huntington invited Irish Hawaiian surfer George Freeth to LA to help promote real-estate developments – California has never been the same since.

The state has plenty of easily accessible world-class surf spots, with the lion's share in SoCal. You won't find many killer spots north of the San Francisco Bay Area, but if your travels take you up there, check out www .northerncaliforniasurfing.com. Famous surf spots southbound include Mavericks, past Half Moon Bay; Steamers Lane in Santa Cruz; Rincon Point, outside Santa Barbara; Surfrider in Malibu; and Trestles, south of San Clemente in the OC. All are point breaks, known for their consistently clean, glassy, big waves.

Generally speaking, the most powerful swells arrive in winter (especially at Mavericks, world-famous for its big-wave surfing competition), while early summer sees the flattest conditions (except at Trestles, which still goes off then) but also warmer waters. Bring or rent a wet suit.

Scuba Diving & Snorkeling

All along the coast, rocky reefs, shipwrecks and kelp forests teem with sea creatures ready for their close-up. Santa Catalina Island and Channel Islands National Park are hot spots for diving and snorkeling. Thanks to the Monterey Bay National Marine Sanctuary, Monterey Bay offers year-round, world-renowned diving and snorkeling, though you'll need to don a wet suit. Nearby Point Lobos State Reserve is another diving gem. North of San Francisco, dive boats depart from windy Bodega Bay.

Move Your Bod

If you don't have the time or inclination to master the art of surfing, there are other ways to catch your 'dream wave' at many SoCal beaches. Bodysurfing and body boarding (or boogie boarding) can extend your ride on the waves, sometimes as much as 100ft (30.5m) or more. Both sports benefit from the use of flippers to increase speed and control. If you're not sure how to do it, watch others or strike up a watery kinship and simply ask for pointers. But it's really pretty easy, and you'll be howling with glee once you catch that first wave.

Windsurfing & Kitesurfing

Experienced windsurfers tear up the waves up and down the coast, while newbies (or those who want a mellower ride) skim along calm bays and protected beaches. There's almost always a breeze, with the best winds springing up from April through October, but the water is cold year-round and, unless you're a polar bear, a wet suit is a necessity. Any place that has good windsurfing has good kitesurfing. Look for surfers doing aerial acrobatics while parachute-like kites propel them over the waves.

Kayaking

Few water sports are as accessible or as much fun for the whole family as kayaking. Prior experience is rarely necessary. Lots of rental outfitters can be found along the Central Coast, for example in Morro Bay, whose waters are protected by a gorgeous 4-mile sand spit, and from Monterey north to Santa Cruz, especially around Elkhorn Slough. Sausalito in Marin County is a mere paddle's-length away from San Francisco's skyline, while sheltered Tomales Bay at Point Reyes National Seashore and Bodega Bay are also popular spots.

As you head further up the chilly north coast, various small towns offer challenging put-in points for experienced sea kayakers. On the Redwood Coast, you can take a scenic spin around Humboldt Bay, Trinidad Cove or Humboldt Lagoons State Park, with outfitters in Eureka and Arcata. Meanwhile, SoCal's warmer waters beckon sea kayakers to Santa Catalina Island and Channel Islands National Park offshore, and San Diego's Mission Bay and La Jolla.

Whale-Watching

During summer, majestic gray whales feed in the Arctic waters between Alaska and Siberia, and every October they start moving south down the Pacific Coast to the sheltered lagoons of the Gulf of California in Mexico's Baja California. While there, pregnant whales give birth to calves weighing up to 1500lb (680kg; which go on to live up to 60 years, grow to 50ft in length and weigh up to 40 tons). Around mid-March, these whales turn around and head back to the Arctic. Luckily for us, during their 12,000-mile round-trip, these whales pass just off the California coast.

Mothers tend to keep newborn calves closer to shore for safety, so your best chances of catching a glimpse may be during the whales' northbound migration. You can try your luck from shore (free, but you're less likely to see anything and are more removed from the action) or by taking a boat cruise. A few of the best dockside spots from which to point your binoculars include Point Reyes Lighthouse, Bodega Head on the North Coast, and Cabrillo National Monument at San Diego's Point Loma.

Hiking

California is perfect for exploring on foot, whether you've got your heart set on peak-bagging in the Sierra Nevada, trekking to desert palm-tree oases, rambling among the world's tallest, largest or most ancient trees, or simply heading for a coastal walk accompanied by booming surf. The best trails are generally found among the jaw-dropping scenery in national and state parks, national forests and wilderness areas. You can choose from an infinite variety of routes, from easy, interpretive nature walks negotiable by wheelchairs and baby strollers to multiday backpacking routes through rugged wilderness. Parks and forests almost always have a visitors center or ranger station with clued-in staff to offer route suggestions, trail-specific tips and weather forecasts. The most popular trails may be subject to daily quotas and require wilderness permits.

Camping

All across California, campers are absolutely spoiled for choice. You can pitch a tent beside alpine lakes and streams with views of snaggle-toothed Sierra Nevada peaks, along gorgeous strands of Southern California sand or on the wilder, windswept beaches of the north coast. Take shelter underneath redwoods, the tallest trees on earth, from south of San Francisco north to the Oregon border. Inland, deserts are magical places to camp, especially next to sand dunes on full-moon nights. If you don't have your own tent, you can rent or buy camping gear in most cities and some towns.

Rock Climbing

Rock hounds can test their mettle on world-class climbs on the big walls and granite domes of Yosemite National Park, where the climbing season runs from April through October. In the warmest summer months, climbers move camp from the Yosemite Valley to Tuolumne Meadows, off Tioga Rd, which also has good bouldering. In SoCal, Joshua Tree National Park is another climbing mecca, with over 8000 established routes ranging from boulders and cracks to multipitch faces; the climbing season runs year-round, but beware of blistering summer heat. Both of these national parks are excellent places to try the sport for the first time, and outdoor outfitters offer guided climbs and instruction. Other prime spots for bouldering and rock climbing include Bishop in the Eastern Sierra and Sequoia and Kings Canyon National Parks, south of Yosemite.

Cycling & Mountain Biking

Top up those tires and strap on that helmet! California is outstanding cycling territory, whether you're off for a leisurely spin by the beach, an adrenaline-fueled mountain ride or a multiday cycling tour along the Pacific Coast Hwy.

With few exceptions, mountain biking is not allowed in wilderness areas or on trails in national or state parks, but you can usually cycle on paved or dirt roads that are open to vehicles. Mountain bikers are allowed on single-track trails in national forests and Bureau of Land Management (BLM) land, but must yield to hikers and stock animals.

Snow Sports

High-speed modern ski lifts, mountains of fresh powder, a cornucopia of trails from easy-peasy 'Sesame Street' to black-diamond 'Death Wish,' skyscraping alpine scenery, luxury mountain cabins – they're all hallmarks of a vacation in the snow in California. The Sierra Nevada offers the best slopes and trails for skiers and snowboarders, not to mention the most reliable conditions.

Over a dozen downhill skiing and snowboarding resorts ring Lake Tahoe, and the season at Mammoth Mountain usually lasts through June. For family-friendly sno-parks that offer sledding and snow play, visit http://ohv.parks.ca.gov/?page_id=1233 online.

**The Best...
Places to
Swim**

1 San Diego: La Jolla, Coronado

2 Orange County: Newport Beach, Laguna Beach

3 Los Angeles: Santa Monica, South Bay

4 Central Coast: Ventura, Carpinteria, Santa Barbara

White-Water Rafting

California has scads of mind-blowing rivers, and feeling their surging power is like taking a thrilling ride on nature's roller coaster. Sure, there are serene floats suitable for picnics with grandma and the kiddies, but then there are others. White-water giants swelled by the snowmelt rip through sheer canyons, and roaring cataracts hurtle you through chutes where gushing water compresses through a 10ft gap between menacing boulders. Pour-overs, voracious hydraulics, endless Class III-IV standing waves wrench at your shoulders as you scream and punch on through to the next onslaught. Paddling these giant white-water rapids, your thoughts are reduced to just two simple words: 'survive' and 'damn!' Too much for you? Between the two extremes run myriad others suited to the abilities of any wannabe river rat.

White-water rafting, Kern River
PHOTOGRAPHER: WITOLD SKRYPCZAK/LONELY PLANET IMAGES ©

Land & Wildlife

DOUGLAS STEAKLEY/LONELY PLANET IMAGES ©

From soaring snowcapped peaks, to scorching deserts and dense forests, California is home to a bewildering variety of ecosystems and animals. The state not only has the highest biodiversity in North America, it has more types of climate and more types of soils than nearly any location in the world. California has a Mediterranean climate, characterized by dry summers and mild wet winters.

The Land

The third-largest US state after Alaska and Texas, California covers more than 160,000 sq miles and is larger than the UK. It is bordered to the north by Oregon, to the south by Mexico, with Nevada and Arizona on its eastern border, and 840 miles of glorious Pacific shoreline on the west. Its cool northern border stands at the same latitude as Rome, Italy, while the arid southern border is at the same latitude as Tel Aviv, Israel.

Geology & Earthquakes

California has a complex geologic landscape formed from fragments of rock and earth crust scraped together as the North American continent drifted westward over hundreds of millions of years. Crumpled coast ranges, the downward-bowing Central Valley and the still-rising Sierra Nevada all provide evidence of gigantic forces exerted as the continental and ocean plates crushed together.

Everything changed about 25 million years ago, when the ocean plates stopped colliding and instead started sliding against each other, creating the massive San Andreas Fault. Because this contact zone doesn't slide smoothly, but catches and slips irregularly, it rattles California with an ongoing succession of tremors and earthquakes.

The state's most famous earthquake in 1906 measured 7.8 on the Richter scale and demolished San Francisco, leaving more than 3000 people dead. The Bay Area made headlines again in 1989 when the Loma Prieta earthquake (7.1) caused a section of the Bay Bridge to collapse. Los Angeles' last 'big one' was in 1994, when the Northridge quake (6.7) caused parts of the Santa Monica Fwy to fall down, making it the most costly quake in US history – so far.

Mountains & Valleys

Much of the California coast is fronted by rugged, little-explored coastal mountains that capture winter's water-laden storms. San Francisco divides the coastal ranges roughly in half: the foggy north coast remains sparsely populated, while the central and south coasts have a balmy climate, sandy beaches and lots of people.

On their eastern flanks, the coastal ranges subside into gently rolling hills that give way to the sprawling Central Valley. Further east looms California's most prominent topographic feature, the world-famous Sierra Nevada. At 400 miles long and 50 miles wide, it's one of the largest mountain ranges in the world and a vast wilderness areas with 13 peaks over 14,000ft (4267m).

Deserts

All lands east of the Sierra Nevada crest are dry and desertlike, receiving less than 10in of rain a year. Areas in the northern half of the state, especially on the elevated Modoc Plateau of northeastern California, are a cold desert blanketed with hardy sagebrush shrubs and pockets of juniper trees. Temperatures increase to the south, with a prominent transition occurring when you descend from Mammoth into Bishop and Owens Valley. This hot desert (the Mojave Desert) includes Death Valley, one of the hottest places on earth.

Southern California is a hodgepodge of small mountain ranges and desert basins. Mountains on the eastern border of the Los Angeles Basin continue southward past San Diego and down the spine of northern Baja California, while the Mojave Desert of the southern Sierra Nevada morphs into the Colorado Desert around the Salton Sea. This entire region is dry and rocky, and mostly devoid of vegetation except for pockets of desert-adapted shrubs, cacti and Joshua trees.

National & State Parks

The majority of Californians rank outdoor recreation as vital to their quality of life, and the amount of preserved lands has steadily grown due to important pieces of legislation passed since the 1960s, including the landmark 1976 California Coastal Act, which saved the coastline from further development. Today, California State Parks protect nearly one-third of the state's coastline, along with redwood forests, mountain lakes, desert canyons, waterfalls, wildlife preserves and historical sites.

In recent years, both federal and state budget shortfalls and chronic underfunding have been partly responsible for widespread park closures, more limited visitor services and steadily rising park-entry and outdoor recreation fees. And unfortunately, some of California's parks are also being loved to death. Overcrowding severely impacts the environment, and it's increasingly difficult to balance public access with conservation. Try to visit big-name parks such as Yosemite in the shoulder seasons (ie not summer) to avoid the biggest crowds. Alternatively, lesser-known parks, especially in the northern mountains and southern California deserts, may go relatively untouched most of the year.

Wildlife

Much of California is a biological island cut off from the rest of North America by the soaring heights of the Sierra Nevada and, as on other 'islands' in the world, evolution creates unique plants and animals under these conditions. As a result, California ranks first in the nation for its number of endemic plants, amphibians, reptiles, freshwater fish and mammals. Even more impressive, 30% of all the plant species found in the US, 50% of all the bird species and 50% of all the mammal species exist in California.

Animals

Many types of birds, including ducks and geese, either pass through California or linger through the winter, making the state one of the top destinations in North America for bird-watchers. Year-round, the best places to see birds are the state's beaches, estuaries and bays, where herons, cormorants, shorebirds and gulls gather.

The black bear is one of the most magnificent animal species found in California. This burly omnivore feeds on berries, nuts, roots, grasses, insects, eggs, small mammals and fish, but can become a nuisance around camping grounds and mountain cabins where food is not properly stored.

Mountain lions hunt throughout the mountains and forests of California, especially in areas teeming with deer. Solitary lions, which can grow 8ft in length and weigh 175lb, are formidable predators. The few attacks on humans occur mostly where encroachment has pushed hungry lions to their limits – for example, at the boundaries between wilderness and rapidly developing suburbs.

The coast of California is blessed with a fantastic assortment of marine mammals, including one of the few whale migration routes in the world that can be easily viewed from land or near-shore boats (see p380). It also offers many chances to see sleek seals, bulky sea lions and mammoth 3000lb elephant seals.

Plants

When it comes to plants, California is a land of superlatives: the tallest (coastal redwoods approaching 380ft), the largest (giant sequoias of the Sierra Nevada 38ft across at the base), the oldest (bristlecone pines of the White Mountains that are almost 5000 years old) and the smallest (a pond-dwelling plant that measures a fraction of a tenth of an inch). The giant sequoia, which is unique to California, survives in isolated groves scattered on the Sierra Nevada's western slopes, including in Yosemite, Sequoia and Kings Canyon National Parks.

Water is an overriding issue for many of California's plants because there is almost no rain during the prime growing season. Desert areas begin their peak blooming in March, with other lowland areas of the state producing abundant wildflowers in April.

Environmental Issues

California has the largest human population of any US state and one of the highest projected growth rates in the nation, putting a tremendous strain on California's many precious resources. Although California is in many ways a success story, development and growth have come at great environmental cost.

The Best...
Impressive Peaks

1 Mt Whitney (14,505ft)

2 Mt Shasta (14,162ft)

3 Telescope Peak, Death Valley (11,049ft)

4 Mammoth Mountain, Mammoth Lakes (11,053ft)

5 Half Dome, Yosemite National Park (8842ft)

Elephant Seals

Northern elephant seals follow a precise calendar. In November and December, adult male 'bull seals' return to their colony's favorite Californian beaches and start the ritual struggles to assert superiority; only the largest, strongest and most aggressive 'alpha' males gather a harem. In January and February, adult females, already pregnant from last year's beach antics, give birth to their pups and soon mate with the dominant males, who promptly depart on their next feeding migration.

Female seals leave the beach in March, abandoning their offspring. For up to two months the young seals, now known as 'weaners,' lounge around in groups, gradually learning to swim, first in tidal pools, then in the sea. Then they, too, depart by May.

Between June and October, elephant seals of all ages and both sexes return in smaller numbers to the beaches to molt.

Water, or the lack thereof, has always been at the heart of California's epic environmental struggles and catastrophes. Despite campaigning by California's greatest environmental champion, John Muir, in the 1920s the Tuolumne River was dammed at Hetch Hetchy (inside Yosemite National Park) so that San Francisco could have drinking water. Likewise, the diversion of water to the Los Angeles area has contributed to the destruction of Owens Lake and its fertile wetlands, and the degradation of Mono Lake.

Although air quality in California has improved markedly over the past two decades, auto exhaust and industrial emissions continue to produce smog, making sunny days in Los Angeles and the Central Valley look hazy.

Survival Guide

DIRECTORY	388
Accommodations	388
Business Hours	389
Climate	389
Customs	390
Discount Cards	390
Electricity	391
Food	391
Gay & Lesbian Travelers	391

Health	392
Insurance	392
Internet Access	392
Legal Matters	393
Money	393
Public Holidays	394
Safe Travel	395
Telephone	396
Time	396

Tourist Information	396
Travelers with Disabilities	397
Visas	397

TRANSPORT	398
Getting There & Away	398
Getting Around	399

Swimming pool, Hearst Castle (p190)
PHOTOGRAPHER: DOUGLAS STEAKLEY/LONELY PLANET IMAGES ©

A-Z

Directory

●●●

Accommodations

- Budget-conscious accommodations include campgrounds, hostels and motels. Because midrange properties generally offer better value for money, most of our accommodations fall into this category.

- At midrange motels and hotels, expect clean, comfortable and decent-sized double rooms with at least a private bathroom, and standard amenities such as cable TV, direct-dial telephone, a coffeemaker, and perhaps a microwave and mini fridge.

- Top-end lodgings offer top-notch amenities and perhaps a scenic location, edgy decor or historical ambience. Pools, fitness rooms, business centers, full-service restaurants and bars as well as other convenient facilities are all standard.

- Where an indoor or outdoor pool is available, the swimming icon 🏊 appears with the review.

- In Southern California, nearly all lodgings have air-conditioning, but in Northern California and in coastal areas as far south as Santa Barbara, where it rarely gets hot, the opposite is true, and even fans may not be provided. Where air-con is available, the ❄ icon appears.

- Accommodations offering online computer terminals for guests are designated with the internet icon (@). A fee may apply (eg at full-service business centers inside hotels).

- When wireless internet access is offered, the wi-fi icon (📶) appears. There may be a fee, especially for in-room access. Look for free wi-fi hot spots in hotel public areas (eg lobby, poolside).

- Many lodgings are now exclusively nonsmoking. Where they still exist, smoking rooms are often left unrenovated and in less desirable locations. Expect a hefty 'cleaning fee' ($100 or more) if you light up in designated nonsmoking rooms.

RATES

- This guide lists accommodations in order of author recommendation. Rates are categorized as $ (under $100), $$ ($100 to $200) or $$$ (over $200). Unless noted, rates do not include taxes, which average more than 10%.

- Generally, midweek rates are lower except in hotels geared toward weekday business travelers, which then lure leisure travelers with weekend deals.

- Rates quoted in this book are for high season: June to August everywhere, except the deserts and mountain ski areas, where December through April are the busiest months.

- Demand and prices spike even higher around major holidays (see p394) and for festivals (see p42), when some properties may impose multiday minimum stays.

- Discount cards (p390) and auto-club membership may get you 10% or more off standard rates at participating hotels and motels.

- You might get a better deal by booking through discount-travel websites like **Priceline** (www.priceline.com), **Hotwire** (www.hotwire.com) or **Hotels .com** (www.hotels.com).

- Bargaining may be possible for walk-in guests without reservations, especially during off-peak times.

RESERVATIONS

- Reservations are recommended for weekend and holiday travel year-round, and every day of the week during high season.

- If you book a reservation by phone, always get a

Book Your Stay Online

For more accommodations reviews by Lonely Planet authors, check out hotels.lonelyplanet. com/California. You'll find independent reviews, as well as recommendations on the best places to stay. Best of all, you can book online.

confirmation number and ask about the cancellation policy before you give out your credit-card information.

○ If you plan to arrive late in the evening, call ahead on the day of your stay to let them know. Hotels overbook, but if you've guaranteed the reservation with your credit card, they should accommodate you somewhere else.

B&BS

If you want an atmospheric or perhaps romantic alternative to impersonal motels and hotels, bed-and-breakfast inns typically inhabit fine old Victorian houses or other heritage buildings, bedecked with floral wallpaper and antique furnishings. However, people who like privacy may find California B&Bs too intimate.

Rates often include a home-cooked breakfast, but occasionally breakfast is *not* included (never mind what the name 'B&B' suggests). Amenities vary widely, but rooms with TV and telephone are the exception; the cheapest units share bathrooms. Standards are high at places certified by the **California Association of Bed & Breakfast Inns** (www.cabbi.com).

Most B&Bs require advance reservations, although some will accommodate the occasional drop-in guest. Smoking is generally prohibited and children are usually not welcome. Minimum-stay requirements are common, especially on weekends and in peak season.

HOTELS & MOTELS

Rooms are often priced by the size and number of beds,

rather than the number of occupants. A room with one double or queen-size bed usually costs the same for one or two people, while a room with a king-size bed or two double beds costs more.

There is often a surcharge for the third and fourth person, but children under a certain age (this varies) may stay free. Cribs or rollaway cots usually incur a surcharge.

If you arrive without reservations, ask to see a room before paying for it, especially at motels.

Overnight rates may include breakfast, which could be just a stale donut and wimpy coffee, an all-you-can-eat hot and cold buffet, or anything in between.

Business Hours

Unless noted, standard opening hours for listings in this guide are as follows.

Banks 8:30am to 4:30pm Monday to Friday, some to 5:30pm Friday, 9am to 12:30pm Saturday

Bars 5pm to midnight daily

Business hours (general) 9am to 5pm Monday to Friday

Nightclubs 10pm to 2am Thursday to Saturday

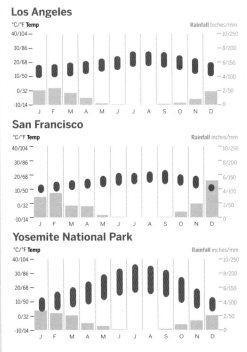

Climate

Los Angeles
°C/°F **Temp**
40/104 —
30/86 —
20/68 —
10/50 —
0/32 —
-10/14 —
J F M A M J J A S O N D
Rainfall Inches/mm
— 10/250
— 8/200
— 6/150
— 4/100
— 2/50
— 0

San Francisco
°C/°F **Temp**
40/104 —
30/86 —
20/68 —
10/50 —
0/32 —
-10/14 —
J F M A M J J A S O N D
Rainfall Inches/mm
— 10/250
— 8/200
— 6/150
— 4/100
— 2/50
— 0

Yosemite National Park
°C/°F **Temp**
40/104 —
30/86 —
20/68 —
10/50 —
0/32 —
-10/14 —
J F M A M J J A S O N D
Rainfall Inches/mm
— 10/250
— 8/200
— 6/150
— 4/100
— 2/50
— 0

Practicalities

o **DVDs** NTSC standard (incompatible with PAL or SECAM); DVDs coded region 1 (USA and Canada only)

o **Newspapers** *Los Angeles Times* (www.latimes.com), *San Francisco Chronicle* (www.sfgate.com), *San Jose Mercury News* (www.mercurynews.com), *Sacramento Bee* (www.sacbee.com)

o **Radio** National Public Radio (NPR), lower end of FM dial

o **TV** PBS (public broadcasting); cable: CNN (news), ESPN (sports), HBO (movies), Weather Channel

o **Weights & Measures** Imperial

Post offices 9am to 5pm Monday to Friday, some 9am to noon Saturday

Restaurants 7am to 10:30am, 11:30am to 2:30pm & 5pm to 9:30pm daily, some later Friday and Saturday

Shops 10am to 6pm Monday to Saturday, noon to 5pm Sunday (malls open later)

Customs

Currently, non-US citizens and permanent residents may import the following:
o 1L of alcohol (if over 21)

o 200 cigarettes (one carton) or 50 (non-Cuban) cigars (if you're over 18)

o $100 worth of gifts

Amounts higher than $10,000 in cash, traveler's checks, money orders and other cash equivalents must be declared. Don't even think about bringing in illegal drugs.

For information, check with **US Customs & Border Protection** (www.cbp.gov).

Discount Cards

For discounts for children and families, see p362.

American Association of Retired Persons (AARP; ☎ 888-687-2277; www.aarp.org; annual membership $16) Advocacy group for Americans 50 years and older offers member discounts (usually 10%) on hotels, car rentals and more.

American Automobile Association (AAA; ☎ 877-428-2277; www.aaa.com; annual membership from $48) Members of AAA and its foreign affiliates (eg CAA, AA) qualify for small discounts (usually 10%) on Amtrak trains, car rentals, motels and hotels, chain restaurants, shopping, tours and theme parks.

America the Beautiful Interagency Annual Pass (http://store.usgs.gov/pass; $80) Admits four adults and all children under 16 years old for free to all national parks and federal recreational lands (eg USFS, BLM) for one year. It can be purchased online or at any national park entrance station. US citizens and permanent residents 62 years and older are eligible for a lifetime Senior Pass ($10) that grants free entry and 50% off some recreational-use fees like camping, as does the lifetime Access Pass (free to US citizens or permanent residents with a permanent disability); these passes are only available in person.

Go Los Angeles Card (1-day pass adult/child $60/50) and **Go San Diego Card** ($70/59) both include admission to major SoCal theme parks (but not Disneyland), while the **Go San Francisco Card** ($55/40) covers museums, bicycle rental and a bay cruise. Note that you've got to do *a lot* of sightseeing over multiple days to make these passes even come close to paying off. For the best prices, buy online in advance at www.smartdestinations.com.

International Student Identity Card (ISIC; www.isic.org; $22) Offers savings on airline fares, travel insurance and local attractions for full-time students. For nonstudents under 26 years of age, an **International Youth Travel Card** (IYTC; $22) grants similar benefits. Cards are issued by student unions, hostelling organizations and travel agencies.

Seniors People over the age of 65 (sometimes 55, 60 or 62) often qualify for the same discounts as students; any ID showing your birth date should suffice as proof of age.

Southern California CityPass

(www.citypass.com) If you're visiting SoCal theme parks, the CityPass costs from $276 per adult (child aged three to nine $229). It covers three-day admission to Disneyland and Disney California Adventure and one-day admission each to Universal Studios and SeaWorld, with another day at either the San Diego Zoo or Safari Park. Passes are valid for 14 days from the day of the first use. Purchase in person at participating attractions or online in advance for the lowest prices.

Student Advantage Card

(☏ 877-256-4672; www.studentadvantage.com; $23) For international and US students, offers 15% savings on Amtrak and 20% on Greyhound, plus discounts of 10% to 20% on some airlines and chain shops, hotels and motels.

Electricity

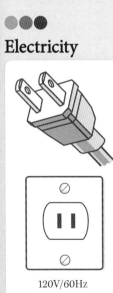

120V/60Hz

Food

In this book, restaurant prices usually refer to an average main course at dinner:

Budget ($) Dinner mains under $10

Midrange ($$) Most dinner mains $10 to $20

Top End ($$$) Dinner mains over $20

These prices don't include drinks, appetizers, desserts, taxes or tip. Note the same dishes at lunch will usually be cheaper, maybe even half-price.

Lunch is generally served between 11:30am and 2:30pm, and dinner between 5:30pm and 9pm daily, though some restaurants close later, especially on Friday and Saturday nights. If breakfast is served, it's usually between 7am and 10:30am; some diners and coffee shops keep serving breakfast into the afternoon, or all day. Weekend brunch is a laid-back affair, usually available from 10am until 3pm on Saturdays and Sundays. Full opening hours are given with all restaurant reviews in this book.

Like all things Californian, restaurant etiquette tends to be informal. Only a handful of restaurants require more than a dressy shirt, slacks and a decent pair of shoes; most places require far less. Here are more things to keep in mind:

○ Tipping 15% to 20% is expected anywhere you receive table service.

○ Smoking is illegal indoors; some restaurants have patios or sidewalk tables where lighting up is tolerated, though don't expect your neighbors to be happy about secondhand smoke.

○ You can bring your own wine to most restaurants, but expect to pay a 'corkage' fee of $15 to $30. Lunches rarely include booze, though a glass of wine or beer, while uncommon, is usually acceptable.

○ Vegetarians and travelers with food allergies or restrictions are in luck – most restaurants are used to catering to specific dietary needs.

Gay & Lesbian Travelers

California is a magnet for LGBTQ travelers. The hot spots are the Castro in San Francisco, West Hollywood (WeHo), Silver Lake and Long Beach in LA, the Hillcrest area of San Diego, the desert resort of Palm Springs, and Guerneville and Calistoga in the Wine Country. Some scenes are predominantly male-oriented, but women usually won't feel too left out.

California offers gays and lesbians extensive domestic rights but currently stops short of the legalization of same-sex marriage and civil unions. Despite widespread tolerance, make no mistake: homophobic bigotry still exists. In small towns, especially away from the coast, tolerance often comes down to a 'don't ask, don't tell' policy.

HELPFUL RESOURCES

Advocate (www.advocate.com/travel) Online news

articles, gay travel features and destination guides.

Damron (www.damron.com) Classic, advertiser-driven international gay travel guides, including *Men's Travel Guide, Women's Traveller* and *Accommodations;* digital editions and 'Gay Scout' mobile app now available.

Gay.com Daily Travel (www.daily.gay.net/travel) City guides, blog-style travel news and special events.

Gay Travelocity (www.travelocity.com/gaytravel) LGBT travel articles with hotel, guided tour and activity bookings.

Out Traveler (www.outtraveler.com) Free online magazine, trip planner, destination guides and a mobile app.

Purple Roofs (www.purpleroofs.com) Online directory of LGBT accommodations.

Health

HEALTHCARE & INSURANCE

◦ Medical treatment in the USA is of the highest caliber, but the expense could kill you. Many health-care professionals demand payment at the time of service, especially from out-of-towners or international visitors.

◦ Except for medical emergencies (in which case call ☏ 911 or go to the nearest 24-hour hospital emergency room, or ER), phone around to find a doctor who will accept your insurance.

◦ Some health-insurance policies require you to get pre-authorization for medical treatment before seeking help.

◦ Overseas visitors with travel health-insurance policies may need to contact a call center for an assessment by phone before getting medical treatment.

◦ Carry any medications you may need in their original containers, clearly labeled. Bring a signed, dated letter from your doctor describing all medical conditions and medications (including generic names).

Insurance

See p400 for information about car insurance.

TRAVEL INSURANCE

Getting travel insurance to cover theft, loss and medical problems is highly recommended. Some policies do not cover 'risky' activities such as scuba diving, motorcycling and skiing so read the fine print. Make sure the policy at least covers hospital stays and an emergency flight home.

Paying for your airline ticket or rental car with a credit card may provide limited travel accident insurance. If you already have private health insurance or a homeowners or renters policy, find out what those policies cover and only get supplemental insurance. If you have prepaid a large portion of your vacation, trip cancellation insurance may be a worthwhile expense.

Worldwide travel insurance is available at www.lonelyplanet.com/bookings. You can buy, extend and claim online anytime – even if you're already on the road.

Internet Access

◦ Internet cafes listed throughout this guide typically charge $6 to $12 per hour for online access.

◦ With branches in most cities and towns, **FedEx Office** (☏ 800-254-6567; www.fedex.com) offers internet access at self-service computer workstations (20¢ to 30¢ per minute) and sometimes free wi-fi, plus digital-photo printing and CD-burning stations.

◦ Accommodations, cafes, restaurants, bars etc that provide guest computer terminals for going online are identified in this book by the internet icon @; the wi-fi icon 🛜 indicates that wireless access is available. There may be a charge for either service.

◦ Wi-fi hot spots (free or fee-based) can be found at major airports; many hotels, motels and coffee shops (eg Starbucks); and some tourist information centers, RV parks (eg KOA), museums, bars, restaurants (including fast-food chains such as McDonalds) and stores (eg Apple).

◦ To find more public wi-fi hot spots, search www.wififreespot.com/ca.html or www.jiwire.com.

◦ Public libraries have internet terminals, but online

time may be limited, advance sign-up required and a nominal fee charged for out-of-network visitors. Increasingly, libraries offer free wi-fi access.

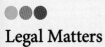

Legal Matters

DRUGS & ALCOHOL

- Possession of under 1oz of marijuana is a misdemeanor in California. Possession of any other drug or more than an ounce of weed is a felony punishable by lengthy jail time. For foreigners, conviction of any drug offense is grounds for deportation.

- Police can give roadside sobriety checks to assess if you've been drinking or using drugs. If you fail, they'll require you to take a breath, urine or blood test to determine if your blood-alcohol level is over the legal limit (0.08%). Refusing to be tested is treated the same as if you had taken and failed the test.

- Penalties for driving under the influence (DUI) of drugs or alcohol range from license suspension and fines to jail time.

- It's illegal to carry open containers of alcohol inside a vehicle, even if they're empty. Unless they're full and still sealed, store them in the trunk.

- Consuming alcohol anywhere other than at a private residence or licensed premises is a no-no, which puts most parks and beaches off-limits (although many campgrounds allow it).

- Bars, clubs and liquor stores often ask for photo ID to prove you are of legal drinking age (ie 21). Being 'carded' is standard practice; don't take it personally.

POLICE & SECURITY

- If you are stopped by the police, be courteous. Don't get out of the car unless asked. Keep your hands where the officer can see them (eg on the steering wheel).

- There is no system of paying fines on the spot. Attempting to pay the fine to the officer may lead to a charge of attempted bribery.

- For traffic violations the ticketing officer will explain the options to you. There is usually a 30-day period to pay a fine; most matters can be handled by mail.

- If you are arrested, you have the right to remain silent and are presumed innocent until proven guilty. Everyone has the right to make one phone call. If you don't have a lawyer, one will be appointed to you free of charge. Foreign travelers who don't have a lawyer, friends or family to help should call their embassy or consulate; the police can provide the number upon request.

- For police, fire and ambulance emergencies, dial ☎911. For nonemergency police assistance, call directory assistance (☎411) for the number of the nearest local police station.

- Due to security concerns about terrorism, never leave your bags unattended, especially not at airports or bus and train stations.

- Carrying mace or cayenne-pepper spray is legal in California, as long as the spray bottle contains no more than 2.5oz of active product. Federal law prohibits it from being carried on planes.

- In cases of sexual assault, rape crisis center and hospital staff can advocate on your behalf and act as a liaison to community services, including the police. Telephone books have listings of local crisis centers, or call the 24-hour **National Sexual Assault Hotline** (☎800-656-4673; www.rainn.org).

SMOKING

- Smoking is generally prohibited inside all public buildings, including airports, shopping malls and train and bus stations.

- There is no smoking allowed inside restaurants, although lighting up may be tolerated at outdoor patio or sidewalk tables (ask first, however).

- At hotels, you must specifically request a smoking room, but note some properties are entirely nonsmoking by law (as noted in this book by the ⊖ icon).

- In some cities and towns, smoking outdoors within a certain distance of any public business is now forbidden.

Money

For US dollar exchange rates and setting your trip budget, see p48.

ATMS

- ATMs are available 24/7 at most banks, shopping malls, airports and grocery and convenience stores.

- Expect a minimum surcharge of $2 to $3 per transaction, in addition to any fees charged by your home bank.

- Most ATMs are connected to international networks and offer decent foreign-exchange rates.

- Withdrawing cash from an ATM using a credit card usually incurs a hefty fee and high interest rates; check with your credit-card company for a PIN number.

CASH

- Most people do not carry large amounts of cash for everyday use, relying instead on credit cards, ATMs and debit cards. Some businesses refuse to accept bills over $20.

CREDIT CARDS

- Major credit cards are almost universally accepted. In fact, it's almost impossible to rent a car, book a room or buy tickets over the phone without one. A credit card may also be vital in emergencies.

- Visa, MasterCard and American Express are the most widely accepted.

MONEYCHANGERS

- You can exchange money at major airports, some banks and all currency-exchange offices such as **American Express** (www .americanexpress.com). Always enquire about rates and fees.

- Outside big cities, exchanging money may be a problem, so make sure you have a credit card and sufficient cash on hand.

TAXES

- A California state sales tax of 8.25% is added to the retail price of most goods and services (gasoline is an exception).

- Local and city sales taxes may tack on an additional 1.5% or more.

- Tourist lodging taxes vary statewide, but currently average over 10%.

TRAVELER'S CHECKS

- Traveler's checks have pretty much fallen out of use.

- Larger restaurants, hotels and department stores will often accept traveler's checks (in US dollars only), but small businesses, markets and fast-food chains may refuse them.

- Visa and American Express are the most widely accepted issuers of traveler's checks.

Public Holidays

On the following national holidays, banks, schools and government offices (including post offices) are closed, and transportation, museums and other services operate on a Sunday schedule. Holidays falling on a weekend are usually observed the following Monday.

New Year's Day January 1

Martin Luther King Jr Day Third Monday in January

Presidents' Day Third Monday in February

Easter Sunday March/April

Memorial Day Last Monday in May

Independence Day July 4 (aka Fourth of July)

Labor Day First Monday in September

Tipping

Tipping is *not* optional. Only withhold tips in cases of outrageously bad service.

Airport skycaps & hotel bellhops	$2 per bag, minimum $5 per cart
Bartenders	10% to 15% per round, minimum $1 per drink
Concierges	Nothing for simple information, up to $20 for securing last-minute restaurant reservations, sold-out show tickets etc
Housekeeping staff	$2 to $4 daily, left under the card provided; more if you're messy
Parking valets	At least $2 when handed back your car keys
Restaurant servers & room service	15% to 20%, unless a gratuity is already charged
Taxi drivers	10% to 15% of metered fare, rounded up to the next dollar

Columbus Day Second Monday in October

Veterans' Day November 11

Thanksgiving Day Fourth Thursday in November

Christmas Day December 25

SCHOOL HOLIDAYS

○ Colleges take a one- or two-week 'spring break' around Easter, sometime in March or April. Some hotels and resorts, especially along the coast, near SoCal's theme parks and in the deserts, raise their rates during this time.

○ School summer vacations run from early June to late August, making July and August the busiest travel months.

Safe Travel

Despite its seemingly apocalyptic list of dangers – guns, violent crime, riots, earthquakes – California is a reasonably safe place to visit. The greatest danger is posed by car accidents (buckle up – it's the law), while the biggest annoyances are city traffic and crowds. Wildlife poses some small threats, and of course there is the dramatic, albeit unlikely, possibility of a natural disaster.

EARTHQUAKES

Earthquakes happen all the time but most are so tiny they are detectable only by sensitive seismological instruments. If you're caught in a serious shaker:

○ If indoors, get under a desk or table or stand in a doorway.

○ Protect your head and stay clear of windows, mirrors or anything that might fall.

○ Don't head for elevators or go running into the street.

○ If you're in a shopping mall or large public building, expect the alarm and/or sprinkler systems to come on.

○ If outdoors, get away from buildings, trees and power lines.

○ If you're driving, pull over to the side of the road away from bridges, overpasses and power lines. Stay inside the car until the shaking stops.

○ If you're on a sidewalk near buildings, duck into a doorway to protect yourself from falling bricks, glass and debris.

○ Prepare for aftershocks.

○ Turn on the radio and listen for bulletins.

○ Use the telephone only if absolutely necessary.

RIPTIDES

If you find yourself being carried offshore by a dangerous ocean current called a riptide, the important thing is to just keep afloat. Don't panic or try to swim against the current, as this will quickly exhaust you and you could drown. Instead, swim parallel to the shoreline and once the current stops pulling you out, swim back to shore.

WILDLIFE

○ Never feed or approach wild animals – it causes them to lose their innate fear of humans, which in turn makes them more aggressive.

○ Disturbing or harassing specially protected species (eg many marine mammals) is a crime, subject to enormous fines.

○ Black bears are often attracted to campgrounds, where they may find food, trash and any other scented items left out on picnic tables or stashed in tents and cars. Always use bear-proof containers where provided.

○ If you encounter a black bear in the wild, don't run. Stay together, keeping small children next to you and picking up little ones. Keep back at least 100yd. If the bear starts moving toward you, back away slowly off-trail and let it pass by, being careful not to block any of the bear's escape routes or to get caught between a mother and her cubs. Sometimes a black bear will 'bluff charge' to test your dominance. Stand your ground by making yourself look as big as possible (eg waving your arms above your head) and shouting menacingly.

○ Mountain lion attacks on humans are rare. If you encounter one, stay calm, pick up small children, face the animal and retreat slowly. Try to appear larger by raising your arms or grabbing a stick. If the lion becomes aggressive, shout or throw rocks at it. If attacked, fight back aggressively.

○ Snakes and spiders are common throughout California, not just in wilderness areas. Always look inside your shoes before putting them back on outdoors, especially when camping. Snake bites are rare, but occur most often when a snake is stepped on or provoked (eg picked up or poked with a stick). Antivenom is available at most hospitals.

Telephone

CELL (MOBILE) PHONES

● You'll need a multiband GSM phone in order to make calls in the US, which differs from most other countries. Popping in a US prepaid rechargeable SIM card is usually cheaper than using your network.

● SIM cards are sold at telecommunications and electronics stores. These stores also sell inexpensive prepaid phones, including some airtime.

● You can rent a cell phone in Los Angeles and San Francisco from **TripTel** (☎877-874-7835; www.triptel.com); pricing plans vary, but typically are expensive.

DIALING CODES

● US phone numbers consist of a three-letter area code followed by a seven-digit local number.

● When dialing a number within the same area code, use the seven-digit number; however, some places require you to dial the entire 10-digit number even for a local call.

● If you are calling long distance, dial ☎1 plus the area code plus the phone number.

● Toll-free numbers begin with ☎800, ☎866, ☎877 or ☎888 and must be preceded by ☎1.

● For direct international calls, dial ☎011 plus the country code plus the area code (usually without the initial '0') plus the local phone number.

● For international call assistance, dial ☎00.

● If you're calling from abroad, the country code for the US is ☎1 (the same as Canada, but international rates apply between the two countries).

PAYPHONES & PHONECARDS

● Where payphones still exist, they are usually coin-operated, although some may only accept credit cards (eg in national parks).

● Local calls usually cost 50¢ minimum.

● For long-distance calls, you're usually better off buying a prepaid phonecard, sold at convenience stores, supermarkets, newsstands and electronics stores.

Time

● California is on Pacific Standard Time (GMT minus eight hours). When it's noon in LA, it's 3pm in New York, 8pm in London and 5am (the next day) in Sydney.

● Daylight Saving Time (DST) starts on the second Sunday in March, when clocks are set one hour ahead, and ends on the first Sunday in November.

Tourist Information

● For pretrip planning, peruse the information-packed website of the **California Travel and Tourism Commission** (www.visit california.com).

● This state-run agency also operates several **California Welcome Centers** (www.visitcwc.com), where staff dispense maps and brochures and help find accommodations.

● Almost every city and town has a local visitor center or a chamber of commerce where you can pick up maps, brochures and information; these are listed in the destination chapters.

ⓘ Important Numbers

All phone numbers have a three-digit area code followed by a seven-digit local number. For long-distance and toll-free calls, dial 1 plus all 10 digits.

Country code	☎1
International dialing code	☎011
Operator	☎0
Emergency (ambulance, fire & police)	☎911
Directory assistance (local)	☎411

- For helpful tourist information websites, see p48 and individual destinations.

Travelers with Disabilities

Southern California is reasonably well-equipped for travelers with disabilities.

COMMUNICATIONS

- Telephone companies provide relay operators (dial 📞711) for the hearing impaired.

- Many banks provide ATM instructions in Braille.

HELPFUL RESOURCES

Access Northern California (www.accessnca .com) Extensive links to accessible-travel resources, publications, tours and transportation, including outdoor recreation opportunities and car and van rentals, plus a searchable lodgings database and an events calendar.

California Coastal Conservancy (www.wheel ingcalscoast.org) Free accessibility information covering beaches, parks and trails, plus downloadable wheelchair riders' guides to the San Francisco, Los Angeles and Orange County coasts.

California State Parks (http://access.parks.ca.gov) Online searchable map and database to find accessible features at parks statewide.

Los Angeles for Disabled Visitors (http:// discoverlosangeles.com /guides/la-living/) Tips for accessible sightseeing, entertainment, museums, theme parks and transportation.

Theme-Park Access Guide (www.mouseplanet .com/tag) An insider's view of Disneyland and other Southern California theme parks 'on wheels.'

Yosemite Access Guide (www.nps.gov/yose/plan yourvisit/upload/access.pdf) Detailed, if somewhat dated downloadable information for Yosemite National Park.

MOBILITY & ACCESSIBILITY

- Most intersections have dropped curbs and sometimes audible crossing signals.

- The Americans with Disabilities Act (ADA) requires public buildings built after 1993 to be wheelchair accessible, including restrooms.

- Motels and hotels built after 1993 must have at least one Americans with Disabilities Act (ADA)–compliant accessible room; state your specific needs when making reservations.

- For nonpublic buildings built prior to 1993, including hotels, restaurants, museums and theaters, there are no accessibility guarantees; call ahead for information.

- Most national and many state parks and some other outdoor recreation areas offer paved or boardwalk-style nature trails accessible

by wheelchairs; for a free national-parks pass, see p390.

PUBLIC TRANSPORTATION

- All major airlines, Greyhound buses and Amtrak trains can accommodate people with disabilities, usually with 48 hours of advance notice.

- Major car-rental agencies offer hand-controlled vehicles and vans with wheelchair lifts at no extra charge, but you must reserve these well in advance.

- For wheelchair-accessible van rentals, try **Wheelchair Getaways** (📞800-642-2042; www.wheelchairgetaways .com) in LA, San Diego and San Francisco or **Mobility Works** (📞877-275-4915; www .mobilityworks.com) in LA.

- Local buses, trains and subway lines usually have wheelchair lifts.

- Seeing-eye dogs are permitted to accompany passengers on public transportation.

- Taxi companies have at least one wheelchair-accessible van, but you'll usually need to call and then wait for one.

Visas

- All of the following information is highly subject to change. Depending on your country of origin, the rules for entering the USA keep changing. Double-check current visa requirements *before* coming to the USA.

- Currently, under the US Visa Waiver Program (VWP), visas are not required for citizens of 36 countries for stays up to 90 days (no extensions) as long as your passport meets current US standards.

- Citizens of VWP countries must also register with the Electronic System for Travel Authorization (ESTA; $14) online (https://esta.cbp.dhs .gov/) at least 72 hours before travel. Once approved, the registration is valid for up to two years.

- Citizens from all other countries or whose passports don't meet US standards will need to apply for a visa in their home country. The process costs a nonrefundable $140, involves a personal interview and can take several weeks, so apply as early as possible.

- For more information, consult http://travel.state .gov/visa.

Transport

GETTING THERE & AWAY

Getting to California by air or overland by bus, car or train is easy, although it's not always cheap. Flights, tours and train tickets can be booked online at lonelyplanet.com/ bookings.

ENTERING THE REGION

California is an important agricultural state. To prevent the spread of pests and diseases, certain food items (including meats, fresh fruit and vegetables) may not be brought into the state. Bakery items, chocolates and hard-cured cheeses are admissible. If you drive into California across the border from Mexico or from the states of Oregon, Nevada or Arizona, you may have to stop for a quick inspection and questioning by California Department of Food and Agriculture agents.

PASSPORT

- Under the Western Hemisphere Travel Initiative (WHTI), all travelers must have a valid machine-readable (MRP) passport when entering the USA by air, land or sea.

- The only exceptions are for most US citizens and some Canadian and Mexican citizens traveling *by land* who can present other WHTI-compliant documents (eg preapproved 'trusted traveler' cards). For details, check www .getyouhome.gov.

- All foreign passports must meet current US standards and be valid for at least six months longer than your intended stay.

- MRP passports issued or renewed after October 26, 2006 must be e-passports (ie have a digital photo and integrated chip with biometric data). For more information, consult www.cbp.gov/travel.

✈ AIR

- To get through airport security checkpoints (30-minute wait times are standard), you'll need a boarding pass and photo ID.

- Some travelers may be required to undergo a secondary screening, involving hand pat-downs and carry-on bag searches.

- Airport security measures restrict many common items (eg pocket knives) from being carried on planes. Check current restrictions with the **Transportation Security Administration** (TSA; ☏866-289-9673; www.tsa .gov).

- Currently, TSA requires that all carry-on liquids and gels be stored in 3oz or smaller bottles placed inside a quart-sized clear plastic zip-top bag. Exceptions, which must be declared to checkpoint security officers, include medications.

- All checked luggage is screened for explosives. TSA may open your suitcase for visual confirmation, breaking the lock if necessary. Leave your bags unlocked or use a TSA-approved lock such as **Travel Sentry** (www .travelsentry.org).

AIRPORTS

California's primary international airports:

Los Angeles International Airport (LAX; www.lawa.org /lax) California's largest and busiest airport, 20 miles southwest of downtown LA, near the coast.

San Francisco International Airport (SFO; www.flysfo.com) Northern California's major hub, 14 miles south of downtown, on San Francisco Bay. Regional airports that offer limited international services include the following:

LA/Ontario International Airport (ONT; www.lawa.org/ont) In Riverside County, east of LA.

Mineta San José International Airport (SJC; www.flysanjose.com) In San Francisco's South Bay.

Oakland International Airport (OAK; www.flyoakland.com) In San Francisco's East Bay.

Palm Springs International Airport (PSP; www.palmspringsairport.com) In the desert, east of LA.

San Diego International Airport (SAN; www.san.org) Four miles northwest of downtown.

LAND

TRAIN

○ **Amtrak** (📞800-872-7245; www.amtrak.com) operates a fairly extensive rail system throughout the USA.

○ Trains are comfortable, if a bit slow, and are equipped with dining and lounge cars on long-distance routes.

○ Amtrak's **USA Rail Pass** (www.amtrak.com) is valid for coach-class travel for 15 ($389), 30 ($579) or 45 ($749) days; children aged two to 15 pay half-price.

○ For Amtrak's California Rail Pass, see p404.

⬤⬤⬤

GETTING AROUND

Most people drive around California, although you can also travel by airplane (if time is limited) or you can save money by taking buses or often scenic trains.

✈ AIR

Apart from California's major international airports, domestic flights also depart from smaller regional airports in Arcata, Burbank, Fresno, Santa Ana, Long Beach, Monterey, Redding, Sacramento, San Luis Obispo and Santa Barbara.

Several major US carriers fly within California. Flights are often operated by their regional subsidiaries, such as American Eagle, Delta Connection and United Express. Alaska Airlines and partner Horizon Air serve many regional airports, as do popular low-cost airlines Southwest and JetBlue. Virgin America currently flies out of San Francisco, Los Angeles and San Diego.

🚲 BICYCLE

Although it's a nonpolluting 'green' way to travel, the distances involved in cycling around California demand a high level of fitness and make it hard to cover much ground. Forget about the deserts in

Climate Change & Travel

Every form of transport that relies on carbon-based fuel generates CO_2, the main cause of human-induced climate change. Modern travel is dependent on airplanes, which might use less fuel per kilometer per person than most cars but travel much greater distances. The altitude at which aircraft emit gases (including CO_2) and particles also contributes to their climate change impact. Many websites offer 'carbon calculators' that allow people to estimate the carbon emissions generated by their journey and, for those who wish to do so, to offset the impact of the greenhouse gases emitted with contributions to portfolios of climate-friendly initiatives throughout the world. Lonely Planet offsets the carbon footprint of all staff and author travel.

summer or the mountains in winter.

ROAD RULES

○ Cycling is allowed on all roads and highways – even along freeways if there's no suitable alternative, such as a smaller parallel road; all mandatory exits are marked.

○ Some cities have designated bicycle lanes, but make sure you have your wits about you when venturing out into heavy traffic.

○ Cyclists must follow the same rules of the road as vehicles. Don't expect drivers to always respect your right of way.

• Wearing a helmet is mandatory for riders under 18 years old.

• Ensure you have proper lights and reflective gear, especially if you're pedaling at night or in fog.

RENTAL

• You can rent bikes by the hour, day or week in most cities and major towns.

• Rentals start around $10 per day for beach cruisers up to $45 or more for mountain bikes; ask about multiday and weekly discounts.

• Most rental companies require a credit-card security deposit of $200 or more.

BOAT

Boats won't get you around California, although there are a few offshore routes, notably to Catalina Island off the coast of Los Angeles and Orange County, and to Channel Islands National Park from Ventura or Oxnard, north of LA. On San Francisco Bay, regular ferry routes operate between San Francisco and Sausalito, Larkspur, Tiburon, Angel Island, Oakland, Alameda and Vallejo.

BUS

Greyhound (☎ 800-231-2222; www.greyhound.com) buses are an economical way to travel between major cities and to points along the coast, but won't get you off the beaten path or to national parks.

Travelers with disabilities who need special assistance should call ☎ 800-752-4841 (TDD/TTY ☎ 800-345-3109) at least 48 hours before

traveling. Wheelchairs are accepted as checked baggage and service animals are allowed on board.

CAR, MOTORCYCLE & RV

California's love affair with cars runs so deep it often verges on pathological, and it's here to stay for at least one practical reason: the state is so big, public transportation can't cover it. For flexibility and convenience, you'll want a car. Independence costs you, though: rental rates and gas prices can eat up a good chunk of your trip budget.

AUTOMOBILE ASSOCIATIONS

For 24-hour emergency roadside assistance, free maps and discounts on lodging, attractions, entertainment, car rentals and more:

....

American Automobile Association (AAA; ☎ 877-428-2277; www.aaa.com) Walk-in offices throughout California, add-on coverage for RVs and motorcycles, and reciprocal agreements with some international auto clubs (eg CAA in Canada, AA in the UK) – bring your membership card from home.

....

Better World Club (☎ 866-238-1137; www.betterworldclub.com) Ecofriendly alternative supports environmental causes and also offers cyclists emergency roadside assistance.

DRIVER'S LICENSE

• Visitors may legally drive a car in California for up to 12 months with their home driver's license.

• If you're from overseas, an International Driving Permit (IDP) will have more credibility with traffic police and simplify the car-rental process, especially if your license doesn't have a photo or isn't written in English.

• To drive a motorcycle, you'll need a valid US state motorcycle license or a specially endorsed IDP.

• International automobile associations can issue IDPs, that are valid for one year, for a fee. Always carry your home license together with the IDP.

FUEL

• Gas stations in California, nearly all of which are self-service, are ubiquitous, except in national parks and some sparsely populated desert and mountain areas.

• Gas is sold by the gallon (1 US gallon equals 3.78L). At press time, the cost for mid-grade fuel ranged from $3.75 to $4.25.

INSURANCE

California law requires liability insurance for all vehicles. When renting a car, check your auto insurance policy from home or your travel insurance policy to see if you're already covered. If not, expect to pay about $20 per day.

Insurance against damage to the car itself, called Collision Damage Waiver (CDW) or Loss Damage Waiver (LDW), costs another $20 per day; the deductible may require you to pay the first $100 to $500 for any repairs. Some credit cards cover this, provided you charge the entire cost of the car rental to the card. If there's an accident you may have to pay the rental-car company first, then seek reimbursement from the credit-card company. Check your credit-card's policy carefully before renting.

PARKING

❍ Parking is usually plentiful and free in small towns and rural areas, but scarce and expensive in cities.

❍ Look for the free-parking icon (P) used in the San Francisco, Los Angeles and San Diego chapters of this book.

❍ You can pay municipal parking meters with coins (eg quarters) or sometimes credit cards.

❍ Expect to pay at least $25 to park overnight in a city lot or garage.

❍ Flat-fee valet parking at hotels and restaurants is common in major cities.

❍ When parking on the street, read all posted regulations and restrictions (eg street-cleaning hours, permit-only residential areas) and pay attention to colored curbs, or you may be ticketed and towed.

RENTAL
Cars

To rent your own wheels, you'll typically need to be at least 25 years old, hold a valid driver's license and have a major credit card, *not* a check or debit card. A few companies may rent to drivers under 25 but over 21 for a surcharge (around $25 per day). If you don't have a credit card, you may occasionally be able to make a large cash deposit instead.

With advance reservations, you can often get an economy-size vehicle with unlimited mileage from around $30 per day, plus insurance, taxes and fees. Weekend and weekly rates are usually more economical. Airport locations may have cheaper rates but higher fees; if you get a fly-drive package, local taxes may be extra when you pick up the car. City-center branches may offer free pickups and drop-offs.

Rates generally include unlimited mileage, but expect surcharges for additional drivers and one-way rentals. Some rental companies let you pay for your last tank of gas upfront. Child or infant safety seats are compulsory (reserve them when booking),

ROAD DISTANCES (miles)

	Anaheim	Arcata	Bakersfield	Death Valley	Las Vegas	Los Angeles	Monterey	Napa	Palm Springs	Redding	Sacramento	San Diego	San Francisco	San Luis Obispo	Santa Barbara	Sth Lake Tahoe
Arcata	680															
Bakersfield	135	555														
Death Valley	285	705	235													
Las Vegas	265	840	285	140												
Los Angeles	25	650	110	290	270											
Monterey	370	395	250	495	535	345										
Napa	425	265	300	545	590	400	150									
Palm Springs	95	760	220	300	280	110	450	505								
Redding	570	140	440	565	725	545	315	190	650							
Sacramento	410	300	280	435	565	385	185	60	490	160						
San Diego	95	770	230	350	330	120	465	520	140	665	505					
San Francisco	405	280	285	530	570	380	120	50	490	215	85	500				
San Luis Obispo	225	505	120	365	405	200	145	265	310	430	290	320	230			
Santa Barbara	120	610	145	350	360	95	250	370	205	535	395	215	335	105		
Sth Lake Tahoe	505	400	375	345	460	480	285	160	485	260	100	600	185	390	495	
Yosemite	335	465	200	300	415	310	200	190	415	325	160	430	190	230	345	190

and cost about $10 per day (maximum $50 per rental).

If you'd like to minimize your carbon footprint, a few major car-rental companies (including Avis, Budget, Enterprise, Fox, Hertz and Thrifty) offer 'green' fleets of hybrid or biofuel rental cars, but they're in short supply. Reserve well in advance and expect to pay significantly more for these models. Also consider:

Simply Hybrid (☎ 323-653-0011, 888-359-0055; www.simplyhybrid.com) In Los Angeles. Free delivery and pickup from some locations with a three-day minimum rental.

Zipcar (☎ 866-494-7227; www.zipcar.com) Currently available in 20 California cities (mostly along the coast), this car-sharing club charges usage fees (per hour or daily), including free gas, insurance (a damage fee of up to $500 may apply) and limited mileage. Apply online (foreign drivers OK); annual membership $50, application fee $25.

To find and compare independent car-rental companies, try **Car Rental Express** (www.carrentalexpress.com) – especially useful for searching out cheaper long-term rentals. Some independent companies may rent to drivers under 25:

Rent-a-Wreck (☎ 877-877-0700; www.rentawreck.com) Minimum rental age and surcharges vary by location. Ten locations, mostly around LA and the San Francisco Bay area.

Super Cheap Cars (www.supercheapcar.com) Normally a surcharge for drivers aged 21 to 24; daily fee applies for drivers aged 18 to 21. Three locations in San Francisco, Los Angeles and Orange County. For wheelchair-accessible van rentals, see p397.

Motorcycles

Motorcycle rentals and insurance are not cheap, especially if you have your eye on a Harley. Depending on the model, renting a motorcycle costs $100 to $200 per day plus taxes and fees, including helmets, unlimited miles and liability insurance; one-way rentals and collision insurance (CDW) cost extra. Discounts may be available for three-day and weekly rentals. Security deposits range from $1000 to $3000 (credit card required).

Motorcycle and scooter rental agencies:

Dubbelju (☎ 415-495-2774, 866-495-2774; www.dubbelju.com; 698a Bryant St, San Francisco) Harley-Davidson, BMW, Japanese-import and electric motorcycles for rent.

Eagle Rider (☎ 888-900-9901; www.eaglerider.com) Nationwide company with 12 locations in California, as well as Reno, Nevada. One-way rental surcharge $250.

Route 66 (☎ 310-578-0112, 888-434-4473; www.route66riders.com; 4161 Lincoln Blvd, Marina del Rey) Harley-Davidson rentals in LA's South Bay.

Recreational Vehicles

It's easy to find campgrounds throughout California with electricity and water hookups for RVs, but in big cities RVs are a nuisance, since there are few places to park or plug them in. RVs are also cumbersome to drive and they burn fuel at an alarming rate. That said, they do solve transportation, accommodation and cooking needs in one fell swoop. Even so, there are many places in national and state parks and in the mountains that RVs can't go.

Book RV rentals as far in advance as possible. Rental costs vary by size and model, but you can expect to pay over $100 per day for a campervan or 25ft-long RV sleeping up to five people. Rates often don't include mileage (from 35¢ per mile), bedding or kitchen kits (rental fee $50 to $100), vehicle prep ($100 surcharge) or taxes. Pets may be allowed, sometimes for an additional surcharge.

RV rental agencies:

Cruise America (☎ 480-464-7300, 800-671-8042; www.cruiseamerica.com) Two dozen pickup locations statewide.

El Monte (☎ 562-483-4956, 888-337-2214; www.elmonterv.com) Ask about AAA discounts.

Happy Travel Campers (☎ 310-928-3980, 800-370-1262; www.camperusa.com) LA-based.

Moturis (☎ 877-297-3687; www.moturis.com) In LA, San Diego, San Francisco and Sacramento.

Road Bear (☎ 818-865-2925, 866-491-9853; www.roadbearrv.com) In LA and San Francisco.

ROAD CONDITIONS & HAZARDS

For up-to-date highway conditions in California, including road closures and construction updates, dial ☎800-427-7623 or visit www.dot.ca.gov. For Nevada highways, call ☎877-687-6237 or check www.nvroads.com.

In places where winter driving is an issue, snow tires and tire chains may be required in mountain areas. Ideally, carry your own chains and learn how to use them before you hit the road. Otherwise, chains can usually be bought (but not cheaply) on the highway, at gas stations or in the nearest town. Most car-rental companies don't permit the use of chains. Driving off-road, or on dirt roads, is also prohibited by most rental-car companies, and it can be dangerous in wet weather.

In rural areas, livestock sometimes graze next to unfenced roads. These areas are typically signed as 'Open Range', with the silhouette of a steer. Where deer and other wild animals frequently appear roadside, you'll see signs with the silhouette of a leaping deer. Take these signs seriously, particularly at night. In coastal areas thick fog may impede driving – slow down and if it's too soupy, get off the road. Along coastal cliffs and in the mountains, watch out for falling rocks, mudslides and avalanches that could damage or disable your car if struck.

ROAD RULES

○ Drive on the right-hand side of the road.

○ Talking on a cell phone while driving is illegal.

○ The use of seat belts is required for drivers, front-seat passengers and children under age 16.

○ Infant and child safety seats are required for children under six years old or weighing less than 60lb.

○ All motorcyclists must wear a helmet. Scooters are not allowed on freeways.

○ High-occupancy (HOV) lanes marked with a diamond symbol are reserved for cars with multiple occupants, sometimes only during morning and afternoon rush hours.

○ Unless otherwise posted, the speed limit is 65mph on freeways, 55mph on two-lane undivided highways, 35mph on major city streets and 25mph in business and residential districts and near schools.

○ It's forbidden to pass a school bus when its rear red lights are flashing.

○ Except where indicated, turning right at red lights after coming to a full stop is permitted, although intersecting traffic still has the right of way.

○ At four-way stop signs, cars proceed in the order in which they arrived. If two cars arrive simultaneously, the one on the right has the right of way. When in doubt, politely wave the other driver ahead.

○ When emergency vehicles (ie police, fire or ambulance) approach from either direction, carefully pull over to the side of the road.

○ California has strict anti-littering laws; throwing trash from a vehicle may incur a $1000 fine. Like Woody says, 'Give a hoot, don't pollute.'

○ Driving under the influence of alcohol or drugs is illegal.

○ It's also illegal to carry open containers of alcohol inside a vehicle, even empty ones. Unless containers are full and still sealed, store them in the trunk.

LOCAL TRANSPORTATION

Except in cities, public transit is rarely the most convenient option, and coverage to outlying towns and suburbs can be sparse. However, it is usually cheap, safe and reliable. See the regional chapters for details.

BICYCLE

○ Cycling is a feasible way of getting around smaller cities and towns, but it's not much fun in traffic-dense areas such as LA.

○ Davis, San Francisco, San Luis Obispo, Santa Barbara and Santa Cruz are among California's most bike-friendly communities, as rated by the **League of American Bicyclists** (www.bikeleague.org).

○ Bicycles may be transported on many buses and trains, sometimes during non-commute hours only.

○ For rentals, see p400.

BUS, CABLE CAR, STREETCAR & TROLLEY

○ Most cities and larger towns have reliable local bus systems (average $1 to $3 per ride), but they may be designed for commuters and provide only limited evening and weekend service.

○ San Francisco's extensive Municipal Railway (MUNI) network includes not only buses and trains, but also historic streetcars and those famous cable cars.

○ San Diego runs trolleys around some neighborhoods and to the Mexican border.

TRAIN

○ In LA, the Metro is a combined, ever-expanding network of subway and light-rail, while Metrolink commuter trains connect LA with surrounding counties.

○ San Diego operates *Coaster* commuter trains along the coast between downtown and Oceanside in the North County.

○ To get around the San Francisco Bay Area, hop aboard Bay Area Rapid Transit (BART) or Caltrain.

TAXI

○ Taxis are metered, with flag-fall fees of $2.50 to $3.50 to start, plus $2 to $3 per mile. Credit cards may be accepted.

○ Taxis may charge extra for baggage and airport pickups.

○ Drivers expect a 10% to 15% tip, rounded up to the next dollar.

○ Taxis cruise the busiest areas in large cities, but elsewhere you may need to call a cab company.

🚆 TRAIN

Amtrak (☎ 800-872-7245; www.amtrak.com) runs comfortable, if occasionally tardy, trains to major California cities and limited towns. At some stations Thruway buses provide onward connections. Smoking is prohibited on board trains and buses.

○ Amtrak's California Rail Pass costs $159 ($80 for children aged two to 15).

○ The pass is valid on all trains (except certain long-distance routes) and most connecting Thruway buses for seven days of travel within a 21-day period.

○ Passholders must make advance reservations for each leg of travel and obtain hard-copy tickets prior to boarding.

Behind the Scenes

This Book

This 2nd edition of *Discover California* was coordinated by Beth Kohn. Bridget Gleeson wrote the San Diego & the Deserts and Disneyland & Orange County chapters. Andrew Bender, Sara Benson, Alison Bing, Nate Cavalieri, Andrea Schulte-Peevers and John A Vlahides also researched and wrote the On the Road chapters. Adam Skolnick wrote the Los Angeles walking tour. Alex Leviton co-wrote the previous edition. This guidebook was commissioned in Lonely Planet's Oakland office, and produced by the following:

Commissioning Editor Suki Gear
Coordinating Editors Laura Crawford, Justin Flynn
Coordinating Cartographers Enes Basic, Mick Garrett, Andrew Smith
Coordinating Layout Designer Wibowo Rusli
Managing Editors Annelies Mertens, Anna Metcalfe
Managing Cartographers Shahara Ahmed, Corey Hutchinson, Alison Lyall
Managing Layout Designer Jane Hart
Assisting Editors Andi Jones, Evan Jones, Helen Koehne, Shawn Low, Dianne Schallmeiner
Assisting Cartographer Jane Chapman
Cover Research Naomi Parker
Internal Image Research Aude Vauconsant
Thanks to Lucy Birchley, Ryan Evans, Yvonne Kirk, Gerard Walker

Author Thanks

BETH KOHN

All the usual suspects get thanks again, especially the fabulous multi-tasking Suki Gear and the dynamo known as Sam Benson. California cohorts and experts this time around included Claude Moller, Felix Thomson, Jenny G, Dillon Dutton and Julia Brashares, plus all the helpful and patient rangers at Yosemite National Park.

BRIDGET GLEESON

Thank you to my lovely sister Molly, my brother-in-law Germán, my dear friend Starla and her family for their hospitality – and to their friends for dining and drinking suggestions. Thanks to my mother Margaret, my faithful travel companion, and to Lisa Robertson and Carrie Tayloe for their expert advice.

Acknowledgments

Climate map data adapted from Peel MC, Finlayson BL & McMahon TA (2007) 'Updated World Map of the Köppen-Geiger Climate Classification', *Hydrology and Earth System Sciences*, 11, 163344.

Cover photographs: Front: Yosemite Falls, Yosemite National Park, Gary Crabbe/Alamy © 2012; Back: Golden Gate Bridge and Fort Point, San Francisco, California, John Elk III/ Lonely Planet Images © 2012. Many of the images in this guide are available for licensing from Lonely Planet Images: www.lonelyplanetimages.com.

SEND US YOUR FEEDBACK

Index

17-Mile Drive 184

A

accommodations 49, 364, 388-9, see also individual locations
activities 378-82, see also individual activities, individual locations
Aguereberry Point 319
air travel 398-9
airports 398-9
Alabama Hills 271
Alcatraz 96, 107
amusement parks 330, see also Disneyland
  Balboa Fun Zone 346
  Disney California Adventure 328, 337-8
  Knott's Berry Farm 345
  Santa Cruz Beach Boardwalk 176
  Santa Monica Pier 72
  SeaWorld 300
  Traintown 229-30
  Universal Studios Hollywood 65
Anchor Bay 154
Andrew Molera State Park 186-7
animals 385-6, see also individual animals, whale-watching, wildlife watching
Año Nuevo State Reserve 175

aquariums
  Birch Aquarium 298
  Long Beach 83
  Monterey Bay Aquarium 180
  Seymour Marine Discovery Center 176
Arcata 165-6
Arcata Marsh & Wildlife Sanctuary 165
architecture 21, 371-2
area codes 396
art galleries, see museums & galleries
arts 369-72
Asian Art Museum 102-3
ATMs 48, 393-4
Auburn State Recreation Area 274
Avenue of the Giants 131, 158-9

B

Badger Pass Ski Area 261
Badwater 318
Baker Beach 105
Balboa Fun Zone 346
Balboa Park 280, 291-3
ballooning 203, 219
Bay Area Discovery Museum 142
beaches 17, 331, 364, 378-9
  Baker Beach 105
  Carmel-by-the-Sea 183
  Corona del Mar 349
  El Matador 81
  Huntington Beach 344
  Klamath 168
  Laguna Beach 19, 329, 348
  Long Beach 83
  Los Angeles 58
  Malibu 81
  Manhattan 81
  Muir Beach 145-6
  Navy Beach 267
  Newport Beach 329
  Ocean Beach 119

Pescadero 174
  Pfeiffer Beach 134, 187
  San Diego 302
  Santa Barbara 134, 193-5
  Santa Cruz 176
  Santa Monica 81
  Seal Beach 349
  Sonoma Coast State Beach 153
  Stinson Beach 134, 146
  Venice 81
bears 385, 395
beer 305, 376
Berkeley 151
Beverly Hills 69
bicycling, see cycling, mountain biking
Big Basin Redwoods State Park 131, 177
Big Sur 21, 185-9
Big Trees State Park 275
Birch Aquarium 298
Bixby Bridge 186
boat travel 400
Bodega Bay 152-3
Bodega Head 152
Bodie State Historic Park 243, 272
Bolsa Chica State Ecological Reserve 344
books 47, see also literature
Bowers Museum of Cultural Art 328, 348
budget 49
bus travel 400, 403-4
business hours 389-90

C

cable cars 97, 123, 404
Cabot's Pueblo Museum 307
Cabrillo, Juan Rodriguez 355
Cabrillo National Monument 297
California Academy of Sciences 95, 110
California Building & Museum of Man 291

California Palace of the Legion of Honor 106
California State Fair 44
California State Railroad Museum 274
camping 381
Cannery Row 178
canoeing & kayaking 380
    Healdsburg 234
    Mendocino 155
    Monterey 182
    Point Reyes National Seashore 150
    San Diego 298-9
Capitola 154
car travel 48, 49, 400-3, *see also* scenic drives
Carmel-by-the-Sea 183-5
Carson Mansion 163
Cathedral of Our Lady of the Angels 63
Cedar Grove 264
cell phones 48, 396
Central Coast 173-97, **128**
    highlights 130-3
    itineraries 136-7, **136**
    planning 135
    travel within 135
    websites 135
Chandelier Drive-Thru Tree 158
Charles M Schulz Museum 231
children, travel with 362-5
    Los Angeles 58, 87
    San Francisco 98
    Santa Barbara 197
climate 48, 389
climate change 399
coffee 377
Coit Tower 121
Conservatory of Flowers 95, 106
Contemporary Jewish Museum 106
Corona del Mar 349
Costa Mesa 346
Covington Flats 315
credit cards 48, 394

Crissy Field 104
Crystal Cave 268
Crystal Cove State Park 346
Culinary Institute of America at Greystone 205, 219
currency 48
customs regulations 390
cycling 399-400, 403, *see also* mountain biking
    Joshua Tree National Park 314
    Los Angeles 56, 73
    San Francisco 108
    Santa Barbara 195
    Sausalito 142-3

D

dangers, *see* safety
Dante's View 318
Death Valley National Park 16, 283, 317-21
Deserts, the 306-21, **278-9**
    highlights 280-3
    itineraries 286-7, **286**
    planning 285
    travel within 285
    websites 285
Devil's Golf Course 318
Devils Postpile National Monument 273
disabilities, travelers with 397
discount cards 390-1
Disney California Adventure 328, 337-8
Disneyland 15, 326-7, 334-7, **336**
    accommodations 339-40
    drinking 342
    entertainment 342
    food 340-2
    itineraries 332-3, **332**
    planning 331
    shopping 342-3
    sights & attractions 334-8
    travel to/from 343-4
    travel within 344
    websites 331

diving & snorkeling 379
    Monterey Bay 182
    San Diego 297-8
Donner Lake 253-4
Donner Memorial State Park 253
Donner Party 253
Drake, Sir Francis 355
drinks 375-7, *see also* beer, wine
driver's licenses 400
driving, *see* car travel, scenic drives
driving distances 401
Dry Creek Valley 234
DVDs 390

E

earthquakes 49, 383-4, 395
East Beach 134
El Capitan 257
electricity 391
elephant seals 386
Elk 154
Elvis Honeymoon Hideaway 312
Emerald Bay State Park 252
emergencies 396
environmental issues 385-6
environmentalism 353
Eureka 163-5
events, *see* festivals & events
exchange rates 49
Exploratorium 103

F

family travel 362-5
Fannette Island 252
farmers markets
    Oxbow Public Market 215
    San Francisco 102
    San Luis Obispo 191
    Santa Monica 81
Ferndale 159-63
Ferry Building 102

festivals & events 42-5, *see also individual locations*
 film 43
 gay & lesbian 43, 111
 music 43, 109
 surfing 45
 wine 44
film industry 65, 75-6, 369-70
films 43, 47
fireworks 339
Fisherman's Wharf 103
fishing
 Bodega Bay 152
 Mammoth Lakes 269
food 13, 28, 29, 96, 330, 353, 373-5, 391, *see also individual locations*
food trucks 46, 115, 375
Founders Grove 158
Furnace Creek 318

G

galleries, *see* museums & galleries
gardens, *see* parks & gardens
gay marriage 367
gay travelers 391-2
 festivals 43, 111
 Los Angeles 88
 museums 46
 San Francisco 111, 120
General Grant Grove 264
geology 30, 383-4
Geology Tour Rd 315
Getty Center 56, 75
Getty Villa 56
Giant Forest 265-6
Giant Forest Museum 265-6
Gingerbread Mansion 160
Glacier Point 241, 259
Gold Country 28, 271-5
gold rush 28, 242, 273, 357
Golden Gate Bridge 16, 102
Golden Gate Park 94, 95

Grammy Museum 63-4
Grauman's Chinese Theatre 64-5
Great Depression 358-9
Griffith Observatory 57, 67
Griffith Park 67
Gualala 154

H

Healdsburg 233-5
health 392
Hearst Castle 190
Heavenly Gondola 249
Hetch Hetchy 258-9
Hidden Valley 313
hiking 14, 380-1
 Death Valley National Park 319
 Humboldt Redwoods State Park 158
 Indian Canyons 309
 Joshua Tree National Park 314
 Lassen Volcanic National Park 170-1
 Los Angeles 73-4
 Mammoth Lakes 269
 Marin Headlands 139
 Point Reyes National Seashore 149-50
 Prairie Creek Redwoods State Park 168
 Redwood National & State Parks 167
 Tahquitz Canyon 309
 Yosemite National Park 259-60
 Yosemite Valley 257-8
historic houses & mansions, *see also* missions
 Carson Mansion 163
 Gingerbread Mansion 160
 Hearst Castle 190
 Vallejo Home 229
 Whaley House 294
history 354-61, *see also* gold rush

holidays 394-5
Hollywood 17, 54, 55, 64-8, **66**, **70-1**
homelessness 367
horseback riding
 Bodega Bay 152
 Humboldt Redwoods State Park 158
 San Diego 299
hot springs, *see* spas & hot springs
hot-air ballooning 203, 219
Humboldt Redwoods State Park 131, 158-9
Humboldt State University 165
Huntington Beach 344-5

I

immigration 357, 367-8
Indian Canyons 309
Indian Springs 203
insurance 392, 400-1
International Surfing Museum 344
internet access 48, 392-3
internet resources, *see* websites
itineraries 32-41, *see also individual locations*

J

Jack London State Historic Park 231-2
Jedediah Smith Redwoods State Park 131
Joshua Tree National Park 30, 283, 313-16
Julia Pfeiffer Burns State Park 187

K

kayaking, *see* canoeing & kayaking
Kings Canyon National Park 243, 264-5

Kings Canyon Scenic Byway 245, 265
kitesurfing 380
Klamath 168
Klamath Basin National Wildlife Refuges 167
Knott's Berry Farm 345

L

La Brea Tar Pits 57, 68
La Jolla 297-8
Lady Bird Johnson Grove 167
Laguna Beach 19, 329, 348-9
Lake Tahoe 23, 242, 248-54, **250**
language 48
Lassen Volcanic National Park 24, 133, 170-1
Lava Beds National Monument 173
legal matters 393
lesbian travelers 391-2
festivals 43, 111
Los Angeles 88
museums 46
San Francisco 111, 120
lighthouses
Pigeon Point 174
Point Arena 154
Point Bonita 139
Point Cabrillo 154-5
Point Piedras Blancas 189
Point Reyes 149
Point Sur State Historic Park 186
literature 370-1, see also books
Lombard St 103-4
Long Beach 83
Los Angeles 51-89, **52-3, 70-1**
accommodations 77-9
activities 73-4
drinking 82
entertainment 83-4
festivals & events 76
food 79-82, 373-4

highlights 54-7
itineraries 60-1, **60**
shopping 84-6
sights & attractions 62-73
tourist offices 86
tours 74-6
travel to/from 86-7
travel within 59, 87-9
websites 59
Los Angeles County Museum of Art 72

M

Malibu 69-71
Mammoth Lakes 268-70
Mammoth Mountain 244, 269
mansions, see historic houses & mansions
Manzanar National Historic Site 270-1
marijuana 352
Marin County 138-51, **140-1**
Marin Headlands 138-42
Mariposa Grove 241, 258
Maritime Museum 289
markets 58, see also farmers markets
Los Angeles 60, 79
Napa 215
Point Reyes Station 148
San Diego 306
Marshall Gold Discovery State Historic Park 242, 273
McCloud 172-3
McWay Falls 187
measures 390
Mendocino 25, 133, 154-7, **156**
Mendocino Art Center 154
Mendocino Headlands State Park 155
MH de Young Memorial Museum 95, 106
Mission Basilica San Diego de Alcalá 294
Mission Beach 302
Mission District 97

missions 20, 355-6, see also historic houses & mansions
Mission Basilica San Diego de Alcalá 294
Mission San Luis Obispo de Tolosa 189-91
Mission Santa Barbara 192
mobile phones 48, 396
Mojave National Preserve 316
money 48, 49, 393-4
Mono Lake 243, 266-8
Monterey 19, 133, 178-83
Monterey Bay Aquarium 180
Monterey History & Maritime Museum 181
Montgomery Woods State Reserve 131
Morro Bay 154
motorcycle travel 402
mountain biking
Furnace Creek 319
Mammoth Mountain 269
Prairie Creek Redwoods State Park 168
mountain lions 385, 395
Mt Shasta 171
Mt Shasta City 171-3
Muir Beach 145-6
Muir Woods National Monument 147
Musée Mecanique 103
museums & galleries 22, 364
Asian Art Museum 102-3
Bay Area Discovery Museum 142
Bowers Museum of Cultural Art 328, 348
Cabot's Pueblo Museum 307
California Building & Museum of Man 291
California Palace of the Legion of Honor 106
California State Railroad Museum 274
Charles M Schulz Museum 231
Contemporary Jewish Museum 106
Exploratorium 103

museums & galleries
continued
Getty Center 56, 75
Giant Forest Museum 265-6
GLBT History Museum 46
Grammy Museum 63-4
International Surfing Museum 344
Los Angeles County Museum of Art 72
Maritime Museum 289
Mendocino Art Center 154
MH de Young Memorial Museum 95, 106
Monterey History & Maritime Museum 181
Musée Mecanique 103
Museum of Contemporary Art (Los Angeles) 63
Museum of Contemporary Art (San Diego) 289
Museum of the American West 67
Museum of Tolerance 69
Newport Harbor Nautical Museum 345
Ocean Institute 345
Pacific Design Center 67
Page Museum 57, 68
Palm Springs Art Museum 307
Petersen Automotive Museum 68
San Diego Chinese Historical Museum 289
San Diego Museum of Art 292
San Diego Natural History Museum 291
San Francisco Museum of Modern Art 105-6
Silverado Museum 219
Timken Museum of Art 292
Yosemite Museum 258
music 47, 371
festivals 43, 109
Mystery Spot 175

N

Napa 214-17
Napa Valley 27, 202, 212-25, **213**
Napa Wine Country 212-25, **201**
highlights 202-5
itineraries 208-9, **208**
planning 207
tours 211-12
travel to/from 210-11
travel within 207, 212
websites 207
national & state parks 364, 384
Andrew Molera State Park 186-7
Año Nuevo State Reserve 175
Auburn State Recreation Area 274
Big Basin Redwoods State Park 131, 177
Big Trees State Park 275
Bodie State Historic Park 243, 272
Bolsa Chica State Ecological Reserve 344
Crystal Cove State Park 346
Death Valley National Park 16, 283, 317-21
Donner Memorial State Park 253
Emerald Bay State Park 252
Humboldt Redwoods State Park 131, 158-9
Jack London State Historic Park 231-2
Jedediah Smith Redwoods State Park 131
Joshua Tree National Park 30, 283, 313-16
Julia Pfeiffer Burns State Park 187
Kings Canyon National Park 243, 264-5
Lassen Volcanic National Park 24, 133, 170-1
Mendocino Headlands State Park 155
Mojave National Preserve 316
Montgomery Woods State Reserve 131
Pfeiffer Big Sur State Park 187
Point Lobos State Natural Reserve 183
Prairie Creek Redwoods State Park 167-8
Redwood National & State Parks 166-7
Robert Louis Stevenson State Park 224
Salt Point State Park 153-4
Sequoia National Park 243, 265-6
Shasta-Trinity National Forest 171
Sonoma State Historic Park 228-9
Sutter's Fort State Historic Park 274
Torrey Pines State Natural Reserve 298
Yosemite National Park 15, 240, 254-63, **238-9**, **256-7**
native peoples 354-5
Navy Beach 267
Nevada City 272-3
Newport Beach 329, 345
Newport Harbor Nautical Museum 345
newspapers 390
Newton B Drury Scenic Parkway 167-8
North Beach 29, 97, 118
Northern California 138-73, **128-9**
highlights 130-3
itineraries 136-7, **136**
planning 135
travel within 135
websites 135
Northstar-at-Tahoe 244, 248-9

000 Map pages

O

Ocean Beach 119, 302
Ocean Institute 345
Old Faithful Geyser 205, 222
opening hours 389-90
Orange 349
Orange County 344-9, **324-5**
  highlights 326-9
  itineraries 332-3, **332**
  planning 331
  websites 331
Oxbow Public Market 215

P

Pacific Beach 302
Pacific Coast Highway 12
Pacific Design Center 67
Page Museum 57, 68
Palace of Fine Arts 103
Palm Springs 24, 283,
  306-13, **308**
Palm Springs Aerial Tramway
  307
Palm Springs Art Museum 307
Panamint Springs 319
Paramount Studios 75
parks & gardens
  Balboa Park 280, 291-3
  Botanical Gardens
    (Los Angeles) 67
  Botanical Gardens
    (San Francisco) 95, 108
  Conservatory of Flowers
    95, 106
  Cornerstone Gardens 229
  Crissy Field 104
  Golden Gate Park 94, 95
  Griffith Park 67
  Sequoia Park 164
passports 398
Pescadero 173-5
Petersen Automotive Museum
  68
Petrified Forest 225
Pfeiffer Beach 134, 187

Pfeiffer Big Sur State Park 187
phonecards 396
photography 372
Piedras Blancas 167
Pigeon Point Light Station 174
Pinnacles National
  Monument 167
Pinto Basin Rd 315
planning, see also individual
  locations
  budgeting 49
  calendar of events 42-5
  California basics 48-9
  children, travel with 362-5
  itineraries 32-41
  repeat visitors 46
  resources 47
  travel seasons 48
plants 385, see also redwood
  trees
Point Arena 154
Point Bonita Lighthouse 139
Point Cabrillo Lighthouse
  154-5
Point Lobos State Natural
  Reserve 183
Point Piedras Blancas 134, 189
Point Reyes Lighthouse 149
Point Reyes National Seashore
  26, 132, 148-51
Point Reyes Station 146-8
Point Sur State Historic Park
  186
politics 352
population 352, 367-8
Prairie Creek Redwoods State
  Park 167-8
public holidays 394-5

R

radio 390
rafting 382
  Auburn State Recreation
    Area 274
  Shasta-Trinity National
    Forest 171
  Yosemite National Park 260-1

Redwood Coast 151
Redwood National & State
  Parks 166-7
redwood trees 130, 131, 158-9
religion 352
Reuben H Fleet Science
  Center 281
riptides 395
road rules 403
road-distance chart 401
Roaring River Falls 264
Robert Louis Stevenson State
  Park 224
rock climbing 381
Rockefeller Forest 158
Route 66 316-17
Russian River Valley 232-3
RV travel 402

S

Sacramento 273-5
safety 395-6, 403
Salt Point State Park 153-4
San Diego 288-306, **290**,
  292-3
  accommodations 299-301
  activities 298-9
  drinking 304-5
  entertainment 305
  food 301-4
  highlights 280-3
  itineraries 286-7, **286**
  planning 285
  shopping 305-6
  sights & attractions 288-98
  tourist offices 306
  tours 299
  travel to/from 306
  travel within 285, 306
  websites 285
San Diego Chinese Historical
  Museum 289
San Diego Museum of Art 292
San Diego Natural History
  Museum 291
San Diego Zoo 18, 281, 282,
  296

San Diego Zoo Safari Park 298
San Francisco 16, 91-125, **93**, **104-5**, **112-13**, **116**
  accommodations 109-11
  drinking 118-19
  entertainment 119-22
  festivals & events 109
  food 111-17, 374
  highlights 94-7
  itineraries 100-1, **100**
  shopping 122
  sights & attractions 102-8
  tourist offices 123
  tours 108-9
  travel to/from 123-4
  travel within 99, 124-5
  websites 99
San Francisco Museum of Modern Art 105-6
San Luis Obispo 189-91
Santa Barbara 20, 132, 134, 191-7, **194**
Santa Cruz 175-8
Santa Cruz Beach Boardwalk 176
Santa Monica 31, 71-2, 81, **76**
Sausalito 142-4
scenic drives 18
  17-Mile Drive 184
  Artists Drive 318
  Avenue of the Giants 131, 158-9
  Covington Flats 315
  Geology Tour Rd 315
  Hwy 395 245
  Kings Canyon Scenic Byway 245, 265
  Klamath 168
  Mt Shasta 171
  Newton B Drury Scenic Parkway 167-8
  Pacific Coast Highway 12
  Pinto Basin Rd 315
  Route 66 316-17
  Tioga Road 245, 258

Seal Beach 349
SeaWorld 300
senior travelers 390
Sequoia National Park 243, 265-6
Sequoia Park 164
Seymour Marine Discovery Center 176
Shrine Drive-Thru Tree 158
Sierra Nevada 266-75, **238-9**
  highlights 240-3
  itineraries 246-7, **246**
  planning 245
  travel within 245
  websites 245
Silicon Valley 360
Silverado Museum 219
Skidoo 319
skiing & snowboarding 381
  Badger Pass Ski Area 261
  Heavenly 244, 248
  Lake Tahoe 248-9
  Mammoth Mountain 244, 269
  Mt Shasta 171
  Northstar-at-Tahoe 244, 248-9
  Squaw Valley 244, 248
smog 49, 386
smoking 393
snakes 395-6
snorkeling, see diving & snorkeling
snowboarding, see skiing & snowboarding
Sonoma 204, 227-31
Sonoma Coast State Beach 153
Sonoma State Historic Park 228-9
Sonoma Valley 13, 225-32, **228**
Sonoma Wine Country 225-35, **201**
  highlights 202-5
  itineraries 208-9, **208**
  planning 207
  tours 211-12

  travel to/from 210-11
  travel within 207, 212
  websites 207
Sony Pictures Studios 75
South Bay Bicycle Trail 56
spas & hot springs
  Calistoga 221-2
  Palm Springs 313
spiders 395-6
spirits 376-7
sports 368, see also individual sports
Squaw Valley 244, 248
St Helena 219-20
state parks, see national & state parks
Stinson Beach 134, 146
Stovepipe Wells 318-19
surfing 45, 379
  Huntington Beach 344
  Los Angeles 73-4
  Monterey 182
  San Diego 298
  Santa Cruz 176-7
  Wedge 346
Sutter's Fort State Historic Park 274
swimming 378-9, see also beaches

T

Tahoe City 251-3
Tahquitz Canyon 309
Tall Trees Grove 167
taxes 394
taxi travel 404
telephone services 48, 396
Tenaya Lake 241
theme parks, see amusement parks
Tiburon 144-5
time 396
Timken Museum of Art 292
Tioga Road 254, 258
tipping 48, 394
Torrey Pines State Natural Reserve 298

Tour Thru Tree 158
Tournament of Roses 42, 76
tours, *see individual locations*
train travel 399, 404
Traintown 229-30
traveler's checks 394
Trees of Mystery 168
trekking, *see* hiking
Truckee 253-4
Tuolumne Meadows 258
TV 390
TV industry 369-70

U

Ukiah 159
Universal Studios Hollywood 65
University of California, Berkeley 151

V

vacations 394-5
Vallejo Home 229
Venice Beach 31, 57, 81, **76**
visas 48, 397-8

W

Walk of Fame 17
walking, *see* hiking

Walt Disney Concert Hall 63
Warner Bros Studios 75-6
water 386
Wawona 258
weather 48, 389
websites 47, *see also individual locations*
weights 390
whale-watching 380
  Bodega Bay 152
  Julia Pfeiffer Burns State Park 187
  Klamath 168
  Mendocino Headlands State Park 155
  Monterey 181-2
  Pescadero 174
Whaley House 294
white-water rafting, *see* rafting
wi-fi 48, 392-3
wildlife watching 26, 42, *see also* whale-watching
  Arcata Marsh & Wildlife Sanctuary 165
  Klamath Basin National Wildlife Refuges 167
  Piedras Blancas 167
  Pinnacles National Monument 167
windsurfing 380
wine 44, 204, 375-6

wine regions, *see also* Napa Valley Wine Country, Sonoma Valley Wine Country
  Dry Creek Valley 234
  Russian River Valley 232-3
  Santa Barbara 196
Wine Train 205
WWII 359

Y

Yosemite Falls 241, 257
Yosemite Museum 258
Yosemite National Park 15, 240, 254-63, **238-9**, **256-7**
  accommodations 261-2
  activities 259-61
  drinking 263
  food 262-3
  highlights 240-3
  itineraries 246-7, **246**
  planning 245
  sights & attractions 255-9
  tours 261
  travel to/from 263
  travel within 245, 263
  websites 245
Yosemite Valley 255-8, **260**
Yountville 217-19

Z

Zabriskie Point 318

How to Use This Book

These symbols will help you find the listings you want:

- ⊙ Sights
- 🐋 Beaches
- ✈ Activities
- 🍃 Courses
- 📷 Tours
- 🎉 Festivals & Events
- 🛏 Sleeping
- 🍴 Eating
- 🍷 Drinking
- ⭐ Entertainment
- 🛍 Shopping
- ℹ Information/Transport

These symbols give you the vital information for each listing:

- 📞 Telephone Numbers
- ☺ Opening Hours
- Ⓟ Parking
- ⊖ Nonsmoking
- ❄ Air-Conditioning
- @ Internet Access
- 📶 Wi-Fi Access
- ⊠ Swimming Pool
- 🍃 Vegetarian Selection
- 📋 English-Language Menu
- 🌴 Family-Friendly
- 🐾 Pet-Friendly
- 🚌 Bus
- 🚢 Ferry
- Ⓜ Metro
- Ⓢ Subway
- ⊖ London Tube
- 🚋 Tram
- 🚆 Train

Reviews are organised by author preference.

Look out for these icons:

FREE No payment required

🍃 A green or sustainable option

Our authors have nominated these places as demonstrating a strong commitment to sustainability – for example by supporting local communities and producers, operating in an environmentally friendly way, or supporting conservation projects.

Map Legend

Sights
- 🐋 Beach
- ☸ Buddhist
- 🏰 Castle
- ✝ Christian
- ☪ Hindu
- ☪ Islamic
- ✡ Jewish
- ❶ Monument
- 🏛 Museum/Gallery
- ⊗ Ruin
- 🍷 Winery/Vineyard
- 🐾 Zoo
- ⊙ Other Sight

Activities, Courses & Tours
- 🤿 Diving/Snorkelling
- 🛶 Canoeing/Kayaking
- ⛷ Skiing
- 🏄 Surfing
- 🏊 Swimming/Pool
- 🚶 Walking
- 🏄 Windsurfing
- ❹ Other Activity/Course/Tour

Sleeping
- 🛏 Sleeping
- ⛺ Camping

Eating
- 🍴 Eating

Drinking
- 🍷 Drinking
- ☕ Cafe

Entertainment
- ⭐ Entertainment

Shopping
- 🛍 Shopping

Information
- 📮 Post Office
- ℹ Tourist Information

Transport
- ✈ Airport
- ⊗ Border Crossing
- 🚍 Bus
- +🚠+ Cable Car/Funicular
- 🚲 Cycling
- ⛴ Ferry
- Ⓜ Metro
- 🚝 Monorail
- Ⓟ Parking
- Ⓢ S-Bahn
- 🚕 Taxi
- +🚆+ Train/Railway
- 🚋 Tram
- ⊖ Tube Station
- Ⓤ U-Bahn
- ● Other Transport

Routes
- Tollway
- Freeway
- Primary
- Secondary
- Tertiary
- Lane
- Unsealed Road
- Plaza/Mall
- Steps
-)≡≡ Tunnel
- Pedestrian Overpass
- Walking Tour
- Walking Tour Detour
- Path

Boundaries
- ─── International
- ─── State/Province
- ── Disputed
- Regional/Suburb
- Marine Park
- Cliff
- Wall

Population
- ❸ Capital (National)
- ◉ Capital (State/Province)
- ● City/Large Town
- ● Town/Village

Geographic
- 🏠 Hut/Shelter
- 🔦 Lighthouse
- 👁 Lookout
- ▲ Mountain/Volcano
- 🌴 Oasis
- ❹ Park
-)(Pass
- 🌳 Picnic Area
- 🍃 Waterfall

Hydrography
- River/Creek
- Intermittent River
- Swamp/Mangrove
- Reef
- Canal
- Water
- Dry/Salt/Intermittent Lake
- Glacier

Areas
- Beach/Desert
- Cemetery (Christian)
- Cemetery (Other)
- Park/Forest
- Sportsground
- Sight (Building)
- Top Sight (Building)

ALISON BING

San Francisco Author, arts commentator and adventurous eater Alison Bing was adopted by California 16 years ago. By now she has done everything you're supposed to do here and a few things you're definitely not, including talking up LA bands in San Francisco bars and falling in love on the 7 Haight bus. Alison holds a graduate degree in international diplomacy, which she regularly undermines with opinionated commentary in magazines, newspapers, public radio and more than 20 books.

NATE CAVALIERI

Northern California & Central Coast, Yosemite & the Sierra Nevada A native of central Michigan, Nate Cavalieri lives in Northern California and has crisscrossed the region's back roads by bicycle, bus and rental car on a quest for the biggest trees, the best camping and the hoppiest pints of beer. In addition to authoring guides on California and Latin America for Lonely Planet, he writes about music and professional cycling. He's the Jazz Editor at Rhapsody Music Service. Photos from his travels in Northern California and other writing can be found at www.natecavalieri.com.

Read more about Nate at:
lonelyplanet.com/members/natecavalieri

ANDREA SCHULTE-PEEVERS

San Diego & the Deserts Andrea fell in love with California – its pizzazz, people and sunshine – almost the instant she landed in the Golden State. She grew up in Germany, lived in London and traveled the world before getting a degree from UCLA and embarking on a career in travel writing. Andrea has written or contributed to some 60 Lonely Planet books, including the *California* and *Los Angeles & Southern California* guides.

JOHN A VLAHIDES

Napa & Sonoma Wine Country John A Vlahides co-hosts the TV series *Lonely Planet: Roads Less Travelled,* screening on National Geographic Channels International. John studied cooking in Paris, with the same chefs who trained Julia Child, and is a former luxury-hotel concierge and member of *Les Clefs d'Or,* the international union of the world's elite concierges. He lives in San Francisco, where he sings tenor with the San Francisco Symphony, and spends free time skiing the Sierra Nevada. For more, see JohnVlahides.com and @JohnVlahides on Twitter.

Read more about John at:
lonelyplanet.com/members/johnvlahides

Our Story

A beat-up old car, a few dollars in the pocket and a sense of adventure. In 1972 that's all Tony and Maureen Wheeler needed for the trip of a lifetime – across Europe and Asia overland to Australia. It took several months, and at the end – broke but inspired – they sat at their kitchen table writing and stapling together their first travel guide, *Across Asia on the Cheap*. Within a week they'd sold 1500 copies. Lonely Planet was born.

Today, Lonely Planet has offices in Melbourne, London and Oakland, with more than 600 staff and writers. We share Tony's belief that 'a great guidebook should do three things: inform, educate and amuse'.

Our Writers

BETH KOHN

Coordinating Author, Northern California & Central Coast, Yosemite & the Sierra Nevada A lucky long-time resident of San Francisco, Beth lives to be playing outside or splashing in big puddles of water. For this guide, she hiked and biked Bay Area byways, lugged a bear canister along the John Muir Trail and selflessly soaked in hot springs – for research purposes, of course. She is an author of Lonely Planet's *Yosemite, Sequoia & Kings Canyon National Parks* and *Mexico* guides, and you can see more of her work at www .bethkohn.com.

BRIDGET GLEESON

San Diego & the Deserts, Disneyland & Orange County Though she travels all over Latin America to write about glaciers, penguins and giant turtles, the sunshine and sailboats of southern California always draw Bridget back to the USA. She covers food, wine, hotels and adventure travel for various travel publications and websites.

Read more about Bridget at:
lonelyplanet.com/members/bridgetgleeson

ANDREW BENDER

Los Angeles Andy is a true Angeleno, not because he was born in Los Angeles but because he's made it his own. Two decades ago, this native New Englander packed up the car and drove cross-country to work in film production, and eventually realized that the joy was in the journey (and writing about it). His work has since appeared in the *Los Angeles Times*, *Forbes*, over two dozen Lonely Planet titles, and on his blog, www.wheres-andy-now.com. Current obsessions: discovering LA's next great ethnic enclave, and winter sunsets over the bike path in Santa Monica.

SARA BENSON

Northern California & Central Coast, Yosemite & the Sierra Nevada After graduating from college in Chicago, Sara jumped on a plane to California and has bounced around the Golden State ever since, especially between SF and LA, where she sea kayaked and hiked her way along the coast to update this guide, and in the Sierra Nevada Mountains, where she has worked as a national park ranger. Sara has authored over 40 travel and nonfiction books, and contributed to Lonely Planet's *USA* and *Coastal California* guides. See www.indietraveler.blogspot.com, www.indietraveler.net and @indie_traveler on Twitter.

Read more about Sara at:
lonelyplanet.com/members/Sara_Benson

More Writers

Published by Lonely Planet Publications Pty Ltd
ABN 36 005 607 983
2nd edition – May 2012
ISBN 978 1 74220 561 8
© Lonely Planet 2012   Photographs © as indicated 2012
10 9 8 7 6 5 4 3 2 1
Printed in Singapore